CHAPTERS INTO VERSE

Chapters into Verse

Poetry in English Inspired by The Bible

VOLUME ONE:
Genesis to Malachi

Assembled and Edited by
ROBERT ATWAN &
LAURANCE WIEDER

Oxford New York
OXFORD UNIVERSITY PRESS
1993

Oxford University Press

Oxford New York Toronto
Delhi Bombay Calcutta Madras Karachi
Kuala Lumpur Singapore Hong Kong Tokyo
Nairobi Dar es Salaam Cape Town
Melbourne Auckland Madrid

and associated companies in
Berlin Ibadan

Published by Oxford University Press, Inc.,
198 Madison Avenue, New York, New York , 10016

Library of Congress Cataloging-in-Publication Data
Chapters into verse : poetry in English inspired by the Bible /
assembled and edited by Robert Atwan and Laurance Wieder.
p. cm.
Contents: v. 1. Genesis to Malachi — v. 2. Gospels to Revelation.
ISBN 0-19-506913-7 (v. 1). — ISBN 0-19-508305-9 (v. 2)
1. Bible—History of Biblical events—Poetry. 2. Religious
poetry, English. 3. Religious poetry, American. I. Atwan, Robert, 1940— .
II. Wieder, Laurance, 1946– .
PR1191.C44 1993
821.008′0382—dc20 92-37206

4 6 8 9 7 5

Printed in the United States of America
on acid-free paper

Agee, James. Reprinted by permission of author's estate.

Ashbery, John. "Caesura," from *Shadow Train,* copyright © John Ashbery. Reprinted by permission.

Auden, W.H. "They Wondered Why the Fruit Had Been Forbidden," from *W.H. Auden: Collected Poems* by W.H. Auden, ed. by Edward Mendelson. Copyright 1945 by W.H. Auden. Reprinted by permission of Random House, Inc.

Benet, Stephen Vincent. "King David" from *Selected Works.* Holt, Rinehart & Winston. Copyright 1937 by Stephen Vincent Benet. Copyright renewed © 1965. Reprinted by permission of Brandt & Brandt Literary Agents.

Berryman, John. "King David Dances" from *Collected Poems 1937–1971* by John Berryman. Copyright © 1989 by Kate Donahue Berryman. Reprinted by permission of Farrar, Straus & Giroux, Inc.

Booth, Philip. "Original Sequence from *Letter from a Distant Land* by Philip Booth. Copyright © 1957 by Philip Booth. Used by permission of Viking Penguin, a division of Penguin Books USA Inc.

Ceravolo, Joseph. "Fill and Illumined" from *Spring in this World of Poor Mutts.* Copyright © 1968 Columbia University Press. Used by permission.

Chagy, John. "Aaggai". Copyright 1953 by John Chagy. Reprinted with permission by Alan Chagy.

Crane, Hart. "To Brooklyn Bridge" from *The Complete Poems and Selected Letters and Prose of Hart Crane,* ed. by Brom Weber. Reprinted by permission of W.W. Norton & Co.

Corrie, Joe. "The Image O' God" from *The Image O' God* by Joe Corrie. Reprinted by permission of Faber and Faber Ltd.

Cullen, Countee. "From Life to Love," by Countee Cullen; copyright © 1925 by *Opportunity* copyright renewed 1953 by Ida M. Cullen. "For a Mouthy Woman" from *Color* by Countee Cullen; Copyright © 1925 by Harper & Brothers; copyright renewed 1953 by Ida M. Cullen.

cummings, e.e. From *Poems 1923–1954.* Copyright © 1954 e.e. cummings. Reprinted by permission of Harcourt, Brace, Jovanovich, Inc.

Curzon, David. "Proverbs 6:6" from *Midrashim* by David Curzon. Copyright © 1991 by David Curzon. Reprinted by permission of Cross-Cultural Communications, and the author.

Davison, Peter. "Where the Sun Ends," from *Barn Fever and Other Poems,* © 1981 by Peter Davison.

Dickinson, Emily. Reprinted by permission of the publishers and the Trustees of Amherst College from *The Poems of Emily Dickinson,* Thomas H. Johnson, ed., Cambridge, Mass.: The Belknap Press of Harvard University Press, Copyright © 1951, 1955, 1979, 1983 by the President and Fellows of Harvard College. "It Always Felt to Me—a Wrong" from *The Complete Poems of Emily Dickinson* edited by Thomas H. Johnson. Copyright 1929 by Martha Dickinson Bianchi; copyright © renewed 1957 by Mary L. Hampson. By permission of Little, Brown, and Co.

Frost, Robert. "Sitting by a Basin in Broad Daylight" and "Provide, Provide". From *The Poetry of Robert Frost* edited by Edward Connery Lathem. Copyright 1928, 1934, © 1969 by Holt, Rinehart and Winston. Copyright 1936, © 1956, 1962 by Robert Frost. Copyright © 1964 by Lesley Frost Ballantine. Reprinted by permission of Henry Holt and Company.

George, Diana Hume. "Asenath," reprinted by permission of the author.

Gilbert, Celia. "The Midwives," copyright © 1992 by Celia Gilbert. Reprinted by permission of the author.

Ginsberg, Allen. From *Collected Poems 1947–1980* by Allen Ginsberg. Reprinted by permission of HarperCollins Publishers.

Graves, Robert. From *Collected Poems.* Reprinted by permission of Oxford University Press

Hardy, Thomas. Reprinted with permission of Macmillan Publishing Company from *The Complete Poems of Thomas Hardy,* edited by James Gibson (New York: Macmillan, 1978)

Harris, Robert. "Isaiah by Kerosene Lantern Light" from *Collected Poems.* © Robert Harris 1991. Reprinted by permission of Collins/Angus & Robertson Publishers.

Heath-Stubbs, John. "A Vision of Beasts" from *Six Emblems from the Book of Daniel* (Carcanet Press, 1988). Reprinted by permission.

Hecht, Anthony. "Naming the Animals," from *The Transparent Man* by Anthony Hecht. Copyright © 1990 by Anthony Hecht. Reprinted by permission of Alfred A. Knopf, Inc.

Hejduk, John. Reprinted by permission of the author.

Hill, Geoffrey. From *Collected Poems.* Copyright © 1986 by Oxford University Press. Reprinted by permission.

Hine, Daryl. Reprinted with permission of Atheneum Publishers, an imprint of Macmillan Publishing Company from *Selected Poems of Daryl Hine.* Copyright © 1960, 1980 by Daryl Hine.

Hodgson, Ralph. Reprinted with permission of Macmillan Publishing Company from *Poems* by Ralph Hodgson (New York: Macmillan, 1924)

Hope, A.D. "Easter Hymn" and "A Commination" by A.D. Hope from his *Collected Poems.* © A.D. Hope.

Housman, A.E. "When Israel Out of Egypt Came" and "Ho, Everyone that Thirsteth". From "A Shropshire Lad"—Authorised Edition—from *The Collected Poems of A.E. Housman.* Copyright 1939, 1940 © 1965 by Holt, Rinehart and Winston. Copyright © 1967, 1968 by Robert E. Symons. Reprinted by permission of Henry Holt and Company, Inc. "When Adam Walked in Eden Young" reprinted with permission of Macmillan Publishing Company from *The Collected Poems of A.E. Housman.*

Huxley, Aldous. "The Burning Wheel" from *The Collected Poetry of Aldous Huxley* edited by Donald Watt. Copyright © 1971 by Laura Huxley. Reprinted by permission of HarperCollins Publishers.

Jackson, Laura Riding. From *The Poems of Laura Riding* by Laura (Riding) Jackson. Copyright © 1938, 1980 by Laura (Riding) Jackson. Reprinted by permission of Persea Books, Inc.

Jarrell, Randall. "Jonah" from *The Complete Poems* by Randall Jarrell. Copyright © 1948, 1969 by Mrs. Randall Jarrell. Reprinted by permission of Farrar, Straus & Giroux, Inc.

Johnson, James Weldon. From *God's Trombones* by James Weldon Johnson. Copyright 1927 The Viking Press, Inc., renewed © 1955 by Grace Nail Johnson. Used by permission of Viking Penguin, a division of Penguin Book USA Inc.

Joyce, James. From *Collected Poems* by James Joyce. Copyright 1918 by B.W. Huebsch, Inc., 1927, 1936 by James Joyce, 1946 by Nora Joyce. Used by permission of Viking Penguin, a division of Penguin Books USA Inc.

Kees, Weldon. Reprinted from *The Collected Poems of Weldon Kees,* edited by Donald Justice, by permission of the University of Nebraska Press. Copyright © 1975 by the University of Nebraska Press.

Kelly, Aileen. "The Given Flesh Returns Nothing But Bread". Copyright Aileen Kelly, first published in *Quadrant* (Australia), July 1984.

Kennedy, X.J. "Joshua" from *Cross Ties: Selected Poems.* Reprinted by permission of the University of Georgia Press.

Lawrence, D.H. From *The Complete Poems of D.H. Lawrence* by D.H. Lawrence. Copyright © 1964, 1971 by Angelo Ravagli and C.M. Weekley, Executors of the Estate of Frieda Larence Ravagli. Used by permission of Viking Penguin, a division of Penguin Books USA Inc.

Lee, Li-Young. "The City in Which I Love You" copyright © 1990 by Li-Young Lee. Reprinted from *The City in Which I Love You* by Li-Young Lee with the permission of BOA Editions, Ltd., 92 Park Ave., Brockport, NY 14420.

Levine, Philip. "The Death of Saul" reprinted by permission of the author. Originally appeared in *The Antioch Review.*

Levertov, Denise. *Poems 1960–1967.* Copyright © 1961, 1964 by Denise Levertov Goodman.

Lindsay, Vachel. Reprinted with permission of Macmillan Publishing Company from *Collected Poems of Vachel Lindsay.* Copyright 1920 by Macmillan Publishing Company, renewed 1948 by Elizabeth C. Lindsay.

Lowell, Robert. "The Book of Wisdom" from *Notebook 1967–1968* by Robert Lowell. Copyright © 1969 by Robert Lowell. Reprinted by permission of Farrar, Straus & Giroux, Inc. From "David to Bathsheba in the Public Garden" from *Mills of the Kavanaughs,* copyright 1946 and renewed 1974 by Robert Lowell. Reprinted by permission of Harcourt Brace Jovanovich.

MacCaig, Norman. "The Golden Calf," from *Collected Poems.* Reprinted by permission of the Random Century Group for Chatto & Windus.

MacDiarmid, Hugh. Reprinted with permission of Macmillan Publishing Company from *Collected Poems of Hugh MacDiarmid.* © 1948, 1962 Christopher Murray Grieve.

MacLeish, Archibald. "What the Serpent Said to Adam," from *Songs for Eve* in *Collected Poems 1917–1982* by Archibald MacLeish. Copyright © 1954 by Archibald MacLeish. Copyright © renewed 1982 by Mrs. Ada MacLeish. Reprinted by permission of Houghton Mifflin Co. All rights reserved.

MacNeice, Louis. "Whit Monday" from *The Collected Poems of Louis MacNeice* edited by E.R. Dodds. Reprinted by permission of Faber and Faber Ltd.

Macpherson, Jay. "The Beauty of Job's Daughters" from *Poems Twice Told* by Jay Macpherson, copyright © Oxford University Press Canada 1981. Reprinted by permission of the publisher.

Mahon, Derek. "Ecclesiastes" © Derek Mahon 1979. Reprinted from *Poems 1962–1978* by Derek Mahon (1979) by permission of Oxford University Press.

McAuley, James. "In the Twentieth Century" and "Jesus" from *Collected Poems* © Norma McAuley 1971. Reprinted by permission of Collins/Angus & Robertson Publishers.

McGinley, Phyllis. "Women of Jericho", copyright 1933 Phyllis McGinley; renewed © 1961 by Julie Elizabeth Hayden and Phyllis Hayden Blake, from *Times Three* by Phyllis McGinley. Used by permission of Viking Penguin, a division of Penguin Books, USA Inc.

Meredith, William. "On Falling Asleep by Firelight" from *The Open Sea and Other Poems* by William Meredith. Copyright © 1957 by William Meredith. Reprinted by permission of Alfred A. Knopf, Inc.

Merton, Thomas. *Collected Poems of Thomas Merton.* Copyright © 1946 by New Directions, 1968, 1969, 1977 by the Trustees of the Merton Legacy Trust.

Merwin, W.S. "Leviathan" from *Green with Beasts,* copyright © 1956 by W.S. Merwin. "Noah's Raven" from *The Moving Target,* copyright © 1963 by W.S. Merwin.

Meynell, Alice. Reprinted with permission of Charles Scribner's Sons, an imprint of Macmillan Publishing Company from *Poems of Alice Meynell: Complete Edition* (New York: Charles Scribner's Sons, 1923).

Millay, Edna St. Vincent. "Make Bright the Arrows" by Edna St. Vincent Millay. Copyright © 1940, 1968 by Edna St. Vincent Millay and Norma Millay Ellis. From *Collected Poems,* HarperCollins. Reprinted by permission of Elizabeth Barnett, literary executor.

Moore, Marianne. "Blessed is the Man," copyright © 1970 by Marianne Moore, "O to Be a Dragon," copyright © 1957 by Marianne Moore, renewed 1985 by Lawrence E. Brinn and Louise Crane, Executors of the Estate of Marianne Moore, from *The Complete Poems of Marianne Moore* by Marianne Moore. Used by permission of Viking Penguin, a division of Penguin Books, USA Inc.

Muir, Edwin. From *Collected Poems.* Copyright © 1986 by Oxford University Press. Reprinted by permission.

Noll, Bink. "Abraham's Madness" from *The Center of the Circle.* Copyright © 1962 Bink Noll. Reprinted by permission of Harcourt Brace Jovanovich.

Oppen, George. *Collected Poems.* Copyright © 1972 by George Oppen.

Ostriker, Alicia. "The Story of Joshua." Reprinted by permission of the author. An early version of "The Story of Joshua" appeared in *Lilith* 14, no. 4 (fall 1989).

Owen, Wilfred. *The Collected Poems of Wilfred Owen.* Copyright © 1973 by Chatto & Windus, Ltd.

Porter, Anne. "Oaks and Squirrels". Copyright © 1985 Commonweal Foundation.

Rakosi, Carl. Reprinted by permission of the author.

Rexroth, Kenneth. *The Collected Shorter Poems of Kenneth Rexroth.* Copyright 1940, 1942 by Kenneth Rexroth.

Reznikoff, Charles. "Israel I and II," "Joshua at Shechem," "David," "The Hebrew of your poets, Zion," "Exodus," "Day of Atonement," "I do not believe that David killed Goliath," "The Deum ," "Babylon 539 B.C.E.," by Charles Reznikoff. Copyright © 1976, 1977 by Marie Syrkin Reznikoff. Reprinted from *Poems 1918–1975: The Complete Poems of Charles Reznikoff* with the permission of the Black Sparrow Press.

Roethke, Theodore. "Follies of Adam," copyright 1954 by Beatrice Roethke, administratrix of the estate of Theodore Roethke. From *The Collected Poems of Theodore Roethke* by Theodore Roethke. Used by permission of Doubleday, a division of Bantam Doubleday Dell Publishing Group, Inc.

Rosenberg, David. Reprinted by permission of author.

Rosenberg, Isaac. Reprinted by permission of the Estate of Isaac Rosenberg.

Rowbotham, David. Acknowledgement to David Rowbotham, from his (national prizewinning) volume of verse "The Pen of Feathers" (Angus & Robertson, Sydney, 1971).

Sassoon, Siegfried. From *Collected Poems* by Siegfried Sassoon. Copyright 1918, 1920 by E.P. Dutton. Copyright 1936, 1946, 1947, 1948 by Siegfried Sassoon. Used by permission of Viking Penguin, a division of Penguin Books, USA Inc.

Schubert, David. "A Successful Summer" is reprinted by permission of Theodore Weiss and originally appeared in the *Quarterly Review Poetry Series:* Volume 24.

Schwartz, Delmore. *Selected Poems: Summer Knowledge.* Copyright 1952 by Delmore Schwartz.

Service, Robert. From *The Collected Poems of Robert Service.* Copyright 1907, Dodd, Mead and Co. Reprinted by permission.

Sewell, Elizabeth. "Job" from *Poems 1947–1961* (University of North Carolina Press) Copyright © 1962 by Elizabeth Sewell. Reprinted by permission of the author.

Shapiro, David. "In a Blind Garden," from *House (Blown Apart).* Copyright © 1988 by David Shapiro. Reprinted by permission of the Overlook Press.

Shapiro, Karl. "The Recognition of Eve" © 1953, 1987 by Karl Shapiro by arrangement with Wieser & Wieser, Inc., New York.

Taylor, Edward. From *The Poems of Edward Taylor* © Donald E. Stanford. 1960, 1988. Reprinted by permission.

Thomas, Dylan. *Poems of Dylan Thomas.* Copyright © 1943 by New Directions, 1953 by Dylan Thomas, 1967 by the Trustees for the Copyrights of Dylan Thomas.

Untermeyer, Louis. "Koheleth" from *Burning Bush* by Louis Untermeyer, copyright 1928 by Harcourt Brace Jovanovich, Inc., and renewed 1956 by Louis Untermeyer, reprinted by permission of the publisher.

Walcott, Derek. "The Cloud" from *Sea Grapes* by Derek Walcott. Copyright © 1976 by Derek Walcott. Reprinted by permission of Farrar, Straus & Giroux, Inc.

Wheelwright, John. *Collected Poems of John Wheelwright.* Copyright © 1971 by Louise Wheelwright Damon.

White, J.P. "In Ecclesiastes I read," from *The Pomegranate Tree Speaks from the Dictator's Garden* by J.P. White (Holy Cow! Press, 1988). Reprinted by permission of Holy Cow! Press.

Wilner, Eleanor. "Epitaph" appeared in *Maya* (University of Massachusetts Press, Amherst, 1979).

Wylie, Elinor. "The Pebble," from *Collected Poems* by Elinor Wylie. Copyright 1932 by Alfred A. Knopf, Inc. and renewed 1960 by Edwina C. Rubenstein. Reprinted by permission of the publisher. "Nebuchadnezzar: from *Collected Poems* by Elinor Wylie. Copyright 1923 by Alfred A. Knopf, Inc. Reprinted by permission of the publisher.

Yeats, W.B. "On Woman," is reprinted with permission of Macmillan Publishing Company from *The Poems of W.B. Yeats: A New Edition,* edited by Richard J. Finneran. Copyright 1919 by Macmillan Publishing Company, renewed 1947 by Bertha Georgie Yeats. "Solomon and the Witch" is reprinted with permission of Macmillan Publishing Company from *The Poems of W.B. Yeats: A New Edition,* edited by Richard J. Finneran. Copyright 1924 by Macmillan Publishing Company, renewed 1952 by Bertha George Yeats.

Zukofsky, Louis. From *A,* pages 147–150. Copyright © 1979 by Celia and Louis Zukofsky. Reprinted by permission of the Regents of the university of California and the University of California Press.

ACKNOWLEDGMENTS

We are grateful to many friends and colleagues for the help they gave us throughout the stages of this vast undertaking. We thank Rev. Lawrence E. Frizzell, Professor of Jewish-Christian Studies at Seton Hall University, for the initial inspiration that brought *Chapters into Verse* to life. We wish to thank, too, those people who offered us many valuable suggestions along the way: George Dardess, Glen Hartley, Michael Heyward, Ron Horning, Gen Kanai, Kenneth Koch, Christina Moustakis, Joyce Carol Oates, Charles O'Neill, Alicia Ostriker, Peggy Rosenthal, David Shapiro, J. O. Tate, and Edward W. Tayler. Michael McSpedon and Francis P. J. DiCesare II helped us with research and manuscript preparation. We appreciate the help and guidance we received from the staff at Oxford University Press, particularly from Elizabeth Maguire, our editor, and Susan Chang. We are especially grateful to Jack Roberts, who patiently went through the enormous first draft of the manuscript and helped us scale it down to publishable size. Finally, we dedicate this book to our families: for Helene, Gregory and Emily Atwan; for Andrea and Aiah Wieder.

CONTENTS

THE SECOND BOOK OF MOSES, CALLED EXODUS

THE THIRD BOOK OF MOSES, CALLED LEVITICUS

THE FOURTH BOOK OF MOSES, CALLED NUMBERS

THE FIFTH BOOK OF MOSES, CALLED DEUTERONOMY

THE BOOK OF JOSHUA

THE BOOK OF JUDGES

THE BOOK OF RUTH

THE FIRST BOOK OF SAMUEL

THE SECOND BOOK OF SAMUEL

THE FIRST BOOK OF THE KINGS COMBINED WITH THE FIRST AND SECOND BOOKS OF THE CHRONICLES

THE SECOND BOOK OF THE KINGS COMBINED WITH THE FIRST AND SECOND BOOKS OF THE CHRONICLES

EZRA

THE BOOK OF NEHEMIAH

ESTHER

THE BOOK OF JOB

THE BOOK OF PSALMS

THE PROVERBS

ECCLESIASTES, OR, THE PREACHER

THE SONG OF SOLOMON

THE BOOK OF THE PROPHET ISAIAH

THE BOOK OF THE PROPHET JEREMIAH

THE LAMENTATIONS OF JEREMIAH

THE BOOK OF THE PROPHET EZEKIEL

THE BOOK OF DANIEL

THE MINOR PROPHETS

INTRODUCTION

> There are no songs comparable to the songs of Zion; no orations equal to those of the prophets; and no politics like those which the Scriptures teach.
>
> John Milton

Ezra Pound once tweaked T. S. Eliot for preferring Moses to the Muses. Pound's witty remark reminds us of English poetry's two great heritages: the classical and the scriptural or (as Matthew Arnold named them) the Hellenic and the Hebraic. Poetry inspired by classical Greek and Latin models has dominated the poetic landscape for so many centuries that most readers now consider it the only literary tradition. Although the scriptural tradition in English poetry is every bit as venerable as the classical, it has never received the attention accorded its chosen twin. Like Ishmael and Esau, it has led a shadow existence. We hope that this collection will finally bring the scriptural tradition out of the shadows and into the light.

Chapters into Verse, therefore, is more than just another anthology of English-language poetry. It is (so far as we know) the first collection ever assembled of poems inspired by the Bible. Its two volumes survey and define a literary legacy that has lived and at times flourished in the wilderness, unremarked by the reigning literary culture. All of the poems selected for both the *Old Testament* and *New Testament* editions respond to specific passages of scripture. Arranged in Biblical order, from "Genesis" to "Malachi" (in Volume One), from "Matthew" to "Revelation" (Volume Two), every poem is preceded by at least the kernel of the appropriate chapter and verse. Whenever possible, we print a poem's Biblical source in full; at other times, to save space, we have excerpted chapter and verse so that readers will have in front of them the salient passage(s) for context and comparison. Whenever a poet responds to an extensive Biblical episode, we provide as much text as is convenient, expecting that readers will turn to their own Bibles for further illumination.

We think that this arrangement lets the reader experience not merely an isolated poem or favorite Biblical quotation; it places the dialogue between individual poet and sacred text in plain view. Each poem, as it retells, contemplates, expands, debates with, praises, voices, or reimagines the language and events of the Bible, becomes as well an exegesis of the text. *Chapters into Verse* can thus be read as a poetic commentary upon the scriptures. The authority of this commentary derives from the individual poet's imaginative insight—from an intuitive precision and expressive vitality—rather than from scholarship or sectarian politics or established religion.

The collection covers an enormous range of literary styles, historical periods, and religious backgrounds. Poets from much of the English-speaking world are present, representing a diversity of countries, cultures, communities, and idioms—from the English metaphysical poets of the seventeenth century to the African-American voices of the Harlem Renaissance, from the Scots dialect of Robert Burns to the jaunty music of Australian Victor Daley. Whether writing in the King's English, another English, or their own invented language, the poets of the scriptural also employ the whole range of verse forms and personal tones familiar to readers of English literature: from lyric to dramatic, from blank verse to highly-wrought rhyme, from ridicule to reverence, from the majestic to the demotic, from epic to epigrammatic.

Although each volume of *Chapters into Verse* contains a wide variety of poetic forms, readers may discover that—aside from theological dissimilarities—there are some notable differences between the two books. Poets attracted to the Old Testament apparently prefer a larger scope and a more impassioned, or rhapsodic, language: they will exult in the glory of the creation, reimagine the songs of Moses, of Deborah, David, Solomon, Hezekiah; they will compose dramas, chivalric romances, verse essays, and epics. The poetry of the New Testament is largely lyrical and meditative, verse that seems better suited to the more inward and private response encouraged by the spiritual quest of Jesus. The Old Testament, on the other hand, invites a more public, less personal and introspective, poetry. In addition, far more of the Old Testament poetry is composed of paraphrase, a difference explained by the fact that the Hebrew Scripture is in many ways a poetic work, with approximately one-third of its text taken up with psalms, songs, lamentations, and various forms of narrative or prophetic verse. In contrast, the New Testament is essentially a prose work, encompassing many types of prose forms—biographies, encomiums, sayings, parables, letters, epistles, rabbinical stories, and episodic narratives.

This major literary distinction between the Old and New Testaments has clearly stimulated different poetic responses to the sacred texts. The Old Testament, for example, undoubtedly presents a special challenge to poets because of the extraordinary poetry it already contains; poets responding to the Hebrew Scriptures need to be fearless—as was William Blake—about competition. Walt Whitman, truly one of the fearless, claimed that he was "a thorough believer in the Hebrew Scriptures." Boldly intending his *Leaves of Grass* to be a "new Bible" for a new era, Whitman nevertheless prophesied that "No true Bard will ever contravene the Bible." Recognizing a scriptural tradition, he saw the unspoken covenant that existed between the books of the Bible and the work of poets. "If the time ever comes," he wrote, "when iconoclasm does its extremest in one direction against the books of the Bible in its present form, the collection must still survive in another, and dominate just as much as hitherto, or more than hitherto, through its divine and primal poetic structure."

To be included in *Chapters into Verse*, a poem had to meet two criteria: it had to possess real literary merit (as distinct from admirable sentiment, or propriety, or didactic fervor) and it had to derive from a specific scriptural source. As a result, some prominent figures who never or rarely partook of poetic inspiration from scripture are missing from this anthology, among them Geoffrey Chaucer, William Shakespeare, Andrew Marvell, Percy Bysshe Shelley, Edgar Allan Poe, and Wallace Stevens. In their place will be found such less familiar names as Francis Quarles, Michael Drayton, Thomas Stanley, Anne Finch, Countess of Winchilsea, Christopher Smart, P. Hately Waddell, and, starting in the twentieth century, such Jewish poets as Charles Reznikoff and Delmore Schwartz.

The decision to use the King James Bible was made not so much by us as by the authors we included. So many important poets since the seventeenth century have relied on this Bible's resonant style, regardless of their religious or historical backgrounds, that it made no literary or editorial sense for us to use any other version or translation. Aside from its theological importance, The King James Bible is itself a monumental literary achievement. Built on a foundation laid by William Tyndale, Miles Coverdale, and the learned committee in Geneva, its language informs both the literature and the everyday chatter of the English-speaking world, an influence rivalled by no other vernacular bible. Thomas Macaulay called the King James Bible "a book which, if everything else in our language should perish, would alone suffice to show the whole extent of its beauty and power." Much of that beauty and power emerges in this collection.

The history of the Bible in English runs parallel to the development of English poetry. John Wycliffe, who made an English Bible from the Latin Vulgate, was a contemporary of Friar Herebert. The first translation from the original tongues into English was undertaken by the unfortunate English Catholic priest, William Tyndale. He perished at the stake after falling into the hands of the Inquisition in the 1540s, the same decade that saw the deaths of the first English sonneteers, Sir Thomas Wyatt and Henry Howard, Earl of Surrey. Besides Englishing Petrarch, Wyatt also translated the Seven Penitential Psalms before his execution for leading a rebellion against the Catholic Queen Mary Tudor; Surrey verse-paraphrased Ecclesiastes. The Geneva Bible, issued by a committee of Calvinists in 1560, was for almost a century the Bible of English Protestants, whose cause found a champion and martyr in the ideal courtier and poet, Sir Philip Sidney. Sidney and his sister Mary Herbert, Countess of Pembroke, are mostly remembered for the crypto-virgilian pastoral, *The Countess of Pembroke's Arcadia*. But as Sidney noted in his *An Apologie for Poetrie*, the Psalmist David was first a shepherd, then a king, and so the original pastoral poet. Before he died, Sidney translated the first forty-three Psalms; his sister took up the task, and triumphantly completed the Sidney Psalter. Other Renaissance poets, perhaps uncertain which camp (England or Rome, high or low, Hellenic or Hebraic) would prevail, pursued the double career: Sir John Davies and Thomas Campion, among many, made Psalms; Edmund Spenser epitomised the Book of Revelation in unrhymed sonnets; Michael Drayton translated the songs of the Patriarchs and Prophets, and John Donne the Lamentations of Jeremy. By the time James I's committee dedicated the official English Bible in 1611, Shakespeare's life was nearly over and John Milton was about to be born.

By the eighteenth century, literature and scripture had pretty much parted company. The Augustan poets, for the most part, eschewed religious themes, while the religious poets either used verse as sectarian propaganda or aimed it at a popular and sentimental audience. Isaac Watts, John Keble, and Charles Wesley, the most popular religious poets of their time, are largely remembered now for their contributions to the Protestant Hymnal. Of the eighteenth-century literary poets, both Christopher Smart, author of "A Song to David" and a translator of the Psalms, and William Cowper, who wrote the Olney Hymns, suffered bouts of depression and religious mania which gave a pretext for literary criticism to dismiss their religious verse.

Even William Blake, perhaps the last great poet to take the workings of the divine as his whole theme, has sometimes been prey to unconvinced readers' suspicions that his inspiration partakes more of madness than of the sacred breath. Oddly, the worldly Lord Byron actively engaged the scriptural tradition: his Hebrew Melodies are psalms in the Scots ballad tradition of Robert Burns and Thomas Moore. In the 1870s, P. Hately Waddell, a disciple of Robert Burns, published *The Psalms: frae Hebrew intil Scottis*, a work every bit the equal of the Scots Chaucerian Gawin Douglas' *Aeneid of Virgil*, which Ezra Pound called "the most beautiful book in the language."

It may surprise readers who regard the twentieth century as all Muses and no Moses to find so many modern poets in this collection. Not all literary modernists threw away their Bibles, as Wallace Stevens did in 1907 ("I'm glad the silly thing is gone," he wrote). Some, such as Charles Reznikoff, arranged and paraphrased the Jewish Bible. Perhaps the greatest heir of the poets of the New England Puritans (who called themselves Israel), Robert Frost wrote plain-style poetry that responded to scripture in profound and moral music. D. H. Lawrence knew his King James intimately (he wrote a book on Revelation), and quarreled with the New Testament intensely. Many of his poems read as though they were written directly in the margins of his Bible. Every bit as feisty as Lawrence, Laura (Riding) Jackson regarded herself as "religious in my devotion to poetry. But in saying this I am thinking of religion as it is a dedication to, a will to know and make known, the ultimate knowledge, a will to think, to be, with truth, to voice, to live articulately by, the essentialities of existence." In her Biblical poems, she continued that ongoing debate with the creation which informs the lyric dissents of Anne Bradstreet, Emily Dickinson, and Marianne Moore.

The past fifty years have seen at least three entirely new translations of the Bible from original tongues, and poets' versions of "Genesis," "Job," and the "Book of Psalms." Sparked by a renewed interest in Biblical scholarship, especially recent research into the

Hebrew Bible, many contemporary poets are rediscovering the scriptural tradition. That tradition is also being reinvigorated by the work of women poets from many religious backgrounds who are viewing the Bible from new perspectives.

The range of literary styles and historical periods covered in *Chapters into Verse* compelled us to make several editorial decisions regarding the texts of older poems. At first we thought we should retain the flavor of the archaic spelling, punctuation and typographical conventions of sixteenth-, seventeenth-, and eighteenth-century poetry, but upon reflection that notion struck us as fussy. We wanted the poetry to be as clear as possible, to present the fewest barriers to direct, unmediated reading. So we decided to exhibit the older poetry entirely in contemporary dress, with no quaint frills or peculiar decoration or typographic bombast. We found that outright modernization transforms many inaccessible-looking texts into poems that seem breathtakingly fresh. To avoid clutter on the page, we kept notes and glosses to a minimum.

This volume of *Chapters into Verse* contains poems from every period of English literature, from Friar William Herebert's fourteenth-century paraphrase on a passage from Isaiah to John Ashbery's post-modern meditation on Job. Nearly every book of the Old Testament is also represented in this volume. Indeed, when we were finally able to sort through the heap of material amassed during our research, we found that only Amos and Obadiah lacked for corresponding poems. So much of the Old Testament has been rendered in poets' paraphrases, that we easily might have collaged a nearly complete English verse version of Hebrew Scripture. As might be expected, the "Book of Psalms" has inspired poets in every century, as has the "Song of Songs." We did not anticipate, however, that the five chapters of "Lamentations" could be presented each by a different poet. Further, we might have embellished the poets' text with an elegy by Francis Quarles upon every verse. Considerations of space, tempered in some cases by mercy toward the reader, prevented such an encyclopedic approach. Poets' versions and paraphrases of the Psalms easily fill an entire volume of their own, and we have omitted them here. Considerations of space, too, prevented us from including long poems (such as Christopher Smart's "Song of David") that did not lend themselves to excerpting. Even so, we believe that the historic scope and literary depth of the scriptural tradition is evident in these pages.

CHAPTERS INTO VERSE

Immediate are the Acts of God, more swift
Than time or motion, but to human ears
Cannot without process of speech be told,
So told as earthly notion can receive.

JOHN MILTON,
Paradise Lost, Bk VII, ll. 176–79

EXTRACTS

The Bible is an antique Volume

Emily Dickinson

The Bible is an antique Volume –
Written by faded Men
At the suggestion of Holy Spectres –
Subjects – Bethlehem –
Eden – the ancient Homestead –
Satan – the Brigadier –
Judas – the Great Defaulter –
David – the Troubadour –
Sin – a distinguished Precipice
Others must resist –
Boys that "believe" are very lonesome –
Other Boys are "lost" –
Had but the Tale a warbling Teller –
All the Boys would come –
Orpheus' Sermon captivated –
It did not condemn –

The H. Scriptures I

George Herbert

Oh Book! infinite sweetness! let my heart
Suck every letter, and a honey gain,
Precious for any grief in any part;
To clear the breast, to mollify all pain.

Thou art all health, health thriving till it make
A full eternity: thou art a mass
Of strange delights, where we may wish and take.
Ladies, look here; this is the thankful glass,

That mends the lookers' eyes: this is the well
That washes what it shows. Who can endear
Thy praise too much? thou art heaven's ledger here,
Working against the states of death and hell.

Thou art joy's handsell: heaven lies flat in thee,
Subject to every mounter's bended knee.

God is not Dumb

James Russell Lowell

God is not dumb, that he should speak no more;
If thou hast wanderings in the wilderness
And findest not Sinai, 'tis thy soul is poor;
There towers the mountain of the Voice no less,
Which whoso seeks shall find; but he who bends,
Intent on manna still and mortal ends,
Sees it not, neither hears its thundered lore.

Slowly the Bible of the race is writ,
And not on paper leaves nor leaves of stone;
Each age, each kindred, adds a verse to it,
Texts of despair or hope, of joy or moan.
While swings the sea, while mists the mountains shroud,
While thunder's surges burst on cliffs of cloud,
Still at the prophets' feet the nations sit.

The Books of the Old Testament

Thomas Russell

The great Jehovah speaks to us
In Genesis and Exodus;
Leviticus and Numbers see
Followed by Deuteronomy.
Joshua and Judges sway the land,
Ruth gleans a sheaf with trembling hand;
Samuel and numerous Kings appear

Whose Chronicles we wondering hear.
Ezra and Nehemiah, now,
Esther the beauteous mourner show.
Job speaks in sighs, David in Psalms,
The Proverbs teach to scatter alms;
Ecclesiastes then comes on,
And the sweet Song of Solomon.
Isaiah, Jeremiah then
With Lamentations takes his pen.
Ezekiel, Daniel, Hosea's lyres
Swell Joel, Amos, Obadiah's.
Next Jonah, Micah, Nahum come,
And lofty Habakkuk finds room,—
While Zephaniah, Haggai calls,
Wrapt Zachariah builds his walls;
And Malachi, with garments rent,
Concludes the Ancient Testament.

The Book of Books

Sir Walter Scott

Within this ample volume lies
The mystery of mysteries.
Happiest they of human race
To whom their God has given grace
To read, to fear, to hope, to pray,
To lift the latch, to force the way;
But better had they ne'er been born
That read to doubt or read to scorn.

Taste

Christopher Smart

O guide my judgment and my taste,
    Sweet Spirit, author of the book
Of wonders, told in language chaste
    And plainness, not to be mistook.

O let me muse, and yet at sight
    The page admire, the page believe;
'Let there be light, and there was light,
    Let there be Paradise and Eve!'

Who his soul's rapture can refrain?
    At Joseph's ever-pleasing tale,
Of marvels, the prodigious train,
    To Sinai's hill from Goshen's vale.

The Psalmist and proverbial Seer,
    And all the prophets' sons of song,
Make all things precious, all things dear,
    And bear the brilliant word along.

O take the book from off the shelf,
    And con it meekly on thy knees;
Best panegyric on itself,

    And self-avouched to teach and please.Respect, adore it heart and mind.
    How greatly sweet, how sweetly grand,
Who reads the most, is most refined,
    And polished by the Master's hand.

On the Bible

THOMAS TRAHERNE

When thou dost take this sacred book into thy hand
Think not that thou the included sense dost understand.

It is a sign thou wantest sound intelligence
If that thou think thyself to understand the sense.

Be not deceived thou then on it in vain mayst gaze;
The way is intricate that leads into a maze.

Here's naught but what's mysterious to an understanding eye;
Where reverence alone stands ope, and sense stands by.

The First Book of Moses, called
GENESIS

1:1–2 In the beginning God created the heaven and the earth. And the earth was without form, and void; and darkness was upon the face of the deep. And the Spirit of God moved upon the face of the waters.

from *PARADISE LOST, BK VII*

JOHN MILTON

ll. 205–216; 224–242

Heaven opened wide
Her ever-during gates, harmonious sound
On golden hinges moving, to let forth
The King of Glory in his powerful word
And spirit coming to create new worlds.
On heavenly ground they stood, and from the shore
They viewed the vast immeasurable abyss
Outrageous as a sea, dark, wasteful, wild,
Up from the bottom turned by furious winds
And surging waves, as mountains to assault
Heaven's height, and with the center mix the pole.
Silence, ye troubled waves, and thou Deep, peace. . . .

Then stayed the fervid wheels, and in his hand
He took the golden compasses, prepared
In God's eternal store, to circumscribe
This universe, and all created things:
One foot he centered, and the other turned
Round through the vast profundity obscure,

And said, Thus far extend, thus far thy bounds,
This be thy just circumference, O World.
Thus God the Heaven created, thus the Earth,
Matter unformed and void: Darkness profound
Covered the abyss: but on the watery calm
His brooding wings the spirit of God outspread,
And vital virtue infused, and vital warmth
Throughout the fluid mass, but downward purged
The black tartareous cold infernal dregs
Adverse to life; then founded, then conglobed
Like things to like, the rest to several place
Disparted, and between spun out the air,
And Earth self-balanced on her center hung.

1:3 And God said, Let there be light:

Let There Be Light!

D. H. Lawrence

If ever there was a beginning
there was no god in it
there was no Verb
no Voice
no Word.

There was nothing to say:
Let there be light!
All that story of Mr God switching on day
is just conceit.

Just man's conceit!
—Who made the sun?
—My child, I cannot tell a lie,
I made it!

George Washington's Grandpapa!

All we can honestly imagine in the beginning
is the incomprehensible plasm of life, of creation
struggling
and *becoming* light.

1:3–8 and there was light. And God saw the light, that it was good: and God divided the light from the darkness. And God called the light Day, and the darkness he called Night. And the evening and the morning were the first day.

And God said, Let there be a firmament in the midst of the waters, and let it divide the waters from the waters. And God made the firmament, and divided the waters which were under the firmament from the waters which were above the firmament: and it was so. And God called the firmament Heaven. And the evening and the morning were the second day.

THERE IS NO LAND YET

LAURA (RIDING) JACKSON

The long sea, how short-lasting,
From water-thought to water-thought
So quick to feel surprise and shame.
Where moments are not time
But time is moments.
Such neither yes nor no,
Such only love, to have to-morrow
By certain failure of now and now.

On water lying strong ships and men
In weakness skilled reach elsewhere:
No prouder places from home in bed
The mightiest sleeper can know.
So faith took ship upon the sailor's earth
To seek absurdities in heaven's name—
Discovery but a fountain without source,
Legend of mist and lost patience.

The body swimming in itself
Is dissolution's darling.
With dripping mouth it speaks a truth

That cannot lie, in words not born yet
Out of first immortality,
All-wise impermanence.

And the dusty eye whose accuracies
Turn watery in the mind
Where waves of probability
Write vision in a tidal hand
That time alone can read.

And the dry land not yet,
Lonely and absolute salvation—
Boasting of constancy
Like an island with no water round
In water where no land is.

1:9–13 And God said, Let the waters under the heaven be gathered together unto one place, and let the dry land appear: and it was so. And God called the dry land Earth; and the gathering together of the waters called he Seas: and God saw that it was good. And God said, Let the earth bring forth grass, the herb yielding seed, and the fruit tree yielding fruit after his kind, whose seed is in itself, upon the earth: and it was so. . . .

from MEDITATIONS ON THE SIX DAYS OF THE CREATION

Third Day

THOMAS TRAHERNE

Lo here, within the waters liquid womb
The unborn Earth lay, as in native tomb;
Whilst she at first was buried in the deep,
And all her forms and seeds were fast asleep.
Th' Almighty word then spake, and straight was heard,
The Earth her head up from the waters reared.
The waters soon, as frighted, fled apace,
And all were swiftly gathered to one place.
See now the Earth, with life and verdure crowned,
Spring from her bed, gay, vigorous, and sound:
Her face ten thousand beauties now adorn,
With blessings numberless from plenty's horn.

Here, there, and every where they richly flow,
For us almighty bounty them does strow.
The hills and dales, the lawns and woods around,
God's wisdom, goodness, and his power resound.
Both far and near his wonders they proclaim.
How vilely then is wretched man to blame,
If he forget to praise that liberal hand,
Out-spread from sea to sea, from land to land?

AMEN

1:14–19 And God said, Let there be lights in the firmament of the heaven to divide the day from the night; and let them be for signs, and for seasons, and for days, and years: And let them be for lights in the firmament of the heaven to give light upon the earth: and it was so. And God made two great lights; the greater light to rule the day, and the lesser light to rule the night: he made the stars also. . . . And the evening and the morning were the fourth day.

ODE

JOSEPH ADDISON

The spacious firmament on high
With all the blue ethereal sky,
And spangled heavens, a shining frame,
Their great original proclaim:
The unwearied sun, from day to day,
Does his creator's power display,
And publishes to every land
The work of an almighty hand.

Soon as the evening shades prevail,
The moon takes up the wondrous tale,
And nightly to the listening earth
Repeats the story of her birth:
Whilst all the stars that round her burn,
And all the planets in their turn,
Confirm the tidings as they roll,
And spread the truth from pole to pole.

What though, in solemn silence, all
Move round the dark, terrestrial ball?
What though nor real voice nor sound
Amid their radiant orbs be found?
In reason's ear they all rejoice,
And utter forth a glorious voice,
For ever singing, as they shine,
'The hand that made us is divine'.

1:20–23 And God said, Let the waters bring forth abundantly the moving creature that hath life, and fowl that may fly above the earth in the open firmament of heaven. And God created great whales, and every living creature that moveth, which the waters brought forth abundantly, after their kind, and every winged fowl after his kind: and God saw that it was good. . . .

from *Paradise Lost, Bk VII*

John Milton

ll. 399–446

Forthwith the sounds and seas, each creek and bay
With fry innumerable swarm, and shoals
Of fish that with their fins and shining scales
Glide under the green wave, in sculls that oft
Bank the mid sea: part single or with mate
Graze the sea weed their pasture, and through groves
Of coral stray, or sporting with quick glance
Show to the sun their waved coats dropped with gold,
Or in their pearly shells at ease, attend
Moist nutriment, or under rocks their food
In jointed armor watch: on smooth the seal
And bended dolphins play: part huge of bulk
Wallowing unwieldy, enormous in their gate
Tempest the ocean: there Leviathan
Hugest of living creatures, on the deep
Stretched like a promontory sleeps or swims,
And seems a moving land, and at his gills
Draws in, and at his trunk spouts out a sea.
Meanwhile the tepid caves, and fens and shores
Their brood as numerous hatch, from th' egg that soon

Bursting with kindly rupture forth disclosed
Their callow young, but feathered soon and fledge
They summed their pens, and soaring th' air sublime
With clang despised the ground, under a cloud
In prospect; there the eagle and the stork
On cliffs and cedar tops their eyries build:
Part loosely wing the region, part more wise
In common, ranged in figure wedge their way,
Intelligent of seasons, and set forth
Their airy caravan high over seas
Flying, and over lands with mutual wing
Easing their flight; so steers the prudent crane
Her annual voyage, born on winds; the air
Floats, as they pass, fanned with unnumbered plumes:
From branch to branch the smaller birds with song
Solaced the woods, and spread their painted wings
Till even, nor then the solemn nightingale
Ceased warbling, but all night tuned her soft lays:
Others on silver lakes and rivers bathed
Their downy breast; the swan with archëd neck
Between her white wings mantling proudly, rows
Her state with oary feet: yet oft they quit
The dank, and rising on stiff pennons, tower
The mid aerial sky: others on ground
Walked firm; the crested cock whose clarion sounds
The silent hours, and th' other whose gay train
Adorns him, colored with the florid hue
Of rainbows and starry eyes.

1:24–25 And God said, Let the earth bring forth the living creature after his kind, cattle, and creeping thing, and beast of the earth after his kind: and it was so. And God made the beast of the earth after his kind, and cattle after their kind, and every thing that creepeth upon the earth after his kind: and God saw that it was good.

The Animals

Edwin Muir

They do not live in the world,
Are not in time and space.
From birth to death hurled

No word do they have, not one
To plant a foot upon,
Were never in any place

For with names the world was called
Out of the empty air,
With names was built and walled,
Line and circle and square,
Dust and emerald;
Snatched from deceiving death
By the articulate breath.

But these have never trod
Twice the familiar track,
Never never turned back
Into the memoried day.
All is new and near
In the unchanging Here
Of the fifth great day of God,
That shall remain the same,
Never shall pass away.

On the sixth day we came.

1:26 And God said, Let us make man in our image, after our likeness: and let them have dominion over the fish of the sea, and over the fowl of the air, and over the cattle, and over all the earth, and over every creeping thing that creepeth upon the earth.

Fill and Illumined

Joseph Ceravolo

God created his image.
I love him like the door.
Speak to me now.
Without god there is no god.
Forget everything!
Lie down and be circumscribed
                        and circumcised.
Yet there is no pain.
Yet there is no joy.

1:27 So God created man in his own image, in the image of God created he him; male and female created he them.

A Divine Image

William Blake

Cruelty has a Human Heart,
And Jealousy a Human Face;
Terror the Human Form Divine,
And Secrecy the Human Dress.

The Human Dress is forged Iron,
The Human Form a fiery Forge,
The Human Face a Furnace sealed,
The Human Heart its hungry Gorge.

The Image o' God

Joe Corrie

Crawlin' aboot like a snail in the mud,
    Covered wi' clammy blae
ME, made after the image o' God—
    Jings! but it's laughable, tae.

Howkin' awa' 'neath a mountain o' stane,
    Gaspin' for want o' air,
The sweat makin' streams doon my bare back-bane
    And my knees a' hauckit and sair.

Strainin' and cursin' the hale shift through,
    Half-starved, half-blin', half-mad;
And the gaffer he says, 'Less dirt in that coal
    Or ye go up the pit, my lad!'

So I gi'e my life to the Nimmo squad
    For eicht and fower a day;
Me! made after the image o' God—
    Jings! but it's laughable, tae.

1:28–30 And God blessed them, and God said unto them, Be fruitful, and multiply, and replenish the earth, and subdue it: and have dominion over the fish of the sea, and over the fowl of the air, and over every living thing that moveth upon the earth. . . .

The Pulley

George Herbert

When God at first made man,
Having a glass of blessings standing by,
'Let us' (said he) 'pour on him all we can;
Let the world's riches, which dispersèd lie,
Contract into a span.'

So strength first made a way;
Then beauty flowed, then wisdom, honor, pleasure.
When almost all was out, God made a stay,
Perceiving that alone of all his treasure
Rest in the bottom lay.

'For if I should' (said he)
'Bestow this jewel also on my creature,
He would adore my gifts instead of me,
And rest in nature, not the God of nature:
So both should losers be.

'Yet let him keep the rest,
But keep them with repining restlessness;
Let him be rich and weary, that at least,
If goodness lead him not, yet weariness
May toss him to my breast.'

1:31–2:1 And God saw every thing that he had made, and, behold, it was very good. And the evening and the morning were the sixth day.

Thus the heavens and the earth were finished, and all the host of them.

Genesis

Geoffrey Hill

I

Against the burly air I strode
Crying the miracles of God.

And first I brought the sea to bear
Upon the dead weight of the land;
And the waves flourished at my prayer,
The rivers spawned their sand.

And where the streams were salt and full
The tough pig-headed salmon strove,
Ramming the ebb, in the tide's pull,
To reach the steady hills above.

II

The second day I stood and saw
The osprey plunge with triggered claw,
Feathering blood along the shore,
To lay the living sinew bare.

And the third day I cried: "Beware
The soft-voiced owl, the ferret's smile,
The hawk's deliberate stoop in air,
Cold eyes, and bodies hooped in steel,
Forever bent upon the kill."

III

And I renounced, on the fourth day,
This fierce and unregenerate clay,
Building as a huge myth for man
The watery Leviathan,

And made the long-winged albatross
Scour the ashes of the sea
Where Capricorn and Zero cross,
A brooding immortality –
Such as the charmed phoenix has
In the unwithering tree.

IV

The phoenix burns as cold as frost;
And, like a legendary ghost,
The phantom-bird goes wild and lost,
Upon a pointless ocean tossed.

So, the fifth day, I turned again
To flesh and blood and the blood's pain.

V

On the sixth day, as I rode
In haste about the works of God,
With spurs I plucked the horse's blood.

By blood we live, the hot, the cold,
To ravage and redeem the world:
There is no bloodless myth will hold.

And by Christ's blood are men made free
Though in close shrouds their bodies lie
Under the rough pelt of the sea;

Though Earth has rolled beneath her weight
The bones that cannot bear the light.

2:2–7 . . . And the LORD God formed man of the dust of the ground, and breathed into his nostrils the breath of life; and man became a living soul.

from *Paradise Lost, Bk VIII*

John Milton

ll. 250–271

[*Adam, to the Archangel Raphael*]*:*

For man to tell how human life began
Is hard: for who himself beginning knew?
Desire with thee still longer to converse
Induced me. As new waked from soundest sleep

Soft in the flowery herb I found me laid
In balmy sweat, which with his beams the sun
Soon dried, and on the reeking moisture fed.
Straight toward Heaven my wondering eyes I turned,
And gazed a while the ample sky, till raised
By quick instinctive motion up I sprung,
As thitherward endeavoring, and upright
Stood on my feet; about me round I saw
Hill, dale, and shady woods, and sunny plains,
And liquid lapse of murmuring streams; by these,
Creatures that lived, and moved, and walked, or flew,
Birds on the branches warbling; all things smiled,
With fragrance and with joy my heart o'erflowed.
My self I then perused, and limb by limb
Surveyed, and sometimes ran
With supple joints, as lively vigor led:
But who I was, or where, or from what cause,
Knew not. . . .

The Creation: A Negro Sermon

James Weldon Johnson

And God stepped out on space,
And He looked around and said:
I'm lonely—
I'll make me a world.

And as far as the eye of God could see
Darkness covered everything,
Blacker than a hundred midnights
Down in a cypress swamp.

Then God smiled,
And the light broke,
And the darkness rolled up on one side,
And the light stood shining on the other,
And God said: *That's good!*

Then God reached out and took the light in His hands,
And God rolled the light around in His hands

Until He made the sun;
And He set that sun a-blazing in the heavens.
And the light that was left from making the sun
God gathered it up in a shining ball
And flung it against the darkness,
Spangling the night with the moon and stars.
Then down between
The darkness and the light
He hurled the world;
And God said: *That's good!*

Then God himself stepped down—
And the sun was on His right hand,
And the moon was on His left;
The stars were clustered about His head,
And the earth was under His feet.
And God walked, and where He trod
His footsteps hollowed the valleys out
And bulged the mountains up.

Then He stopped and looked and saw
That the earth was hot and barren.
So God stepped over to the edge of the world
And He spat out the seven seas—
He batted His eyes, and the lightnings flashed—
He clapped His hands, and the thunders rolled—
And the waters above the earth came down,
The cooling waters came down.

Then the green grass sprouted,
And the little red flowers blossomed,
The pine tree pointed his finger to the sky,
And the oak spread out his arms,
The lakes cuddled down in the hollows of the ground,
The rivers ran down to the sea;
And God smiled again,
And the rainbow appeared,
And curled itself around His shoulder.

Then God raised His arm and He waved His hand
Over the sea and over the land,
And He said: *Bring forth! Bring forth!*
And quicker than God could drop His hand,
Fishes and fowls

And beasts and birds
Swam the rivers and the seas,
Roamed the forests and the woods,
And split the air with their wings.
And God said: *That's good!*

Then God walked around,
And God looked around
On all that He had made.
He looked at His sun,
And He looked at His moon,
And He looked at His little stars;
He looked on His world
With all its living things,
And God said: *I'm lonely still.*

Then God sat down—
On the side of a hill where He could think;
By a deep, wide river He sat down;
With His head in His hands,
God thought and thought,
Till He thought: *I'll make me a man!*

Up from the bed of the river
God scooped the clay;
And by the bank of the river
He kneeled Him down;
And there the great God Almighty
Who lit the sun and fixed it in the sky,
Who flung the stars to the most far corner of the night,
Who rounded the earth in the middle of His hand;
This Great God,
Like a mammy bending over her baby,
Kneeled down in the dust
Toiling over a lump of clay
Till He shaped it in His own image;

Then into it He blew the breath of life,
And man became a living soul.
Amen. Amen.

2:8–9 And the LORD God planted a garden eastward in Eden; and there he put the man whom he had formed. And out of the ground made the LORD God to grow every tree that is pleasant to the sight, and good for food; the tree of life also in the midst of the garden, and the tree of knowledge of good and evil.

When Adam Walked in Eden young

A. E. Housman

When Adam walked in Eden young,
Happy, 'tis writ, was he,
While high the fruit of knowledge hung
Unbitten on the tree.

Happy was he the livelong day;
I doubt 'tis written wrong:
The heart of man, for all they say,
Was never happy long.

And now my feet are tired of rest,
And here they will not stay,
And the soul fevers in my breast
And aches to be away.

2:10–18 And a river went out of Eden to water the garden; and from thence it was parted, and became into four heads. . . .
And the LORD God took the man, and put him into the garden of Eden to dress it and to keep it. And the LORD God commanded the man, saying, Of every tree of the garden thou mayest freely eat: But of the tree of the knowledge of good and evil, thou shalt not eat of it: for in the day that thou eatest thereof thou shalt surely die.

Eden

Thomas Traherne

A learnèd and a happy ignorance
Divided me
From all the vanity,
From all the sloth, care, pain and sorrow that advance
The madness and the misery

Of men. No error, no distraction I
Saw soil the Earth, or overcloud the sky.

I knew not that there was a serpent's sting,
Whose poison shed
On men did overspread
The world: nor did I dream of such a thing
As sin, in which mankind lay dead.
They all were brisk and living weights to me,
Yea pure, and full of immortality.

Joy, pleasure, beauty, kindness, glory, love
Sleep, day, life, light,
Peace, melody, my sight,
My ears and heart did fill, and freely move.
All that I saw did me delight:
The *Universe* was then a world of treasure,
To me an universal world of pleasure.

Unwelcome penitence was then unknown;
Vain costly toys,
Swearing and roaring boys,
Shops, markets, taverns, coaches were unshown:
So all things were that drowned my joys.
No thorns choked up my path, nor hid the face
Of bliss and beauty, nor eclipsed the place.

Only what Adam in his first estate,
Did I behold;
Hard silver and dry gold
As yet lay under ground: my blessed fate
Was more acquainted with the old
And innocent delights which he did see
In his Original Simplicity.

Those things which first his Eden did adorn
My infancy
Did crown: simplicity
Was my protection when I first was born.
Mine eyes those treasures first did see
Which God first made: the first effects of love
My first enjoyments upon Earth did prove;

And were so great, and so divine, so pure;
So fair and sweet,
So true; when I did meet
Them here at first, they did my soul allure
And drew away my infant feet
Quite from the works of men; that I might see
The glorious wonders of the Deity.

SONNET IV

E.E. CUMMINGS

this is the garden: colors come and go
frail azures fluttering from night's outer wing
strong silent greens serenely lingering,
absolute lights like baths of golden snow.
This is the garden: pursed lips do blow
upon cool flutes within wide glooms, and sing
(of harps celestial to the quivering string)
invisible faces hauntingly and slow.

This is the garden. Time shall surely reap
and on Death's blade lie many a flower curled,
in other lands where other songs be sung;
yet stand They here enraptured, as among
the slow deep trees perpetual of sleep
some silver-fingered fountain steals the world.

2:19–20 And the LORD God said, It is not good that the man should be alone; I will make him an help meet for him. And out of the ground the LORD God formed every beast of the field, and every fowl of the air; and brought them unto Adam to see what he would call them: and whatsoever Adam called every living creature, that was the name thereof. And Adam gave names to all cattle, and to the fowl of the air, and to every beast of the field;

Naming the Animals

Anthony Hecht

Having commanded Adam to bestow
Names upon all the creatures, God withdrew
To empyrean palaces of blue
That warm and windless morning long ago,
And seemed to take no notice of the vexed
Look on the young man's face as he took thought
Of all the miracles the Lord had wrought,
Now to be labelled, dubbed, yclept, indexed.

Before an addled mind and puddled brow,
The feathered nation and the finny prey
Passed by; there went biped and quadruped.
Adam looked forth with bottomless dismay
Into the tragic eyes of his first cow,
And shyly ventured, "Thou shalt be called 'Fred.' "

2:20–22 but for Adam there was not found an help meet for him. And the LORD God caused a deep sleep to fall upon Adam, and he slept: and he took one of his ribs, and closed up the flesh instead thereof; And the rib, which the LORD God had taken from man, made he a woman, and brought her unto the man.

The Recognition of Eve

Karl Shapiro

Whatever it was she had so fiercely fought
Had fled back to the sky, but still she lay
With arms outspread, awaiting its assault,
Staring up through the branches of the tree,
The fig tree. Then she drew a shuddering breath
And turned her head instinctively his way.
She had fought birth as dying men fight death.

Her sigh awakened him. He turned and saw
A body swollen, as though formed of fruits,
White as the flesh of fishes, soft and raw.

He hoped she was another of the brutes
So he crawled over and looked into her eyes,
The human wells that pool all absolutes.
It was like looking into double skies.

And when she spoke the first word (it was *thou*)
He was terror-stricken, but she raised her hand
And touched his wound where it was fading now,
For he must feel the place to understand.
Then he recalled the longing that had torn
His side, and while he watched it whitely mend,
He felt it stab him suddenly, like a thorn.

He thought the woman had hurt him. Was it she
Or the same sickness seeking to return;
Or was there any difference, the pain set free
And she who seized him now as hard as iron?
Her fingers bit his body. She looked old
And involuted, like the newly-born.
He let her hurt him till she loosed her hold.

Then she forgot him and she wearily stood
And went in search of water through the grove.
Adam could see her wandering through the wood,
Studying her footsteps as her body wove
In light and out of light. She found a pool
And there he followed shyly to observe.
She was already turning beautiful.

The Sleep of Adam

John Hejduk

While Eve waited
inside of Adam
she was his
structure
her volume
filled him
his skin hung
on Eve's form

when God
released her
from Adam
Death rushed in
preventing collapse.

2:23 And Adam said, This is now bone of my bones, and flesh of my flesh: she shall be called Woman, because she was taken out of Man.

The Follies of Adam

Theodore Roethke

Read me Euripides,
Or some old lout who can
Remember what it was
To jump out of his skin.
Things speak to me, I swear;
But why am I groaning here,
Not even out of breath?

What are scepter and crown?
No more than what is raised
By a naked stem:
The rose leaps to this girl;
The earthly lives in her;
A thorn does well in the wind,
At ease with all that flows.

I talked to a shrunken root;
Ah, how she laughed to see
Me staring past my foot,
One toe in eternity;
But when the root replied,
She shivered in her skin,
And looked away.

Father and son of this death,
The soul dies every night;
In the wide white, the known
Reaches of common day,
What eagle needs a tree?
The flesh fathers a dream;
All true bones sing alone.

Poseidon's only a horse,
Laughed a master of hump and snort;
He cared so much for the sport,
He rode all night, and came
Back on the sea-foam;
And when he got to the shore,
He laughed, once more.

2:24 Therefore shall a man leave his father and his mother, and shall cleave unto his wife: and they shall be one flesh.

What the Serpent Said to Adam

Archibald MacLeish

Which is you, old two-in-one?
Which is which, old one of two?
When the doubling is undone
Which one is you?

Is it you that so delights
By that woman in her bed?
Or you the glimmering sky afrights,
Vast overhead?

Are you body, are you ghost?
Were you got or had no father?
Is this you—the guest?—the host?
Who then's the other?

That woman says, old one-of-two,
In body was the soul begun:
Now two are one and one is you:—
Which one? Which one?

2:25 And they were both naked, the man and his wife, and were not ashamed.

The Fall

John Wilmot, Earl of Rochester

How blessed was the created state
    Of man and woman, ere they fell,
Compared to our unhappy fate:
    We need not fear another hell.

Naked beneath cool shades they lay;
    Enjoyment waited on desire;
Each member did their wills obey,
    Nor could a wish set pleasure higher.

But we, poor slaves to hope and fear,
    Are never of our joys secure;
They lessen still as they draw near,
    And none but dull delights endure.

Then, Chloris, while I duly pay
    The nobler tribute of my heart,
Be not you so severe to say
    You love me for the frailer part.

As Adam Early in the Morning

Walt Whitman

As Adam early in the morning,
Walking forth from the bower refreshed with sleep,
Behold me where I pass, hear my voice, approach,
Touch me, touch the palm of your hand to my body as I pass,
Be not afraid of my body.

3:1–6 Now the serpent was more subtil than any beast of the field which the Lord God had made. And he said unto the woman, Yea, hath God said, Ye shall not eat of every tree of the garden?

And the woman said unto the serpent, We may eat of the fruit of the trees of the garden: But of the fruit of the tree which is in the midst of the garden, God hath said, Ye shall not eat of it, neither shall ye touch it, lest ye die.

And the serpent said unto the woman, Ye shall not surely die: For God doth know that in the day ye eat thereof, then your eyes shall be opened, and ye shall be as gods, knowing good and evil.

And when the woman saw that the tree was good for food, and that it was pleasant to the eyes, and a tree to be desired to make one wise, she took of the fruit thereof, and did eat,

from *Paradise Lost, Bk IX*

John Milton

ll. 670–784

As when of old some orator renowned
In Athens or free Rome, where eloquence
Flourished, since mute, to some great cause addressed,
Stood in himself collected, while each part,
Motion, each act won audience ere the tongue,
Sometimes in height began, as no delay
Of preface brooking through his zeal of right.
So standing, moving, or to height upgrown
The Tempter all impassioned thus began:
Sacred, wise, and wisdom-giving plant,
Mother of science, now I feel thy power
Within me cleare, not only to discern
Things in their causes, but to trace the ways
Of highest agents, deemed however wise.
Queen of this universe, do not believe
Those rigid threats of death; ye shall not die:
How should ye? by the fruit? it gives you life
To knowledge: by the threatener? look on me,
Me who have touched and tasted, yet both live,
And life more perfect have attained than fate
Meant me, by venturing higher than my lot.
Shall that be shut to Man, which to the beast
Is open? or will God incense his ire
For such a petty trespass, and not praise
Rather your dauntless virtue, whom the pain

Of death denounced, whatever thing death be,
Deterred not from achieving what might lead
To happier life, knowledge of good and evil;
Of good, how just? of evil, if what is evil
Be real, why not known, since easier shunned?
God therefore cannot hurt ye, and be just;
Not just, not God; not feared then, nor obeyed:
Your fear itself of death removes the fear.
Why then was this forbid? Why but to awe,
Why but to keep ye low and ignorant,
His worshippers; he knows that in the day
Ye eat thereof, your eyes shall seem so clear,
Yet are but dim, shall perfectly be then
Opened and cleared, and ye shall be as Gods,
Knowing both Good and Evil as they know.
That ye should be as gods, since I as Man,
Internal Man, is but proportion meet,
I of brute human, ye of human gods.
So shall ye die perhaps, by putting off
Human, to put on gods, death to be wished,
Though threatened, which no worse than this can bring.
And what are gods that Man may not become
As they, participating god-like food?
The gods are first, and that advantage use
On our belief, that all from them proceeds;
I question it, for this fair Earth I see,
Warmed by the Sun, producing every kind,
Them nothing: If they all things, who enclosed
Knowledge of good and evil in this tree,
That whoso eats thereof, forthwith attains
Wisdom without their leave? and wherein lies
Th' offence, that Man should thus attain to know?
What can your knowledge hurt him, or this tree
Impart against his will if all be his?
Or is it envy, and can envy dwell
In heavenly breasts? these, these and many more
Causes import your need of this fair fruit.
Goddess human, reach then, and freely taste.
He ended, and his words replete with guile
Into her heart too easy entrance won:
Fixed on the fruit she gazed, which to behold
Might tempt alone, and in her ears the sound
Yet rung of his persuasive words, impregn'd
With reason, to her seeming, and with truth;

Meanwhile the hour of noon drew on, and waked
An eager appetite, raised by the smell
So savory of that fruit, which with desire,
Inclinable now grown to touch or taste,
Solicited her longing eye; yet first
Pausing a while, thus to herself she mused:
    Great are thy virtues, doubtless, best of fruits,
Though kept from Man, and worthy to be admired,
Whose taste, too long forborn, at first assay
Gave elocution to the mute, and taught
The tongue not made for speech to speak thy praise:
Thy praise he also who forbids thy use,
Conceals not from us, naming thee the Tree
Of Knowledge, knowledge both of good and evil;
Forbids us then to taste, but his forbidding
Commends thee more, while it infers the good
By thee communicated, and our want:
For good unknown, sure is not had, or had
And yet unknown, is as not had at all.
In plain then, what forbids he but to know,
Forbids us good, forbids us to be wise?
Such prohibitions bind not. But if death
Bind us with after-bands, what profits then
Our inward freedom? In the day we eat
Of this fair fruit, our doom is, we shall die.
How dies the serpent? he hath eaten and lives,
And knows, and speaks, and reasons, and discerns,
Irrational till then. For us alone
Was death invented? or to us denied
This intellectual food, for beasts reserved?
For beasts it seems: yet that one beast which first
Hath tasted, envies not, but brings with joy
The good befallen him, author unsuspect,
Friendly to Man, far from deceit or guile.
What fear I then, rather what know to fear
Under this ignorance of Good and Evil,
Of God or Death, of Law or Penalty?
Here grows the cure of all, this fruit divine,
Fair to the eye, inviting to the taste,
Of virtue to make wise: what hinders then
To reach, and feed at once both body and mind?
    So saying, her rash hand in evil hour
Forth reaching to the fruit, she plucked, she eat:

Earth felt the wound, and nature from her seat
Sighing through all her works gave signs of woe,
That all was lost.

Eve

RALPH HODGSON

Eve, with her basket, was
Deep in the bells and grass,
Wading in bells and grass
Up to her knees,
Picking a dish of sweet
Berries and plums to eat,
Down in the bells and grass
Under the trees.

Mute as a mouse in a
Corner the cobra lay,
Curled round a bough of the
Cinnamon tall. . . .
Now to get even and
Humble proud heaven and—
Now was the moment or
Never at all.

"Eva!" Each syllable
Light as a flower fell,
"Eva!" he whispered the
Wondering maid,
Soft as a bubble sung
Out of a linnet's lung,
Soft and most silverly
"Eva!" he said.

Picture that orchard sprite,
Eve, with her body white,
Supple and smooth to her
Slim finger tips,
Wondering, listening,
Listening, wondering,
Eve with a berry
Half-way to her lips.

Oh, had our simple Eve
Seen through the make-believe!
Had she but known the
Pretender he was!
Out of the boughs he came,
Whispering still her name,
Tumbling in twenty rings
Into the grass.

Here was the strangest pair
In the world anywhere,
Eve in the bells and grass
Kneeling, and he
Telling his story low. . . .
Singing birds saw them go
Down the dark path to
The Blasphemous Tree.

Oh, what a clatter when
Titmouse and Jenny Wren
Saw him successful and
Taking his leave!
How the birds rated him!
How they all hated him!
How they all pitied
Poor motherless Eve.

Picture her crying
Outside in the lane,
Eve, with no dish of sweet
Berries and plums to eat,
Haunting the gate of the
Orchard in vain. . . .
Picture the lewd delight
Under the hill tonight—
"Eva!" the toast goes round,
"Eva!" again.

3:6 and gave also unto her husband with her; and he did eat.

Sharing Eve's Apple

John Keats

O blush not so! O blush not so!
  Or I shall think you knowing;
And if you smile the blushing while,
  Then maidenheads are going.

There's a blush for won't, and a blush for shan't,
  And a blush for having done it:
There's a blush for thought and a blush for nought,
  And a blush for just begun it.

O sigh not so! O sigh not so!
  For it sounds of Eve's sweet pippin;
By these loosened lips you have tasted the pips
  And fought in an amorous nipping.

Will you play once more at nice-cut-core,
  For it only will last our youth out,
And we have the prime of the kissing time,
  We have not one sweet tooth out.

There's a sigh for yes, and a sigh for no,
  And a sigh for I can't bear it!
O what can be done, shall we stay or run?
  O cut the sweet apple and share it!

3:7 And the eyes of them both were opened, and they knew that they were naked; and they sewed fig leaves together, and made themselves aprons.

The Tree of Knowledge

Abraham Cowley

That there is no Knowledge:
Against the Dogmatists

The sacred tree midst the fair orchard grew;
  The Phœnix Truth did on it rest,
  And built his perfumed nest.

That right Porphyrian tree which did true logic shew,
Each leaf did learnëd notions give,
And th' apples were demonstrative.
So clear their color and divine,
The very shade they cast did other lights out-shine.

Taste not, said God; 'tis mine and angels' meat;
A certain death does sit
Like an ill worm i'th' core of it.
Ye cannot know and live, nor live or know and eat.
Thus spoke God, yet man did go
Ignorantly on to know;
Grew so more blind, and she
Who tempted him to this, grew yet more blind than he.

The only science man by this did get,
Was but to know he nothing knew:
He straight his nakedness did view,
His ignorant poor estate, and was ashamed of it.
Yet searches probabilities,
And rhetoric, and fallacies,
And seeks by useless pride
With slight and withering leaves that nakedness to hide.

Henceforth, said God, the wretched sons of earth
Shall sweat for food in vain
That will not long sustain,
And bring with labor forth each fond abortive birth.
That serpent, too, their pride,
Which aims at things denied,
That learned and eloquent lust
Instead of mounting high, shall creep upon the dust.

3:8 And they heard the voice of the Lord God walking in the garden in the cool of the day: and Adam and his wife hid themselves from the presence of the Lord God amongst the trees of the garden.

Songs of Experience

Introduction

WILLIAM BLAKE

Hear the voice of the Bard!
Who Present, Past, and Future, sees;
Whose ears have heard
The Holy Word
That walked among the ancient trees,

Calling the lapsed Soul,
And weeping in the evening dew;
That might control
The starry pole,
And fallen, fallen light renew!

"O Earth, O Earth, return!
"Arise from out the dewy grass:
"Night is worn,
"And the morn
"Rises from the slumberous mass.

"Turn away no more;
"Why wilt thou turn away?
"The starry floor,
"The watery shore,
"Is given thee till the break of day."

3:9–10 And the LORD God called unto Adam, and said unto him, Where art thou?

And he said, I heard thy voice in the garden, and I was afraid, because I was naked; and I hid myself.

Earth's Answer

William Blake

Earth raised up her head
From the darkness dread and drear.
Her light fled,
Stony dread!
And her locks covered with grey despair.

"Prisoned on watery shore,
"Starry Jealousy does keep my den:
"Cold and hoar,
"Weeping o'er,
"I hear the Father of the ancient men.

"Selfish father of men!
"Cruel, jealous, selfish fear!
"Can delight,
"Chained in night,
"The virgins of youth and morning bear?

"Does spring hide its joy
"When buds and blossoms grow?
"Does the sower
"Sow by night,
"Or the plowman in darkness plow?

"Break this heavy chain
"That does freeze my bones around.
"Selfish! vain!
"Eternal bane!
"That free Love with bondage bound."

3:11–13 And he said, Who told thee that thou wast naked? Hast thou eaten of the tree, whereof I commanded thee that thou shouldest not eat?

And the man said, The woman whom thou gavest to be with me, she gave me of the tree, and I did eat.

And the LORD God said unto the woman, What is this that thou hast done? And the woman said, The serpent beguiled me, and I did eat.

Original Sequence

Philip Booth

Time was the apple Adam ate.
Eve bit, gave seconds to his mouth.
and then they had no minute left
to lose. Eyes opened in mid-kiss,
they saw, for once, raw nakedness,
and hid that sudden consequence
behind an hour's stripped leaves.

This is one sequence in the plot,
the garden where God came, that time,
to call. Hands behind him, walking
to and fro, he counted how
the fruit fell, bruised on frozen sod.
This was his orchard, his to pace;
the day was cool, and he was God.

Old Adam heard him humming, talking
to himself: *Winesap, King,*
ripen in sun,
McIntosh and
Northern Spy
fall one by one,
ripen to die.

Adam heard him call his name,
but Adam, no old philosopher,
was not sure what he was after.
We're naked, Lord, and can't come out.
Eve nudged him with the bitter fruit.
God paused. *How do you know? Where is*
that woman that I sprung from you?

Eve held the twisted stem, the pulp;
she heard the low snake hiss, and let fly
blindly with a woman arm, careless
where her new-won anger struck.
The fodder for that two-fold flock
fell, an old brown core, at God's
stopped feet. He reached, and wound the clock.

3:14–20 . . . And unto Adam he said, Because thou hast hearkened unto the voice of thy wife, and hast eaten of the tree, of which I commanded thee, saying, Thou shalt not eat of it: cursed is the ground for thy sake; in sorrow shalt thou eat of it all the days of thy life; Thorns also and thistles shall it bring forth to thee; and thou shalt eat the herb of the field; In the sweat of thy face shalt thou eat bread, till thou return unto the ground; for out of it wast thou taken: for dust thou art, and unto dust shalt thou return. And Adam called his wife's name Eve; because she was the mother of all living.

The Cloud

Derek Walcott

And, laterally,
to Adam's pulsing eye,
the erect ridges would throb and recede.

a sigh under the fig tree and a sky
deflating to the serpent's punctured hiss,
repeating you will die.

The woman lay still as the settling mountains.
There was another silence,
all was thick with it;

the clouds given a mortal destination,
the silent shudder from the broken branch
where the sap dripped

from the torn tree.
When she, his death,
turned on her side and slept,
the breath he drew was his first real breath.

What left the leaves,
the phosphorescent air,
was both God and the serpent leaving him.
Neither could curse or bless.

Pollen was drifting to the woman's hair,
his eye felt brighter,
a cloud's slow shadow slowly covered them,

and, as it moved, he named it Tenderness.

3:21 Unto Adam also and to his wife did the LORD God make coats of skins, and clothed them.

Adam Posed

Anne Finch, Countess of Winchilsea

Could our first father, at his toilsome plough,
Thorns in his path, and labor on his brow,
Clothed only in a rude, unpolished skin,
Could he a vain fantastic nymph have seen,
In all her airs, in all her antic graces,
Her various fashions, and more various faces;
How had it posed that skill, which late assigned
Just appellations to each several kind!
A right idea of the sight to frame;
T'have guessed from what new element she came;
T'have hit the wavering form, or given this thing a name.

3:22 And the LORD God said, Behold, the man is become as one of us, to know good and evil:

from Of Human Knowledge

Sir John Davies

ll. 1–40; 149–180

Why did my parents send me to the schools
    That I with knowledge might enrich my mind?
    Since the desire to know first made men fools,
    And did corrupt the root of all mankind.

For when God's hand had written in the hearts
    Of the first parents all the rules of good,
    So that their skill infused did pass all arts
    That ever were, before or since the flood,

And when their reason's eye was sharp and clear,
    And, as an eagle can behold the sun,
    Could have approached th' eternal light as near
    As the intellectual angels could have done,

Even then to them the spirit of lies suggests
    That they were blind, because they saw not ill,
    And breathes into their incorrupted breasts
    A curious wish, which did corrupt their will.

For that same ill they straight desired to know;
    Which ill, being nought but a defect of good,
    And all God's works the devil could not show
    While man their lord in his perfection stood.

So that themselves were first to do the ill,
    Ere they thereof the knowledge could attain;
    Like him that knew not poison's power to kill,
    Until, by tasting it, himself was slain.

Even so by tasting of that fruit forbid,
    Where they sought knowledge, they did error find;
    Ill they desired to know, and ill they did,
    And to give passion eyes, made reason blind.

* * * * *

If aught can teach us aught, affliction's looks,
    Making us look into ourselves so near,
    Teach us to know ourselves beyond all books,
    Or all the learnëd schools that ever were.

This mistress lately plucked me by the ear,
    And many a golden lesson hath me taught;
    Hath made my senses quick and reason clear,
    Reformed my will and rectified my thought.

So do the winds and thunders cleanse the air;
    So working lees settle and purge the wine;
    So lopped and prunëd trees do flourish fair;
    So doth the fire the drossy gold refine.

Neither Minerva nor the learnëd muse,
    Nor rules of art, nor precepts of the wise,
    Could in my brain those beams of skill infuse,
    As but the glance of this dame's angry eyes.

She within lists my ranging mind hath brought,
    That now beyond myself I list not go;
    Myself am center of my circling thought,
    Only myself I study, learn, and know.

I know my body's of so frail a kind
    As force without, fevers within, can kill;
    I know the heavenly nature of my mind,
    But 'tis corrupted both in wit and will;

I know my soul hath power to know all things,
    Yet is she blind and ignorant in all;
    I know I am one of nature's little kings,
    Yet to the least and vilest things am thrall.

I know my life's a pain and but a span,
    I know my sense is mocked with everything;
    And to conclude, I know myself a man,
    Which is a proud and yet a wretched thing.

3:22–23 and now, lest he put forth his hand, and take also of the tree of life, and eat, and live for ever: Therefore the LORD God sent him forth from the garden of Eden, to till the ground from whence he was taken.

EDEN IS THAT OLD-FASHIONED HOUSE

EMILY DICKINSON

Eden is that old-fashioned House
We dwell in every day
Without suspecting our abode
Until we drive away.

How fair on looking back, the Day
We sauntered from the Door –
Unconscious our returning,
But discover it no more.

3:24 So he drove out the man; and he placed at the east of the garden of Eden Cherubims, and a flaming sword which turned every way, to keep the way of the tree of life.

TO THE GARDEN THE WORLD

WALT WHITMAN

To the garden the world anew ascending,
Potent mates, daughters, sons, preluding,

The love, the life of their bodies, meaning and being,
Curious here behold my resurrection after slumber,
The revolving cycles in their wide sweep having brought me again,
Amorous, mature, all beautiful to me, all wondrous,
My limbs and quivering fire that ever plays through them, for reasons,
most wondrous,
Existing I peer and penetrate still,
Content with the present, content with the past,
By my side or back of me Eve following,
Or in front, and I following her just the same.

They Wondered Why the Fruit Had Been Forbidden

W. H. Auden

They wondered why the fruit had been forbidden;
It taught them nothing new. They hid their pride,
But did not listen much when they were chidden;
They knew exactly what to do outside.

They left: immediately the memory faded
Of all they'd learnt; they could not understand
The dogs now who, before, had always aided;
The stream was dumb with whom they'd always planned.

They wept and quarrelled: freedom was so wild.
In front, maturity, as he ascended,
Retired like a horizon from the child;

The dangers and the punishments grew greater;
And the way back by angels was defended
Against the poet and the legislator.

4:1 And Adam knew Eve his wife; and she conceived, and bare Cain, and said, I have gotten a man from the Lord.

IMPERIAL ADAM

A. D. HOPE

Imperial Adam, naked in the dew,
Felt his brown flanks and found the rib was gone.
Puzzled he turned and saw where, two and two,
The mighty spoor of Jahweh marked the lawn.

Then he remembered through mysterious sleep
The surgeon fingers probing at the bone,
The voice so far away, so rich and deep:
"It is not good for him to live alone."

Turning once more he found Man's counterpart
In tender parody breathing at his side.
He knew her at first sight, he knew by heart
Her allegory of sense unsatisfied.

The pawpaw drooped its golden breasts above
Less generous than the honey of her flesh;
The innocent sunlight showed the place of love;
The dew on its dark hairs winked crisp and fresh.

This plump gourd severed from his virile root,
She promised on the turf of Paradise
Delicious pulp of the forbidden fruit;
Sly as the snake she loosed her sinuous thighs,

And waking, smiled up at him from the grass;
Her breasts rose softly and he heard her sigh—
From all the beasts whose pleasant task it was
In Eden to increase and multiply

Adam had learned the jolly deed of kind:
He took her in his arms and there and then,
Like the clean beasts, embracing from behind,
Began in joy to found the breed of men.

Then from the spurt of seed within her broke
Her terrible and triumphant female cry,
Split upward by the sexual lightning stroke.
It was the beasts now who stood watching by:

The gravid elephant, the calving hind,
The breeding bitch, the she-ape big with young
Were the first gentle midwives of mankind;
The teeming lioness rasped her with her tongue;

The proud vicuña nuzzled her as she slept
Lax on the grass; and Adam watching too
Saw how her dumb breasts at their ripening wept,
The great pod of her belly swelled and grew,

And saw its water break, and saw, in fear,
Its quaking muscles in the act of birth,
Between her legs a pigmy face appear,
And the first murderer lay upon the earth.

4:2 And she again bare his brother Abel. And Abel was a keeper of sheep, but Cain was a tiller of the ground.

Song with Words

James Agee

When Eve first saw the glistering day
    Watch by the wan world side
She learned her worst and down she lay
    In the streaming land and cried.

When Adam saw the mastering night
    First board the wan world's lifted breast
He climbed his bride with all his might
    And sank to tenderest rest.

And night took both and day brought high
The children that must likewise die:
And all our grief and every joy
To time's deep end shall time destroy:

And weave us one and wave us under
Where is neither faith nor wonder.

4:3–10 . . . And the Lord said unto Cain, Where is Abel thy brother? And he said, I know not: Am I my brother's keeper?

And he said, What hast thou done? the voice of thy brother's blood crieth unto me from the ground.

Eve

Christina Rossetti

'While I sit at the door,
Sick to gaze within,
Mine eye weepeth sore
For sorrow and sin:
As a tree my sin stands
To darken all lands;
Death is the fruit it bore.

'How have Eden bowers grown
Without Adam to bend them!
How have Eden flowers blown,
Squandering their sweet breath,
Without me to tend them!
The Tree of Life was ours,
Tree twelvefold-fruited,
Most lofty tree that flowers,
Most deeply rooted:
I chose the Tree of Death.

'Hadst thou but said me nay,
Adam, my brother,
I might have pined away;
I, but none other:
God might have let thee stay
Safe in our garden
By putting me away
Beyond all pardon.

'I, Eve, sad mother
Of all who must live,
I, not another,
Plucked bitterest fruit to give
My friend, husband, lover.
O wanton eyes run over;

Who but I should grieve?—
Cain hath slain his brother:
Of all who must die mother,
Miserable Eve!'

Thus she sat weeping,
Thus Eve our mother,
Where one lay sleeping
Slain by his brother.
Greatest and least
Each piteous beast
To hear her voice
Forgot his joys
And set aside his feast.
The mouse paused in his walk
And dropped his wheaten stalk;
Grave cattle wagged their heads
In rumination;
The eagle gave a cry
From his cloud station:
Larks on thyme beds
Forbore to mount or sing;
Bees drooped upon the wing;
The raven perched on high
Forgot his ration;
The conies in their rock,
A feeble nation,
Quaked sympathetical;
The mocking-bird left off to mock;
Huge camels knelt as if
In deprecation;
The kind hart's tears were falling;
Chattered the wistful stork;
Dove-voices with a dying fall
Cooed desolation
Answering grief by grief.
Only the serpent in the dust,
Wriggling and crawling,
Grinned an evil grin, and thrust
His tongue out with its fork.

ABEL

JOHN WHEELWRIGHT

In the dead night we walk behind a hearse
zigzagging towards a dancing colonnade;
knee-deep, through dust of faded petals wade
past thornless flowers through thorns. Hear us converse:
"Whom do we mourn?" you ask me, half afraid.
"I mourn for you, and whom I mourn, I curse."
And, though I know my answer is perverse,
I do not know who the one was who prayed.

With dawn comes knowledge. The prophet in the fane
withered the valedictory spray we brought,
and swept it out into the empty court.
By scorn in love, by charity in disdain,
our fragmentary fealties attain
foreknowledge of the vacancy he sought.

4:11–16 And now art thou cursed from the earth, which hath opened her mouth to receive thy brother's blood from thy hand; When thou tillest the ground, it shall not henceforth yield unto thee her strength; a fugitive and a vagabond shalt thou be in the earth. . . .

And Cain went out from the presence of the Lord, and dwelt in the land of Nod, on the east of Eden.

from CAIN: A MYSTERY

GEORGE NOEL GORDON, LORD BYRON

Act iii, Scene i, ll. 528–544

Cain. Oh! thou dead
And everlasting witness! whose unsinking
Blood darkens earth and heaven! what thou now art
I know not! but if thou seest what I am,
I think thou wilt forgive him, whom his God
Can ne'er forgive, nor his own soul.— Farewell!
I must not, dare not touch what I have made thee.
I, who sprung from the same womb as thee, drained
The same breast, clasped thee often to my own,

In fondness brotherly and boyish, I
Can never meet thee more, nor even dare
To do that for thee, which thou shouldst have done
For me—compose thy limbs into their grave—
The first grave yet dug for mortality.
But who hath dug that grave? Oh, earth! Oh, earth!
For all the fruits thou hast rendered to me, I
Give thee back this. Now for the wilderness.

The Ghost of Abel

A Revelation in the Visions of Jehovah Seen by

William Blake

To Lord Byron in the Wilderness:
What doest thou here, Elijah?
Can a Poet doubt the Visions of Jehovah? Nature has no Outline, but Imagination has. Nature has no Tune, but Imagination has. Nature has no Supernatural and dissolves: Imagination is Eternity.

Scene—A rocky Country. Eve *fainted over the dead body of* Abel, *which lays near a Grave.* Adam *kneels by her.* Jehovah *stands above.*

Jehovah. Adam!
Adam. I will not hear thee more, thou Spiritual Voice.
Is this Death?
Jehovah. Adam!
Adam. It is in vain. I will not hear thee
Henceforth! Is this thy Promise, that the Woman's Seed
Should bruise the Serpent's head? Is this the Serpent? Ah!
Seven times, O Eve, thou hast fainted over the Dead. Ah! Ah!
Eve *revives.*
Eve. Is this the Promise of Jehovah? O, it is all a vain delusion,
This Death and this Life and this Jehovah!
Jehovah. Woman, lift thine eyes!

A Voice is heard coming on.

Voice. O Earth, cover not thou my Blood! cover not thou my Blood!

Enter the Ghost *of* Abel.

Eve. Thou Visionary Phantasm, thou art not the real Abel.

Abel. Among the Elohim, a Human Victim I wander: I am their House,
Prince of the Air, and our dimensions compass Zenith and Nadir.
Vain is thy Covenant, O Jehovah! I am the Accuser and Avenger
Of Blood. O Earth, Cover not thou the Blood of Abel.
Jehovah. What Vengeance dost thou require?
Abel. Life for Life! Life for Life!
Jehovah. He who shall take Cain's life must also Die, O Abel!
And who is he? Adam, wilt thou, or Eve, thou do this?
Adam. It is all a Vain delusion of the all creative Imagination
Eve, come away, and let us not believe these vain delusions.
Abel is dead, and Cain slew him. We shall also Die a Death,
And then, what then? be, as poor Abel, a Thought, or as
This! O, what shall I call thee, Form Divine, Father of Mercies,
That appearest to my Spiritual Vision? Eve, seest thou also?
Eve. I see him plainly with my Mind's Eye. I see also Abel living,
Though terribly afflicted, as We also are, yet Jehovah sees him
Alive and not Dead; were it not better to believe Vision
With all our might and strength, though we are fallen and lost?
Adam. Eve, thou hast spoken truly: let us kneel before his feet.
They Kneel before Jehovah.
Abel. Are these the Sacrifices of Eternity, O Jehovah, a Broken Spirit
And a Contrite Heart? O, I cannot Forgive! the Accuser hath
Entered into Me as into his House, and I loathe thy Tabernacles.
As thou hast said, so is it come to pass: My desire is unto Cain,
And He doth rule over Me; therefore My Soul in fumes of Blood
Cries for Vengeance, Sacrifice on Sacrifice, Blood on Blood!
Jehovah. Lo, I have given you a Lamb for an Atonement instead
Of the Transgressor, or no Flesh or Spirit could ever Live.
Abel. Compelled I cry, O Earth, cover not the Blood of Abel!
Abel sinks down into the Grave, from which arises Satan,
Armed in glittering scales, with a Crown and a Spear.
Satan. I will have Human Blood and not the blood of Bulls or Goats,
And no Atonement, O Jehovah! the Elohim live on Sacrifice
Of Men: hence I am God of Men: Thou Human, O Jehovah!
By the Rock and Oak of the Druid, creeping Mistletoe and Thorn,
Cain's City built with Human Blood, not Blood of Bulls and
Goats,
Thou shalt Thyself be Sacrificed to Me, thy God, on Calvary.
Jehovah. Such is My Will *Thunders.*
that Thou Thyself go to Eternal Death
In Self Annihilation, even till Satan, Self-subdued, Put off Satan
Into the Bottomless Abyss, whose torment arises for ever and ever.

On each side a Chorus of Angels entering Sing the following:
The Elohim of the Heathen Swore Vengeance for Sin! Then Thou stoodst
Forth, O Elohim Jehovah! in the midst of the darkness of the Oath, All Clothed
In Thy Covenant of the Forgiveness of Sins: Death, O Holy! Is this Brotherhood.
The Elohim saw their Oath Eternal Fire: they rolled apart trembling over The
Mercy Seat each in his station fixed in the Firmament by Peace, Brotherhood and Love.

The Curtain falls.

4:17–5:4 . . . This is the book of the generations of Adam. In the day that God created man, in the likeness of God made he him; Male and female created he them; and blessed them, and called their name Adam, in the day when they were created. . . .

Ancient History

Siegfried Sassoon

Adam, a brown old vulture in the rain,
Shivered below his wind-whipped olive-trees;
Huddling sharp chin on scarred and scraggy knees,
He moaned and mumbled to his darkening brain;
'*He was the grandest of them all – was Cain!*
'A lion laired in the hills, that none could tire:
'Swift as a stag: a stallion of the plain,
'Hungry and fierce with deeds of huge desire.'

Grimly he thought of Abel, soft and fair –
A lover with disaster in his face,
And scarlet blossom twisted in bright hair.
'Afraid to fight; was murder more disgrace? . . .
'*God always hated Cain*' . . . He bowed his head –
The gaunt wild man whose lovely sons were dead.

5:5–24 . . . And all the days of Enoch were three hundred sixty and five years: And Enoch walked with God: and he was not; for God took him.

Enoch

Jones Very

I looked to find a man who walked with God,
Like the translated patriarch of old;—
Though gladdened millions on his footstool trod,
Yet none like him did such sweet converse hold;
I heard the wind in low complaint go by
That none its melodies like him could hear;
Day unto day spoke wisdom from on high,
Yet none like David turned a willing ear;
God walked alone unhonored through the earth;
For him no heart-built temple open stood,
The soul forgetful of her nobler birth
Had hewn him lofty shrines of stone and wood,
And left unfinished and in ruins still
The only temple he delights to fill.

5:25–6:2 . . . And it came to pass, when men began to multiply on the face of the earth, and daughters were born unto them, That the sons of God saw the daughters of men that they were fair; and they took them wives of all which they chose.

The Woman and the Angel

Robert Service

An angel was tired of heaven, as he lounged in the golden street;
His halo was tilted side-ways, and his harp lay mute at his feet;
So the Master stooped in His pity, and gave him a pass to go,
For the space of a moon, to the earth-world, to mix with the men below.

He doffed his celestial garments, scarce waiting to lay them straight;
He bade good-bye to Peter, who stood by the golden gate;
The sexless singers of heaven chanted a fond farewell,
And the imps looked up as they pattered on the red-hot flags of hell.

Never was seen such an angel—eyes of heavenly blue,
Features that shamed Apollo, hair of a golden hue;
The women simply adored him; his lips were like Cupid's bow;
But he never ventured to use them—and so they voted him slow.

Till at last there came One Woman, a marvel of loveliness,
And she whispered to him: "Do you love me?" And he answered that woman, "Yes."
And she said: "Put your arms around me, and kiss me, and hold me—so—"
But fiercely he drew back, saying: "This thing is wrong, and I know."

Then sweetly she mocked his scruples, and softly she him beguiled:
"You, who are verily man among men, speak with the tongue of a child.
We have outlived the old standards; we have burst, like an over-tight thong,
The ancient, outworn, Puritanic traditions of Right and Wrong."

Then the Master feared for His angel, and called him again to His side,
For oh, the woman was wondrous, and oh, the angel was tried!
And deep in his hell sang the Devil, and this was the strain of his song:
"The ancient, outworn, Puritanic traditions of Right and Wrong."

6:3–22 . . . And God said unto Noah, The end of all flesh is come before me; for the earth is filled with violence through them; and, behold, I will destroy them with the earth. . . .

from Noah's Flood

Noah's Sermon

Michael Drayton

A hundred years the Ark in building was,
So long the time ere he could bring to pass
This work intended; all which time just Noy
Cried, that th'Almighty would the world destroy,
And as this good man used many a day
To walk abroad, his building to survey,
These cruel giants coming in to see,
(In their thoughts wondering what this work should be)
He with erected hands to them doth cry,
Either repent ye, or ye all must die,
Your blasphemies, your beastliness, your wrongs,
Are heard to heaven, and with a thousand tongues
Shout in the ears of the Almighty Lord;
So that your sins no leisure him afford
To think on mercy, they so thickly throng,

That when he would your punishment prolong,
Their horror hales him on, that from remorse
In his own nature, you do him enforce,
Nay, wrest plagues from him, upon human kind
Who else to mercy, wholly is inclined.
From Seth which God to Eva gave in lieu
Of her son Abel whom his brother slew,
That cursed Cain, how hath th'Almighty blessed,
The seed of Adam though he so transgressed,
In Enos by whose godliness men came,
At first to call on the Almighty's name,
And Enoch, whose integrity was such,
In whom the Lord delighted was so much,
As in his years he suffered no decay,
But God to Heaven took bodily away;
With long life blessing all that goodly stem,
From the first man down to Mathusalem,
Now from the loins of Lamech sendeth me,
(Unworthy his ambassador to be)
To tell ye yet, if ye at last repent,
He will lay by his wrathful punishment,
That God who was so merciful before,
To our forefathers, likewise hath in store,
Mercy for us their nephews, if we fall
With tears before him, and he will recall,
His wrath sent out already, therefore fly
To him for mercy, yet the threatening sky
Pauses, ere it be the deluge down will pour,
For every tear you shed, he'll stop a shower;
Yet of th'Almighty mercy you may win,
He'll leave to punish, if you leave to sin;
That God eternal, which old Adam cast
Out of the earthly heaven, where he had placed,
That first-made man, for his forbidden deed,
From thence forever banishing his seed,
For us his sinful children doth provide,
And with abundance hath us still supplied,
And can his blessings who respects you thus,
Make you most wicked, most rebellious:
Still is your stubborn obstinacy such?
Have ye no mercy, and your God so much?
Your God, said I, O wherefore said I so?
Your words deny him, and your works say no;
O see the day, doth but too fast approach,

Wherein heaven's maker means to set abroach
That world of water, which shall over-flow
Those mighty mountains whereon now you go,
The dropsied clouds, see, your destruction threat,
The sun and moon both in their course are set
To war by water, and do all they can
To bring destruction upon sinful man,
And every thing shall suffer for your sake,
For the whole earth shall be but one whole lake;
Oh cry for mercy, leave your wicked ways,
And God from time shall separate those days
Of vengeance coming, and he shall disperse
These clouds now threatening the whole universe,
And save the world, which else he will destroy.
But this good man, this terror-preaching Noy,
The bears, and tigers, might have taught as well,
They laughed to hear this godly man to tell
That God would drown the world, they thought him mad,
For their great maker they forgotten had,
They knew none such, th'Almighty God say they,
What might he be? and when shall be the day
Thou talkst of to us? canst thou think that we
Can but suppose that such a thing can be?
What can he do that we cannot defeat?
Whose brawny fists, to very dust can beat
The solidest rock, and with our breasts can bear
The strongest stream backward, dost thou think to fear
Us with these dreams of deluges? to make
Us our own ways and courses to forsake?
Let us but see that God that dares to stand
To what thou speakst, that with his furious hand,
Dare say he'll drown us, and we will defy
Him to his teeth: and if he keep the sky,
We'll dare him thence, and if he then come down,
And challenge us that he the world will drown,
We'll follow him until his threats he stints,
Or we will batter his blue house with flints.

7:11–14 . . . And the rain was upon the earth forty days and forty nights. In the selfsame day entered Noah, and Shem, and Ham, and Japheth, the sons of Noah, and Noah's wife, and the three wives of his sons with them, into the ark; They, and every beast after his kind, and all the cattle after

their kind, and every creeping thing that creepeth upon the earth after his kind, and every fowl after his kind, every bird of every sort.

AUTHOR'S PROLOGUE

DYLAN THOMAS

This day winding down now
At God speeded summer's end
In the torrent salmon sun,
In my seashaken house
On a breakneck of rocks
Tangled with chirrup and fruit,
Froth, flute, fin and quill
At a wood's dancing hoof,
By scummed, starfish sands
With their fishwife cross
Gulls, pipers, cockles, and sails,
Out there, crow black, men
Tackled with clouds, who kneel
To the sunset nets,
Geese nearly in heaven, boys
Stabbing, and herons, and shells
That speak seven seas,
Eternal waters away
From the cities of nine
Days' night whose towers will catch
In the religious wind
Like stalks of tall, dry straw,
At poor peace I sing
To you strangers (though song
Is a burning and crested act,
The fire of birds in
The world's turning wood,
For my sawn, splay sounds),
Out of these seathumbed leaves
That will fly and fall
Like leaves of trees and as soon
Crumble and undie
Into the dogdayed night.
Seaward the salmon, sucked sun slips,
And the dumb swans drub blue
My dabbed bay's dusk, as I hack

This rumpus of shapes
For you to know
How I, a spinning man,
Glory also this star, bird
Roared, sea born, man torn, blood blest.
Hark: I trumpet the place,
From fish to jumping hill! Look:
I build my bellowing ark
To the best of my love
As the flood begins,
Out of the fountainhead
Of fear, rage red, manalive,
Molten and mountainous to stream
Over the wound asleep
Sheep white hollow farms
To Wales in my arms.
Hoo, there, in castle keep,
You king singsong owls, who moonbeam
The flickering runs and dive
The dingle furred deer dead!
Huloo, on plumbed bryns,
O my ruffled ring dove
In the hooting, nearly dark
With Welsh and reverent rook,
Coo rooing the woods' praise,
Who moons her blue notes from her nest
Down to the curlew herd!
Ho, hullaballoing clan
Agape, with woe
In your beaks, on the gabbing capes!
Heigh, on horseback hill, jack
Whisking hare! who
Hears, there, this fox light, my flood ship's
Clangour as I hew and smite
(A clash of anvils for my
Hubbub and fiddle, this tune
On a tongued puffball)
But animals thick as thieves
On God's rough tumbling grounds
(Hail to His beasthood!).
Beasts who sleep good and thin,
Hist, in hogsback woods! The haystacked
Hollow farms in a throng
Of waters cluck and cling,

And barnroofs cockcrow war!
O kingdom of neighbours, finned
Felled and quilled, flash to my patch
Work ark and the moonshine
Drinking Noah of the bay,
With pelt, and scale, and fleece:
Only the drowned deep bells
Of sheep and churches noise
Poor peace as the sun sets
And dark shoals every holy field.
We will ride out alone, and then,
Under the stars of Wales,
Cry, Multitudes of arks! Across
The water lidded lands,
Manned with their loves they'll move,
Like wooden islands, hill to hill.
Huloo, my prowed dove with a flute!
Ahoy, old, sea-legged fox,
Tom tit and Dai mouse!
My ark sings in the sun
At God speeded summer's end
And the flood flowers now.

7:15 And they went in unto Noah into the ark, two and two of all flesh, wherein is the breath of life.

PARLEY OF BEASTS

HUGH MACDIARMID

Auld Noah was at hame wi' them a',
The lion and the lamb,
Pair by pair they entered the Ark
And he took them as they cam'.

If twa o' ilka beist there is
Into this room sud come,
Wad I cud welcome them like him
And no' staun' gowpin' dumb!

Be chief wi' them and they wi' me
And a' wi' ane anither
As Noah and his couples were
There in the Ark thegither.

It's fain I'd mell wi' tiger and tit,
Wi' elephant and ell,
But noo-a-days e'en wi' ain's se
At hame it's hard to feel.

8:4–7 **. . . And it came to pass at the end of forty days, that Noah opened the window of the ark which he had made: And he sent forth a raven, which went forth to and fro, until the waters were dried up from off the earth.**

Noah's Raven

W. S. Merwin

Why should I have returned?
My knowledge would not fit into theirs.
I found untouched the desert of the unknown,
Big enough for my feet. It is my home.
It is always beyond them. The future
Splits the present with the echo of my voice.
Hoarse with fulfillment, I never made promises.

8:9–22 **But the dove found no rest for the sole of her foot, and she returned unto him into the ark, for the waters were on the face of the whole earth: then he put forth his hand, and took her, and pulled her in unto him into the ark. And he stayed yet other seven days; and again he sent forth the dove out of the ark; And the dove came in to him in the evening; and, lo, in her mouth was an olive leaf pluckt off: so Noah knew that the waters were abated from off the earth. . . .**

And Noah builded an altar unto the LORD; . . . and offered burnt offerings on the altar. And the LORD smelled a sweet savour; and the LORD said in his heart, I will not again curse the ground any more for man's sake; for the imagination of man's heart is evil from his youth; neither will I again smite any more every thing living, as I have done. . . .

from The Monarch

After the Flood

Sir David Lindsay

When Noy had made his sacrifice,
Thanking God of his benefice,
He standed on mount Armenie,
Where he the country might espy,
Ye may believe his heart was sore,
Seeing the earth, which was afore
The Flood so pleasant and perfect,
Which to behold was great delight,
That now was barren made and bare,
Afore which fructuous was and fair.
The pleasant trees bearing fruits
Were lying riven up by the roots.
The wholesome herbs and fragrant flowers
Had taint, both virtue and colors.
The fields green and forest meads
Were spoiled of their pleasant weeds.
The earth, which first was so fair formed,
Was, by that furious flood, deformed.
Where once-while were the pleasant plains,
Were hollow glens and high mountains.
From clattering crags, great and gray,
The earth was washing quite away.
    But Noy had greatest displeasures,
    Beholding the dead creatures,
Which was one sight right lamentable
Men, women, beasts innumerable,
Seeing them lie upon the lands,
And some were floating on the strands.
Whales and monsters of the seas
Stuck on stumps, among the trees
And, when the Flood was decreasing,
They were left weltering on the land.
Afore the Flood during that space,
The sea was all into one place.
Right so the earth, as been decided,
In sundry parts was not divided,
As been Europe and Asia
Divided are from Africa.
Ye see, now, diverse famous isles

Stand from the main land many miles:
All their great isles, I understand
Were, then, equal with the firm land.
There was none sea Mediterranean,
But only the great Ocean
Which did not spread such bellowing strands
As it does, now, athwart the lands.
Then, by the raging of that flood,
The earth of virtue was denude,
The which afore was to be prized,
Whose beauty then was disguised.
Then was the malediction known
Which was by God to Adam shown.
I read how clerks do conclude,
In during that most furious flood,
With which the earth was so suppressed,
The wind blew forth of the southwest.
As may be seen, by experience,
How, through the waters violence,
The high mountains, in every art,
Are bare forgainst the southwest part,
As the mountains of Pyrenees,
The Alps, and rocks in the seas,
Right so, the rocks, great and gray,
Which stand into Norway,
The highest hills, in every art,
And in Scotland, for the most part.
Through weltering of that furious flood,
The crags of earth war made denude:
Travelling men may consider best
The mountains bare next the southwest.

9:8–11 And God spake unto Noah, and to his sons with him, saying, . . . I will establish my covenant with you, neither shall all flesh be cut off any more by the waters of a flood; neither shall there any more be a flood to destroy the earth.

Holy Sonnet V

John Donne

I am a little world made cunningly
Of elements, and an angelic sprite,
But black sin hath betrayed to endless night
My world's both parts, and (oh) both parts must die.
You which beyond that heaven which was most high
Have found new spheres, and of new lands can write,
Pour new seas in mine eyes, that so I might
Drown my world with my weeping earnestly,
Or wash it if it must be drowned no more:
But oh it must be burnt! alas the fire
Of lust and envy have burnt it heretofore,
And made it fouler; Let their flames retire
And burn me ô Lord, with a fiery zeal
Of thee and thy house, which doth in eating heal.

9:12–13 And God said, . . . I do set my bow in the cloud, and it shall be for a token of a covenant between me and the earth.

The Rainbow: or curious Covenant

Robert Herrick

Mine eyes, like clouds, were drizzling rain,
And as they thus did entertain
The gentle beams from Julia's sight
To mine eyes levelled opposite:
O thing admired! there did appear
A curious rainbow smiling there;
Which was the Covenant, that she
No more would drown mine eyes, or me.

9:14–21 . . . And Noah began to be an husbandman, and he planted a vineyard: And he drank of the wine, and was drunken; and he was uncovered within his tent.

WINE AND WATER

G. K. CHESTERTON

Old Noah he had an ostrich farm and fowls on the largest scale,
He ate his egg with a ladle in an egg-cup big as a pail,
And the soup he took was Elephant Soup, and the fish he took was
Whale,
But they all were small to the cellar he took when he set out to sail,
And Noah he often said to his wife when he sat down to dine,
"I don't care where the water goes if it doesn't get into the wine."

The cataract of the cliff of heaven fell blinding off the brink
As if it would wash the stars away as suds go down the sink,
The seven heavens came roaring down for the throats of hell to drink,
And Noah he cocked his eye and said, "It looks like rain, I think,
The water has drowned the Matterhorn as deep as a Mendip mine,
But I don't care where the water goes if it doesn't get into the wine."

But Noah he sinned, and we have sinned; on tipsy feet we trod,
Till a great big black teetotaller was sent us for a rod,
And you can't get wine at a P. S. A., or chapel, or Eisteddfod,
For the Curse of Water has come again because of the wrath of God,
And water is on the Bishop's board and the Higher Thinker's shrine,
But I don't care where the water goes if it doesn't get into the wine.

9:22–10:1 And Ham, the father of Canaan, saw the nakedness of his father, and told his two brethren without. And Shem and Japheth took a garment, and laid it upon both their shoulders, and went backward, and covered the nakedness of their father; and their faces were backward, and they saw not their father's nakedness. . . .

from THE FAMILY OF LOVE

Song of Shem

JAMES MCAULEY

When our beasts low in their stalls
And rain renews its antique mode
My superstitious spine recalls
The earth's diluvian episode.

What men were they before the flood?
What speech, what barter then obtained?
What man was I? And did my blood
Freeze then, as now, when the sky rained?

What women, coins, and statues then
Dissolved into that dreadful ooze?
What kings unknown to later men?
What giant lustful residues?

And did we then find grace in living
In some accustomed, unblest way;
Heedless that God was unforgiving,
Not looking for a likelier day?

My thoughts are wrecked upon that sea,
The hauntings of a drowned man's cry:
While Ham and Japhet spread the tea
And Noah hangs his clothes to dry.

10:8–11:4 . . . And the whole earth was of one language, and of one speech. And it came to pass, as they journeyed from the east, that they found a plain in the land of Shinar; and they dwelt there. And they said one to another, Go to, let us make brick, and burn them thoroughly. And they had brick for stone, and slime had they for mortar. And they said, Go to, let us build us a city and a tower, whose top may reach unto heaven; and let us make us a name, lest we be scattered abroad upon the face of the whole earth.

On the Babel-Builders

Francis Quarles

Sure, if those Babel-builders had thought good
To raise their heaven-high tower before the flood,
The wiser sort of people might deride
Their folly, and that folly had salved their pride;
Or had their faiths but enterprised that plot,
Their hearts had finished what their hands could not;
'Twas not for love of heaven: nor did they aim
So much to raise a building, as a name:
They that by works shall seek to make intrusion
To heaven, find nothing but their own confusion.

11:5–9 And the LORD came down to see the city and the tower, which the children of men builded. And the LORD said, Behold, the people is one, and they have all one language; and this they begin to do: and now nothing will be restrained from them, which they have imagined to do. Go to, let us go down, and there confound their language, that they may not understand one another's speech. So the LORD scattered them abroad from thence upon the face of all the earth: and they left off to build the city. Therefore is the name of it called Babel; because the LORD did there confound the language of all the earth: and from thence did the LORD scatter them abroad upon the face of all the earth.

The Tower of Babel

Laurance Wieder

Nimrod gazed across the plain
About the city he had made,
From the horizon to his feet,
The valley where two rivers meet,
And sighed, and stared into the heavens:
A polished stone of mirror blue
By day, an inky pool by night
That flickered in the milky light
Of living stars, and changing moon:
The open pupil of God's eye?
Beyond the city's walls, dunes walked
The earth in scattered generations.
How could he keep these people one?
All Babel came to Nimrod's summons
From the ramparts: "Let's be done
With building cities in the sun,
For none among us has the power
To stop the wind, or stay the hour.
Go to, come, take brick and slime
To raise a tower up to heaven,
To make ourselves a name, one nation,
People, not dispersed or crushed
By storm, or time, or death." A hush,
Then, "Yes," they answered in one voice,
(For they were all of Adam's line
And tongue, and when a thing was named
They could imagine it entire)
"Come, let us stoke the kiln and fire
Bricks. Go to the river, gather

Ooze for mortar, and together
We will build this signal tower."
Donkeys strained, yoked oxen groaned,
Masons trued each handmade brick.
They did not need an architect;
A thousand thousand ziggurats
Stacked each upon the other, left
Mountains, thunderstorms below:
So high rose the first great story.
Spiral ramps gyred up the sides,
With little cities at the edge
For animal and traveler
To rest, as they ascended, ledge
By ledge. "Brick on brick," the hunter
Muttered to the mass, "and soon
We'll reach the porches of the moon
Where heaven and the angels are."
The Lord looked down, and saw the Tower
Rear above its mortar city
And said: "Behold, this human many
Are as one. They speak one tongue,
And this thing they begin to do.
Now no thing will be beyond them,
Nothing they imagine. Go to,"
The Lord said to his angels, "Come,
Let us go down and there confound
Their language and their speech,
That they not understand nor reach
Us, others." But said, then done.
On Shinar's plain once burst
Confusion from the sky, a whirlwind
Hurtling whistled, swamped, dispersed
The people into many nations.
Language lost, a weighty thud
And screech of men in hail of bricks
Puffed dust upon the plain as thick
As polar snow, as fall monsoon.

Where once prayers said were unison,
And conversations harmony,
We now mistake our dearest loves;
Crowds muddle in cacophony.
So far from being of one name
We clash, strive, swindle, beat, and blame

The other for not being nearer
To ourselves, or speaking clearer.
Nimrod's grave magnificence
Redounds as naked arrogance
And God, that made of Babel rubble,
We call in many tongues a father,
Light, indifferent, shepherd, mild,
Stern, an absence, or a bubble.

12:1–13:18 . . . But the men of Sodom were wicked and sinners before the LORD exceedingly. And the LORD said unto Abram, after that Lot was separated from him, Lift up now thine eyes, and look from the place where thou art northward, and southward, and eastward, and westward: For all the land which thou seest, to thee will I give it, and to thy seed for ever. And I will make thy seed as the dust of the earth: so that if a man can number the dust of the earth, then shall thy seed also be numbered. Arise, walk through the land in the length of it and in the breadth of it; for I will give it unto thee. Then Abram removed his tent, and came and dwelt in the plain of Mamre, which is in Hebron, and built there an altar unto the LORD.

RETIREMENT

HENRY VAUGHAN

Fresh fields and woods! the Earth's fair face,
God's foot-stool, and man's dwelling-place.
I ask not why the first Believer
Did love to be a country liver?
Who to secure pious content
Did pitch by groves and wells his tent;
Where he might view the boundless sky,
And all those glorious lights on high:
With flying meteors, mists and showers,
Subjected hills, trees, meads and flowers:
And every minute bless the King
And wise creator of each thing.
    I ask not why he did remove
To happy Mamre's holy grove,
Leaving the cities of the plain
To Lot and his successless train?
All various lusts in cities still

Are found; they are the thrones of ill.
The dismal sinks, where blood is spilled,
Cages with much uncleanness filled.
But rural shades are the sweet fence
Of piety and innocence.
They are the meek's calm region, where
Angels descend, and rule the sphere:
Where heaven lies leiguer, and the dove
Duly as dew, comes from above.
If Eden be on Earth at all,
'Tis that, which we the country call.

17:1–18:15 . . . Now Abraham and Sarah were old and well stricken in age; and it ceased to be with Sarah after the manner of women. Therefore Sarah laughed within herself, saying, After I am waxed old shall I have pleasure, my lord being old also?

And the LORD said unto Abraham, Wherefore did Sarah laugh, saying, Shall I of a surety bear a child, which am old? Is any thing too hard for the LORD? At the time appointed I will return unto thee, according to the time of life, and Sarah shall have a son.

Then Sarah denied, saying, I laughed not; for she was afraid. And he said, Nay; but thou didst laugh.

Sarah

Delmore Schwartz

The angel said to me: "Why are you laughing?"
"Laughing! Not me! Who was laughing? I did not laugh. It was
A cough. I was coughing. Only hyenas laugh.
It was the cold I caught nine minutes after
Abraham married me: when I saw
How I was slender and beautiful, more and more
Slender and beautiful.
I was also
Clearing my throat; something inside of me
Is continually telling me something
I do not wish to hear: A joke: A big joke:
But the joke is always just on me.
He said: you will have more children than the sky's stars
And the seashore's sands, if you just wait patiently.
Wait: patiently: ninety years? You see
The joke's on me!"

18:16–27 . . . And the LORD said, If I find in Sodom fifty righteous within the city, then I will spare all the place for their sakes.

And Abraham answered and said, Behold now, I have taken upon me to speak unto the Lord, which am but dust and ashes:

Oaks and Squirrels

Anne Porter

"I speak to my Lord though I am dust and ashes,"
A handful of ashes the wind will soon send flying
Into the drifted oak-leaves under the hedge.
No gardener ever rakes there
Only the squirrels gather bedding there
When they stack up their rustling nests.

You have granted me more time
On earth than the squirrels, less time than the oak,
Whose secret takes a hundred years to tell.
Out of the acorn in the dirt
Its wooden sticks come up
Already knowing how to grow their leaves
And when to spend them all.
Knowing exactly
How to thread up into a winter sky
A dark-veined map like that of a great river
Spun out in tapering streams,
Twig by twig ascending and unfolding
Until at night its topmost buds
Enter the country of the stars.
By day
The squirrels run like script along its boughs
And write their lives with their light bodies.
They are afraid of us
We can never hold them
And there's no room for us in their invisible ark.
Our home is warring disobedient history.

18:28–19:25 . . . The sun was risen upon the earth when Lot entered into Zoar. Then the LORD rained upon Sodom and upon Gomorrah brim-

stone and fire from the LORD out of heaven; And he overthrew those cities, and all the plain, and all the inhabitants of the cities, and that which grew upon the ground.

The Cities of the Plain

John Greenleaf Whittier

"Get ye up from the wrath of God's terrible day!
Ungirded, unsandalled, arise and away!
'Tis the vintage of blood, 'tis the fulness of time,
And vengeance shall gather the harvest of crime!"

The warning was spoken—the righteous had gone,
And the proud ones of Sodom were feasting alone;
All gay was the banquet—the revel was long,
With the pouring of wine and the breathing of song.

'Twas an evening of beauty; the air was perfume,
The earth was all greenness, the trees were all bloom;
And softly the delicate viol was heard,
Like the murmur of love or the notes of a bird.

And beautiful maidens moved down in the dance,
With the magic of motion and sunshine of glance;
And white arms wreathed lightly, and tresses fell free
As the plumage of birds in some tropical tree.

Where the shrines of foul idols were lighted on high,
And wantonness tempted the lust of the eye;
Midst rites of obsceneness, strange, loathsome, abhorred,
The blasphemer scoffed at the name of the Lord.

Hark! the growl of the thunder,—the quaking of earth!
Woe, woe to the worship, and woe to the mirth!
The black sky has opened; there's flame in the air;
The red arm of vengeance is lifted and bare!

Then the shriek of the dying rose wild where the song
And the low tone of love had been whispered along;
For the fierce flames went lightly o'er palace and bower,
Like the red tongues of demons, to blast and devour!

Down, down on the fallen the red ruin rained,
And the reveller sank with his wine-cup undrained;
The foot of the dancer, the music's loved thrill,
And the shout and the laughter grew suddenly still.

The last throb of anguish was fearfully given;
The last eye glared forth in its madness on Heaven!
The last groan of horror rose wildly and vain,
And death brooded over the pride of the Plain!

The Destruction of Sodom

DARYL HINE

One would never suspect there were so many vices.
It is, I think, a tribute to the imagination
Of those who in these eminently destructible cities
Have made an exact science of perversion
That they, like us, limited by their bodies,
Could put those bodies to such various uses.

Before now men have been punished for their uses
Contrary to nature, though some, indulging phantom vices
Secretly in the brothels of the imagination,
Have escaped so far a condemnation like these cities'
Which were rebuked for innocent perversion
Through the spirit's envy of too simple bodies.

Do not suppose that I intend to praise their bodies,
Though I admit that bodies have their uses,
Nor is my purpose to defend their vices.
Simply as a pervert of the imagination
I pronounce the funeral oration of two cities
Famous for acts of unimaginable perversion.

All love deserves the epitaph 'Perversion',
Being unnaturally concerned, like physics, with foreign bodies,
Inseparable from their uses and abuses.
To those who care for nothing but their vices
Love is the faculty of the imagination.
Fantasy, I say, debauches cities.

Discreetly, Lord, show mercy to these cities,
Not for the sake of their, but your, perversion
That contradicts its own created bodies.
These are precisely the instruments grace uses,
Alchemically reforming virtues of their vices,
To raise a heaven from the imagination.

O, where is that heaven of the imagination,
The first and least accessible of cities,
If not in the impossible kingdom of perversion?
Its angels have no sexes and no bodies,
Its speech, no words, its instruments, no uses.
None enter there but those who know their vices.

Number your vices in imagination:
Would they teach whole cities of perversion?
Forgive us our bodies, forgive our bodies' uses.

19:26–32 . . . And Lot went up out of Zoar, and dwelt in the mountain, and his two daughters with him; for he feared to dwell in Zoar: and he dwelt in a cave, he and his two daughters. And the firstborn said unto the younger, Our father is old, and there is not a man in the earth to come in unto us after the manner of all the earth: Come, let us make our father drink wine, and we will lie with him, that we may preserve seed of our father.

On the Two Great Floods

FRANCIS QUARLES

Two floods I read of; water, and of wine;
The first was Noah's; Lot, the last was thine:
The first was the effect; the last, the cause
Of that foul sin, against the sacred laws
Of God and nature, incest: Noah found
An ark to save him, but poor Lot was drowned;
Good Noah found an ark; but Lot found none:
We're safer in God's hands then in our own:
The former flood of waters did extend
But some few days; this latter has no end;
They both destroyed, I know not which the worst:

The last is even as general, as the first:
The first being ceased, the world began to fill;
The last depopulates, and wastes it still:
Both floods o'erwhelmed both man and beast together;
The last is worst, if there be best of either:
The first are ceased: Heaven vowed it by a sign;
When shall we see a rainbow after wine?

19:33–35 And they made their father drink wine that night: and the firstborn went in, and lay with her father; and he perceived not when she lay down, nor when she arose. And it came to pass on the morrow, that the firstborn said unto the younger, Behold, I lay yesternight with my father: let us make him drink wine this night also; and go thou in, and lie with him, that we may preserve seed of our father. And they made their father drink wine that night also: and the younger arose, and lay with him; and he perceived not when she lay down, nor when she arose.

Lot and his Daughters I

A. D. Hope

The ruddy fire-glow, like her sister's eyes,
Flickered on her bare breasts and licked along
The ripeness of her savage flanks; a tongue
Of darkness curled between her restless thighs.

Black as the Syrian night, on her young head
Clustered the tendrils of their ancient vine;
The cave gaped with its drunken mouth; the wine
Babbled, unceasing, from the old man's bed:

'I have two daughters . . . let them serve your need
. . . virgins . . . but these, my guests . . . you understand'—
She crept in and lay down. Her Promised Land
Lay waiting for the sower with his seed.

She felt him stir; she felt herself embraced;
The tough old arms bit hard on loin and breast;
The great beard smothered her. She was possessed.
A lioness roared abruptly in the waste.

But Lot's grim heart was far away. Beside
The Jordan stream, in other days, he stood
And kept the great beast, raging, from her brood,
And drove his javelin through her tawny hide.

19:36–38 Thus were both the daughters of Lot with child by their father. And the firstborn bare a son, and called his name Moab: the same is the father of the Moabites unto this day. And the younger, she also bare a son, and called his name Benammi: the same is the father of the children of Ammon unto this day.

Lot and his Daughters II

A. D. Hope

The sun above the hills raged in the height.
Within Lot's cave, his vine-stock's living screen
Filtered the noon-day glare to a dim green
And hung the fat grapes bunched against the light.

The rascal patriarch, the bad old man,
Naked and rollicking on his heap of straw,
Scratching his hairy cods—one drunken paw
Spilled the red liquor from its silver can.

His beard, white as a blossoming branch, gaped wide;
Out flew a laugh: 'By God, the wine is out!
More wine!'
The cavern rumbled to his shout.
Brown fingers pushed the leafy screen aside.

And, padding broadly with their bare-foot tread,
Calm-eyed, big-bellied, purposeful and slow,
Lot's delicate daughters, in the bloom and glow
Of their fulfilment stood beside his bed.

Crafty from fear, reckless with joy and greed,
The old man held them in his crapulous eye:
Mountains of promise bulging in his sky;
Ark of his race; God's covenant to his seed.

They stooped to take his cup, tilted and poured;
The must rose mantling to the glittering rim;
And, as the heart of Lot grew bold in him,
It boasted and exulted in the Lord.

'The one Just Man from Sodom saved alive
Did not His finger point me to this cave?
Behold His hand once more stretched out to save
For Jahweh too is just. My seed shall thrive.

'Shall not the Judge of all the earth do right?
Why did his angels take me by the hand?
My tribe shall yet be numbered with the sand
Upon the shore and with the stars of night.

'With me it shall be as with Abraham.
Dark are His ways, but sure and swift to bless—
How should my ewes breed in the wilderness ?
And lo, the Lord himself provides a ram!'

But Lot's resourceful daughters, side by side,
Smiled back, inscrutable, patient and content;
Their slender bodies, ripe and eloquent,
Swayed like the standing corn at harvest-tide.

And, conscious of what trouble stirred below
His words and flickered in his shrewd old eyes,
They placed the cup that kept their father wise
In that best wisdom, which is not to know.

21:1–22:13 . . . And it came to pass after these things, that God did tempt Abraham, and said unto him, Abraham: and he said, Behold, here I am.

And he said, Take now thy son, thine only son Isaac, whom thou lovest, and get thee into the land of Moriah; and offer him there for a burnt offering upon one of the mountains which I will tell thee of.

And Abraham rose up early in the morning, and saddled his ass, and took two of his young men with him, and Isaac his son, and clave the wood for the burnt offering, and rose up, and went unto the place of which God had told him.

Then on the third day Abraham lifted up his eyes, and saw the place afar off. And Abraham said unto his young men, Abide ye here with the

ass; and I and the lad will go yonder and worship, and come again to you. And Abraham took the wood of the burnt offering, and laid it upon Isaac his son; and he took the fire in his hand, and a knife; and they went both of them together.

And Isaac spake unto Abraham his father, and said, My father: and he said, Here am I, my son. And he said, Behold the fire and the wood: but where is the lamb for a burnt offering?

And Abraham said, My son, God will provide himself a lamb for a burnt offering: so they went both of them together.

And they came to the place which God had told him of; and Abraham built an altar there, and laid the wood in order, and bound Isaac his son, and laid him on the altar upon the wood. And Abraham stretched forth his hand, and took the knife to slay his son.

And the angel of the LORD called unto him out of heaven, and said, Abraham, Abraham: and he said, Here am I. And he said, Lay not thine hand upon the lad, neither do thou any thing unto him: for now I know that thou fearest God, seeing thou hast not withheld thy son, thine only son from me.

And Abraham lifted up his eyes, and looked, and behold behind him a ram caught in a thicket by his horns: and Abraham went and took the ram, and offered him up for a burnt offering in the stead of his son.

FAITH

CHRISTOPHER SMART

The Father of the Faithful said,
At God's first calling, 'Here am I';
Let us by his example swayed,
Like him submit, like him reply,

'Go take thy son, thine only son,
And offer him to God thy King.'
The word was given: the work begun,
'The altar pile, the victim bring.'

But lo! th' angelic voice above
Bade the great Patriarch stop his hands;
'Know God is everlasting love,
And must revoke such harsh commands.'

Then let us imitate the Seer,
    And tender with compliant grace
Ourselves, our souls, and children here,
    Hereafter in a better place.

Abraham to kill him

Emily Dickinson

Abraham to kill him
Was distinctly told –
Isaac was an urchin –
Abraham was old –

Not a hesitation –
Abraham complied –
Flattered by obeisance –
Tyranny demurred–

Isaac – to his children
Lived to tell the tale –
Moral – with a mastiff
Manners may prevail.

The Parable of the Old Man and the Young

Wilfred Owen

So Abram rose, and clave the wood, and went,
And took the fire with him, and a knife.
And as they sojourned both of them together,
Isaac the first-born spake and said, My Father,
Behold the preparations, fire and iron,
But where the lamb for this burnt offering?
Then Abram bound the youth with belts and straps,
And builded parapets and trenches there,
And stretchèd forth the knife to slay his son.
When lo! an angel called him out of heaven,

Saying, Lay not thy hand upon the lad,
Neither do anything to him. Behold,
A ram, caught in a thicket by its horns;
Offer the Ram of Pride instead of him.
But the old man would not so, but slew his son,
And half the seed of Europe, one by one.

Abraham

Delmore Schwartz

To J. M. Kaplan

I was a mere boy in a stone-cutter's shop
When, early one evening, my raised hand
Was halted and the soundless voice said:
"Depart from your father and your country
And the things to which you are accustomed.
Go now into a country unknown and strange.
I will make of your children a great nation,
Your generations will haunt every generation of all the nations,
They will be like the stars at midnight, like the sand of the sea."
Then I looked up at the infinite sky,
Star-pointing and silent, and it was then, on that evening, that I
Became a man: that evening of my manhood's birthday.

I went then to Egypt, the greatest of nations.
There I encountered the Pharaoh who built the tombs,
Great public buildings, many theatres, and seashore villas:
And my wife's beauty was such that, fearing his power and lust,
I called her my sister, a girl neither for him nor for me.
And soon was fugitive, a nomad again.
Living alone with my sister, becoming very rich
In all but children, in herds, in possessions, the herds continually
Increased my possessions through prodigies of progeny.

From time to time, in the afternoon's revery
In the late sunlight or the cool of the evening
I called to mind the protracted vanity of that promise
Which had called me forth from my father's house unwillingly
Into the last strangeness of Egypt and the childless desert.

Then Sarah gave me her handmaid, a young girl
That I might at least at last have children by another
And later, when a great deal else had occurred,
I put away Hagar with the utmost remorse
Because the child was the cause of so much rivalry and jealousy.
At last when all this had passed or when
The promise seemed the parts of dream,
When we were worn out and patient in all things
The stranger came, suave and elegant,
A messenger who renewed the promise, making Sarah
Burst out laughing hysterically!

But the boy was born and grew and I saw
What I had known, I knew what I had seen, for he
Possessed his mother's beauty and his father's humility,
And was not marked and marred by her sour irony and my endless
anxiety.

Then the angel returned, asking that I surrender
My son as a lamb to show that humility
Still lived in me, and was not altered by age and prosperity.

I said nothing, shocked and passive. Then I said but to myself alone:
"This was to be expected. These promises
Are never unequivocal or unambiguous, in this
As in all things which are desired the most:
I have had great riches and great beauty.
I cannot expect the perfection of every wish
And if I deny the command, who knows what will happen?"

But his life was forgiven and given back to me:
His children and their children are an endless nation:
Dispersed on every coast. And I am not gratified
Nor astonished. It has never been otherwise:
Exiled, wandering, dumbfounded by riches,
Estranged among strangers, dismayed by the infinite sky,
An alien to myself until at last the caste of the last alienation
The angel of death comes to make the alienated and indestructible one a
part of his famous society.

22:14–18 And Abraham called the name of that place Jehovahjireh: as it is said to this day, In the mount of the LORD it shall be seen.

And the angel of the LORD called unto Abraham out of heaven the second time, And said, By myself have I sworn, saith the LORD, for because thou hast done this thing, and hast not withheld thy son, thine only son: That in blessing I will bless thee, and in multiplying I will multiply thy seed as the stars of the heaven, and as the sand which is upon the sea shore; and thy seed shall possess the gate of his enemies; And in thy seed shall all the nations of the earth be blessed; because thou hast obeyed my voice.

ABRAHAM'S MADNESS

BINK NOLL

When Isaac watched his father strain back
the ram's head, its throat separate and bleed,
evisceration, and fat turn to smoke,

not *he* had heard any angel speak
but felt sharply where the rope still cut,
how his own neck cracked, his own flesh burned.

I likewise learned to distrust my sire
whose god in our house was powerful
as revenge shuddering through a plot.

Mornings, his story would begin,
"My dear boy, God will provide the lamb,"
when I knew I went the only lamb,

knew the god had repeated his demand
and violence on this man who adored
both of us past any hope of reason.

I was proving tall, bright, soft of voice.
Then he—his love wild to get me grown—
would change and cheat the law, then reach out

to slay some cheap and easy innocent,
then stop the silence raging in his ear
by reports of angels I never heard.

How we sons lay awake to ponder
the misery of such divided men
to whom the patriarchal lies come true.

My son shall not watch me in a fury
of faith take fire to the altar where
I sacrifice nothing I cherish.

He may feel my hands grab like priest hands,
his eyes may die in the brightness
that I have meant obedience entire.

So much I walked with my mad Abraham.

ISAAC: A POISE

PETER COLE

His sun's arms and grappling
hooks and spears
stripping him
fleabane bare
on its abstract field—

in the fume-like shimmer and blur.

A kiln-pure sky
the cypresses touch.
'His eyes like the dying moon.'
His hope at home in the finally darkness
where what should happen would.

He waited.

Blood on the wood
where his head had been.
Where the body buried what its father had planned.
Spirit.
Thicket.

The strained way home.

'A host'
it says.
A host of them shouting
Praise Him.
goat-meat and ox-ash and noise.

With fire, and whisper, and gall.

A host.
While the gold tackle tore at his will.
Consigned.
Among thistle and rubble,
and caper

and dill.

24:1–63 . . . And Isaac went out to meditate in the field at the eventide: and he lifted up his eyes, and saw, and, behold, the camels were coming.

Isaac's Marriage

Henry Vaughan

Praying and to be married? It was rare,
But now 'tis monstrous; and that pious care
Though of our selves, is so much out of date,
That to renew't were to degenerate.
But thou a chosen sacrifice wert given,
And offered up so early unto heaven
Thy flames could not be out; religion was
Rayed into thee, like beams into a glass,
Where, as thou grewst, it multiplied and shined
The sacred constellation of thy mind.
But being for a bride, prayer was such
A decried course, sure it prevailed not much.
Hadst ne'er an oath, nor compliment? thou wert
An odd dull suitor; hadst thou but the art
Of these our days, thou couldst have coined thee
New several oaths, and compliments (too) plenty;
O sad, and wild excess! and happy those
White days, that durst no impious mirth expose!

When conscience by lewd use had not lost sense,
Nor bold-faced custom banished innocence;
Thou hadst no pompous train, nor antic crowd
Of young, gay swearers, with their needless, loud
Retinue; all was here smooth as thy bride
And calm like her, or that mild evening-tide:
Yet, hadst thou nobler guests: Angels did wind
And rove about thee, guardians of thy mind,
These fetched thee home thy bride, and all the way
Advised thy servant what to do, and say;
These taught him at the well, and thither brought
The chaste, and lovely object of thy thought;
But here was ne'er a compliment, not one
Spruce, supple cringe, or studied look put on,
All was plain, modest truth: Nor did she come
In rolls and curls, mincing and stately dumb,
But in a virgin's native blush and fears
Fresh as those roses, which the day-spring wears.
O sweet, divine simplicity! O grace
Beyond a curled lock, or painted face!
A pitcher too she had, nor thought it much
To carry that, which some would scorn to touch;
With which in mild, chaste language she did woo
To draw him drink, and for his camels too.
And now thou knewest her coming, it was time
To get thee wings on, and devoutly climb
Unto thy God, for marriage of all states
Makes most unhappy, or most fortunates;
This brought thee forth, where now thou didst undress
Thy soul, and with new pinions refresh
Her wearied wings, which so restored did fly
Above the stars, a track unknown, and high,
And in her piercing flight perfumed the air
Scattering the myrrh, and incense of thy prayer.
So from Lahai-roi's well some spicy cloud*
Wooed by the sun swells up to be his shroud,
And from his moist womb weeps a fragrant shower,
Which, scattered in a thousand pearls, each flower
And herb partakes, where having stood awhile
And something cooled the parched, and thirsty isle,

* *A well in the South Country where Jacob dwelt, between* Cadesh, & Bered; Heb. *the well of him that liveth, and seeth me.* [Vaughan's note.]

The thankful Earth unlocks her self, and blends,
A thousand odors, which (all mixed,) she sends
Up in one cloud, and so returns the skies
That dew they lent, a breathing sacrifice.
    Thus soared thy soul, who (though young,) didst inherit
Together with his blood, thy father's spirit,
Whose active zeal, and tried faith were to thee
Familiar ever since thy infancy.
Others were timed, and trained up to't but thou
Didst thy swift years in piety out-grow,
Age made them reverend, and a snowy head,
But thou wert so, ere time his snow could shed;
Then, who would truly limn thee out, must paint
First, a young Patriarch, then a married Saint.

24:64–67 **And Rebekah lifted up her eyes, and when she saw Isaac, she lighted off the camel. For she had said unto the servant, What man is this that walketh in the field to meet us? And the servant had said, It is my master: therefore she took a vail, and covered herself.**

And the servant told Isaac all things that he had done. And Isaac brought her into his mother Sarah's tent, and took Rebekah, and she became his wife; and he loved her: and Isaac was comforted after his mother's death.

Genesis XXIV

Arthur Hugh Clough

Who is this Man
    that walketh in the field,
O Eleazar,
    steward to my lord?

And Eleazar
    answered her and said,
Daughter of Bethuel,
    it is other none
But my lord Isaac,
    son unto my lord;
Who, as his wont is,
    walketh in the field

In the hour of evening
    meditating there.

Therefore Rebekah
    hasted where she sat,
And from her camel
    lighting to the earth
Sought for a veil,
    and put it on her face.
Wherefore he came,
    and met them on the field,
Whom, when Rebekah
    saw, she came before,
Saying, Behold
    the handmaid of my lord,
Who for my lord's sake
    travel from my land.

But he said, O
    thou blessed of our God,
Come, for the tent
    is eager for thy face.
Shall not thy husband
    be unto thee more than
Hundreds of kinsmen
    living in thy land?

And Eleazar answered,
    Thus and thus,
Even according
    as thy father bade,
Did we; and thus and
    thus it came to pass;
Lo! is not this
    Rebekah, Bethuel's child?

And as he ended
    Isaac spoke and said,
Surely my heart
    went with you on the way,
When with the beasts
    ye came unto the place.

Truly, O child
    of Nahor, I was there,
When to thy mother
    and thy mother's son
Thou madest answer,
    saying, I will go.
And Isaac brought her
    to his mother's tent.

25:5–10 . . . Then Abraham gave up the ghost, and died in a good old age, an old man, and full of years; and was gathered to his people. And his sons Isaac and Ishmael buried him in the cave of Machpelah, in the field of Ephron the son of Zohar the Hittite, which is before Mamre; The field which Abraham purchased of the sons of Heth: there was Abraham buried, and Sarah his wife.

Abraham

Edwin Muir

The rivulet-loving wanderer Abraham
Through waterless wastes tracing his fields of pasture
Led his Chaldean herds and fattening flocks
With the meandering art of wavering water
That seeks and finds, yet does not know its way.
He came, rested and prospered, and went on,
Scattering behind him little pastoral kingdoms,
And over each one its own particular sky,
Not the great rounded sky through which he journeyed,
That went with him but when he rested changed.
His mind was full of names
Learned from strange peoples speaking alien tongues,
And all that was theirs one day he would inherit.
He died content and full of years, though still
The Promise had not come, and left his bones,
Far from his father's house, in alien Canaan.

25:11–34 . . . And Jacob sod pottage: and Esau came from the field, and he was faint: And Esau said to Jacob, Feed me, I pray thee, with that same red pottage; for I am faint: therefore was his name called Edom.

And Jacob said, Sell me this day thy birthright. And Esau said, Behold, I am at the point to die: and what profit shall this birthright do to me? And Jacob said, Swear to me this day; and he sware unto him: and he sold his birthright unto Jacob. . . .

ON JACOB'S PURCHASE

FRANCIS QUARLES

How poor was Jacob's motion, and how strange
His offer! How unequal was th' exchange!
A mess of porridge for inheritance?
Why could not hungry Esau strive t' enhance
His price a little? So much underfoot?
Well might he give him bread and drink to boot:
An easy price! The case is even our own;
For toys we often sell our Heaven, our Crown.

27:1–28:12 . . . And Jacob went out from Beersheba, and went toward Haran. And he lighted upon a certain place, and tarried there all night, because the sun was set; and he took of the stones of that place, and put them for his pillows, and lay down in that place to sleep. And he dreamed, and behold a ladder set up on the earth, and the top of it reached to heaven: and behold the angels of God ascending and descending on it.

THE JACOB'S LADDER

DENISE LEVERTOV

The stairway is not
a thing of gleaming strands
a radiant evanescence
for angels' feet that only glance in their tread, and need not
touch the stone.

It is of stone.
A rosy stone that takes
a glowing tone of softness
only because behind it the sky is a doubtful, a doubting
night gray.

A stairway of sharp
angles, solidly built.
One sees that the angels must spring
down from one step to the next, giving a little
lift of the wings:

and a man climbing
must scrape his knees, and bring
the grip of his hands into play. The cut stone
consoles his groping feet. Wings brush past him.
The poem ascends.

28:13–19 . . . And Jacob awaked out of his sleep, and he said, Surely the LORD is in this place; and I knew it not. And he was afraid, and said, How dreadful is this place! this is none other but the house of God, and this is the gate of heaven. And Jacob rose up early in the morning, and took the stone that he had put for his pillows, and set it up for a pillar, and poured oil upon the top of it. . . .

from "A-12"

LOUIS ZUKOFSKY

Like Grandpa Paul.
The water is all of my mind,
I walk the bridge
And the only word I think of is *high*
Man who lives, his speech rattles in throat and head
The sky a tine;
How great the Soul is, Lord Dexter,
Do you not all admire and wonder to
See and behold and hear?
Can you all believe half
The truth and admire to hear —
Illiterate lord of a court of ships figureheads—
How a man *drownded* in the sea
What a great bubble comes up at the top of the water
This is the wind—the bubble's the soul.
All these dead years.
My mother sat away from the stoop, the new bridge going up,
To catch her breath in the hottest summer.

Some old landmarks down
The bridge is aging
Effaced their ties
And their sorrow—
History, all its cornices.
Where is, moping?
New York's skyline's a mist of Egypt?
Where, my son, are my dead breathing friends
Effaced in my lines, my growing sun
Who imitates my steps
Whose profile's likeness to me shocks
Who says "My God—
Good gracious"
As the bridge trolley darts
And breathes himself
And understands me best
Because he does not understand.

There is too much air in the air.
Too many stars too high.
A spring mattress pronouncedly spring
This is a "fall to" table, it leans
From New England, not Manhattan.
When I sit down to eat, my father drowses.
This is a "fall to" bench-trestle
It leans to the table.
My guest Henry (masculine)
What a face has the great American novelist
It says: Fie! Nancy, finance.
I have just met him on Rutgers Street, New York
Henry James, Jr.,
Opposite what stood out in my youth
As a frightening
Copy of a Norman church in red brick
Half a square block, if I recall,
Faced with a prospect of fire escapes—
Practically where I was born.
Breathing quite affectively in the mind
Ready to chance the sea of conversation
And unshamefacedly—it has been like a warm day—
The look of a shaven Chassid,
Were it possible to either him or Chassid,
Takes an impressed step forward
Pleased, not ominous in behalf of the blind or the publicist—

Said the Chassid:
If you do not, Lord, yet wish to redeem
Israel, at least redeem the Gentiles.

I cannot be too grateful for what you did for Rutgers Street
(Or for Baltimore, "That cheerful little city of the dead")
You went down-town once
At that no beard shaking the head

—Let me go, the dawn is on us
—No, not until you bless me first
—Your name?
And the sun rose (chaos to come)
And he halted.
And once before, toward Haran
Lighted upon a certain place
And stayed there, the sun had set.
Stones for pillows.
He dreamed
There were angels going up and down a ladder.
Standing over him a Voice:
—I will give you the land where you sleep on stone,
Seed the dust of the earth.
Blest. And in you everybody—west, east, north, south.
And awoke afraid
—How dreadful is this place
None other but His—the gate to Him.
Said: Keep me in the way I go
With bread,
A coat to put on—
To come back to my father—

28:20–22 . . . And this stone, which I have set for a pillar, shall be God's house: and of all that thou shalt give me I will surely give the tenth unto thee.

Jacob's Pillow, and Pillar

Henry Vaughan

I see the temple in thy pillar reared,
And that dread glory, which thy children feared,
In mild, clear visions, without a frown,

Unto thy solitary self is shown.
'Tis number makes a schism: throngs are rude,
And God himself died by the multitude.
This made him put on clouds, and fire and smoke,
Hence he in thunder to thy off-spring spoke;
The small, still voice, at some low cottage knocks,
But a strong wind must break thy lofty rocks.

The first true worship of the world's great King
From private and elected hearts did spring,
But he most willing to save all mankind,
Enlarged that light, and to the bad was kind.
Hence Catholic or Universal came
A most fair notion, but a very name.
For this rich pearl, like some more common stone,
When once made public, is esteemed by none.
Man slights his Maker, when familiar grown,
And sets up laws, to pull his honor down.
This God foresaw: And when slain by the crowd
(Under that stately and mysterious cloud
Which his death scattered) he foretold the place,
And form to serve him in, should be true grace
And the meek heart, not in a mount, nor at
Jerusalem, with blood of beasts, and fat.
A heart is that dread place, that awful cell,
That secret ark, where the mild dove doth dwell
When the proud waters rage: when heathens rule
By God's permission, and man turns a mule.
This little Goshen, in the midst of night,
And Satan's seat, in all her coasts hath light,
Yea Bethel shall have tithes (saith Israel's stone)
And vows and visions, though her foes cry, None.
Thus is the solemn temple sunk again
Into a pillar, and concealed from men.
And glory be to his eternal Name!
Who is contented, that this holy flame
Shall lodge in such a narrow pit, till he
With his strong arm turns our captivity.

But blessed Jacob, though thy sad distress
Was just the same with ours, and nothing less,
For thou a brother, and blood-thirsty too
Didst fly, whose children wrought thy childrens woe:
Yet thou in all thy solitude and grief,

On stones didst sleep and foundst but cold relief;
Thou from the day-star a long way didst stand
And all that distance was Law and command.
But we a healing sun by day and night,
Have our sure guardian, and our leading light;
What thou didst hope for and believe, we find
And fell a friend most ready, sure and kind.
Thy pillow was but type and shade at best,
But we the substance have, and on him rest.

29:1–30:13 . . . And when Rachel saw that she bare Jacob no children, Rachel envied her sister; and said unto Jacob, Give me children, or else I die. And Jacob's anger was kindled against Rachel: and he said, Am I in God's stead, who hath withheld from thee the fruit of the womb? And she said, Behold my maid Bilhah, go in unto her; and she shall bear upon my knees, that I may also have children by her. And she gave him Bilhah her handmaid to wife: and Jacob went in unto her. . . .

The Patriarch

Robert Burns

As honest Jacob on a night,
Wi' his beloved beauty,
Was duly laid on wedlock's bed,
And noddin' at his duty
Tal de dal, & c.

'How lang, she says, ye fumblin' wretch,
'Will ye be f——g at it?
'My eldest wean might die of age,
'Before that ye could get it.

'Ye pegh, and grane, and groazle there,
'And mak an unco splutter,
'And I maun ly and thole you here,
'And fient a hair the better.'

Then he, in wrath, put up his graith,
'The deevil's in the hizzie!
'I m–w you as I m–w the lave,
'And night and day I'm bisy.

'I've bairn'd the servant gypsies baith,
'Forbye your titty Leah;
'Ye barren jad, ye put me mad,
'What mair can I do wi' you.

'There's ne'er a m–w I've gi'en the lave,
'But ye ha'e got a dizzen;
'And d—n'd a ane ye 'se get again,
'Altho' your c—t should gizzen.'

Then Rachel calm, as ony lamb,
She claps him on the waulies,
Quo' she, 'ne'er fash a woman's clash,
'In trowth, ye m–w me braulies.

'My dear 'tis true, for mony a m–w,
'I'm your ungratefu' debtor;
'But ance again, I dinna ken,
'We'll aiblens happen better.'

Then honest man! wi' little wark,
He soon forgot his ire;
The patriarch, he coost the sark,
And up and till 't like fire!!!

30:14–32:10 . . . And Jacob said, O God of my father Abraham, and God of my father Isaac, the LORD which saidst unto me, Return unto thy country, and to thy kindred, and I will deal well with thee: I am not worthy of the least of all the mercies, and of all the truth, which thou hast shewed unto thy servant; for with my staff I passed over this Jordan; and now I am become two bands.

The Posie

George Herbert

Let wits contest,
And with their words and posies windows fill:
Less than the least
Of all thy mercies, is my posie still.

This on my ring,
This by my picture, in my book I write:
Whether I sing,
Or say, or dictate, this is my delight.

Invention rest,
Comparisons go play, wit use thy will:
Less than the least
Of all God's mercies,[*] is my posie still.

32:11–29 . . . And Jacob was left alone; and there wrestled a man with him until the breaking of the day. And when he saw that he prevailed not against him, he touched the hollow of his thigh; and the hollow of Jacob's thigh was out of joint, as he wrestled with him. And he said, Let me go, for the day breaketh. And he said, I will not let thee go, except thou bless me. And he said unto him, What is thy name? And he said, Jacob. And he said, Thy name shall be called no more Jacob, but Israel: for as a prince hast thou power with God and with men, and hast prevailed. And Jacob asked him, and said, Tell me, I pray thee, thy name. And he said, Wherefore is it that thou dost ask after my name? And he blessed him there.

A LITTLE EAST OF JORDAN

EMILY DICKINSON

A little East of Jordan,
Evangelists record,
A Gymnast and an Angel
Did wrestle long and hard –

Till morning touching mountain –
And Jacob, waxing strong,
The Angel begged permission
To Breakfast – to return –

Not so, said cunning Jacob!
"I will not let thee go
Except thou bless me" – Stranger!
The which acceded to –

[*] Herbert's personal motto.

Light swung the silver fleeces
"Peniel" Hills beyond,
And the bewildered Gymnast
Found he had worsted God!

Jacob Wrestling with the Angel

Jones Very

The Patriarch wrestled with the angel long,
For though of mortal race, yet he was strong;
Nor would release him at the break of day,
That he might take his upward heavenly way.
"Bless me," he cried, "ere I shall let thee go;
Thou art an angel, and no mortal foe,
Who through the night's dark hours couldst thus maintain
With me a contest on the starry plain."
"What is thy name?" the angel asked again,
"For thou hast power alike with God and men."
"Jacob," he said. The angel blessed him there:
"Henceforth the name of Israel thou shalt bear;
Thou hast prevailed, thou art a Prince indeed:
A blessing rest on thee, and on thy seed."
Deem not that to those ancient times belong
The wonders told in history and in song:
Men may with angels now, as then, prevail;
Too oft, alas, they in the contest fail.
Their blessed help is not from man withdrawn;
Contend thou with the angel till the dawn:
A blessing he to earth for thee doth bring,
Then back to heaven again his flight will wing.

34:1–14 And Dinah the daughter of Leah, which she bare unto Jacob, went out to see the daughters of the land. And when Shechem the son of Hamor the Hivite, prince of the country, saw her, he took her, and lay with her, and defiled her. And his soul clave unto Dinah the daughter of Jacob, and he loved the damsel, and spake kindly unto the damsel. And Shechem spake unto his father Hamor, saying, Get me this damsel to wife. . . . And the sons of Jacob answered Shechem and Hamor his father

deceitfully, and said, because he had defiled Dinah their sister: And they said unto them, We cannot do this thing, to give our sister to one that is uncircumcised; for that were a reproach unto us:

On Dinah

Francis Quarles

When Dinah's careless eye was grown too lavish
To entertain, Shechem found time to ravish:
It is no less than silent invitation,
Although we scorn the sin, to give th' occasion:
Sure, Dinah's resolution was too strong,
Or to admit, or not resist a wrong,
And scorns to stoop to the adulterer's arms;
We often burn, intending but to warm's:
She went but out to see; perchance, to hear
What lust could say: What harm to lend an ear?
Another's sin, sometimes, procures our shames:
It stains our bodies; or, at least, our names.

35:9–37:3 . . . Now Israel loved Joseph more than all his children, because he was the son of his old age: and he made him a coat of many colours.

Joseph's Coat

George Herbert

Wounded I sing, tormented I indite,
Thrown down I fall into a bed, and rest:
Sorrow hath changed its note: such is his will,
Who changeth all things, as him pleaseth best.
For well he knows, if but one grief and smart
Among my many had his full career,
Sure it would carry with it even my heart,
And both would run until they found a bier
To fetch the body; both being due to grief.
But he hath spoiled the race; and given to anguish
One of joy's coats, ticing it with relief

To linger in me, and together languish.
 I live to show his power, who once did bring
 My joys to weep, and now my griefs to sing.

37:4–11 And when his brethren saw that their father loved him more than all his brethren, they hated him, and could not speak peaceably unto him. And Joseph dreamed a dream, and he told it his brethren: and they hated him yet the more. . . .

Jacob

Delmore Schwartz

All was as it is, before the beginning began, before
We were bared to the cold air, before
Pride. Fullness of bread. Abundance of idleness.
No one has ever told me what now I know:
Love is unjust, justice is loveless.

So, as it was to become, it was, in the black womb's ignorance
Coiled and bound, under the mother's heart.
There in the womb we wrestled, and writhed, hurt
Each other long before each was other and apart,
Before we breathed: who then committed greed,
Impersonation, usurpation? So, in the coming forth,
In the noose and torment of birth, Esau went first,
He was red all over. I followed him, clutching his heel,
And we were named: Esau, the one of the vivid coat,
Jacob, the one who clutches the heel of the one
Who has a vivid coat. The names were true
As the deceptive reality into which we were thrown.
For I did not know what clutching was, nor had I known
Would I have known whose heel I clutched, my brother's or my own!

So, the world we entered then and thus was one
In which the second must be second that the first may be first.
The world of precedence, order, other, under and above,
The darkness, sweetness, confusion and unity of love!
How the truth of our names became, as we grew, more true,
Growing like truth. How could it be otherwise? For truth abides
Hidden in the future, in the ambush of the marvellous,
Unknown and monstrous, at the very heart of surprise.

The gift was mind. The gift was eminence. The gift
Like every gift, was guilt. The guilt began
In the darkness and dark mystery where all begins.
The mystery of the perpetual invisible fires whence flow
The very beasts and woods where—
with what happiness!
what innocence!—
Esau my brother hunted, cantering like the horses of summer.
And sleeping, when he returned, the sleep of winter farms,
Spontaneous and blessed, like energy itself, sleeping or awake.
Until the hour when the angel struck!

So it was: so:
O angel of the unspeakable,
Why must a gift be guilt and hurt the gifted one?
O angel of the unspeakable, power of powers,
Locking my reins, my arms, my heart all night
So that my body was burdened as with the load of all stones
Dost thou remember what, in the darkness, I cried,
During the desperation in which I died
The last death of hope and the little deaths of the heart
Wrestling and writhing between two rivers—on one bank,
Esau, awaiting me, like a river slept—beneath me once more.
"Hast thou not seen," I cried aloud, to the unspeakable.
"Esau my brother: his handsome hunting heart upon a horse?"
How should it seem so strange that I should win,
Since victory was my gift? Unjust, like every gift,
A something neither deserved, nor gained by toil . . .
How else could it be gift and given?
Favor: favored: favorite:
Gold hair: great strength: Esau was very tall,
Possessed by the supple grace of the sea's waves, breaking.

Now Joseph is, as I was: in Egypt's pit,
In that accustomed depth and isolated height
The solitude of eminence, the exiled intelligence,
Which separated me even as it created me:
Estranged and unloved, gifted and detested,
Denied the love of the servants and the dogs.
Joseph a stranger in Egypt may only know
What I have known: my gifts, my victory, my guilt.
For Egypt is a country like a gift.
The gift is loved but not the gifted one.
The coat of many colors is much admired

By everyone, but he who wears the coat
Is not made warm. Why should the gift be the cause of pain,
O thou unspeakable? Must the vivid coat
Of eminence elect the favored favorite
As scapegoat or turncoat, exile or fugitive,
The loved of mother and God, and by all others
Shunned in fear or contempt?
                                        I knew what it was,
When Joseph became my favorite: knew the sympathy
Of the long experience of the unasked-for gift:
Knew the nature of love: how many colors
Can a coat have? What should we wish, if
We could choose? What should I desire
—Not to have loved my son, the best of sons?
Rejected the choice of love? Should I have hidden
My love of him? Or should he have concealed the self
I loved, above all others, wearing the coat
Which is customary, the coats his brothers wore?
To how many coats can a color give vividness?
How can the heart know love, and not love one the more?
Love is unjust: justice is loveless.

37:12–27 . . . And it came to pass, when Joseph was come unto his brethren, that they stript Joseph out of his coat, his coat of many colours that was on him; And they took him, and cast him into a pit: and the pit was empty, there was no water in it. And they sat down to eat bread: and they lifted up their eyes and looked, and, behold, a company of Ishmaelites came from Gilead with their camels bearing spicery and balm and myrrh, going to carry it down to Egypt. And Judah said unto his brethren, What profit is it if we slay our brother, and conceal his blood? Come, and let us sell him to the Ishmaelites, and let not our hand be upon him; for he is our brother and our flesh. And his brethren were content.

Israel I

CHARLES REZNIKOFF

Our eldest son is like Ishmael, Jacob is like you;
therefore, you like Esau better:
because he is a hunter, a man of the fields,
can bring you venison from distant cliffs,

is strong, and covered with hair like a ram;
but Jacob who is like you, a quiet man, dwelling in tents, is the better.
Esau is like a club, Jacob a knife,
Esau is stupid, Jacob shrewd,
Jacob is like my brother Laban.

My father, sit and eat of my venison.
How is it that you have found it so quickly?
God helped me.
Come near that I may feel you, my son,
whether you are my very son Esau or not;
the voice is Jacob's voice, but the hands are Esau's.
Are you my son Esau?
I am.
Come near now and kiss me, my son.

How dreadful are these cliffs!
I who have always lived in booths,
seldom far from the song of women at the doors,
or at the farthest, near the shepherd's flute—.
When Abraham's servant came to us,
he brought gifts of clothing, jewels of silver and gold;
you came with empty hands, it seemed;
but my cattle have been well cared for.
(Can Jacob match himself against Laban,
a young man who has nothing among strangers,
against a man grown grizzled among strong and crafty men?)

The seven years that I served for you, Rachel,
were but a few days.

Why have you cheated me?
In our place the younger is not given before the first-born.
Had Rachel been married first, the tears of Leah
would have made your marriage bitter.

When this beauty of which you keep telling me is gone,
as the petals are shaken from a tree—
surely, although they are so many, at last they have all fallen—
Leah now hires you of me with the mandrakes
her eldest finds in the field,
but who will find me anything in those days?

My companions so many nights,
physicians to whom I told my secrets,
I touch you:
you are wood;
so is the staff that helps us on our way,
the spoon that feeds us, and at last our coffin.
Does Laban among sons and brothers need you?
We need you,
a shepherd, women, children, and a flock of sheep,
among the mountains in the wilderness. (*She steals the idols.*)

Why have you stolen away,
and carried away my daughters as if they were captives of the sword?
Why did you not tell me,
that I might have sent you away with mirth and songs,
with drum and harp?
Why did you not let me kiss my sons and daughters?
The daughters are my daughters, the children are my children,
and the flocks my flocks,
all that you see is mine;
but what can I do to these, my daughters,
or to the children whom they have borne?

How unworthy I am of the kindness which you have shown me,
God of Abraham and Isaac,
for with my staff I crossed the Jordan,
and am now two companies.
Deliver me now from the hand of Esau!
And whose are the children?
My children.
And what meant the company I met?
To find favor in your sight.
I have enough. Let that which you have be yours.

Look, Joseph is coming, the master of dreams.
What do the camels carry?
Spicery and balm and myrrh to Egypt.
What profit shall we have in the death of our brother?
Lift him out of the pit and sell him to these for pieces of silver;
and dip his coat in a goat's blood,
and send it to our father,
and say, we have found this and do not know whether it is your son's
coat or not;
and he will think a beast tore Joseph to pieces.

39:1–7 And Joseph was brought down to Egypt; and Potiphar, an officer of Pharaoh, captain of the guard, an Egyptian, bought him of the hands of the Ishmelites, which had brought him down thither. And the LORD was with Joseph, and he was a prosperous man; and he was in the house of his master the Egyptian. And his master saw that the LORD was with him, and that the LORD made all that he did to prosper in his hand. And Joseph found grace in his sight, and he served him: and he made him overseer over his house, and all that he had he put into his hand. And it came to pass from the time that he had made him overseer in his house, and over all that he had, that the LORD blessed the Egyptian's house for Joseph's sake; and the blessing of the LORD was upon all that he had in the house, and in the field. And he left all that he had in Joseph's hand; and he knew not ought he had, save the bread which he did eat. And Joseph was a goodly person, and well favoured.

And it came to pass after these things, that his master's wife cast her eyes upon Joseph; and she said, Lie with me.

from THE MAIDENS BLUSH; OR JOSEPH

JOSHUA SYLVESTER

But, fair Iëmpsar (wife of Potiphar)
Above the rest, his parts did high prefer;
Him more than all she inly did admire,
And still beholds him with a young desire.
Yet, ignorant what fury would ensue
The pleasing passion she did so pursue;
What wily godling to beguile her, sought
To snare her freedom in a servile thought;
As yet she vented neither sigh nor tear:
All yet was sweet, no bitter fit, no fear.
Which th' envious Prince of Styx and Acheron,
Malignant father of confusion,
Man's deadly foe, observing; and beside,
That Isaac's seed still happy multiplied;
In fell despite and full of desperate rage,
He calls a bird of his infernal cage,
A cruel harpy, full of wicked wile,
A thousand ways the wisest to beguile.
Go, hie, saith He, my darling, hie thee quick
To fair Iëmpsar; she is fant'sy-sick
Already: Therefore so insinuate,
That more and more thou her intoxicate:
Breathe in her bosom, blow in new infection,
Kindle the tinder of her light affection,

To such a flame, that neither gods nor men
May be of power to put it out again:
And do the best (for that I most desire)
If possible, set Joseph (too) afire:
But if on him, thou nothing canst prevail,
Return to her, her fancy re-assail.
Fill her with frenzy, and with fury double
Still burn her fell, till all her friends she trouble:
Till with disgrace, disdained, and desperate,
She turn her dear love to as deadly hate:
Till then, desist not; but persist and ply
To play thy part with art and subtilty.
He, glad and ready for the worst of ills,
With Stygian puddle half a vial fills,
Blending so ne bitter, sharp-sweet wine withal.
Then snatching quick one of the snakes that crawl
About Alecto's grim and ghastly brows,
Away he hies to Potiphar his house,
Within his bosom hiding what he had.
And formally just in the form him clad
Of Iphicle, the Lady Iëmpsar's nurse;
With better credit, to beguile the worse.
Then to her Lady having made a duck,
Sweet Madame (said she, fie on all ill luck)
What sad disaster, what misfortune rife,
Hath made poor Joseph weary of his life?
My self, of late have seen him oft, forlorn
Sit sole and sighing, and have heard him mourn,
Wishing for death. And when I sought to know
The secret cause of his exceeding woe:
O! Mother (said he) or whether I conceal it
Needs die I must, or whether I reveal it.
Inquire not therefore; for, 'tis better end,
With my sad life my sorrow's cause unkenned.
Not so, my Son (said I) for oft a wound
Discovered, is recovered, and made sound;
Which, hid a while, would gangrene to the bone:
Tell boldly (lad) art thou in love with none?
If that be cause of thy distress: Why boy
Be of good cheer, thou shalt thy dear enjoy,
Hope well, and have well: So shalt thou; or else
I'll charm Love's Passion with some stronger spell.
With bashful blush, then said he, Yes, I love:
Be witness, gods, how earnest I have strove

To strangle it! How I have labored long!
How loth (alas!) my Lord in thought to wrong!
More wishing death: Death, now make good my trial:
Happy were I to live and die so loyal.
And, saying so, on his fair cheeks he pours
A sea of tears, in pearl and crystal showers:
So that I see, without quick remedy,
For love of you, Madame, the youth will die.
    Alas! then said the lady, Woe is me
For his misfortune and his misery;
To me right tragic is the tale you tell:
For, truth to say, I love him but too well,
And would enjoy him if I could or durst;
But, O! I cannot: O! I may not: first,
For sacred laws, for Hymen's secret yoke,
(Which never any yet, unpunished, broke)
For fear of danger, and dishonor's brand,
And dreadful vengeance of my husband's hand.
    Why, my dear daughter, damned nurse replies,
The gods do laugh at lovers' injuries:
And with thy wedlock thou mayest well dispense,
On so good ground of so great consequence,
As is the saving of a life so young,
So innocent, that never yet did wrong;
Unless it be a wrong to love too much,
Or die for love. (Who would not die for such?)
Lovers must dare, and wise-men must not dread
The worst of dangers that is threatened:
For, even the gods have lovers in their guard,
And love and pity they will still reward.
I have a water of a sovereign use
(Th' extracted spirit of many a chymick-juice)
Which inly ta'en in a perplexed case,
Expels the doubt, and shows truth's naked face:
That, far from ambage, th' undistract affection
May of the better freely make election.
If therefore, Madame, yet you stand divided,
What part to take; to have your doubts decided,
I'll give it you: and, as she spake, she gave
The hellish philtre, made of Stygian wave.
    Thanks, dearest Mother, said her Ladyship:
And, taking all, not with a fearful sip,
But full carouse, lifting her hand on high,

Quaffed off the poison, drew the goblet dry.
      This done, the demon, with a beldame's face,
Towards Joseph's chamber hies with hobbling pace;
Where he was praying, and devoutly praising
The God of gods, for his so gracious raising:
But when the false fiend in his portal spied
A heavenly warder (both his guard and guide)
With threatful brandish of a shining blade,
More speed then good, headlong he downward made
In dreadful maze; and, as the foulest fowl,
Transforms him quick into a screeching-owl,
Night's horrid monster, hovering long aloof,
At last perched on Iëmpsar's chamber roof.
      Wretched Iëmpsar, having quaffed up
The brim and bottom of the Stygian cup,
Now all alone, she feels her all a-fire,
Blood, bones and marrow, burning in desire;
Sad, silent, sighing: in a wondrous fit;
And all for Joseph, nigh beside her wit:
Now on her bed she falls, and by and by
Flings up again; and to and fro doth fly
From place to place; soon weary of the best,
Runs every where, and no where findeth rest;
Like one whose breast a burning fever fries,
Or whom some serpent's sting doth agonize.
At last she breaks out; and Alas! quoth she,
What, what is this that thus tormenteth me?
O! is it love? or was it not the drink
I took right now? No: it is love I think,
'Tis surely love, love in extremity,
And but fair Joseph gently help, I die.

39:8–23 . . . And she laid up his garment by her, until his lord came home. And she spake unto him according to these words, saying, The Hebrew servant, which thou hast brought unto us, came in unto me to mock me: And it came to pass, as I lifted up my voice and cried, that he left his garment with me, and fled out. And it came to pass, when his master heard the words of his wife, which she spake unto him, saying, After this manner did thy servant to me; that his wrath was kindled. And Joseph's master took him, and put him into the prison, a place where the king's prisoners were bound: and he was there in the prison. . . .

from EGYPT'S FAVORITE

Joseph in Carcere: OR, The Innocent Prisoner

FRANCIS HUBERT

'Tis wretchedness too much to be cast down;
What is it then to fall with infamy!
But he that is to any greatness grown
Upon a change must look for obloquy.

Unhappy virtue cannot be secure,
Scarce from the hands not from the tongues assault;
Fair actions foul constructions must endure
When our misfortunes shall be thought our fault.

Nay Potiphar himself is construed too
And pierced, perhaps, by the plebeian wind,
In that he would so undiscreetly do
As lay such trust upon an unknown hind.

Thou many-headed monster that art bred
Out of the vulgar mud, without all brain,
How easily is thy erring judgement led?
To pass a sudden sentence, idle, vain,

Without all certain ground, without all weight,
Nay, without any scanning of the matter!
But thou art swayed with a received conceit
And thy light air soon turneth into water:

For rashly-heady thou art easily borne
Now unto one, straight to another mind:
So have I seen a field of eared corn
Bending all south, blown with a southern wind,

And let the same but shift into the north
Then stalks and heads and all do bend that way:
And can that man be wise, of real worth,
That doth on such light puffs his fortunes lay?

But stay! Me thinks my self forgets my course
And I begin to sail without my card.
Though empty casks without all true discourse
Are in their censures sudden, sour and hard,

Yet he that looks with other eyes than men
And finds the heart untainted with offence,
Binds whom we free and frees whom we condemn;
'Tis he alone that safeguards innocence.

And oft he works beyond the reach of man.
We cannot fathom him with our short line;
We may as well grasp Heaven within our span
As sound the depth of what he doth design.

How could it be conceived by man's discourse
That gyves and fetters were the means to rise?
Yet all-commanding God doth take that course,
And Joseph must be raised by enemies.

40:1–41:45 . . . And Pharaoh called Joseph's name Zaphnathpaaneah; and he gave him to wife Asenath the daughter of Potipherah priest of On. And Joseph went out over all the land of Egypt.

Asenath

Diana Hume George

Why did you choose me for your wife, Joseph?
You could have had any woman,
but you asked Pharaoh for me.
When you lived in our house,
you never looked on me at all,
though I tried to catch your eye.

I know what my mother said you did, Joseph.
You say it isn't true,
and I believe you.
But you broke her.
She never was herself again.
She couldn't sleep at night.
Even the potions did her no good.
She woke up staring every night,
dreaming she was drowning,
sea creatures pulling at her feet,
dreaming she was strangled
by snakes wound about her throat,

dreaming she was dead.
When she did die,
she died in slow sleep,
unconscious for weeks.
I stood over her breathing body,
watching her eyes crawling
under their lids.

She wailed on our wedding night.
I know it.
I could hear her miles away
from our bed.
I can hear her years away now.
She paid for her desire with her soul,
Joseph, with the curse of the ages
upon her nameless head.

I stare at your sleeping face.
You are a good man, Joseph,
wise and true and chosen.
Your eyes are running in their lids.
Where are you going?
What do you want?
What are you dreaming,
diviner of dreams?

41:46–45:11 . . . Then Joseph could not refrain himself before all them that stood by him; and he cried, Cause every man to go out from me. And there stood no man with him, while Joseph made himself known unto his brethren. And he wept aloud: and the Egyptians and the house of Pharaoh heard. And Joseph said unto his brethren, I am Joseph; doth my father yet live? And his brethren could not answer him; for they were troubled at his presence. And Joseph said unto his brethren, Come near to me, I pray you. And they came near. And he said, I am Joseph your brother, whom ye sold into Egypt. . . .

ISRAEL II

CHARLES REZNIKOFF

Since Potiphar made you his overseer,
he has been blessed in house and field;
all that he has is in your hand,

and he knows of nothing but the bread that he eats.
And you in our house have become comely—
you were nothing but a bag of bones.
Come here!
Your cheeks were sunken so,
your eyes staring and your hair
dishevelled like this, like this.
Are not my hands soft?
You stepped as lightly as a deer,
as slim and graceful as a deer,
and held your head as proudly.
Sit here.
Kiss me.
Not so.
Oh, you don't know how to kiss.
Kiss me so.
Wet your lips and kiss me so.
Kiss my eyes, my throat,
now my mouth—
oh, you fool! You fool!

You are magicians and wise men at my feasts;
now, what is the meaning of my dreams?

"Have me in mind when it shall be well with you,
make mention of me to Pharaoh, and bring me out of this house;
for I was stolen from the land of the Hebrews;
and here also I have done nothing that they should put me into the
dungeon."
Since then, two full years have passed, and until this day I have
forgotten Joseph.

Therefore, let Pharaoh set a man, discreet and wise,
to appoint overseers, and these gather in the cities from the fields
about them
grain in the good years against the years of famine.
Where can we find such a man?
I have no one discreet and wise as you.
You shall be over my house, and according to your word shall my
people be ruled;
only I, on the throne, will be greater.
Clothe him in fine linen and put a gold chain about his neck,
he shall ride in the second chariot and all cry out before him, Bend the
knee!

You are spies, you come to see the nakedness of the land.
No, my lord, we are not spies, we have come to buy food.
We are brothers, the sons of one man in Canaan.
And is your father yet alive?
He is.
Have you another brother?
We have.
We were twelve,
the youngest is with our father,
and one is no more.

My lord, we have brought you a present of the fruit of our land:
A little balm, a little honey, spicery and myrrh, pistachios and almonds.
Is your father well, the old man of whom you spoke? Is he yet alive?
Is this your youngest brother of whom you spoke?

Why have you rewarded evil for good? Where is the cup from which my lord drinks?
The man in whose hand the cup was found shall be my bondsman.

Now when I come to the servant your father and the lad is not with us—
his brother is dead, and he alone is left of his mother, and his father loves him—
let me remain instead of the lad, a bondsman to my lord.

Let every man go out but these.
I am Joseph.
Come nearer.
I am Joseph, your brother, whom you sold into Egypt.
And now be not grieved, nor angry with yourselves,
for I was sent before you to save us all alive;
you meant evil against me, but it was meant for good.
Go up to our father and say to him,
your son Joseph has become head of all Egypt;
without Joseph no man, except Pharaoh on the throne, lifts hand or foot throughout Egypt.
You have not thought to see his face and you shall see his sons also.
Come to him and you shall dwell in the land of Goshen—
and he shall be near me and his children and his children's children
and bring all your flocks and herds and all that you have;
for there are yet five years of famine.
You shall tell my father of all my glory in Egypt;
you shall take wagons out of Egypt for your little ones and your wives, and bring our father and come;

and I will give you all the good of the land of Egypt.
I will establish my people like a pyramid,
no longer to be blown along like sand.

47:7–10 And Joseph brought in Jacob his father, and set him before Pharaoh: and Jacob blessed Pharaoh. And Pharaoh said unto Jacob, How old art thou? And Jacob said unto Pharaoh, The days of the years of my pilgrimage are an hundred and thirty years: few and evil have the days of the years of my life been, and have not attained unto the days of the years of the life of my fathers in the days of their pilgrimage. And Jacob blessed Pharaoh, and went out from before Pharaoh. . . .

On Mortality

Henry Colman

Thc world's deceitful, and man's life at best
Is but a life undressed,
And void of rest,
Scarce a span-long, frail as the brittlest glass,
And like the withered grass
It hence doth pass;
Who trusts the world then, or man's brittle fate,
Reckons without his host, betrays his state.

Each bubble (fitly) represents to man
His life, and (broken) can
Show him his span,
So vain, and frail's the greatest mortals stay,
That every moment may
His life betray;
Grant then ô Lord that I may trust in none,
Neither the world, nor man, but thee alone.

No sooner are we born into the light,
But presently we fright,
And bid good night,
As if our birth-day were but given to spy
The world, and at it cry,
And straightway die,
Thus as soon dead, as born, as soon forgot,
Scarce any knowing that we were or not.

If God do please to lengthen out our days,
And give us time to raise
His name, and praise;
Our longest time is but an hundred years,
And those so full of fears,
So mixed with cares
That never any so long-lived was seen,
But all his days have few, and evil been.

Our infancy is altogether cross,
Our childish-age but loss,
Our youth mere dross,
Once grown up to be men, we then presume
We may our lives consume
In drink, and fume,
And our old age (mere dotage) is the worst;
So each scene fills up but a life accursed.

If while we live here we do health enjoy,
Honor, or wealth us cloy
And make us coy,
If we have all delights the world can give,
Yet we shall wretched live
Only to grieve;
For the world's pomp, and earth's felicity,
Is only constant in unconstancy.

Shall I then dote, and be in love with earth,
Or any mortal birth?
Or fear a death
That I must pay? O rather let me strive
(While I am here alive)
Only to give
My life to thee; and grant that when I die
Lord, I may reign with thee eternally.

47:27–49:33 . . . And the time drew nigh that Israel must die: and he called his son Joseph, and said unto him, If now I have found grace in thy sight, put, I pray thee, thy hand under my thigh, and deal kindly and truly with me; bury me not, I pray thee, in Egypt: But I will lie with my fathers, and thou shalt carry me out of Egypt, and bury me in their buryingplace. And he said, I will do as thou hast said. And he said, Swear

unto me. And he sware unto him. And Israel bowed himself upon the bed's head. . . . And Israel said unto Joseph, Behold, I die: but God shall be with you, and bring you again unto the land of your fathers.

And Jacob called unto his sons, and said, Gather yourselves together, that I may tell you that which shall befall you in the last days. Gather yourselves together, and hear, ye sons of Jacob; and hearken unto Israel your father. . . . And he charged them, and said unto them, I am to be gathered unto my people: bury me with my fathers in the cave that is in the field of Ephron the Hittite, In the cave that is in the field of Machpelah, which is before Mamre, in the land of Canaan, which Abraham bought with the field of Ephron the Hittite for a possession of a buryingplace. . . .

MUSE IN LATE NOVEMBER

JONATHAN HENDERSON BROOKS

I greet you, son, with joy and winter rue:
For you the fatted calf, the while I bind
Sackcloth against my heart for siring you
At sundown and the twilight. Child, you find
A sire sore tired of striving with the winds;
Climbing Mount Nebo with laborious breath
To view the land of promise through blurred lens,
Knowing he can not enter, feeling death.

And, as old Israel called his dozen sons
And placed his withered hands upon each head
Ere he was silent with the skeletons
In Mamre of the cold, cave-chambered dead,
So would I bless you with a dreamer's will:
The dream that baffles me, may you fulfill.

The Second Book of Moses, called EXODUS

1:6–19 And Joseph died, and all his brethren, and all that generation. . . .

Now there arose up a new king over Egypt, which knew not Joseph. And he said unto his people, Behold, the people of the children of Israel are more and mightier than we: Come on, let us deal wisely with

them; . . . Therefore they did set over them taskmasters to afflict them with their burdens. . . . But the more they afflicted them, the more they multiplied and grew. . . .

And the king of Egypt spake to the Hebrew midwives, of which the name of the one was Shiphrah, and the name of the other Puah: And he said, When ye do the office of a midwife to the Hebrew women, and see them upon the stools; if it be a son, then ye shall kill him: but if it be a daughter, then she shall live. But the midwives feared God, and did not as the king of Egypt commanded them, but saved the men children alive. And the king of Egypt called for the midwives, and said unto them, Why have ye done this thing, and have saved the men children alive? And the midwives said unto Pharaoh, Because the Hebrew women are not as the Egyptian women; for they are lively, and are delivered ere the midwives come in unto them. . . .

The Midwives

Celia Gilbert

Low huts, groans muffled,
babes slide to waiting arms
and afterbirth's
the buried plumage
of angels fallen
in travail,
but the mothers,
dazzled, tend
clandestine liberty
at hand—
sweet new bodies,
every one redeemer.

1:22–2:4 **And Pharaoh charged all his people, saying, Every son that is born ye shall cast into the river, and every daughter ye shall save alive.**

And there went a man of the house of Levi, and took to wife a daughter of Levi. And the woman conceived, and bare a son: and when she saw him that he was a goodly child, she hid him three months. And when she could not longer hide him, she took for him an ark of bulrushes, and daubed it with slime and with pitch, and put the child therein; and she laid it in the flags by the river's brink. And his sister stood afar off, to wit what would be done to him.

Moses in Infancy

Jones Very

How! Canst thou see the basket wherein lay
The infant Moses by the river's side,
And her who stood and watched it on the tide;
Will Time bring back to thee that early day?
And canst thou to the distant Nile be near,
Where lived that mother, tossed with hope and fear
Yet more than was her infant by the wave?
No: Time will not his dark domain unbar;
Himself he cannot from oblivion save,
Nor canst thou make come nearer what is far;
But thou hast human sympathies to feel
What eye, nor ear, nor sense can e'er reveal;
Hope too is thine, that past the ocean sails,
And Memory, that over Time himself prevails!

2:5–6 And the daughter of Pharaoh came down to wash herself at the river; and her maidens walked along by the river's side; and when she saw the ark among the flags, she sent her maid to fetch it. And when she had opened it, she saw the child:

Pharao's Daughter

Michael Moran—'Zozimus'

In Agypt's land contaygious to the Nile,
Old Pharao's daughter went to bathe in style,
She tuk her dip and came unto the land,
And for to dry her royal pelt she ran along the strand:

A bull-rush tripped her, whereupon she saw
A smiling babby in a wad of straw,
She took it up and said in accents mild,
'Tare-an-ages, girls, which o'yees own the child?'

EPITAPH

ELEANOR WILNER

Though only a girl,
the first born of the Pharaoh,
I was the first to die.

Young then,
we were bored already,
rouged pink as oleanders
on the palace grounds, petted
by the eunuchs, overfed
from gem-encrusted bowls, barren
with wealth, until the hours of the afternoon
seemed to outlast even
my grandmother's mummy, a perfect
little dried apricot
in a golden skin. We would paint
to pass the time, with delicate
brushes dipped in char
on clay, or on our own blank lids.
So it was that day we found him
wailing in the reeds, he seemed
a miracle to us, plucked
from the lotus by the ibis' beak,
the squalling seed of the sacred
Nile. He was permitted
as a toy; while I pretended play
I honed him like a sword.
For him, I was as polished and as perfect
as a pebble in a stutterer's mouth.
While the slaves' fans beat
incessantly as insect wings,
I taught him how to hate
this painted Pharaoh's tomb
this palace built of brick
and dung, and gilded like a poet's
tongue; these painted eyes.

2:6–10 and, behold, the babe wept. And she had compassion on him, and said, This is one of the Hebrews' children. Then said his sister to

Pharaoh's daughter, Shall I go and call to thee a nurse of the Hebrew women, that she may nurse the child for thee? And Pharaoh's daughter said to her, Go. And the maid went and called the child's mother. And Pharaoh's daughter said unto her, Take this child away, and nurse it for me, and I will give thee thy wages. And the woman took the child, and nursed it. And the child grew, and she brought him unto Pharaoh's daughter, and he became her son. And she called his name Moses: and she said, Because I drew him out of the water.

from MOSES HIS BIRTH AND MIRACLES

MICHAEL DRAYTON

. . . In time the Princess playing with the child,
In whom she seemed her chief delight to take,
With whom she oft the weary time beguiled,
That as her own did of this Hebrew make:
It so fell out as Pharaoh was in place,
Seeing his daughter in the child to joy,
To please the Princess, and to do it grace,
Himself vouchsafes to entertain the boy:
Whose shape and beauty when he did behold
With much content his princely eye that fed,
Giving to please it, any thing it would,
Set his rich crown upon the infant's head,
Which this weak child regarding not at all
(As such a baby carelessly is meet)
Unto the ground the diadem let fall
Spurning it from him with neglectful feet.
Which as the priests beheld this ominous thing
(That else had passed unnoted as a toy)
As from their skill report unto the King,
This was the man that Egypt should destroy.
Told by the Magi that were learn'd and wise,
Which might full well the jealous King enflame,
Said by th'Egyptian ancient prophecies
That might give credit eas'lier to the same.
She as discreet as she was chaste and fair,
With princely gesture and with countenance mild
By things that hurtful and most dangerous were
Shows to the King the weakness of the child:
Hot burning coals doth to his mouth present,

Which he to handle simply doth not stick,
This little fool, this reckless innocent
The burning gleed with his soft tongue doth lick:
Which though in Pharaoh her desire it wrought,
His babish imbecility to see,
To the child's speech impediment it brought,
From which he after never could be free.

3:1–6 Now Moses kept the flock of Jethro his father in law, the priest of Midian: and he led the flock to the backside of the desert, and came to the mountain of God, even to Horeb. And the angel of the LORD appeared unto him in a flame of fire out of the midst of a bush: and he looked, and, behold, the bush burned with fire, and the bush was not consumed. And Moses said, I will now turn aside, and see this great sight, why the bush is not burnt.

And when the LORD saw that he turned aside to see, God called unto him out of the midst of the bush, and said, Moses, Moses. And he said, Here am I. And he said, Draw not nigh hither: put off thy shoes from off thy feet, for the place whereon thou standest is holy ground. Moreover he said, I am the God of thy father, the God of Abraham, the God of Isaac, and the God of Jacob. And Moses hid his face; for he was afraid to look upon God.

Sitting by a Bush in Broad Daylight

ROBERT FROST

When I spread out my hand here today
I catch no more than a ray
To feel of between thumb and fingers;
No lasting effect of it lingers.

There was one time and only the one
When dust really took in the sun;
And from that one intake of fire
All creatures still warmly suspire.

And if men have watched a long time
And never seen sun-smitten slime
Again come to life and crawl off,
We must not be too ready to scoff.

God once declared he was true
And then took the veil and withdrew,
And remember how final a hush
Then descended of old on the bush.

God once spoke to people by name.
The sun once imparted its flame.
One impulse persists as our breath.
The other persists as our faith.

3:7–14 . . . And Moses said unto God, Behold, when I come unto the children of Israel, and shall say unto them, The God of your fathers hath sent me unto you; and they shall say to me, What is his name? what shall I say unto them?

And God said unto Moses, I AM THAT I AM: and he said, Thus shalt thou say unto the children of Israel, I AM hath sent me unto you.

ON EXODUS 3:14. 'I AM THAT I AM'

An Ode

MATTHEW PRIOR

Man! Foolish Man!
Scarce knowst thou how thy self began;
Scarce has thou thought enough to prove thou art;
Yet steeled with studied boldness, thou dar'st try
To send thy doubting reason's dazzled eye
Through the mysterious gulf of vast immensity.
Much thou canst there discern, much thence impart.
    Vain wretch! suppress thy knowing pride;
        Mortify thy learned lust:
Vain are thy thoughts, while thou thyself art dust.

Let wit her sails, her oars let wisdom lend;
The helm let politic experience guide:
Yet cease to hope thy short-lived bark shall ride
Down spreading Fate's unnavigable tide.
    What, though still it farther tend?
    Still 'tis farther from its end;
And in the bosom of that boundless sea,
Still finds its error lengthen with its way.

With daring pride and insolent delight
Your doubts resolved you boast, your labors crowned;
And *Eureka!* your God forsooth is found
Incomprehensible and Infinite.
How is He therefore found? Vain searcher! no:
Let your imperfect definition show
That nothing you, the weak definer, know.

Say, why should the collected main
Itself within itself contain?
Why to its caverns should it sometimes creep,
And with delighted silence sleep
On the loved bosom of its parent's deep?
Why should its numerous waters stay
In comely discipline, and fair array,
Till winds and tides exert their high commands?
Then, prompt and ready to obey,
Why do the rising surges spread
Their opening ranks o'er Earth's submissive head,
Marching through different paths to different lands?

Why does the constant sun
With measured steps his radiant journeys run?
Why does he order the diurnal hours
To leave Earth's other part, and rise in ours?
Why does he wake the correspondent moon,
And fill her willing lamp with liquid light,
Commanding her with delegated powers
To beautify the world, and bless the night?
Why does each animated star
Love the just limits of its proper sphere?
Why does each consenting sign
With prudent harmony combine
In turns to move, and subsequent appear,
To gird the globe, and regulate the year?

Man does with dangerous curiosity
Those unfathomed wonders try:
With fancied rules and arbitrary laws
Matter and motion he restrains;
And studied lines and fictious circles draws:
Then with imagined sovereignty
Lord of his new Hypothesis he reigns.
He reigns: How long? 'til some usurper rise;

And he too, mighty thoughtful, mighty wise,
Studies new lines, and other circles feigns.
From this last toil again what knowledge flows?
Just as much, perhaps, as shows
That all his predecessor's rules
Were empty cant, all Jargon of the schools;
That he on t'other's ruin rears his throne;
And shows his friend's mistake, and thence confirms his own.

On earth, in air, amidst the seas and skies,
Mountainous heaps of wonders rise;
Whose towering strength will ne'er submit
To reason's batteries, or the mines of wit:
Yet still enquiring, still mistaking Man,
Each hour repulsed, each hour dare onward press;
And levelling at God his wandering guess
(That feeble engine of his reasoning war,
Which guides his doubts, and combats his despair),
Laws to his Maker the learned wretch can give:
Can bound that Nature, and prescribe that will,
Whose pregnant word did either ocean fill:
Can tell us whence all Beings are, and how they move and live.
Through either ocean, foolish Man!
That pregnant word sent forth again,
Might to a world extend each Atom there;
For every drop call forth a sea, a heaven for every star.

Let cunning earth her fruitful wonders hide;
And only lift thy staggering reason up
To trembling Calvary's astonished top;
Then mock thy knowledge, and confound thy pride,
Explaining how Perfection suffered pain,
Almighty languished, and Eternal died:
How by her patient victor Death was slain;
And Earth profaned, yet blessed, with deicide.
Then down with all thy boasted volumes, down;
Only reserve the sacred one:
Low, reverently low,
Make thy stubborn knowledge bow;
Weep out thy reason's, and thy body's, eyes;
Deject thyself, that thou mayst rise;
To look to Heaven, be blind to all below.

Then faith, for reason's glimmering light, shall give
Her immortal perspective;
And grace's presence nature's loss retrieve:
Then thy enlivened soul shall see
That all the volumes of philosophy,
With all their comments, never could invent
So politic an instrument
To reach the Heaven of Heavens, the high abode
Where Moses places his mysterious God,
As was that ladder which old Jacob reared,
When light divine had human darkness cleared;
And his enlarged ideas found the road
Which faith had dictated, and angels trod.

3:15–4:5 . . . And Moses answered and said, But, behold, they will not believe me, nor hearken unto my voice: for they will say, The LORD hath not appeared unto thee.

And the LORD said unto him, What is that in thine hand? And he said, A rod.

And he said, Cast it on the ground. And he cast it on the ground, and it became a serpent; and Moses fled from before it. And the LORD said unto Moses, Put forth thine hand, and take it by the tail. And he put forth his hand, and caught it, and it became a rod in his hand: That they may believe that the LORD God of their fathers, the God of Abraham, the God of Isaac, and the God of Jacob, hath appeared unto thee.

On God's Law

Francis Quarles

Thy sacred law, O God,
Is like to Moses' rod:
If we but keep it in our hand,
It will do wonders in the land;
If we slight and throw it to the ground;
'Twill turn a serpent, and inflict a wound;
A wound that flesh and blood cannot endure,
Nor salve, until the brazen serpent cure:
I wish not, Lord, thou shouldst withhold it;
Nor would I have it, and not hold it:
O teach me then, my God,
To handle Moses' rod.

9:13–14 And the LORD said unto Moses, Rise up early in the morning, and stand before Pharaoh, and say unto him, Thus saith the LORD God of the Hebrews, Let my people go, that they may serve me. For I will at this time send all my plagues upon thine heart, and upon thy servants, and upon thy people; that thou mayest know that there is none like me in all the earth.

THE COMING OF THE PLAGUE

WELDON KEES

September was when it began.
Locusts dying in the fields; our dogs
Silent, moving like shadows on a wall;
And strange worms crawling; flies of a kind
We had never seen before; huge vineyard moths;
Badgers and snakes, abandoning
Their holes in the field; the fruit gone rotten;
Queer fungi sprouting; the fields and woods
Covered with spiderwebs; black vapors
Rising from the earth— all these,
And more, began that fall. Ravens flew round
The hospital in pairs. Where there was water,
We could hear the sound of beating clothes
All through the night. We could not count
All the miscarriages, the quarrels, the jealousies.
And one day in a field I saw
A swarm of frogs, swollen and hideous,
Hundreds upon hundreds, sitting on each other,
Huddled together, silent, ominous,
And heard the sound of rushing wind.

13:17–22 And it came to pass, when Pharaoh had let the people go, that God led them not through the way of the land of the Philistines, . . . But God led the people about, through the way of the wilderness of the Red sea: and the children of Israel went up harnessed out of the land of Egypt. And Moses took the bones of Joseph with him: for he had straitly sworn the children of Israel, saying, God will surely visit you; and ye shall carry up my bones away hence with you. . . . And the LORD went before them by day in a pillar of a cloud, to lead them the way; and by night in a pillar of fire, to give them light; to go by day and night: He took not away the pillar of the cloud by day, nor the pillar of fire by night, from before the people.

THE PILLAR OF THE CLOUD

JOHN HENRY, CARDINAL NEWMAN

Lead, Kindly Light, amid the circling gloom,
    Lead Thou me on!
The night is dark, and I am far from home—
    Lead Thou me on!
Keep Thou my feet; I do not ask to see
The distant scene,—one step enough for me.

I was not ever thus, nor prayed that Thou
    Shouldst lead me on!
I loved to choose and see my path; but now
    Lead Thou me on!
I loved the garish day, and, spite of fears,
Pride ruled my will: remember not past years.

So long Thy power hath blest me, sure it still
    Will lead me on,
O'er moor and fen, o'er crag and torrent, till
    The night is gone;
And with the morn those angel faces smile
Which I have loved long since, and lost awhile.

14:24–29 And it came to pass, that in the morning watch the LORD looked unto the host of the Egyptians through the pillar of fire and of the cloud, and troubled the host of the Egyptians, And took off their chariot wheels, that they drave them heavily: so that the Egyptians said, Let us flee from the face of Israel; for the LORD fighteth for them against the Egyptians.

And the LORD said unto Moses, Stretch out thine hand over the sea, that the waters may come again upon the Egyptians, upon their chariots, and upon their horsemen. And Moses stretched forth his hand over the sea, and the sea returned to his strength when the morning appeared; and the Egyptians fled against it; and the LORD overthrew the Egyptians in the midst of the sea. And the waters returned, and covered the chariots, and the horsemen, and all the host of Pharaoh that came into the sea after them; there remained not so much as one of them. But the children of Israel walked upon dry land in the midst of the sea; and the waters were a wall unto them on their right hand, and on their left.

Exodus

George Oppen

Miracle of the children   the brilliant
Children   the word
Liquid as woodlands   Children?

When she was a child I read Exodus
To my daughter   'The children of Israel . . .'

Pillar of fire
Pillar of cloud

We stared at the end
Into each other's eyes   Where
She said hushed

Were the adults   We dreamed to each other
Miracle of the children
The brilliant children   Miracle

Of their brilliance   Miracle
of

14:30–31 Thus the LORD saved Israel that day out of the hand of the Egyptians; and Israel saw the Egyptians dead upon the sea shore. And Israel saw that great work which the LORD did upon the Egyptians: and the people feared the LORD, and believed the LORD, and his servant Moses.

Mock on, Mock on Voltaire, Rousseau

William Blake

Mock on, Mock on Voltaire, Rousseau:
Mock on, Mock on: 'tis all in vain!
You throw the sand against the wind,
And the wind blows it back again.

And every sand becomes a Gem
Reflected in the beams divine;
Blown back they blind the mocking Eye,
But still in Israel's paths they shine.

The Atoms of Democritus
And Newton's Particles of light
Are sands upon the Red sea shore,
Where Israel's tents do shine so bright.

15:1–3 Then sang Moses and the children of Israel this song unto the LORD, and spake, saying, I will sing unto the LORD, for he hath triumphed gloriously: the horse and his rider hath he thrown into the sea.

The LORD is my strength and song, and he is become my salvation: he is my God, and I will prepare him an habitation; my father's God, and I will exalt him.

The LORD is a man of war: the LORD is his name. . . .

The first Song of Moses

George Wither

Now shall the praises of the Lord be sung:
For, he a most renownèd triumph won:
Both horse and man into the sea he flung;
And them together there hath overthrown.
The Lord is He, whose strength doth make me strong;
And he is my salvation and my song.
My God, for whom I will a house prepare;
My fathers God, whose praise I will declare.

Well knows the Lord to war what doth pertain;
The Lord-almighty is his glorious name:
He Pharaoh's chariots, and his armed train,
Amid the sea o'erwhelming, overcame:
Those of his army that were most renowned,
He hath together in the Red Sea drowned;
The deeps, a covering over them were thrown,
And, to the bottom sunk they, like a stone.

Lord, by thy power thy right hand famous grows:
Thy right hand, Lord, thy foe destroyed hath:
Thy glory thy opposers overthrows;
And, stubble-like, consumes them in thy wrath.
A blast but from thy nostrils forth did go,
And up together did the waters flow;

Yea, rolled up on heaps; the liquid flood
Amid the sea, as if congealed, stood.

I will pursue them (their pursuer cried)
I will o'ertake them, and the spoil enjoy:
My lust upon them shall be satisfied:
With sword unsheathed my hand shall them destroy.
    Then from thy breath a gale of wind was sent:
    The billows of the sea quite o'er them went:
And they the mighty waters sunk into,
Even as a weighty piece of lead will do.

Lord, who like thee among the gods is there!
In holiness so glorious who may be!
Whose praises so exceeding dreadful are!
In doing wonders, who can equal thee!
Thy glorious right hand on high didst rear,
    And in the earth they quickly swallowed were:
But thou, in mercy, onward hast conveyed
Thy people, whose redemption thou hast paid.

Them, by thy strength, thou hast been pleased to bear
Unto a holy dwelling place of thine:
The nations at report thereof shall fear;
And grieve shall they that dwelt in Palestine,
    On Edom's princes shall amazement fall:
    The mighty men of Moab tremble shall;
And, such as in the land of Canaan dwell,
Shall pine away, of this when they hear tell.

They shall be seized with a horrid fear:
Stone-quiet thy right hand shall make them be,
Till passed over, Lord, thy people are;
(Till those pass over, that were brought by thee.)
    For, thou shalt make them to thy hill repair,
    And plant them there (oh Lord) where thou art heir;
Even there, where thou thy dwelling hast prepared;
That holy place, which thine own hands have reared.

The Lord shall ever, and for ever reign:
(His sovereignty shall never have an end)
For, when as Pharaoh did into the main
With chariots, and with horsemen down descend,
    The Lord did back again the sea recall,
    And with those waters overwhelmed them all:

But, through the very inmost of the same,
The seed of Israel safe and dry-shod came.

15:20–21 And Miriam the prophetess, the sister of Aaron, took a timbrel in her hand; and all the women went out after her with timbrels and with dances. And Miriam answered them, Sing ye to the LORD, for he hath triumphed gloriously; the horse and his rider hath he thrown into the sea.

Sound the Loud Timbrel

Thomas Moore

Sound the loud timbrel o'er Egypt's dark sea!
Jehovah has triumphed—his people are free.
Sing—for the pride of the tyrant is broken,
    His chariots, his horsemen, all splendid and brave—
How vain was their boast, for the Lord hath but spoken,
    And chariots and horsemen are sunk in the wave.
Sound the loud timbrel o'er Egypt's dark sea;
Jehovah has triumphed—his people are free.

Praise to the Conqueror, praise to the Lord!
His word was our arrow, his breath was our sword.
Who shall return to tell Egypt the story
    Of those she sent forth in the hour of her pride?
For the Lord hath looked out from his pillar of glory,
    And all her brave thousands are dashed in the tide.
Sound the loud timbrel o'er Egypt's dark sea;
Jehovah has triumphed—his people are free.

15:22–23 So Moses brought Israel from the Red sea, and they went out into the wilderness of Shur; and they went three days in the wilderness, and found no water. And when they came to Marah, they could not drink of the waters of Marah, for they were bitter: therefore the name of it was called Marah.

THE JEWISH CEMETERY AT NEWPORT

HENRY WADSWORTH LONGFELLOW

How strange it seems! These Hebrews in their graves,
Close by the street of this fair seaport town,
Silent beside the never-silent waves,
At rest in all this moving up and down!

The trees are white with dust, that o'er their sleep
Wave their broad curtains in the southwind's breath,
While underneath these leafy tents they keep
The long, mysterious Exodus of Death.

And these sepulchral stones, so old and brown,
That pave with level flags their burial-place,
Seem like the tablets of the Law, thrown down
And broken by Moses at the mountain's base.

The very names recorded here are strange,
Of foreign accent, and of different climes;
Alvares and Rivera interchange
With Abraham and Jacob of old times.

"Blessed be God! for he created Death!"
The mourners said, "and Death is rest and peace;"
Then added, in the certainty of faith,
"And giveth Life that nevermore shall cease."

Closed are the portals of their Synagogue,
No Psalms of David now the silence break,
No Rabbi reads the ancient Decalogue
In the grand dialect the Prophets spake.

Gone are the living, but the dead remain,
And not neglected, for a hand unseen,
Scattering its bounty, like a summer rain,
Still keeps their graves and their remembrance green.

How came they here? What burst of Christian hate,
What persecution, merciless and blind,
Drove o'er the sea—that desert desolate—
These Ishmaels and Hagars of mankind?

They lived in narrow streets and lanes obscure,
    Ghetto and Judenstrass, in mirk and mire;
Taught in the school of patience to endure
    The life of anguish and the death of fire.

All their lives long, with the unleavened bread
    And bitter herbs of exile and its fears,
The wasting famine of the heart they fed,
    And slaked its thirst with marah of their tears.

Anathema maranatha! was the cry
    That rang from town to town, from street to street;
At every gate the accursed Mordecai
    Was mocked and jeered, and spurned by Christian feet.

Pride and humiliation hand in hand
    Walked with them through the world where'er they went;
Trampled and beaten were they as the sand
    And yet unshaken as the continent.

For in the background figures vague and vast
    Of patriarchs and of prophets rose sublime,
And all the great traditions of the Past
    They saw reflected in the coming time.

And thus forever with reverted look
    The mystic volume of the world they read,
Spelling it backward, like a Hebrew book,
    Till life became a Legend of the Dead.

But ah! what once has been shall be no more!
    The groaning earth in travail and in pain
Brings forth its races, but does not restore,
    And the dead nations never rise again.

20:1–6. . . And God spake all these words, saying, I am the LORD thy God, which have brought thee out of the land of Egypt, out of the house of bondage. Thou shalt have no other gods before me. Thou shalt not make unto thee any graven image, or any likeness of any thing that is in heaven above, or that is in the earth beneath, or that is in the water under the earth. Thou shalt not bow down thyself to them, nor serve them: for I the LORD thy God am a jealous God, visiting the iniquity of the fathers upon the children unto the third and fourth generation of them that hate me; And shewing mercy unto thousands of them that love me, and keep my commandments.

Neutrality Loathesome

Robert Herrick

God will have all, or none; serve Him, or fall
Down before Baal, Bel, or Belial:
Either be hot, or cold: God doth despise,
Abhor, and spew out all Neutralities.

20:7–17 Thou shalt not take the name of the LORD thy God in vain; for the LORD will not hold him guiltless that taketh his name in vain.Remember the sabbath day, to keep it holy. Six days shalt thou labour, and do all thy work: But the seventh day is the sabbath of the LORD thy God: in it thou shalt not do any work, thou, nor thy son, nor thy daughter, thy manservant, nor thy maidservant, nor thy cattle, nor thy stranger that is within thy gates: For in six days the LORD made heaven and earth, the sea, and all that in them is, and rested the seventh day: wherefore the LORD blessed the sabbath day, and hallowed it. Honour thy father and thy mother: that thy days may be long upon the land which the LORD thy God giveth thee. Thou shalt not kill.Thou shalt not commit adultery. Thou shalt not steal. Thou shalt not bear false witness against thy neighbour. Thou shalt not covet thy neighbour's house, thou shalt not covet thy neighbour's wife, nor his manservant, nor his maidservant, nor his ox, nor his ass, nor any thing that is thy neighbour's.

from TAYLOR'S ARITHMETIC FROM ONE TO TWELVE

JOHN TAYLOR

The 10 Commandments, are the Law Divine,
(To keep those laws, Good Lord our hearts incline;)
But from those 10, should 10 men each pluck one,
Tis to be feared that left we should have none.
The atheist (which the Psalmist fool doth call)
As he believes will have no God at all.
Th' idolater will stock, block, idols have
To save him, though themselves they cannot save.
The roarer that delights to damn and swear,
From the Commandments he the third would tear,
The Sabbath-breaker would pluck out the fourth,
The fifth (with rebels) is of little worth,
The sixth the murderer would stab and wound,
The seventh the hot adult'rer would confound,
The thief would steal the eighth away, and then
False witness spoil the ninth: and for the ten,
The wretch that's covetous would rend and bite,
And pluck the rest in pieces if he might.
Thus would there 10 (this cursed catalogue)
Each 'rase out one, and spoil the Decalogue.

THE LAW GIVEN AT SINAI

ISAAC WATTS

Arm thee with thunder, heavenly muse,
And keep th' expecting world in awe;
Oft hast thou sung in gentler mood
The melting mercies of thy God;
Now give thy fiercest fires a loose,
And sound his dreadful law:
To Israel first the words were spoke,
To Israel freed from Egypt's yoke,
Inhuman bondage! the hard galling load
Over-pressed their feeble souls,
Bent their knees to senseless bulls,
And broke their ties to God.
Now had they passed the Arabian bay,

And marched between the cleaving sea;
The rising waves stood guardians of their wondrous way,
But fell with most impeteous force
On the pursuing swarms
And buried Egypt all in arms.
Blending in watery death the rider and the horse:
O'er struggling Pharaoh rolled the mighty tide,
And saved the labors of a pyramid.
Apis and Ore in vain he cries,
And all his horned gods beside,
He swallows fate with swimming eyes,
And cursed the Hebrews as he died.

Ah! foolish Israel, to comply
With Memphian idolatry!
And bow to brutes, (a stupid slave)
To idols impotent to save!
Behold thy God, the sovereign of the sky,
Has wrought salvation in the deep,
Has bound thy foes in iron sleep,
And raised thine honors high;
His grace forgives thy follies past,
Behold he comes in majesty,
And Sinai's top proclaims his law:
Prepare to meet thy God in haste!
But keep an awful distance still:
Let Moses round the sacred hill
The circling limits draw.

Hark! the shrill echoes of the trumpet roar,
And call the trembling armies near;
Slow and unwilling they appear,
Rails kept them from the mount before,
Now from the rails their fear:
'Twas the same herald, and the trump the same
Which shall be blown by high command,
Shall bid the wheels of nature stand,
And heaven's eternal will proclaim,
That 'Time shall be no more.'

Thus while the laboring angel swelled the sound,
And rent the skies, and shook the ground,
Up rose th' Almighty; round his sapphire seat
Adoring thrones in order fell;
The lesser powers at distance dwell,
And cast their glories down successive at his feet:
Gabriel the great prepares his way,
'Lift up your heads, eternal doors,' he cries;
Th' eternal doors his word obey,
Open and shoot celestial day
Upon the lower skies.
Heaven's mighty pillars bowed their head,
As their Creator bid,
And down Jehovah rode from the superior sphere,
A thousand guards before, and myriads in the rear.

His chariot was a pitchy cloud,
The wheels beset with burning gems;
The winds in harness with the flames
Flew o'er th' ethereal road:
Down through his magazines he past
Of hail, and ice, and fleecy snow,
Swift rolled the triumph, and as fast
Did hail, and ice, in melted rivers flow.
The day was mingled with the night,
His feet on solid darkness trod,
His radiant eyes proclaimed the God,
And scattered dreadful light;
He breathed, and sulphur ran, a fiery stream:
He spoke, and (though with unknown speed he came)
Chid the slow tempest, and the lagging flame.

Sinai received his glorious flight,
With axle red, and glowing wheel,
Did the wingéd chariot light,
And rising smoke obscured the burning hill.
Lo, it mounts in curling waves,
Lo, the gloomy pride out-braves
The stately pyramids of fire
The pyramids to heaven aspire,

And mix with stars, but see their gloomy offspring higher.
So you have seen ungrateful ivy grow
Round the tall oak that six score years has stood,
And proudly shoot a leaf or two
Above its kind supporter's utmost bough,
And glory there to stand the loftiest of the wood.

Forbear, young muse, forbear;
The flowery things that poets say,
The little arts of simile
Are vain and useless here;
Nor shall the burning hills of old
With Sinai be compared,
Nor all that lying Greece has told,
Or learnéd Rome has heard;
Ætna shall be named no more,
Ætna, the torch of Sicily;
Not half so high
Her lightnings fly,
Not half so loud her thunders roar
Cross the Sicanian sea, to fright th' Italian shore.
Behold the sacred hill: Its trembling spire
Quakes at the terrors of the fire,
While all below its verdant feet
Stagger and reel under th' almighty weight:
Pressed with a greater than feigned Atlas' load
Deep groaned the mount; it never bore
Infinity before,
It bowed, and shook beneath the burden of a God.

Fresh horror seize the camp, despair
And dying groans, torment the air,
And shrieks, and swoons, and deaths were there;
The bellowing thunder, and the lightning's blaze,
Spread through the host a wild amaze;
Darkness on every soul, and pale was every face:
Confused and dismal were the cries,
'Let Moses speak, or Israel dies:'
Moses the spreading terror feels,
No more the man of God conceals
His shivering and surprise:

Yet, with recovering mind, commands
Silence, and deep attention, through the Hebrew bands.
    Hark! from the center of the flame,
    All armed and feathered with the same,
Majestic sounds break through the smoky cloud:
    Sent from the all-creating tongue
    A flight of cherubs guard the words along,
And bear their fiery law to the retreating crowd.

    'I am the Lord: 'Tis I proclaim
    'That glorious and that fearful name,
    'Thy God and King: 'Twas I, that broke
    'Thy bondage, and th' Egyptian yoke;
    'Mine is the right to speak my will,
    'And thine the duty to fulfil.

'Adore no God beside me, to provoke mine eyes:
'Nor worship me in shapes and forms that men devise;
'With reverence use my name, nor turn my words to jest;
'Observe my sabbath well, nor dare profane my rest;
'Honor, and due obedience, to thy parents give;
'Nor spill the guiltless blood, nor let the guilty live:
'Preserve thy body chaste, and flee th' unlawful bed;
'Nor steal thy neighbour's gold, his garment, or his bread:
'Forbear to blast his name with falsehood, or deceit;
'Nor let thy wishes loose upon his large estate.'

26:30–27:20 And thou shalt rear up the tabernacle according to the fashion thereof which was shewed thee in the mount. . . . All the vessels of the tabernacle in all the service thereof, and all the pins thereof, and all the pins of the court, shall be of brass. And thou shalt command the children of Israel, that they bring thee pure oil olive beaten for the light, to cause the lamp to burn always.

The Jew

Isaac Rosenberg

Moses, from whose loins I sprung,
Lit by a lamp in his blood
Ten immutable rules, a moon
For mutable lampless men.

The blond, the bronze, the ruddy,
With the same heaving blood,
Keep tide to the moon of Moses.
Then why do they sneer at me?

28:4–34 And these are the garments which they shall make; a breastplate, and an ephod, and a robe, and a broidered coat, a mitre, and a girdle: and they shall make holy garments for Aaron thy brother, and his sons, that he may minister unto me in the priest's office. And they shall take gold, and blue, and purple, and scarlet, and fine linen. And they shall make the ephod of gold, of blue, and of purple, of scarlet, and fine twined linen, with cunning work. . . . And thou shalt make the breastplate of judgment with cunning work; after the work of the ephod thou shalt make it; of gold, of blue, and of purple, and of scarlet, and of fine twined linen, shalt thou make it. . . . And thou shalt put in the breastplate of judgment the Urim and the Thummim; and they shall be upon Aaron's heart, when he goeth in before the LORD: and Aaron shall bear the judgment of the children of Israel upon his heart before the LORD continually. And thou shalt make the robe of the ephod all of blue. And there shall be an hole in the top of it, in the midst thereof: it shall have a binding of woven work round about the hole of it, as it were the hole of an habergeon, that it be not rent. And beneath upon the hem of it thou shalt make pomegranates of blue, and of purple, and of scarlet, round about the hem thereof; and bells of gold between them round about: A golden bell and a pomegranate, a golden bell and a pomegranate, upon the hem of the robe round about.

AARON

GEORGE HERBERT

Holiness on the head,
Light and perfections on the breast,
Harmonious bells below, raising the dead
To lead them unto life and rest.
Thus are true Aarons dressed.

Profaneness in my head,
Defects and darkness in my breast,
A noise of passions ringing me for dead
Unto a place where is no rest.
Poor priest thus am I dressed.

Only another head
I have, another heart and breast,
Another music, making live not dead,
Without whom I could have no rest:
In him I am well dressed.

Christ is my only head,
My alone only heart and breast,
My only music, striking me even dead;
That to the old man I may rest,
And be in him new dressed.

So holy in my head,
Perfect and light in my dear breast,
My doctrine tuned by Christ, (who is not dead,
But lives in me while I do rest)
Come people; Aaron's dressed.

32:1–34 . . . And the LORD said unto Moses, Go, get thee down; for thy people, which thou broughtest out of the land of Egypt, have corrupted themselves: They have turned aside quickly out of the way which I commanded them: they have made them a molten calf, and have worshipped it, and have sacrificed thereunto, and said, These be thy gods, O Israel, which have brought thee up out of the land of Egypt. . . .

And it came to pass on the morrow, that Moses said unto the people, Ye have sinned a great sin: and now I will go up unto the LORD; peradventure I shall make an atonement for your sin. And Moses returned unto the LORD, and said, Oh, this people have sinned a great sin, and have made them gods of gold. Yet now, if thou wilt forgive their sin—; and if not, blot me, I pray thee, out of thy book which thou hast written.

And the LORD said unto Moses, Whosoever hath sinned against me, him will I blot out of my book. . . .

The Book of the World

William Drummond of Hawthornden

Of this fair volume which we World do name,
If we the sheets and leaves could turn with care,
Of Him who it corrects, and did it frame,
We clear might read the art and wisdom rare?
Find out his Power which wildest powers doth tame,

His Providence extending everywhere,
His Justice which proud rebels doth not spare.
In every page, no, period of the same:
But silly we (like foolish children) rest
Well pleased with colored vellum, leaves of gold,
Fair dangling ribbons, leaving what is best,
On the great Writer's sense ne'er taking hold;
    Or if by chance our minds do muse on ought,
    It is some picture on the margin wrought.

33:9–34:20 . . . All that openeth the matrix is mine; and every firstling among thy cattle, whether ox or sheep, that is male. But the firstling of an ass thou shalt redeem with a lamb: and if thou redeem him not, then shalt thou break his neck. All the firstborn of thy sons thou shalt redeem. And none shall appear before me empty.

The Ass

Robert Herrick

God did forbid the Israelites, to bring
An Ass unto Him, for an offering:
Only, by this dull creature, to express
His detestation to all slothfulness.

34:21–28 . . . And the LORD said unto Moses, Write thou these words: for after the tenor of these words I have made a covenant with thee and with Israel. And he was there with the LORD forty days and forty nights; he did neither eat bread, nor drink water. And he wrote upon the tables the words of the covenant, the ten commandments.

The Latest Decalogue

Arthur Hugh Clough

Thou shalt have one God only; who
Would be at the expense of two?
No graven images may be

Worshipped, except the currency:
Swear not at all; for, for thy curse
Thine enemy is none the worse:
At church on Sunday to attend
Will serve to keep the world thy friend:
Honour thy parents; that is, all
From whom advancement may befall:
Thou shalt not kill; but needst not strive
Officiously to keep alive:
Do not adultery commit;
Advantage rarely comes of it:
Thou shalt not steal; an empty feat
When it's so lucrative to cheat:
Bear not false witness; let the lie
Have time on its own wings to fly:
Thou shalt not covet; but tradition
Approves all forms of competition.
The sum of all is, thou shalt love,
If any body, God above:
At any rate shall never labour
More than thyself to love thy neighbor.

40:1–10 And the LORD spake unto Moses, saying, On the first day of the first month shalt thou set up the tabernacle of the tent of the congregation. And thou shalt put therein the ark of the testimony, and cover the ark with the vail. And thou shalt bring in the table, and set in order the things that are to be set in order upon it; and thou shalt bring in the candlestick, and light the lamps thereof. And thou shalt set the altar of gold for the incense before the ark of the testimony, and put the hanging of the door to the tabernacle. And thou shalt set the altar of the burnt offering before the door of the tabernacle of the tent of the congregation. And thou shalt set the laver between the tent of the congregation and the altar, and shalt put water therein. And thou shalt set up the court round about, and hang up the hanging at the court gate. And thou shalt take the anointing oil, and anoint the tabernacle, and all that is therein, and shalt hallow it, and all the vessels thereof: and it shall be holy. And thou shalt anoint the altar of the burnt offering, and all his vessels, and sanctify the altar: and it shall be an altar most holy.

Tabernacle

D. H. Lawrence

Come, let us build a temple to oblivion
with seven veils, and an innermost
Holy of Holies of sheer oblivion.

And there oblivion dwells, and the silent soul
may sink into god at last, having passed the veils.

But anyone who shall ascribe attributes to God or oblivion
let him be cast out, for blasphemy.
For God is a deeper forgetting far than sleep
and all description is a blasphemy.

40:17–38 . . . Then a cloud covered the tent of the congregation, and the glory of the LORD filled the tabernacle. And Moses was not able to enter into the tent of the congregation, because the cloud abode thereon, and the glory of the LORD filled the tabernacle. And when the cloud was taken up from over the tabernacle, the children of Israel went onward in all their journeys: But if the cloud were not taken up, then they journeyed not till the day that it was taken up. For the cloud of the LORD was upon the tabernacle by day, and fire was on it by night, in the sight of all the house of Israel, throughout all their journeys.

Exodus

Charles Reznikoff

We who had known the desert's grit and granite,
saw the river, the wide and brimming river,
watering the fields of wheat and barley,
of cucumbers and onions, and bringing fish for food.
Come, he had said, I am no Egyptian—
who fears and hates the tribesmen of the desert—
I am your brother, Joseph.
Come and bring your herds and flocks;
here is land, ample land, for grazing;
here is plenty; come and prosper.

We who had known the desert's angry god,
saw the well-ordered life of Egypt,

its fields and ancient cities;
shelter from the heat by day, the wind at night;
saw the ancient river, wide and brimming—
all of Egypt's plenty;
and, turning to each other who had famished in the desert,
languished in the desert,
said: let us stay in Egypt;
here the gods are many—kind and wise.

But there came a Pharaoh who knew not Joseph
and set us building treasuries and cities,
set us making brick for him and building cities:
we who had been masters of our days and daylight,
free to wander, free to stay.
King and servants, priests and laymen;
soldiers, overseers, and slaves:
this was Egypt's peace and order,
and in this order we were slaves:
Israel like a bird that a creeping weasel has wounded in the head
or a man knocked against a wall;
the cattle have trampled it—but still it flutters.

But there came a shepherd from the desert,
speaking in the ancient tongue
all but our eldest had forgotten;
and we saw an old man—withered hands and haunches;
and he said to us, stuttering as he spoke:
I bring a message from the God of your fathers
and, in place of these burdens,
I bring you—the yoke of His law.
How pleasant it is, distinguished from the beasts,
to feed upon His law
tasting in each syllable
the radiance of our Lord!
If there is bone enough to make the tooth of a key
and ink enough to write two letters of the alphabet—
then fear not the rush of tramping shoes nor the sound of the shouting
and hurry out of this land!*

* The three lines at the very end of the third stanza and those at the end of the last stanza (lines 13–15) are from the Mishnah (Hullin 3:3 and other places, Danby's translation). [Charles Reznikoff's note.]

The Third Book of Moses, called
LEVITICUS

11:1–4 And the LORD spake unto Moses and to Aaron, saying unto them, Speak unto the children of Israel, saying, These are the beasts which ye shall eat among all the beasts that are on the earth. Whatsoever parteth the hoof, and is clovenfooted, and cheweth the cud, among the beasts, that shall ye eat. Nevertheless these shall ye not eat of them that chew the cud, or of them that divide the hoof: as the camel, because he cheweth the cud, but divideth not the hoof; he is unclean unto you.

The Chewing the Cud

Robert Herrick

When well we speak, and nothing do that's good,
We not divide the hoof, but chew the cud:
But when good words, by good works, have their proof,
We then both chew the cud, and cleave the hoof.

11:13–20 And these are they which ye shall have in abomination among the fowls; they shall not be eaten, they are an abomination: the eagle, and the ossifrage, and the ospray, And the vulture, and the kite after his kind; Every raven after his kind; And the owl, and the night hawk, and the cuckow, and the hawk after his kind, And the little owl, and the cormorant, and the great owl, And the swan, and the pelican, and the gier eagle, And the stork, the heron after her kind, and the lapwing, and the bat. All fowls that creep, going upon all four, shall be an abomination unto you.

A Paraphrase on . . . Leviticus Chap. XI. Vers. 13, &c.

Fashioned after the Manner of Master Geoffrey Chaucer in his Assembly of Fowls

Thomas Warton the Elder

Containing the Reasons of the several Prohibitions

Of feathered fouls, that fan the buxom air,
Not all alike were made for food to men;

For, these thou shalt not eat, doth God declare,
Twice ten their number, and their flesh unclean:
First the great eagle, bird of feigned Jove,
Which Thebans worship, and diviners love:

Next ossifrage, and osprey, (both one kind)
Of luxury, and rapine, emblems meet,
That haunt the shores, the choicest prey to find,
And burst the bones, and scoop the marrow sweet:
The vulture, void of delicace, and fear,
Who spareth not the pale dead man to tear:

The tall-built swan, fair type of pride confessed;
The pelican, whose sons are nursed with blood,
Forbid to man! — She stabbeth deep her breast,
Self murderess through fondness to her brood:
They too that range the thirsty wilds among,
The ostriches, unthoughtful of their young:

The raven ominous, (as Gentiles hold)
What time she croaketh hoarsely *A la Morte*;
The hawk, aerial hunter, swift, and bold,
In feats of mischief trained for disport;
The vocal cuckoo, of the falcon race,
Obscene intruder in her neighbor's place:

The owl demure, who loveth not the light,
(Ill semblance she of wisdom to the Greek)
The smallest fowls dread foe, the coward kite,
And the still her'n, arresting fishes meek;
The glutton cormorant, of sullen mood:
Regarding no distinction in her food.

The stork, which dwelleth on the fir tree-top,
And trusteth that no Power shall her dismay,
As kings on their high stations place their hope,
Nor wist that there be higher far than they:
The gay ger-eagle, beautiful to view,
Bearing within a savage heart untrue:

The ibis whom in Egypt Israel found,
Fell bird! that living serpents can digest;
The crested lapwing, wailing shrill around,
Solicitous, with no contentment blessed:
Last the foul bat, of bird, and beast first bred,
Flitting, with little leathern sails dispread.

16:1–24 . . . And Aaron shall lay both his hands upon the head of the live goat, and confess over him all the iniquities of the children of Israel, and all their transgressions in all their sins, putting them upon the head of the goat, and shall send him away by the hand of a fit man into the wilderness: And the goat shall bear upon him all their iniquities unto a land not inhabited: and he shall let go the goat in the wilderness. And Aaron shall come into the tabernacle of the congregation, and shall put off the linen garments, which he put on when he went into the holy place, and shall leave them there: And he shall wash his flesh with water in the holy place, and put on his garments, and come forth, and offer his burnt offering, and the burnt offering of the people, and make an atonement for himself, and for the people.

Day of Atonement

Charles Reznikoff

The great Giver has ended His disposing;
the long day
is over and the gates are closing.
How badly all that has been read
was read by us,
how poorly all that should be said.

All wickedness shall go in smoke.
It must, it must!
The just shall see and be glad.
The sentence is sweet and sustaining;
for we, I suppose, are the just;
and we, the remaining.

If only I could write with four pens between five fingers
and with each pen a different sentence at the same time—
but the rabbis say it is a lost art, a lost art.
I well believe it. And at that of the first twenty sins that we confess,
five are by speech alone;
little wonder that I must ask the Lord to bless
the words of my mouth and the meditations of my heart.

Now, as from the dead, I revisit the earth and delight
in the sky, and hear again
the noise of the city and see
earth's marvelous creatures—men.
Out of nothing I became a being,

and from a being I shall be
nothing—but until then
I rejoice, a mote in Your world,
a spark in Your seeing.

The Fourth Book of Moses, called
NUMBERS

13:17–27 And Moses sent them to spy out the land of Canaan. . . . Now the time was the time of the first ripe grapes. So they went up, and searched the land from the wilderness of Zin unto Rehob, as men come to Hamath. And they ascended by the south, and came unto Hebron; where Ahiman, Sheshai, and Talmai, the children of Anak, were. (Now Hebron was built seven years before Zoan in Egypt.) And they came unto the brook of Eshcol, and cut down from thence a branch with one cluster of grapes, and they bare it between two upon a staff; and they brought of the pomegranates, and of the figs. The place was called the brook Eshcol, because of the cluster of grapes which the children of Israel cut down from thence. And they returned from searching of the land after forty days. And they went and came to Moses, and to Aaron, and to all the congregation of the children of Israel, . . . and shewed them the fruit of the land. And they told him, and said, We came unto the land whither thou sentest us, and surely it floweth with milk and honey; and this is the fruit of it.

The bunch of Grapes

George Herbert

Joy, I did lock thee up: but some bad man
Hath let thee out again:
And now, me thinks, I am where I began
Seven years ago: one vogue and vain,
One air of thoughts usurps my brain.
I did toward Canaan draw; but now I am
Brought back to the Red sea, the sea of shame.

For as the Jews of old by God's command
Traveled, and saw no town:
So now each Christian hath his journeys spanned:
Their story pens and sets us down.
A single deed is small renown.
God's works are wide, and let in future times;
His ancient justice overflows our crimes.

Then have we too our guardian fires and clouds;
Our Scripture-dew drops fast:
We have our sands and serpents, tents and shrouds;
Alas! our murmurings come not last.
But where's the cluster? where's the taste
Of mine inheritance? Lord, if I must borrow,
Let me as well take up their joy, as sorrow.

But can he want the grape, who hath the wine?
I have their fruit and more.
Blessed be God, who prospered Noah's vine,
And made it bring forth grapes good store.
But much more him I must adore,
Who of the law's sour juice sweet wine did make,
Even God himself, being pressed for my sake.

13:28–14:2 . . . Caleb stilled the people before Moses, and said, Let us go up at once, and possess it; for we are well able to overcome it. But the men that went up with him said, . . . The land, through which we have gone to search it, is a land that eateth up the inhabitants thereof; and all the people that we saw in it are men of a great stature. And there we saw the giants, the sons of Anak, which come of the giants: and we were in our own sight as grasshoppers, and so we were in their sight. And all the congregation lifted up their voice, and cried; and the people wept that night. And all the children of Israel murmured against Moses and against Aaron: and the whole congregation said unto them, Would God that we had died in the land of Egypt! or would God we had died in this wilderness!

On Death

Anne Killigrew

Tell me thou safest end of all our woe,
Wretched mortals do avoid thee so:
Thou gentle drier o'th'afflicted's tears,
Thou noble ender of the coward's fears;
Thou sweet repose to lovers' sad despair,
Thou calm t'ambitions rough tempestuous care.
If in regard of bliss thou wert a curse,
And then the joys of Paradise art worse;
Yet after man from his first station fell,
And God from Eden Adam did expel,
Thou wert no more an evil, but relief;
The balm and cure to every human grief:
Through thee (what man had forfeited before)
He now enjoys, and ne'er can lose it more.
No subtle serpents in the grave betray.
Worms on the body there, not soul do prey;
No vice there tempts, no terrors there affright,
No cozening sin affords a false delight:
No vain contentions do that peace annoy,
No fierce alarms break the lasting joy.

Ah since from thee so many blessings flow,
Such real good as life can never know;
Come when thou wilt, in thy affrighting'st dress,
Thy shape shall never make thy welcome less.
Thou mayst to joy, but ne'er to fear give birth,
Thou best, as well as certain'st thing on Earth.
Fly thee? May travellers then fly their rest,
And hungry infants fly the proferred breast.
No, those that faint and tremble at thy name,
Fly from their good on a mistaken fame.
Thus childish fear did Israel of old
From plenty and the Promised Land withhold;
They fancied giants, and refused to go,
When Canaan did with milk and honey flow.

14:3–16 . . . And the LORD said unto Moses, How long will this people provoke me? and how long will it be ere they believe me, for all the signs which I have shewed among them? I will smite them with the pestilence, and disinherit them, and will make of thee a greater nation and mightier than they.

And Moses said unto the LORD, Then the Egyptians shall hear it, (for thou broughtest up this people in thy might from among them;) And they will tell it to the inhabitants of this land: for they have heard that thou LORD art among this people, that thou LORD art seen face to face, and that thy cloud standeth over them, and that thou goest before them, by day time in a pillar of a cloud, and in a pillar of fire by night. Now if thou shalt kill all this people as one man, then the nations which have heard the fame of thee will speak, saying, Because the LORD was not able to bring this people into the land which he sware unto them, therefore he hath slain them in the wilderness. . .

NUMERI XIII

JOHN HALL

Let now thy power be great O Lord,
Like as thy lips did once repeat:
And as we find it in thy word,
Thy suffrance long, thy mercy great.

For as thou dost our sins forgive
And trespasses, when we repent:
So are we sure no man alive
From sin is free and innocent.

And of their father the misdeed
Thou visitest upon the child,
His generation and his seed,
In four degrees therewith defiled.

But now oh Lord be gracious
Unto thy flock and their offence:
And of thy mercy bounteous
Remember not our negligence.

Thy people as thou didst forbear,
From Egypt into wilderness,
We thee beseech in like manner,
That we may taste thy gentleness.

14:28–35 Say unto them, As truly as I live, saith the LORD, . . . your children shall wander in the wilderness forty years, and bear your whoredoms, until your carcases be wasted in the wilderness. After the number of the days in which ye searched the land, even forty days, each day for a year, shall ye bear your iniquities, even forty years, and ye shall know my breach of promise. I the LORD have said, I will surely do it unto all this evil congregation, that are gathered together against me: in this wilderness they shall be consumed, and there they shall die.

Golden Calf

NORMAN MACCAIG

If all the answer's to be the Sinai sort
The incorruptible lava of the word
Made alphabetic in a stormspout, what
Mere human vocables you've ever heard,
Poor golden calf, could overbear, I wonder,
The magniloquence of thunder?

You're for another flame. The Moses in me
Looks with a stone face on our gaudy lives.
His fingers, scorched with godhead, point, and loose
An influence of categorical negatives
That make an image of love, a trope of lover.
Our dancing days are over.

The buckles tarnish at the thought of it.
The winecup shatters. The bragging music chokes
To the funeral silence it was awkward in.
And before the faggot of salvation smokes,
Your knees are loosed, your wreathed neck bows lowly
In presence of the holy.

What's a disgruntled cloud to you or me?
Listen to my multitudes, and beam for them,
Making a plinth of this dark wilderness.
Utter such rigmaroles an apothegm,
Doing its head-stroke, drowns in such wild water
And proves itself no matter.

Or where's the desert cat, or hunching shade
That ambles hugely in the dark outside,
Or hospitable anguish beckoning
To its foul ceremony a sorry bride
Could bear the darts struck from your hide by torches
　　That guard our pleasure's marches?

Forty years. Small wilderness to unravel
Such an unknotted thread of wandering.
The desert is in Moses' skull, the journey
To the white thalamus whose cradling
Enfolds the foetus of the law—gestation
　　Of Moses as a nation.

A chosen people, since they have no choice.
The doors are locked, the flesh-pots on the shelves,
And a long line of lamentation moves
Led by the nose through their own better selves
To buy with blood a land of milk and honey
　　Where's no need of money.

The smoke and thunder die. And here I stand
Smelling of gunpowder and holiness.
The great fire does its belly-dance and in it
You shine unharmed, not knowing what's to confess;
And the desert, seeing the issue grows no clearer,
　　Takes one long slow step nearer.

16:1–33 Now Korah, the son of Izhar, the son of Kohath, the son of Levi, and Dathan and Abiram, the sons of Eliab, and On, the son of Peleth, sons of Reuben, took men: And they rose up before Moses. . . . And Moses said, Hereby ye shall know that the LORD hath sent me to do all these works; for I have not done them of mine own mind. . . . And it came to pass, as he had made an end of speaking all these words, that the ground clave asunder that was under them: And the earth opened her mouth, and swallowed them up, and their houses, and all the men that appertained unto Korah, and all their goods. They, and all that appertained to them, went down alive into the pit, and the earth closed upon them: and they perished from among the congregation.

Lines Written Under the Influence of Delirium

William Cowper

composed while under the care of Dr. Cotton, at St. Albans

Hatred and vengeance,—my eternal portion
Scarce can endure delay of execution,—
Wait with impatient readiness to seize my
Soul in a moment.

Damned below Judas; more abhorred than he was,
Who for a few pence sold his holy Master!
Twice betrayed, Jesus me, the last delinquent,
Deems the profanest.

Man disavows, and Deity disowns me,
Hell might afford my miseries a shelter;
Therefore, Hell keeps her ever-hungry mouths all
Bolted against me.

Hard lot! encompassed with a thousand dangers;
Weary, faint, trembling with a thousand terrors,
I'm called, if vanquished, to receive a sentence
Worse than Abiram's.

Him the vindictive rod of angry Justice
Sent quick and howling to the centre headlong;
I fed with judgment, in a fleshy tomb, am
Buried above ground.

22:1–30 . . . And Balaam rose up in the morning, and saddled his ass, and went with the princes of Moab. And God's anger was kindled because he went: and the angel of the LORD stood in the way for an adversary against him. Now he was riding upon his ass, and his two servants were with him. And the ass saw the angel of the LORD standing in the way, and his sword drawn in his hand: and the ass turned aside out of the way, and went into the field: and Balaam smote the ass, to turn her into the

way. . . . And the LORD opened the mouth of the ass, and she said unto Balaam, What have I done unto thee, that thou hast smitten me these three times? And Balaam said unto the ass, Because thou hast mocked me: I would there were a sword in mine hand, for now would I kill thee. And the ass said unto Balaam, Am not I thine ass, upon which thou hast ridden ever since I was thine unto this day? was I ever wont to do so unto thee? And he said, Nay.

On Balaam's Ass

FRANCIS QUARLES

The ass, that for her slowness, was forbid
To be employed in God's service, did
Perform good service now, in being slow:
The ass received stripes, but would not go:
She balked the way, and Balaam could not guide her:
The ass had far more wisdom than the rider:
The message being bad, the ass was loth
To be the bearer: 'Twas a happy sloth;
'Twas well for Balaam: had his ass but tried
Another step, Balaam had surely died:
Poor ass! And was thy faithful service paid
With oft-repeated strokes? Hadst thou obeyed,
Thy Lord had bought thy travel, with his blood:
Such is man's payment, often bad for good:
The ass begins to question with his master,
Argues the case, pleads why he went no faster:
Nay, shows him mysteries, far beyond his reach;
Sure, God wants prophets, when dull asses preach:
The ass perceives the angel, and falls down;
When Balaam sees him not; or sees, unknown:
Nor is 't a wonder: for God's spirit did pass
From blindfold Balaam, into Balaam's ass.

24:1–5 **And when Balaam saw that it pleased the LORD to bless Israel, he went not, as at other times, to seek for enchantments, but he set his face toward the wilderness. And Balaam lifted up his eyes, and he saw**

Israel abiding in his tents according to their tribes; and the spirit of God came upon him. And he took up his parable, and said, Balaam the son of Beor hath said, and the man whose eyes are open hath said: He hath said, which heard the words of God, which saw the vision of the Almighty, falling into a trance, but having his eyes open:

How goodly are thy tents, O Jacob, and thy tabernacles, O Israel!

from *Davideis, Book I*

Abraham Cowley

So covetous Balaam with a fond intent
Of cursing the blessed Seed, to Moab went.
But as he went his fatal tongue to sell;
His Ass taught him to speak, God to speak well.
How comely are thy Tents, oh Israel!
(Thus he began) what conquests they foretell!
Less fair are orchards in their autumn pride,
Adorned with trees on some fair river's side.
Less fair are valleys their green mantles spread!
Or mountains with tall cedars on their head!
'Twas God himself (thy God who must not fear?)
Brought thee from bondage to be master here.
Slaughter shall wear out these; new weapons get;
And death in triumph on thy darts shall sit.
When Judah's Lion starts up to his prey,
The beasts shall hang their ears, and creep away.
When he lies down, the woods shall silence keep,
And dreadful tygers tremble at his sleep.
Thy cursers, Jacob, shall twice cursed be;
And he shall bless himself that blesses Thee.

28:1–10 And the LORD spake unto Moses, saying, Command the children of Israel, and say unto them, My offering, and my bread for my sacrifices made by fire, for a sweet savour unto me, shall ye observe to offer unto me in their due season. And thou shalt say unto them, This is the offering made by fire which ye shall offer unto the LORD; two lambs of the first year without spot day by day, for a continual burnt offering. The one lamb shalt thou offer in the morning, and the other lamb shalt thou

offer at even; And a tenth part of an ephah of flour for a meat offering, mingled with the fourth part of an hin of beaten oil. It is a continual burnt offering, which was ordained in mount Sinai for a sweet savour, a sacrifice made by fire unto the LORD. . . . And on the sabbath day two lambs of the first year without spot, . . .

MEDITATION TWENTY-FIVE

Second Series

EDWARD TAYLOR

One Lamb shalt thou offer in the Morning, and the other at Even.
And on the Sabbath day two Lambs etc.

Guilty, my Lord, what can I more declare?
    Thou knowst the case, and cases of my soul.
A box of tinder: sparks that falling o'er
    Set all on fire, and work me all in shoals.
    A pouch of passion is my pericard.
    Sparks fly when e'er my flint and steel strike hard.

I am a dish of dumps: yea ponderous dross,
    Black blood all clotted, burdening my heart,
That anger's anvil, and my bark bears moss.
    My spirits soaked are drunk with blackish art.
    If any virtue stir, it is but feeble.
    Th' Earth magnet is, my heart's the trembling needle.

My Manna breedeth worms: thoughts flyblown are.
    My heart's the temple of the God of Flies.
My tongue's an altar of forbidden ware
    Fancy a foolish fire enflamed by toys
    Perfumed with reeking offerings of sins
    Whose steaming reeks delight hobgoblins.

My Lord, is there no help for this with thee?
    Must I abuse, and be abused thus?

There morn, and even sacrifices be:
    To cleanse the sins of day, and night from us.
    Christ is the lamb: my prayer each morn and night
    As incense offer I up in thy sight.

My morn, and evening sacrifice I bring
    With incense sweet upon mine altar Christ,
With oil and wine two quarters of an hin
    With flower for a meat offering all well spiced,
    On bended knees, with hands that tempt the skies.
    This is each day's atoning sacrifice.

And thou the Sabbath settledst at the first
    And wilt continue it till last. Wherefore,
Who strike down Gospel Sabbaths are accursed.
    Two lambs, a meat, and drink offering God more
    Conferred on it than any other day
    As types the Gospel Sabbaths to display.

Here is atonement made: and spiritual wine
    Poured out to God: and sanctified bread
From Heaven's given us: What! shall we decline
    With God communion, thus to be fed?
    This Heavenly fare will make true grace to thrive.
    Such as deny this thing are not alive.

I'll tend thy Sabbaths: at thine altar feed.
    And never make thy type a nullity.
The ceremonies cease, but yet the creed
    Contained therein, continues gospelly,
    That make my feeble spirits will grow frim.
    Hence I in Sabbath Service love to swim.

My vespers and my matins I'll attend:
    My Sabbath service carry on I will.
Atoning efficacy God doth send
    To sinners in this path, and grace here stills.
    Still this on me until I glory gain.
    And then I'll sing thy praise in better strain.

32:39–42 And the children of Machir the son of Manasseh went to Gilead, and took it, and dispossessed the Amorite which was in it. And Moses gave Gilead unto Machir the son of Manasseh; and he dwelt therein. And Jair the son of Manasseh went and took the small towns thereof, and called them Havothjair. And Nobah went and took Kenath, and the villages thereof, and called it Nobah, after his own name.

Place Names

THOMAS MERTON

Jair the son of Manasseh went and seized the encampments
And called them the Encampments of Jair
Nobah went and seized Kenath
With its outlying villages
And called it Nobah
After himself
(*Numbers 32: 41-42*)

1871-1883

Baron Nikolai Miklouho-Maclay
(Tibud Maclay)
Comes and goes
Exploring
Recording the language
As a reward for hospitality
Leaves the coast with
To further honor
The place where he landed
He called it "Constantine Harbour"
(Grand Duke Constantine
President of the Imperial Russian Geographical Society
Had paid for the trip.)

1878

Australian gold-prospectors
Put in at Bongu
In the good ship Dove
But leave at once
Forgetting to name the place
"Dove Harbor"

But there is a "Dove Point"
A hundred miles up the coast.

1884

Herr Finsch
Representing the Neu Guinea Kompagnie
Hoists the German flag
Over "Bismarck (naturally)
Archipelago" "Kaiser
(Of course) Wilhelmsland"
And last but not least
"Finschhafen."

The Fifth Book of Moses, called DEUTERONOMY

16:19 Thou shalt not wrest judgment; thou shalt not respect persons, neither take a gift: for a gift doth blind the eyes of the wise, and pervert the words of the righteous.

To his Conscience

Robert Herrick

Can I not sin, but thou wilt be
My private Protonotary?
Can I not woo thee to pass by
A short and sweet iniquity?
I'll cast a mist and cloud, upon
My delicate transgression,
So utter dark, as that no eye
Shall see the hugged impiety:
Gifts blind the wise, and bribes do please,

And wind all other witnesses:
And wilt not thou, with gold, be tied
To lay thy pen and ink aside?
That in the murk and tongueless night,
Wanton I may, and thou not write?
It will not be: And, therefore, now,
For times to come, I'll make this vow,
From aberrations to live free;
So I'll not fear the Judge, or thee.

27:2–3 And it shall be on the day when ye shall pass over Jordan unto the land which the LORD thy God giveth thee, that thou shalt set thee up great stones, and plaister them with plaister: And thou shalt write upon them all the words of this law, when thou art passed over, that thou mayest go in unto the land which the LORD thy God giveth thee, a land that floweth with milk and honey; as the LORD God of thy fathers hath promised thee.

The Altar

George Herbert

A broken ALTAR, Lord, thy servant rears,
Made of a heart, and cemented with tears:
Whose parts are as thy hand did frame;
No workmans tool hath touched the same.
A HEART alone
Is such a stone,
As nothing but
Thy power doth cut.
Wherefore each part
Of my hard heart
Meets in this frame,
To praise thy name.
That if I chance to hold my peace,
These stones to praise thee may not cease.
O let thy blessed SACRIFICE be mine,
And sanctify this ALTAR to be thine.

30:11–14 For this commandment which I command thee this day, it is not hidden from thee, neither is it far off. It is not in heaven, that thou shouldest say, Who shall go up for us to heaven, and bring it unto us, that we may hear it, and do it? Neither is it beyond the sea, that thou shouldest say, Who shall go over the sea for us, and bring it unto us, that we may hear it, and do it? But the word is very nigh unto thee, in thy mouth, and in thy heart, that thou mayest do it.

from A Song for Occupations

Walt Whitman

Will you seek afar off? you surely come back at last,
In things best known to you finding the best, or as good as the best,
In folks nearest to you finding the sweetest, strongest, lovingest,
Happiness, knowledge, not in another place but this place, not for another hour but this hour,
Man in the first you see or touch, always in friend, brother, nighest neighbor—woman in mother, sister, wife,
The popular tastes and employments taking precedence in poems or anywhere,
You workwomen and workmen of these States having your own divine and strong life,
And all else giving place to men and women like you.

When the psalm sings instead of the singer,
When the script preaches instead of the preacher,
When the pulpit descends and goes instead of the carver that carved the supporting desk,
When I can touch the body of books by night or by day, and when they touch my body back again,
When a university course convinces like a slumbering woman and child convince,
When the minted gold in the vault smiles like the night-watchman's daughter,
When warrantee deeds loaf in chairs opposite and are my friendly companions,
I intend to reach them my hand, and make as much of them as I do of men and women like you.

30:15–20 See, I have set before thee this day life and good, and death and evil; In that I command thee this day to love the LORD thy God, to walk in his ways, and to keep his commandments and his statutes and his judgments, that thou mayest live and multiply: and the LORD thy God shall bless thee in the land whither thou goest to possess it. . . .

I call heaven and earth to record this day against you, that I have set before you life and death, blessing and cursing: therefore choose life, that both thou and thy seed may live: That thou mayest love the LORD thy God, and that thou mayest obey his voice, and that thou mayest cleave unto him: for he is thy life, and the length of thy days: that thou mayest dwell in the land which the LORD sware unto thy fathers, to Abraham, to Isaac, and to Jacob, to give them.

Deuteronomy 30. 19

Francis Quarles

The world's a floor, whose swelling heaps retain
The mingled wages of the ploughman's toil;
The world's a heap, whose yet unwinnowed grain
Is lodged with chaff and buried in her soil;
All things are mixed, the useful with the vain;
The good with bad, the noble with the vile;
The world's an ark, wherein things pure and gross
Present their lossfull gain, and gainfull loss;
Where every dram of gold contains a pound of dross.

This furnished ark presents the greedy view
With all that earth can give, or Heaven can add;
Here, lasting joys; here, pleasures hourly new,
And hourly fading, may be wished and had:
All points of honor, counterfeit and true,
Salute thy soul, and wealth both good and bad:
Here mayst thou open wide the two-leaved door
Of all thy wishes, to receive that store
Which being empty most, does overflow the more.

Come then, my soul, approach this royal Bourse,
And see what wares our great Exchange retains;

Come, come; here's that shall make a firm divorce
    Betwixt thy wants and thee, if want complains;
No need to sit in council with thy purse,
    Here's nothing good shall cost more price then pains:
        But O my soul, take heed; if thou rely
        Upon thy faithless Optics, thou wilt buy
Too blind a bargain: know, fools only trade by th' eye.

The worldly wisdom of the foolish man
    Is like a sieve, that does alone retain
The grosser substance of the worthless bran:
    But thou, my soul, let thy brave thoughts disdain
So coarse a purchase; O be thou a fan
    To purge the chaff, and keep the winnowed grain:
        Make clean thy thoughts, and dress thy mixed desires,
        Thou art Heaven's tasker; and thy God requires
The purest of thy floor, as well as of thy fires.

Let grace conduct thee to the paths of peace,
    And wisdom bless thy soul's unblemished ways;
No matter then, how short or long's the lease,
    Whose date determines thy self-numbered days:
No need to care for wealth's or fame's increase,
    Nor Mars his palm, nor high Apollo's bays.
        Lord, if thy gracious bounty please to fill
        The floor of my desires, and teach me skill
To dress and choose the corn, take those the chaff that will.

31:24–32:2 And it came to pass, when Moses had made an end of writing the words of this law in a book, until they were finished, That Moses commanded the Levites, which bare the ark of the covenant of the LORD, saying, Take this book of the law, and put it in the side of the ark of the covenant of the LORD your God, that it may be there for a witness against thee. And Moses spake in the ears of all the congregation of Israel the words of this song, until they were ended.

Give ear, O ye heavens, and I will speak; and hear, O earth, the words of my mouth.

My doctrine shall drop as the rain, my speech shall distil as the dew, as the small rain upon the tender herb, and as the showers upon the grass: . . .

Give Ear, O Heavens, to That Which I Declare

Henry Ainsworth

Give ear, O heavens, to that which I declare;
And hear, O earth, what my mouth's sayings are.

Drop down as doth the rain shall my doctrine;
Distill as dew so shall my speech divine,

As on the tender herb the small rain pours,
And as upon the grass the greater showers,

For I Jehovah's name proclaim abroad;
O give ye greatness unto him our God.

Do ye Jehovah in this wise regard,
O foolish folk, and wanting wise regard?

Thy Father, that hath brought thee, is not he?
Hath he not made thee and established thee?

Remember thou the days that were of old;
Mind ye the years of ages manifold;

Ask thou thy Father, and thee show will he;
Thine elders ask, and they will tell it thee.

32:44–52 And Moses came and spake all the words of this song in the ears of the people, he, and Hoshea the son of Nun. . . . And the LORD spake unto Moses that selfsame day, saying, Get thee up into this mountain Abarim, unto mount Nebo, which is in the land of Moab, that is over against Jericho; and behold the land of Canaan, which I give unto the children of Israel for a possession: And die in the mount whither thou goest up, and be gathered unto thy people; as Aaron thy brother died in mount Hor, and was gathered unto his people: Because ye trespassed against me among the children of Israel at the waters of MeribahKadesh, in the wilderness of Zin; because ye sanctified me not in the midst of the children of Israel. Yet thou shalt see the land before thee; but thou shalt not go thither unto the land which I give the children of Israel.

It always felt to me – a wrong

EMILY DICKINSON

It always felt to me – a wrong
To that Old Moses – done –
To let him see – the Canaan –
Without the entering –

And tho' in soberer moments –
No Moses can there be
I'm satisfied – the Romance
In point of injury –

Surpasses sharper stated –
Of Stephen – or of Paul –
For these – were only put to death –
While God's adroiter will

On Moses – seemed to fasten
With tantalizing Play
As Boy – should deal with lesser Boy –
To prove ability.

The fault – was doubtless Israel's –
Myself – had banned the Tribes –
And ushered Grand Old Moses
In Pentateuchal Robes

Upon the Broad Possession
'Twas little – But titled Him – to see –
Old Man on Nebo! Late as this –
My justice bleeds – for Thee!

34:1–4 And Moses went up from the plains of Moab unto the mountain of Nebo, to the top of Pisgah, that is over against Jericho. And the LORD shewed him all the land of Gilead, unto Dan, And all Naphtali, and the land of Ephraim, and Manasseh, and all the land of Judah, unto the utmost sea, And the south, and the plain of the valley of Jericho, the city of palm trees, unto Zoar. And the LORD said unto him, This is the land

which I sware unto Abraham, unto Isaac, and unto Jacob, saying, I will give it unto thy seed: I have caused thee to see it with thine eyes, but thou shalt not go over thither.

Pisgah-Sights. I & II

Robert Browning

Over the ball of it,
Peering and prying,
How I see all of it,
Life there, outlying!
Roughness and smoothness,
Shine and defilement,
Grace and uncouthness:
One reconcilement.

Orbed as appointed,
Sister with brother
Joins, ne'er disjointed
One from the other.
All's lend-and-borrow;
Good, see, wants evil,
Joy demands sorrow,
Angel weds devil!

'Which things must – *why* be?'
Vain our endeavour!
So shall things aye be
As they were ever.
'Such things should *so* be!'
Sage our desistence!
Rough-smooth let globe be,
Mixed – man's existence.

Man – wise and foolish,
Lover and scorner,
Docile and mulish –
Keep each his corner!
Honey yet gall of it!
There's the life lying,
And I see all of it,
Only, I'm dying!

Could I but live again,
    Twice my life over,
Would I once strive again?
    Would I not cover
Quietly all of it –
    Greed and ambition–
So, from the pall of it,
    Pass to fruition?

'Soft!' I'd say, 'Soul mine!
    Three-score and ten years,
Let the blind mole mine
    Digging out deniers!
Let the dazed hawk soar,
    Claim the sun's rights too!
Turf 'tis thy walk's o'er,
    Foliage thy flight's to.'

Only a learner,
    Quick one or slow one,
Just a discerner,
    I would teach no one.
I am earth's native:
    No rearranging it!
I be creative,
    Chopping and changing it?

March, men, my fellows!
    Those who, above me,
(Distance so mellows)
    Fancy you love me:
Those who, below me,
    (Distance makes great so)
Free to forego me,
    Fancy you hate so!

Praising, reviling,
    Worst head and best head,
Past me defiling,
    Never arrested,
Wanters, abounders,
    March, in gay mixture,

Men, my surrounders!
I am the fixture.

So shall I fear thee,
Mightiness yonder!
Mock-sun – more near thee,
What is to wonder?
So shall I love thee,
Down in the dark, – lest
Glowworm I prove thee,
Star that now sparklest!

When Israel Out of Egypt Came

A. E. Housman

When Israel out of Egypt came
Safe in the sea they trod;
By day in cloud, by night in flame,
Went on before them God.

He brought them with a stretched out hand
Dry-footed through the foam,
Past sword and famine, rock and sand,
Lust and rebellion, home.

I never over Horeb heard
The blast of advent blow;
No fire-faced prophet brought me word
Which way behoved me go.

Ascended is the cloudy flame,
The mount of thunder dumb;
The tokens that to Israel came,
To me they have not come.

I see the country far away
Where I shall never stand;
The heart goes where no footstep may
Into the promised land.

The realm I look upon and die
Another man will own;
He shall attain the heaven that I
Perish and have not known.

But I will go where they are hid
That never were begot,
To my inheritance amid
The nation that is not,

When mixed with me the sandstorms drift
And nerve and thew and brain
Are ashes for the air to lift
And lightly shower again.

34:5–8 So Moses the servant of the LORD died there in the land of Moab, according to the word of the LORD. And he buried him in a valley in the land of Moab, over against Bethpeor: but no man knoweth of his sepulchre unto this day. And Moses was an hundred and twenty years old when he died: his eye was not dim, nor his natural force abated. And the children of Israel wept for Moses in the plains of Moab thirty days: so the days of weeping and mourning for Moses were ended.

Weep, Children of Israel

Thomas Moore

Weep, weep for him, the Man of God—
In yonder vale he sunk to rest;
But none of earth can point the sod
That flowers above his sacred breast.
Weep, children of Israel, weep!

His doctrine fell like Heaven's rain,
His words refreshed like Heaven's dew—
Oh, ne'er shall Israel see again
A Chief, to God and her so true.
Weep, children of Israel, weep!

Remember ye his parting gaze,
His farewell song by Jordan's tide,
When, full of glory and of days,
He saw the promised land—and died.
Weep, children of Israel, weep!

Yet died he not as men who sink,
Before our eyes, to soulless clay
But, changed to spirit, like a wink
Of summer lightning, passed away.
Weep, children of Israel, weep!

34:10 And there arose not a prophet since in Israel like unto Moses, whom the LORD knew face to face,

The Death of Moses

George Eliot

Moses, who spake with God as with his friend,
And ruled his people with the twofold power
Of wisdom that can dare and still be meek,
Was writing his last word, the sacred name
Unutterable of that Eternal Will
Which was and is and evermore shall be.
Yet was his task not finished, for the flock
Needed its shepherd and the life-taught sage
Leaves no successor; but to chosen men,
The rescuers and guides of Israel,
A death was given called the Death of Grace,
Which freed them from the burden of the flesh
But left them rulers of the multitude
And loved companions of the lonely. This
Was God's last gift to Moses, this the hour
When soul must part from self and be but soul.

God spake to Gabriel, the messenger
Of mildest death that draws the parting life
Gently, as when a little rosy child
Lifts up its lips from off the bowl of milk
And so draws forth a curl that dipped its gold
In the soft white—thus Gabriel draws the soul.
"Go bring the soul of Moses unto me!"
And the awe-stricken angel answered, "Lord,
How shall I dare to take his life who lives
Sole of his kind, not to be likened once
In all the generations of the earth?"

Then God called Michaël, him of pensive brow,
Snow-vest and flaming sword, who knows and acts:
"Go bring the spirit of Moses unto me!"
But Michaël with such grief as angels feel,
Loving the mortals whom they succor, pled:
"Almighty, spare me; it was I who taught
Thy servant Moses; he is part of me
As I of thy deep secrets, knowing them."

Then God called Zamaël, the terrible,
The angel of fierce death, of agony
That comes in battle and in pestilence
Remorseless, sudden or with lingering throes
And Zamaël, his raiment and broad wings
Blood-tinctured, the dark lustre of his eyes
Shrouding the red, fell like the gathering night
Before the prophet. But that radiance
Won from the heavenly presence in the mount
Gleamed on the prophet's brow and dazzling pierced
Its conscious opposite: the angel turned
His murky gaze aloof and inly said:
"An angel this, deathless to angel's stroke."

But Moses felt the subtly nearing dark:
"Who art thou? and what wilt thou?" Zamaël then:
"I am God's reaper; through the fields of life
I gather ripened and unripened souls
Both willing and unwilling. And I come
Now to reap thee." But Moses cried,
Firm as a seer who waits the trusted sign:
"Reap thou the fruitless plant and common herb—
Not him who from the womb was sanctified
To teach the law of purity and love."
And Zamaël baffled from his errand fled.

But Moses, pausing, in the air serene
Heard now that mystic whisper, far yet near,
The all-penetrating Voice, that said to him,
"Moses, the hour is come and thou must die."
"Lord, I obey; but thou rememberest
How thou, Ineffable, didst take me once
Within thy orb of light untouched by death."
Then the voice answered, "Be no more afraid:
With me shall be thy death and burial."
So Moses waited, ready now to die.

And the Lord came, invisible as a thought,
Three angels gleaming on his secret track,
Prince Michaël, Zamaël, Gabriel, charged to guard
The soul-forsaken body as it fell
And bear it to the hidden sepulchre
Denied forever to the search of man.
And the Voice said to Moses: "Close thine eyes."
He closed them. "Lay thine hand upon thine heart,
And draw thy feet together." He obeyed.
And the Lord said, " O spirit! child of mine!
A hundred years and twenty thou hast dwelt
Within this tabernacle wrought of clay.
This is the end: come forth and flee to heaven."

But the grieved soul with plaintive pleading cried,
"I love this body with a clinging love:
The courage fails me, Lord, to part from it."

"O child, come forth! for thou shalt dwell with me
About the immortal throne where seraphs joy
In growing vision and in growing love."

Yet hesitating, fluttering, like the bird
With young wing weak and dubious, the soul
Stayed. But behold! upon the death-dewed lips
A kiss descended, pure, unspeakable—
The bodiless Love without embracing Love
That lingered in the body, drew it forth
With heavenly strength and carried it to heaven.

But now beneath the sky the watchers all,
Angels that keep the homes of Israel
Or on high purpose wander o'er the world
Leading the Gentiles, felt a dark eclipse:
The greatest ruler among men was gone.
And from the westward sea was heard a wail,
A dirge as from the isles of Javanim,
Crying, "Who now is left upon the earth
Like him to teach the right and smite the wrong?"
And from the East, far o'er the Syrian waste,
Came slowlier, sadlier, the answering dirge:
"No prophet like him lives or shall arise
In Israel or the world forevermore."

But Israel waited, looking toward the mount,
Till with the deepening eve the elders came
Saying, "His burial is hid with God.
We stood far off and saw the angels lift
His corpse aloft until they seemed a star
That burnt itself away within the sky."

The people answered with mute orphaned gaze
Looking for what had vanished evermore.
Then through the gloom without them and within
The spirit's shaping light, mysterious speech,
Invisible Will wrought clear in sculptured sound,
The thought-begotten daughter of the voice,
Thrilled on their listening sense: "He has no tomb.
He dwells not with you dead, but lives as Law."

The Book of JOSHUA

3:9–11 And Joshua said unto the children of Israel, Come hither, and hear the words of the LORD your God. And Joshua said, Hereby ye shall know that the living God is among you, and that he will without fail drive out from before you the Canaanites, and the Hittites, and the Hivites, and the Perizzites, and the Girgashites, and the Amorites, and the Jebusites. Behold, the ark of the covenant of the Lord of all the earth passeth over before you into Jordan.

The Story of Joshua

Alicia Ostriker

The New Englanders are a people of God settled
in those which were once the devil's territories.
—Cotton Mather, The Wonders of the Invisible World, *1692*

We reach the promised land
Forty years later
The original ones who were slaves

Have died
The young are seasoned soldiers
There is wealth enough for everyone and God
Here at our side, the people
Are mad with excitement.
Here is what to do, to take
This land away from the inhabitants:
Burn their villages and cities
Kill their men
Kill their women
Consume the people utterly.
God says: is that clear?
I give you the land, but
You must murder for it.
You will be a nation
Like other nations,
Your hands are going to be stained like theirs
Your innocence annihilated.
Keep listening, Joshua.
Only to you among the nations
Do I also give knowledge
The secret
Knowledge that you are doing evil
Only to you the commandment:
Love ye therefore the stranger, for you were
Strangers in the land of Egypt, a pillar
Of fire to light your passage
Through the blank desert of history forever.
This is the agreement.
Is it entirely
Clear, Joshua,
Said the Lord.
I said it was. He then commanded me
To destroy Jericho.

6:2–25 . . . So the people shouted when the priests blew with the trumpets: and it came to pass, when the people heard the sound of the trumpet, and the people shouted with a great shout, that the wall fell down flat, so that the people went up into the city, every man straight before him, and they took the city. And they utterly destroyed all that was in the city, both man and woman, young and old, and ox, and sheep, and ass, with the edge of the sword. . . .

Women of Jericho

Phyllis McGinley

Though seven times, or seventy times seven,
Your armies circle our beleaguered town,
Not with their clamor may our gates be riven;
O, not by trumpets shall the walls go down!
Send out your troops to trample the fresh grasses
With horns and banners! They shall find defeat.
These walls can bear the insolence of brasses
Sounded at noonday in the dust and heat.

It is the whisper, only, that we dread:
The hushed and delicate murmur like low weeping
Which shall assail us, when, as do the dead,
The warders sleep and all the town lies sleeping.
That holy word is whispered which can fell
These armored walls, and raze the citadel.

7:21 When I saw among the spoils a goodly Babylonish garment, and two hundred shekels of silver, and a wedge of gold of fifty shekels weight, then I coveted them, and took them; and, behold, they are hid in the earth in the midst of my tent, and the silver under it.

The H. Communion

George Herbert

Not in rich furniture, or fine array
Nor in a wedge of gold,
Thou, who from me wast sold,
To me dost now thy self convey;
For so thou shouldst without me still have been,
Leaving within me sin:

But by the way of nourishment and strength
Thou creepst into my breast;
Making thy way my rest,
And thy small quantities my length;

Which spread their forces into every part,
        Meeting sins force and art.

Yet can these not get over to my soul,
        Leaping the wall that parts
        Our souls and fleshly hearts;
    But as th' outworks, they may control
My rebel-flesh, and carrying thy name,
        Affright both sin and shame.

Only thy grace, with which these elements comes,
        Knoweth the ready way,
        And hath the privy key,
    Op'ning the souls most subtle rooms;
While those to spirits refined, at door attend
        Dispatches from their friend.

Give me my captive soul, or take
    My body also thither.
Another lift like this will make
    Them both to be together.

Before that sin turned flesh to stone,
    And all our lump to leaven;
A fervent sigh might well have blown
    Our innocent earth to heaven.

For sure when Adam did not know
    To sin, or sin to smother;
He might to heaven from Paradise go,
    As from one room t'another.

Thou hast restored us to this ease
    By this thy heavenly blood;
Which I can go in, when I please,
    And leave th' earth to their food.

10:1–13 . . . Then spake Joshua to the LORD in the day when the LORD delivered up the Amorites before the children of Israel, and he said in the sight of Israel, Sun, stand thou still upon Gibeon; and thou, Moon, in the valley of Ajalon. And the sun stood still, and the moon stayed, until the people had avenged themselves upon their enemies. Is

not this written in the book of Jasher? So the sun stood still in the midst of heaven, and hasted not to go down about a whole day.

JOSHUA

X. J. KENNEDY

Earth stopped. The Holy City hit a mountain
As a tray of dishes meets a swinging door.
Oceans lunged to converge, one with another.
He who had called that halt stood bemused there.

Who would have thought a simple invocation . . . ?
As brazen leaves, troops fell. His walking stick
Tapped as he limped across a foiled battalion.
Sun and moon hung stone still, their axles stuck.

No cricket sprang from upright walls of grass.
Clouds swung in bunches, wingless. Who could look
Long on so high a carnage: all creation
Crushed like a sprig of heather in a book?

Futile to wail, wear sackcloth, tear his tongue out—
How could he feel commensurate remorse?
At last the sun, God resting noncommittal,
Rose in confusion and resumed its course.

24:1–13 . . . And I have given you a land for which ye did not labour, and cities which ye built not, and ye dwell in them; of the vineyards and oliveyards which ye planted not do ye eat.

JOSHUA AT SCHECHEM

CHARLES REZNIKOFF

You Hebrews are too snug in Ur,
said God; wander about waste places,
north and south leave your dead;
let kings fight against you,
and the heavens rain fire and brimstone

on you. And it was so.
And God looked again and saw
the Hebrews with their sons and daughters
rich in flocks and herds,
with jewels of silver
and jewels of gold.
And God said, Be slaves
to Pharaoh. And it was so.
And God looked again and saw
the Hebrews at the fleshpots,
with fish to eat,
cucumbers and melons.
And God said, Be gone
into the wilderness by the Red Sea
and the wilderness of Shur and the wilderness
of Shin; let Amalek come upon you,
and fiery serpents bite you. And it was so.
And God looked again and saw in a land of brooks and springs and fountains,
wheat and barley,
the Hebrews, in a land on which they did not labor,
in cities which they did not build,
eating of vineyards and olive trees which they did not plant.
And God scattered them—
through the cities of the Medes, beside the waters of Babylon;
they fled before Him into Egypt and went down to the sea in ships;
the whales swallowed them,
the birds brought word of them to the king;
the young men met them with weapons of war,
the old men with proverbs—
and God looked and saw the Hebrews
citizens of the great cities,
talking Hebrew in every language under the sun.

24:19–27 And Joshua said unto the people, Ye cannot serve the LORD: for he is an holy God; he is a jealous God; he will not forgive your transgressions nor your sins. If ye forsake the LORD, and serve strange gods, then he will turn and do you hurt, and consume you, after that he hath done you good. . . . And Joshua wrote these words in the book of the law of God, and took a great stone, and set it up there under an oak, that was by the sanctuary of the LORD. And Joshua said unto all the people, Behold, this stone shall be a witness unto us; for it hath heard all the

words of the LORD which he spake unto us: it shall be therefore a witness unto you, lest ye deny your God.

The Stone

Henry Vaughan

I have it now:
But where to act, that none shall know,
Where I shall have no cause to fear
An eye or ear,
What man will show?
If nights, and shades, and secret rooms,
Silent as tombs,
Will nor conceal nor assent to
My dark designs, what shall I do?
Man I can bribe, and woman will
Consent to any gainful ill,
But these dumb creatures are so true,
No gold nor gifts can them subdue.
'Hedges have ears,' said the old sooth,
'And every bush is something's booth;'
This cautious fools mistake, and fear
Nothing but man, when ambushed there.

But I (Alas!)
Was shown one day in a strange glass
That busy commerce kept between
God and his creatures, though unseen.

They hear, see, speak,
And into loud discoveries break,
As loud as blood. Not that God needs
Intelligence, whose spirit feeds
All things with life, before whose eyes,
Hell and all hearts stark naked lies.
But *he that judgeth as he hears,
He that accuseth none, so steers
His righteous course, that though he knows
All that man doth, conceals or shows,

* John chap. 5. ver. 30. 45. [Vaughan's note.]

Yet will not he by his own light
(Though both all-seeing and all right,)
Condemn men; but will try them by
A process, which even man's own eye
Must needs acknowledge to be just.

Hence sand and dust
Are shaked for witnesses, and stones
Which some think dead, shall all at once
With one attesting voice detect
Those secret sins we least suspect.
For know, wild men, that when you err
Each thing turns scribe and register,
And in obedience to his Lord,
Doth your most private sins record.

The Law delivered to the Jews,
Who promised much, but did refuse
Performance, will for that same deed
Against them by a stone proceed;
Whose substance, though 'tis hard enough,
Will prove their hearts more stiff and tough.
But now, since God on himself took
What all mankind could never brook,
If any (for he all invites)
His easy yoke rejects or slights,
The *Gospel* then (for 'tis his word
And not himself *shall judge the world)
Will by loose dust that man arraign,
As one than dust more vile and vain.

* St. John, chap. 12. ver. 47, 48. [Vaughan's note.]

The Book of JUDGES

11:30–35 And Jephthah vowed a vow unto the LORD, and said, If thou shalt without fail deliver the children of Ammon into mine hands, Then it shall be, that whatsoever cometh forth of the doors of my house to meet me, when I return in peace from the children of Ammon, shall surely be the LORD'S, and I will offer it up for a burnt offering. So Jephthah passed over unto the children of Ammon to fight against them; and the LORD delivered them into his hands. . . . Thus the children of Ammon were subdued before the children of Israel. And Jephthah came to Mizpeh unto his house, and, behold, his daughter came out to meet him with timbrels and with dances: and she was his only child; beside her he had neither son nor daughter. And it came to pass, when he saw her, that he rent his clothes, and said, Alas, my daughter! thou hast brought me very low, and thou art one of them that trouble me: for I have opened my mouth unto the LORD, and I cannot go back.

JEPHTHA'S DAUGHTER

GEORGE NOEL GORDON, LORD BYRON

Since our country, our God—Oh, my sire!
Demand that thy daughter expire;
Since thy triumph was bought by thy vow—
Strike the bosom that's bared for thee now!

And the voice of my mourning is o'er,
And the mountains behold me no more:
If the hand that I love lay me low,
There cannot be pain in the blow!

And of this, oh, my father! be sure—
That the blood of thy child is as pure
As the blessing I beg ere it flow,
And the last thought that soothes me below.

Though the virgins of Salem lament,
Be the judge and the hero unbent!
I have won the great battle for thee,
And my father and country are free!

When this blood of thy giving hath gushed,
When the voice that thou lovest is hushed,
Let my memory still be thy pride,
And forget not I smiled as I died!

11:36–40 And she said unto him, My father, if thou hast opened thy mouth unto the LORD, do to me according to that which hath proceeded out of thy mouth; forasmuch as the LORD hath taken vengeance for thee of thine enemies, even of the children of Ammon. And she said unto her father, Let this thing be done for me: let me alone two months, that I may go up and down upon the mountains, and bewail my virginity, I and my fellows. And he said, Go. And he sent her away for two months: and she went with her companions, and bewailed her virginity upon the mountains. And it came to pass at the end of two months, that she returned unto her father, who did with her according to his vow which he had vowed: and she knew no man. And it was a custom in Israel, That the daughters of Israel went yearly to lament the daughter of Jephthah the Gileadite four days in a year.

The Dirge of Jephthah's Daughter

Sung by the Virgins

Robert Herrick

O thou, the wonder of all days!
O paragon, and pearl of praise!
O virgin-martyr, ever blessed
Above the rest
Of all the maiden-train! We come,
And bring fresh strewings to thy tomb.

Thus, thus, and thus we compass round
Thy harmless and unhaunted ground;

And as we sing thy dirge, we will
    The daffodill,
And other flowers, lay upon
(The altar of our love) thy stone.

Thou wonder of all maids, liest here,
Of daughters all, the dearest dear;
The eye of virgins; nay, the Queen
    Of this smooth green,
And all sweet meads; from whence we get
The primrose, and the violet.

Too soon, too dear did Jephthah buy,
By thy sad loss, our liberty:
His was the bond and covenant, yet
    Thou paidst the debt,
Lamented maid! he won the day,
But for the conquest thou didst pay.

Thy father brought with him along
The olive branch, and victors song:
He slew the Ammonites, we know,
    But to thy woe;
And in the purchase of our peace,
The cure was worse than the disease.

For which obedient zeal of thine,
We offer here, before thy shrine,
Our sighs for storax, tears for wine;
    And to make fine,
And fresh thy hearse-cloth, we will, here,
Four times bestrew thee every year.

Receive, for this thy praise, our tears:
Receive this offering of our hairs:
Receive these crystal vials filled
    With tears, distilled
From teeming eyes; to these we bring,
Each maid, her silver filleting,

To gild thy tomb; besides, these cauls,
These laces, ribbons, and these falls,
These veils, wherewith we used to hide
    The bashful bride,
When we conduct her to her groom:
All, all we lay upon thy tomb.

No more, no more, since thou art dead,
Shall we e'er bring coy brides to bed;
No more at yearly festivals
We cowslip balls,
Or chains of columbines shall make,
For this, or that occasions sake.

No, no; our maiden-pleasures be
Wrapped in the winding-sheet, with thee:
'Tis we are dead, though not i'th' grave:
Or, if we have
One seed of life left, 'tis to keep
A Lent for thee, to fast and weep.

Sleep in thy peace, thy bed of spice;
And make this place all Paradise:
May sweets grow here! and smoke from hence,
Fat frankincense:
Let balm, and cassia send their scent
From out thy maiden-monument.

May no wolf howl, or screech-owl stir
A wing about thy sepulcher!
No boisterous winds, or storms, come hither,
To starve, or wither
Thy soft sweet earth! but (like a spring)
Love keep it ever flourishing.

May all shy maids, at wonted hours,
Come forth, to strew thy tomb with flowers:
May virgins, when they come to mourn,
Male-incense burn
Upon thine altar! then return,
And leave thee sleeping in thy urn.

13:2–16:9 And there was a certain man of Zorah, of the family of the Danites, whose name was Manoah; and his wife was barren, and bare not. And the angel of the LORD appeared unto the woman, and said unto her, Behold now, thou art barren, and bearest not: but thou shalt conceive, and bear a son. Now therefore beware, I pray thee, and drink not wine nor strong drink, and eat not any unclean thing: For, lo, thou shalt conceive, and bear a son; and no razor shall come on his head: for the child shall be a Nazarite unto God from the womb: and he shall begin to

deliver Israel out of the hand of the Philistines. . . . And the woman bare a son, and called his name Samson. . . .

And it came to pass afterward, that he loved a woman in the valley of Sorek, whose name was Delilah. And the lords of the Philistines came up unto her, and said unto her, Entice him, and see wherein his great strength lieth, and by what means we may prevail against him, that we may bind him to afflict him; and we will give thee every one of us eleven hundred pieces of silver. And Delilah said to Samson, Tell me, I pray thee, wherein thy great strength lieth, and wherewith thou mightest be bound to afflict thee. And Samson said unto her, If they bind me with seven green withes that were never dried, then shall I be weak, and be as another man. Then the lords of the Philistines brought up to her seven green withes which had not been dried, and she bound him with them. Now there were men lying in wait, abiding with her in the chamber. And she said unto him, The Philistines be upon thee, Samson. And he brake the withes, as a thread of tow is broken when it toucheth the fire. So his strength was not known.

ANGRY SAMSON

ROBERT GRAVES

Are they blind, the lords of Gaza
    In their strong towers,
Who declare Samson pillow-smothered
    And stripped of his powers?

O stolid Philistines
    Stare now in amaze
At my foxes running in your cornfields
    With their tails ablaze,

At swung jaw-bone, at bees swarming
    In the stark lion's hide,
At these, the gates of well-walled Gaza
    A-clank to my stride.

16:10–16 And Delilah said unto Samson, Behold, thou hast mocked me, and told me lies: now tell me, I pray thee, wherewith thou mightest be bound. And he said unto her, If they bind me fast with new ropes that never were occupied, then shall I be weak, and be as another man. Delilah therefore took new ropes, and bound him therewith, and said unto him, The Philistines be upon thee, Samson. And there were liers in wait abiding in the chamber. And he brake them from off his arms like a

thread. And Delilah said unto Samson, Hitherto thou hast mocked me, and told me lies: tell me wherewith thou mightest be bound. And he said unto her, If thou weavest the seven locks of my head with the web. And she fastened it with the pin, and said unto him, The Philistines be upon thee, Samson. And he awaked out of his sleep, and went away with the pin of the beam, and with the web. And she said unto him, How canst thou say, I love thee, when thine heart is not with me? thou hast mocked me these three times, and hast not told me wherein thy great strength lieth. And it came to pass, when she pressed him daily with her words, and urged him, so that his soul was vexed unto death;

from *Poetical Sketches*:

Samson

William Blake

. . . For Dalila's fair arts have long been tried in vain; in vain she wept in many a treacherous tear. "Go on, fair traitress; do thy guileful work; ere once again the changing moon her circuit hath performed, thou shalt overcome, and conquer him by force unconquerable, and wrest his secret from him. Call thine alluring arts and honest-seeming brow, the holy kiss of love, and the transparent tear; put on fair linen, that with the lily vies, purple and silver; neglect thy hair, to seem more lovely in thy loose attire; put on thy country's pride, deceit; and eyes of love decked in mild sorrow, and sell thy Lord for gold."—For now, upon her sumptuous couch reclined, in gorgeous pride, she still intreats, and still she grasps his vigorous knees with her fair arms.—"Thou lov'st me not! thou'rt war, thou art not love! O foolish Dalila! O weak woman! it is death clothed in flesh thou lovest, and thou hast been incircled in his arms!—Alas, my Lord, what am I calling thee? Thou art my God! To thee I pour my tears for sacrifice morning and evening: My days are covered with sorrow! Shut up, darkened. By night I am deceived! Who says that thou wast born of mortal kind? Destruction was thy father, a lioness suckled thee, thy young hands tore human limbs, and gorged human flesh! Come hither, Death; art thou not Samson's servant? 'Tis Dalila that calls, thy master's wife; no, stay, and let thy master do the deed: one blow of that strong arm would ease my pain; then should I lay at quiet, and have rest. Pity forsook thee at thy birth! O Dagon furious, and all ye gods of Palestine, withdraw your hand! I am but a weak woman. Alas, I am wedded to your enemy! I will go mad, and tear my crisped hair; I'll run about, and pierce the ears o' th' gods! O Samson, hold me not; thou lovest me not! Look not upon me with those deathful eyes! Thou wouldst my death, and death approaches fast."—Thus, in false tears, she bathed his feet, and thus she day by day oppressed his soul: he seemed a mountain, his brow among the clouds; she seemed a silver stream, his feet embracing. Dark thoughts rolled to and fro in his mind, like thunder clouds, troubling the sky; his visage was troubled; his soul was distressed.— "Though I should tell her all my heart, what can I fear? Though I should tell this secret of my birth, the utmost may be warded off as well when told as now." She saw him moved, and thus resumes her wiles.— "Samson, I'm thine; do with me what thou wilt; my friends are enemies; my life is death; I am a traitor to my nation, and despised; my joy is given into the hands of him who hates me, using deceit to the wife of his bosom. Thrice hast thou mocked me, and grieved my soul. Didst thou not tell me with green withes to bind thy nervous arms, and after that, when I had found thy falsehood, with new ropes to bind thee fast? I knew thou didst but mock me. Alas, when in thy sleep I bound thee with them to try thy truth, I cried, 'The Philistines be upon thee, Samson!' Then did suspicion wake thee; how didst thou rend the feeble ties! Thou fearest nought, what shouldst thou fear? Thy power is more than mortal, none can hurt thee; thy bones are brass, thy sinews are iron! Ten thousand spears are like the summer grass; an army of mighty men are as flocks in the valleys; what canst thou fear? I drink my tears like water; I live upon sorrow! O worse than wolves and tygers, what canst thou give when such a trifle is denied me? But O at last thou mockest me, to shame my over-fond inquiry! Thou toldest me to weave thee to the beam by thy strong hair; I did even that to try thy truth: but when I cried, 'The Philistines be upon thee!' then didst thou leave me to bewail that Samson loves me not."—He sat, and inward grieved; he saw and loved the beauteous suppliant, nor could conceal aught that might appease her; then, leaning on her bosom, thus he spoke: "Hear, O Dalila! doubt no more of Samson's love; for that fair breast was made the ivory palace of my inmost heart, where it shall lie at rest; for sorrow is the lot of all of woman born: for care was I brought forth, and labour is my lot: nor matchless might, nor wisdom, nor every gift enjoyed, can from the heart of man hide sorrow. . . . "

16:17–21 That he told her all his heart, and said unto her, There hath not come a razor upon mine head; for I have been a Nazarite unto God from my mother's womb: if I be shaven, then my strength will go from me, and I shall become weak, and be like any other man. And when Delilah saw that he had told her all his heart, she sent and called for the lords of the Philistines, saying, Come up this once, for he hath shewed me all his heart. Then the lords of the Philistines came up unto her, and brought money in their hand. And she made him sleep upon her knees; and she called for a man, and she caused him to shave off the seven locks of his head; and she began to afflict him, and his strength went from him.

And she said, The Philistines be upon thee, Samson. And he awoke out of his sleep, and said, I will go out as at other times before, and shake myself. And he wist not that the LORD was departed from him. But the Philistines took him, and put out his eyes, and brought him down to Gaza, and bound him with fetters of brass; and he did grind in the prison house.

SAMSON TO HIS DELILAH

RICHARD CRASHAW

Could not once blinding me, cruel, suffice?
When first I looked on thee, I lost mine eyes.

16:22 Howbeit the hair of his head began to grow again after he was shaven.

from SAMSON AGONISTES

JOHN MILTON

ll. 53–114

But what is strength without a double share
Of wisdom, vast, unwieldy, burdensome,
Proudly secure, yet liable to fall
By weakest subtleties, not made to rule,
But to subserve where wisdom bears command.
God, when he gave me strength, to show withal
How slight the gift was, hung it in my hair.
But peace, I must not quarrel with the will
Of highest dispensation, which herein
Haply had ends above my reach to know:
Suffices that to me strength is my bane,
And proves the source of all my miseries;
So many, and so huge, that each apart
Would ask a life to wail, but chief of all,
O loss of sight, of thee I most complain!
Blind among enemies, O worse than chains,
Dungeon, or beggary, or decrepit age!
Light the prime work of God to me is extinct,

And all her various objects of delight
Annulled, which might in part my grief have eased,
Inferior to the vilest now become
Of man or worm; the vilest here excel me,
They creep, yet see, I dark in light exposed
To daily fraud, contempt, abuse, and wrong,
Within doors, or without, still as a fool,
In power of others, never in my own;
Scarce half I seem to live, dead more than half.
O dark, dark, dark, amid the blaze of noon,
Irrecoverably dark, total eclipse
Without all hope of day!
O first created Beam, and thou great Word,
"Let there be light, and light was over all";
Why am I thus bereaved thy prime decree?
The sun to me is dark
And silent as the moon,
When she deserts the night
Hid in her vacant interlunar cave.
Since light so necessary is to life,
And almost life itself, if it be true
That light is in the soul,
She all in every part; why was the sight
To such a tender ball as th' eye confined?
So obvious and so easy to be quenched,
And not as feeling through all parts diffused,
That she might look at will through every pore?
Then had I not been thus exiled from light;
As in the land of darkness yet in light,
To live a life half dead, a living death,
And buried; but O yet more miserable!
My self, my sepulcher, a moving grave,
Buried, yet not exempt
By privilege of death and burial
From worst of other evils, pains and wrongs,
But made hereby obnoxious more
To all the miseries of life,
Life in captivity
Among inhuman foes.
But who are these?

16:23–30 Then the lords of the Philistines gathered them together for to offer a great sacrifice unto Dagon their god, and to rejoice: for they said,

Our god hath delivered Samson our enemy into our hand. And when the people saw him, they praised their god: for they said, Our god hath delivered into our hands our enemy, and the destroyer of our country, which slew many of us. And it came to pass, when their hearts were merry, that they said, Call for Samson, that he may make us sport. And they called for Samson out of the prison house; and he made them sport: and they set him between the pillars. And Samson said unto the lad that held him by the hand, Suffer me that I may feel the pillars whereupon the house standeth, that I may lean upon them. . . .

The Warning

Henry Wadsworth Longfellow

Beware! The Israelite of old, who tore
The lion in his path,—when, poor and blind,
He saw the blessed light of heaven no more
Shorn of his noble strength and forced to grind
In prison, and at last led forth to be
A pander to Philistine revelry,—

Upon the pillars of the temple laid
His desperate hands, and in its overthrow
Destroyed himself, and with him those who made
A cruel mockery of his sightless woe;
The poor, blind slave, the scoff and jest of all,
Expired, and thousands perished in the fall!

There is a poor, blind Samson in this land,
Shorn of his strength and bound in bonds of steel,
Who may, in some grim revel, raise his hand,
And shake the pillars of this Commonweal,
Till the vast temple of our liberties
A shapeless mass of wreck and rubbish lies.

The Book of RUTH

2:1–17 . . . And when she was risen up to glean, Boaz commanded his young men, saying, Let her glean even among the sheaves, and reproach her not: And let fall also some of the handfuls of purpose for her, and leave them, that she may glean them, and rebuke her not. So she gleaned in the field until even, and beat out that she had gleaned: and it was about an ephah of barley.

Ruth

THOMAS HOOD

She stood breast high amid the corn,
Clasped by the golden light of morn,
Like the sweetheart of the sun,
Who many a glowing kiss had won.

On her cheek an autumn flush,
Deeply ripened;—such a blush
In the midst of brown was born,
Like red poppies grown in corn.

Round her eyes her tresses fell,
Which were blackest none could tell,
But long lashes veiled a light,
That had else been all too bright.

And her hat, with shady brim,
Made her tressy forehead dim;—
Thus she stood amid the stooks,
Praising God with sweetest looks:—

Sure, I said, heaven did not mean,
Where I reap thou shouldst but glean;
Lay thy sheaf adown and come,
Share my harvest and my home.

The First Book of SAMUEL

OTHERWISE CALLED THE FIRST BOOK OF KINGS

1:1–20 Now there was a certain man of Ramathaimzophim, of mount Ephraim, and his name was Elkanah, the son of Jeroham, the son of Elihu, the son of Tohu, the son of Zuph, an Ephrathite: And he had two wives; the name of the one was Hannah, and the name of the other Peninnah: and Peninnah had children, but Hannah had no children. . . . And she was in bitterness of soul, and prayed unto the LORD, and wept sore. And she vowed a vow, and said, O LORD of hosts, if thou wilt indeed look on the affliction of thine handmaid, and remember me, and not forget thine handmaid, but wilt give unto thine handmaid a man child, then I will give him unto the LORD all the days of his life, and there shall no razor come upon his head. . . . Wherefore it came to pass, when the time was come about after Hannah had conceived, that she bare a son, and called his name Samuel, saying, Because I have asked him of the LORD.

Hope

Christopher Smart

Ah! Hannah, why shouldst thou despair,
Quick to the tabernacle speed;
There on thy knees prefer thy prayer,
And there thy cause to mercy plead.

Her pious breathings now ascend,
As from her heart the sighs she heaves;
And angels to her suit attend,
Till strong in hope she now conceives.

Then Samuel soon was brought to light
To serve the Lord, as yet a child—
O what a heart-reviving sight!
Sure cherubims and seraphs smiled.

Thus yet a child may I begin
 To serve the Lord with all my heart;
To shun the wily lures of sin,
 And claim the prize, or e'er I start.

1:21–3:18 . . . And the child Samuel grew on, and was in favour both with the LORD, and also with men. . . . And the child Samuel ministered unto the LORD before Eli. And the word of the LORD was precious in those days; there was no open vision. And it came to pass at that time, when Eli was laid down in his place, and his eyes began to wax dim, that he could not see; And ere the lamp of God went out in the temple of the LORD, where the ark of God was, and Samuel was laid down to sleep; That the LORD called Samuel: and he answered, Here am I. . . .

Then Eli called Samuel, and said, Samuel, my son. And he answered, Here am I. And he said, What is the thing that the Lord hath said unto thee? I pray thee hide it not from me: God do so to thee, and more also, if thou hide any thing from me of all the things that he said unto thee. And Samuel told him every whit, and hid nothing from him. . . .

Samuel's Prayer

John Keble

With joy the guardian Angel sees
A duteous child upon his knees,
And writes in his approving book
Each upward, earnest, holy look.

Light from his pure aërial dream
He springs to meet morn's orient beam,
And pours towards the kindling skies
His clear adoring melodies.

Some glorious seraph, waiting by,
Receives the prayer to waft on high,
And wonders, as he soars, to read
More than we know, and all we need.

More than we know, and all we need,
Is in young children's prayer and creed.
They, for their home, before Him fall,
He, for his church, receives their call.

They cry with simple voice and clear,
"Bless Father, Mother, Brethren dear."
He for the priests of his dread Son
Accounts the blessing asked and won.

For holy priests and matrons mild,
For penitents and undefiled,
For dying saints, for babes new-born,
He takes their offering, eve and morn.

He gives the frail and feeble tongue
A doom to speak on sin and wrong;
Unconscious they stern lightnings aim,
When His ten Precepts they proclaim.

Thus in the tabernacle shade
At morn and eve young Samuel prayed,
Nor knew God's ark should win,
Forfeit by priest's and people's sin.

To Eli thus dread words he spake:—
Ye hearts profane, with penance ache;—
A wondrous peal o'er Israel rung,
Heaven's thunder from a child's meek tongue.

3:19–10:1 And Samuel grew, and the LORD was with him, and did let none of his words fall to the ground. . . .

Now the LORD had told Samuel in his ear a day before Saul came, saying, To morrow about this time I will send thee a man out of the land of Benjamin, and thou shalt anoint him to be captain over my people Israel, that he may save my people out of the hand of the Philistines. . . . And when Samuel saw Saul, the LORD said unto him, Behold the man whom I spake to thee of! this same shall reign over my people. . . . And as they were going down to the end of the city, Samuel said to Saul, Bid the servant pass on before us, (and he passed on), but stand thou still a while, that I may shew thee the word of God. Then Samuel took a vial of oil, and poured it upon his head, and kissed him, and said, Is it not because the LORD hath anointed thee to be captain over his inheritance?

ON SAUL AND DAVID

FRANCIS QUARLES

Sure, Saul as little looked to be a king,
As I: and David dreamed of such a thing,
As much as he; when both alike did keep,
The one his father's asses; t'other, sheep:
Saul must forsake his whip: And David flings
His crook aside; and they must both be kings:
Saul had no sword; and David, then, no spear;
These was none conquered, nor no conqueror there;
There was no sweat; there was no blood, to shed:
The unsought crown besought the wearer's head;
There was no stratagem; no opposition;
No taking parts; no jealous competition:
There needs no art; there needs no sword to bring,
And place the crown, where God appoints the king.

10:5–16:1 . . . And the LORD said unto Samuel, How long wilt thou mourn for Saul, seeing I have rejected him from reigning over Israel? fill thine horn with oil, and go, I will send thee to Jesse the Bethlehemite: for I have provided me a king among his sons.

from DAVID AND GOLIAH

MICHAEL DRAYTON

Our sacred Muse, of Israel's Singer sings,
That heavenly harper, whose harmonious strings
Expelled that evil spirit which Saul possessed,
And of his torments often him released;
That princely prophet David, whose high lays,
Immortal God, are trumpets of thy praise,
Thou Lord of hosts be helping then to me,
To sing of him who hath so sung of thee. . . .
His curled tresses on his shoulders hung,
To which the dews at morn and eve so clung,
To the beholders that they did appear
As nature threaded pearl with every hair:

The bees, and wasps, in wildernesses wild
Have with his beauties often been beguiled,
Roses and lilies thinking they had seen,
But finding there they have deceived been,
Play with his eyes, which them that comfort bring,
That those two suns would shortly get a spring;
His lips in their pure coral liveries mock
A row of pales cut from a crystal rock,
Which stood within them, all of equal height.
From top to toe each limb so clean and straight,
By every joint of his that one might try,
Or give true laws to perfect symmetry;
The vermin (oft) his sheep that would surprise
Became so charmed with the splendor of his eyes,
That they forgot their ravine, and have lain
Down by his flocks, as they would glad and fain
Keep them from others, that on them would prey,
Or tend upon them, that they should not stray.
Whether in cotes he had his flock in hold,
Or for the fallows kept them in the fold,
He was not idle, though not taking pains,
Celestial lyrics singing to the swains,
And often sitting in the silent shade,
When his fair flock to rest themselves were laid,
On his lyre tuned such harmonious lays,
That the birds perched upon the tender sprays,
Mad at his music, strain themselves so much
To imitate th'unimitable touch,
Breaking their hearts, that they have dropped to ground,
And died for grief in malicing the sound.
Sometimes a stag he with his sling would slay,
Or with his sheephook kill a boar at bay,
Or run a roe so long (he was so fleet)
Till it lay trembling, breathless, at his feet,
Sometimes again, he practised a fight,
That from the desert, should a dragon light
Upon his sheep, the serpent to assail,
How by clear skill through courage to prevail.
Then with a small stone thrown out of his sling
To hit a swallow on her height of wing,

And home at night when they their sheep should drive,
The sluggish shepherds lastly to revive,
He took his harp so excellently strung,
In a broad baldrick at his back that hung,
And on the same stroke such melodious strains,
That from the coverts as the neighboring plains,
The echoes waked with sweetness of his notes,
Which each to other diligently rotes;
And thus his time the Lord's beloved passed;
Till God to Samuel calling at the last. . . .

16:19–17:49 Wherefore Saul sent messengers unto Jesse, and said, Send me David thy son, which is with the sheep. . . . And David came to Saul, and stood before him: and he loved him greatly; and he became his armourbearer. And Saul sent to Jesse, saying, Let David, I pray thee, stand before me; for he hath found favour in my sight. And it came to pass, when the evil spirit from God was upon Saul, that David took an harp, and played with his hand: so Saul was refreshed, and was well, and the evil spirit departed from him.

Now the Philistines gathered together their armies to battle. . . . And there went out a champion out of the camp of the Philistines, named Goliath, of Gath, whose height was six cubits and a span. . . .

And David said to Saul, Let no man's heart fail because of him; thy servant will go and fight with this Philistine. . . . And he took his staff in his hand, and chose him five smooth stones out of the brook, and put them in a shepherd's bag which he had, even in a scrip; and his sling was in his hand: and he drew near to the Philistine. . . .

And it came to pass, when the Philistine arose, and came, and drew nigh to meet David, that David hasted, and ran toward the army to meet the Philistine. And David put his hand in his bag, and took thence a stone, and slang it, and smote the Philistine in his forehead, that the stone sunk into his forehead; and he fell upon his face to the earth.

The Pebble

Elinor Wylie

If any have a stone to shy,
Let him be David and not I;
The lovely shepherd, brave and vain,
Who has a maggot in the brain,

Which, since the brain is bold and pliant,
Takes the proportions of a giant.
Alas, my legendary fate!
Who sometimes rage, but never hate.
Long, long before the pebble flieth
I see a virtue in Goliath;
Yea, in the Philistine his face,
A touching majesty and grace;
Then like the lights of evening shine
The features of the Philistine
Until my spirit faints to see
The beauty of my enemy.
If any have a stone to fling
Let him be a shepherd-king,
Who is himself so beautiful
He may detest the gross and dull
With holy rage and heavenly pride
To make a pebble sanctified
And feather its course with wings of scorn.
But, from the day that I was born
Until like corn I bow to the sickle,
I am in hatred false and fickle.
I am most cruel to anyone
Who hates me with devotion;
I will not freeze, I will not burn;
I make his heart a poor return
For all the passion that he spends
In swearing we shall never be friends;
For all the pains his passion spent
In hatred I am impotent;
The sad perversity of my mind
Sees in him my kin and kind.
Alas, my shameful heritage,
False in hate and fickle in rage!
Alas, to lack the power to loathe!
I like them each; I love them both;
Philistine and shepherd-king
They strike the pebble from my sling;
My heart grows cold, my spirit grows faint;
Behold, a hero and a saint
Where appeared, a moment since,
A giant and a heathen prince;
And I am bound and given over
To be no better than a lover,

Alas, who strove as a holy rebel!
They have broke my sling and stole my pebble:
If any have a stone to throw
It is not I, ever or now.

17:50 So David prevailed over the Philistine with a sling and with a stone, and smote the Philistine, and slew him; but there was no sword in the hand of David.

I took my Power in my Hand –

EMILY DICKINSON

I took my Power in my Hand –
And went against the World –
'Twas not so much as David – had –
But I – was twice as bold –

I aimed my Pebble – but Myself
Was all the one that fell –
Was it Goliath – was too large –
Or was myself – too small?

17:51 Therefore David ran, and stood upon the Philistine, and took his sword, and drew it out of the sheath thereof, and slew him, and cut off his head therewith. And when the Philistines saw their champion was dead, they fled.

David and Goliath

P. HATELY WADDELL

This bit lilt o' his ain till David's Praise,
Whan he fought again Goliath,
Stan's like a to-fa' till the Psalms

[Quo' the LXX.]

Sma' was I, amang brether o' mine;
An' the bairn was I, i' my faither's ha';
My faither's fe I was hirdin:

My han's, they wrought the organ fine;
An' my fingers, wi' thairms, the harp an' a'
They war girdin.

An' wha was 't tell'd the Lord o' me?
The Lord himsel, he hearken'd till me;
An' his rinner he sent, an' he cried me awa—
Cried me awa frae my faither's fe;
An' wi' chrystin oyle o' his ain an' a',
He chrystit me:
Brether o' mine, they war brave an' braw;
An' the Lord o' them wad hae nought ava'.

Furth gaed I, till fecht wi' the frem;
Syne by his eidols he swure at me:
Bot that swurd o' his ain, I claught it frae him;
An' I sned his head frae his shouthirs trim;
An' the skaith an' the scorn I carried it a',
Frae the folk o' Israel, hame wi' me!

18:14 And David behaved himself wisely in all his ways; and the LORD was with him.

I DO NOT BELIEVE THAT DAVID KILLED GOLIATH

CHARLES REZNIKOFF

I do not believe that David killed Goliath.
It must have been—
you will find the name in the list of David's captains.
But, whoever it was, he was no fool
when he took off the helmet
and put down the sword and the spear and the shield
and said, The weapons you have given me are good,
but they are not mine:
I will fight in my own way
with a couple of pebbles and a sling.

18:15–23 Wherefore when Saul saw that he behaved himself very wisely, he was afraid of him. But all Israel and Judah loved David, because he went out and came in before them. . . .

And Michal Saul's daughter loved David: and they told Saul, and the thing pleased him. And Saul said, I will give him her, that she may be a snare to him, and that the hand of the Philistines may be against him. Wherefore Saul said to David, Thou shalt this day be my son in law in the one of the twain. And Saul commanded his servants, saying, Commune with David secretly, and say, Behold, the king hath delight in thee, and all his servants love thee: now therefore be the king's son in law. And Saul's servants spake those words in the ears of David. And David said, Seemeth it to you a light thing to be a king's son in law, seeing that I am a poor man, and lightly esteemed?

from *Davideis, Book III*

Abraham Cowley

Michal her modest flames sought to conceal,
But Love even th'art to hide it does reveal.
Her soft unpracticed eyes betrayed the theft,
Love passed through them, and there such footsteps left.
She blushed when he approached, and when he spoke,
And suddenly her wandering answers broke,
At his names sound, and when she heard him praised,
With concerned haste her thoughtful looks she raised.
Uncalled-for sighs oft from her bosom flew,
And Adriel's active friend she abruptly grew.
Oft when the court's gay youth stood waiting by,
She strove to act a cold indifferency;
In vain she acted so constrained a part,
For thousand nameless things disclosed her heart.
On th'other side David with silent pain
Did in respectful bounds his fires contain.
His humble fear t'offend, and trembling awe,
Imposed on him a no less rigorous law
Than modesty on her, and though he strove
To make her see't, he durst not tell his love.
To tell it first the timorous youth made choice
Of music's bolder and more active voice
And thus beneath her window, did he touch
His faithful lyre; the words and numbers such,
As did well worth my memory appear,
And may perhaps deserve your princely ear.

Awake, awake my Lyre,
And tell thy silent master's humble tale,
In sounds that may prevail;
Sounds that gentle thoughts inspire,
Though so exalted she
And I so lowly be,
Tell her such different notes make all thy harmony.

Hark, how the strings awake,
And though the moving hand approach not near,
Themselves with awful fear,
A kind of numerous trembling make.
Now all thy forces try,
Now all thy charms apply,
Revenge upon her ear the conquests of her eye.

Weak Lyre! thy virtue sure
Is useless here, since thou art only found
To cure, but not to wound,
And she to wound, but not to cure.
Too weak, too, wilt thou prove
My passion to remove,
Physic to other ills, thou'rt nourishment to Love.

Sleep, sleep again, my Lyre;
For thou canst never tell my humble tale,
In sounds that will prevail,
Nor gentle thoughts in her inspire;
All thy vain mirth lay by,
Bid thy strings silent lie,
Sleep, sleep again, my Lyre, and let thy master die.

She heard all this, and the prevailing sound
Touched with delightful pain her tender wound.

31:1 Now the Philistines fought against Israel: and the men of Israel fled from before the Philistines, and fell down slain in mount Gilboa.

Song of Saul Before his Last Battle

George Noel Gordon, Lord Byron

Warriors and chiefs! should the shaft or the sword
Pierce me in leading the host of the Lord,
Heed not the corse, though a king's, in your path:
Bury your steel in the bosoms of Gath!

Thou who art bearing my buckler and bow,
Should the soldiers of Saul look away from the foe,
Stretch me that moment in blood at thy feet!
Mine be the doom which they dared not to meet!

Farewell to others, but never we part,
Heir to my royalty, son of my heart!
Bright is the diadem, boundless the sway,
Or kingly the death, which awaits us to-day!

31:2–6 And the Philistines followed hard upon Saul and upon his sons; and the Philistines slew Jonathan, and Abinadab, and Melchishua, Saul's sons. And the battle went sore against Saul, and the archers hit him; and he was sore wounded of the archers. Then said Saul unto his armourbearer, Draw thy sword, and thrust me through therewith; lest these uncircumcised come and thrust me through, and abuse me. But his armourbearer would not; for he was sore afraid. Therefore Saul took a sword, and fell upon it. And when his armourbearer saw that Saul was dead, he fell likewise upon his sword, and died with him. So Saul died, and his three sons, and his armourbearer, and all his men, that same day together.

The Death of Saul

Philip Levine

"Is Saul also among the prophets?" I Samuel 10

The sleeping armies of the living God
Embraced the King who could not wake or sleep.

Their faith in him who had no will to faith
Or faith but theirs was more than he could bear.
Hearing their leader scream, they roused, unarmed,
Unsure of what they heard—the needs of terror
Calling through sleep—nor did they understand
When, later, beside a stream, they strapped on armour,
Blessed and buckled halters, received their vows,
The soldier's vows which they would not fulfill
Until they clasped the final lack of peace.

All roads led upward to the mountain top
Where he would flush the partridge of the hills,
David the stave with which God whipped his fury:
A fury that was love, a love of self.
He thought he saw him riding next to him,
Turned on his mount, thrilling the wayward flanks
That stretched below. This time he could not speak,
And when they leaned to touch he saw his son.
Not for the loss of David did he weep,
But for the knowledge gained: the fear of death
Was but a shadow of the power of love,
Though death had fixed those eyes which turned toward his.
Beyond the olive line, on sun-bleached rocks,
The Philistines were closing ranks to charge.
Violent, Godless, their prayer for strength at arms
Descended like the driving words of God
On those below, aching for certitude.
The archers done, the first waves met and broke;
The flanks closed in and locked; both forces joined,
Their differences obscured in smoke and dust.
Habit or need? His dead and dying troops
Would never know what drove King Saul to kneel,
A penitent upon those burning slopes,
Finding, too late, in every Godless act
And every act of will the will of God.

And Jonathan was dead; the hope of Saul
A trophy wrapped in scarlet, lovingly;
His brothers slain, their armour-bearers fled
And crouched and wept by Saul, who knew too well
The messages they lacked the strength to give.
A King of God in death, he persevered;
Pride against pride deployed until it failed.
His wounded ceased their cries. He was alone.

The sword by which he lived was all he had,
And so he turned to it, knowing the act
Would end his name and heritage forever,
Knowing the way, far from his living love,
Far from the shepherd boy conceived in grace,
And further still from Him he could not name.

31:7–9 And when the men of Israel that were on the other side of the valley, and they that were on the other side Jordan, saw that the men of Israel fled, and that Saul and his sons were dead, they forsook the cities, and fled; and the Philistines came and dwelt in them. And it came to pass on the morrow, when the Philistines came to strip the slain, that they found Saul and his three sons fallen in mount Gilboa. And they cut off his head, and stripped off his armour, and sent into the land of the Philistines round about, to publish it in the house of their idols, and among the people.

In Which Roosevelt Is Compared to Saul*

Vachel Lindsay

Where is David? . . . Oh God's people
Saul has passed, the good and great.
Mourn for Saul, the first anointed,
Head and shoulders o'er the state.

He was found among the prophets:
Judge and monarch, merged in one.
But the wars of Saul are ended,
And the works of Saul are done.

Where is David, ruddy shepherd,
God's boy-king for Israel?
Mystic, ardent, dowered with beauty,
Singing where still waters dwell?

Prophet, find that destined minstrel
Wandering on the range today,
Driving sheep, and crooning softly
Psalms that cannot pass away.

* Written and published in 1913, and republished five years later, in the *Boston Transcript*, on the death of Theodore Roosevelt.

"David waits," the prophet answers,
"In a black, notorious den,
In a cave upon the border,
With four hundred outlaw men.

"He is fair and loved of women,
Mighty-hearted, born to sing:
Thieving, weeping, erring, praying,
Radiant royal rebel-king.

"He will come with harp and psaltry,
Quell his troop of convict swine,
Quell his mad-dog roaring rascals,
Witching them with tunes divine.

"They will ram the walls of Zion.
They will win us Salem hill,
All for David, shepherd David,
Singing like a mountain rill."

The Second Book of SAMUEL

OTHERWISE CALLED THE SECOND BOOK OF KINGS

1:1–20 . . . And David lamented with this lamentation over Saul and over Jonathan his son:

The beauty of Israel is slain upon thy high places: how are the mighty fallen! Tell it not in Gath, publish it not in the streets of Askelon; lest the daughters of the Philistines rejoice, lest the daughters of the uncircumcised triumph.

DAVID'S EPITAPH ON JONATHAN

FRANCIS QUARLES

Here lies the fairest flower, that stood
In Israel's garden; now, in blood;
Which, Death to make her garland gay,

Hath cropped, against her triumph day:
Here, here lies he, whose actions penned
The perfect copy of a friend;
Whose milk-white vellum did incur
No least suspicion of a blur:
Here lies th' example of a brother,
Not to be followed by another;
The fair-indented counterpart
Of David's joy, of David's heart:
Rest then; for ever, rest alone;
Thy ashes can be touched by none,
Till Death hath picked out such another:
Here lies a flower, a friend, a brother.

3:1–6:15 . . . Then came all the tribes of Israel to David unto Hebron, . . . and king David made a league with them in Hebron before the LORD: and they anointed David king over Israel. David was thirty years old when he began to reign, and he reigned forty years. . . .

Again, David gathered together all the chosen men of Israel, thirty thousand. And David arose, and went with all the people that were with him from Baale of Judah, to bring up from thence the ark of God, whose name is called by the name of the LORD of hosts that dwelleth between the cherubims. And they set the ark of God upon a new cart, and brought it out of the house of Abinadab that was in Gibeah: and Uzzah and Ahio, the sons of Abinadab, drave the new cart. . . .

And David danced before the LORD with all his might; and David was girded with a linen ephod. So David and all the house of Israel brought up the ark of the LORD with shouting, and with the sound of the trumpet.

David

CHARLES REZNIKOFF

The shadow does not leave my feet,
how shrunken now it lies;
with sunshine I am anointed king,
I leap before the ark, I sing;
I seem to walk but I dance about,
you think me silent but I shout.

6:16–20 And as the ark of the LORD came into the city of David, Michal Saul's daughter looked through a window, and saw king David leaping and dancing before the LORD; and she despised him in her heart. And they brought in the ark of the LORD, and set it in his place, in the midst of the tabernacle that David had pitched for it: and David offered burnt offerings and peace offerings before the LORD. . . .

Then David returned to bless his household. And Michal the daughter of Saul came out to meet David, and said, How glorious was the king of Israel to day, who uncovered himself to day in the eyes of the handmaids of his servants, as one of the vain fellows shamelessly uncovereth himself!

KING DAVID DANCES

JOHN BERRYMAN

Aware to the dry throat of the wide hell in the world,
O trampling empires, and mine one of them,
and mine one gross desire against His sight,
slaughter devising there,
some good behind, ambiguous ahead,
revolted sons, a pierced son, bound to hear,
mid hypocrites amongst idolaters,
mocked in abysm by one shallow wife,
with the ponder both of priesthood & of State
heavy upon me, yea,
all the black same I dance my blue head off!

11:2 And it came to pass in an eveningtide, that David arose from off his bed, and walked upon the roof of the king's house: and from the roof he saw a woman washing herself; and the woman was very beautiful to look upon.

from LOVE OF KING DAVID AND FAIR BETHSABE

GEORGE PEELE

Hot sun, cool fire, tempered with sweet air,
Black shade, fair nurse, shadow my white hair.
Shine, sun; burn, fire; breathe, air, and ease me;
Shadow, my sweet nurse, keep me from burning,

Make not my glad cause cause of mourning.
Let not my beauty's fire
Inflame unstaid desire,
Nor pierce any bright eye
That wandereth lightly.

11:3–12:7 And David sent and enquired after the woman. And one said, Is not this Bathsheba, the daughter of Eliam, the wife of Uriah the Hittite? And David sent messengers, and took her; and she came in unto him, and he lay with her. . . .

And the LORD sent Nathan unto David. And he came unto him, and said unto him, There were two men in one city; the one rich, and the other poor. The rich man had exceeding many flocks and herds: But the poor man had nothing, save one little ewe lamb, which he had bought and nourished up: and it grew up together with him, and with his children; it did eat of his own meat, and drank of his own cup, and lay in his bosom, and was unto him as a daughter. And there came a traveller unto the rich man, and he spared to take of his own flock and of his own herd, to dress for the wayfaring man that was come unto him; but took the poor man's lamb, and dressed it for the man that was come to him.

And David's anger was greatly kindled against the man; and he said to Nathan, As the LORD liveth, the man that hath done this thing shall surely die: And he shall restore the lamb fourfold, because he did this thing, and because he had no pity.

And Nathan said to David, Thou art the man. . . .

from Penitential Psalms

Prologue

Sir Thomas Wyatt

Love to give law unto his subject hearts
Stood in the eyes of Barsabe the bright,
And in a look anon himself converts
Cruelly pleasant before King David's sight;
First dazed his eyes, and further forth he starts
With venomed breath, as softly as he might
Touched his senses, and overruns his bones
With creeping fire, sparpled for the nonce.

And when he saw that kindled was the flame,
The moist poison in his heart he lanced,

So that the soul did tremble with the same.
And in this brawl as he stood and tranced,
Yielding unto the figure and the frame
That those fair eyes had in his presence glanced,
The form that Love had printed in his breast
He honoreth as thing of things the best.

So that forgot the wisdom and forecast
(Which woes to realms when that these kings doth lack),
Forgetting eke God's majesty as fast,
Yea, and his own, forthwith he doth to make
Uriah to go into the field in haste,
Uriah I say, that was his idols make,
Under pretence of certain victory
For enemies' swords a ready prey to die.

Whereby he may enjoy her out of doubt
Whom more than God or himself he mindeth.
And after he had brought this thing about
And of that lust possessed himself, he findeth
That hath and doth reverse and clean turn out
Kings from kingdoms, and cities undermineth:
He blinded thinks this train so bold and close
To blind all thing that nought may it disclose.

But Nathan hath spied out this treachery,
With rueful cheer and sets afore his face
The offence, outrage and injury
That he hath done to God, as in this case
By murder for to cloak adultery.
He showeth him eke from heaven the threats alas
So sternly sore, this prophet, this Nathan,
That all amazed this aged woeful man.

Like him that meets with horror and with fear
The heat doth straight forsake the limbs cold;
The color eke droopeth down from his cheer,
So doth he feel his fire manifold;
His heat, his lust and pleasure all in fear
Consume and waste, and straight his crown of gold,
His purple pall, his sceptre he lets fall,
And to the ground he throwth himself withal.

The pompous pride of state and dignity
Forthwith rebates repentant humbleness;
Thinner vile cloth than clotheth poverty
Doth scantly hide and clad his nakedness;
His fair hoar beard of reverent gravity
With ruffled hair, knowing his wickedness,
More like was he the selfsame repentance
Than stately prince of worldly governance.

His harp he taketh in hand to be his guide,
Wherewith he offereth his plaints his soul to save
That from his heart distills on every side,
Withdrawing him into a dark cave
Within the ground, wherein he might him hide,
Fleeing the light, as in prison or grave:
In which as soon as David entered had
The dark horror did make his soul adrad.

But he without prolonging or delay
Of that that might his Lord his God appease
Fallth on his knees, and with his harp I say
Afore his breast, fraughted with disease
Of stormy sighs, his cheer coloured like clay,
Dressed upright, seeking to counterpese
His song with sighs and touching of the strings
With tender heart, . . . to God he sings.

12:7–13 Thus saith the LORD God of Israel, I anointed thee king over Israel, and I delivered thee out of the hand of Saul; And I gave thee thy master's house, and thy master's wives into thy bosom, and gave thee the house of Israel and of Judah; and if that had been too little, I would moreover have given unto thee such and such things. Wherefore hast thou despised the commandment of the LORD, to do evil in his sight? thou hast killed Uriah the Hittite with the sword, and hast taken his wife to be thy wife, and hast slain him with the sword of the children of Ammon. Now therefore the sword shall never depart from thine house; because thou hast despised me, and hast taken the wife of Uriah the Hittite to be thy wife. Thus saith the LORD, Behold, I will raise up evil against thee out of thine own house, and I will take thy wives before thine eyes, and give them unto thy neighbour, and he shall lie with thy wives in the sight of this sun. For thou didst it secretly: but I will do this thing before all Israel, and before the sun.

And David said unto Nathan, I have sinned against the LORD.

DAVID'S *PECCAVI*

ROBERT SOUTHWELL

In eaves sole sparrow sits not more alone,
Nor mourning pelican in desert wild,
Than seely I, that solitary moan,
From highest hopes to hardest hap exiled:
Sometime, O blissful time! was virtue's mead.
Aim to my thoughts, guide to my word and deed.

But fears are now my feres, grief my delight,
My tears my drink, my famished thoughts my bread;
Day full of dumps, nurse of unrest the night,
My garments gyves, a bloody field my bed;
My sleep is rather death than death's ally,
Yet killed with murdering pangs I cannot die.

This is the change of my ill changèd choice,
Ruth for my rest, for comforts cares I find:
To pleasing tunes succeeds a plaining voice,
The doleful echo of my wailing mind;
Which, taught to know the worth of virtue's joys,
Doth hate itself, for loving fancy's toys.

If wiles of wit had overwrought my will,
Or subtle trains mislead my steps awry,
My foil had found excuse in want of skill,
Ill deed I might, though not ill doom, deny.
But wit and will must now confess with shame,
Both deed and doom to have deservèd blame.

I fancy deemed fit guide to lead my way,
And as I deemed I did pursue her track,
Wit lost his aim and will was fancy's prey;
The rebel won, the ruler went to wrack.
But now since fancy did with folly end,
Wit bought with loss, will taught by wit, will mend.

12:13–24 And Nathan said unto David, The LORD also hath put away thy sin; thou shalt not die. Howbeit, because by this deed thou hast given great occasion to the enemies of the LORD to blaspheme, the child also

that is born unto thee shall surely die. And Nathan departed unto his house.

And the LORD struck the child that Uriah's wife bare unto David, and it was very sick. David therefore besought God for the child; and David fasted, and went in, and lay all night upon the earth. And the elders of his house arose, and went to him, to raise him up from the earth: but he would not, neither did he eat bread with them. And it came to pass on the seventh day, that the child died. And the servants of David feared to tell him that the child was dead: for they said, Behold, while the child was yet alive, we spake unto him, and he would not hearken unto our voice: how will he then vex himself, if we tell him that the child is dead? But when David saw that his servants whispered, David perceived that the child was dead: therefore David said unto his servants, Is the child dead? And they said, He is dead.

Then David arose from the earth, and washed, and anointed himself, and changed his apparel, and came into the house of the LORD, and worshipped: then he came to his own house; and when he required, they set bread before him, and he did eat. Then said his servants unto him, What thing is this that thou hast done? thou didst fast and weep for the child, while it was alive; but when the child was dead, thou didst rise and eat bread. And he said, While the child was yet alive, I fasted and wept: for I said, Who can tell whether GOD will be gracious to me, that the child may live? But now he is dead, wherefore should I fast? can I bring him back again? I shall go to him, but he shall not return to me.

And David comforted Bathsheba his wife, and went in unto her, and lay with her: and she bare a son, and he called his name Solomon: and the LORD loved him.

King David

Stephen Vincent Benet

David sang to his hook-nosed harp:
"The Lord God is a jealous God!
His violent vengeance is swift and sharp!
And the Lord is King above all gods!

"Blest be the Lord, through years untold,
The Lord Who has blessed me a thousand fold!

"Cattle and concubines, corn and hives
Enough to last me a dozen lives.

"Plump, good women with noses flat,
Marrowful blessings, weighty and fat.

"I wax in His peace like a pious gourd,
The Lord God is a pleasant God,
Break mine enemy's jaw, O Lord!
For the Lord is King above all gods!"

His hand dropped slack from the tunable strings,
A sorrow came on him—a sorrow of kings.

A sorrow sat on the arm of his throne,
An eagle sorrow with claws of stone.

"I am merry, yes, when I am not thinking,
But life is nothing but eating and drinking.

"I can shape my psalms like daggers of jade,
But they do not shine like the first I made.

"I can harry the heathen from North to South,
But no hot taste comes into my mouth.

"My wives are comely as long-haired goats,
But I would not care if they cut their throats!

"Where are the maids of the desert tents
With lips like flagons of frankincense?

"Where is Jonathan? Where is Saul?
The captain-towers of Zion wall?

"The trees of cedar, the hills of Nod,
The kings, the running lions of God?

"Their words were a writing in golden dust,
Their names are myrrh in the mouths of the just.

"The sword of the slayer could never divide them—
Would God I had died in battle beside them!"

The Lord looked down from a thunder-clap.
(The Lord God is a crafty God.)
He heard the strings of the shrewd harp snap.
(The Lord Who is King above all gods.)

He pricked the king with an airy thorn,
It burnt in his body like grapes of scorn.

The eyelids roused that had drooped like lead.
David lifted his heavy head.

The thorn stung at him, a fiery bee,
"The world is wide. I will go and see
From the roof of my haughty palace," said he.

2

Bathsheba bathed on her vine-decked roof.
(The Lord God is a mighty God.)
Her body glittered like mail of proof.
(And the Lord is King above all gods.)

Her body shimmered, tender and white
As the flesh of aloes in candlelight.

King David forgot to be old or wise.
He spied on her bathing with sultry eyes.

A breath of spice came into his nose.
He said, "Her breasts are like two young roes."

His eyes were bright with a crafty gleam.
He thought, "Her body is soft as cream."

He straightened himself like an unbent bow
And called a servant and bade him go.

3

Uriah the Hittite came to his lord,
Dusty with war as a well-used sword.

A close, trim man like a belt, well-buckled;
A jealous gentleman, hard to cuckold.

David entreated him, soft and bland,
Offered him comfits from his own hand.

Drank with him deep till his eyes grew red,
And laughed in his beard as he went to bed.

The days slipped by without hurry or strife,
Like apple-parings under a knife,
And still Uriah kept from his wife.

Lean fear tittered through David's psalm,
"This merry husband is far too calm."

David sent for Uriah then,
They greeted each other like pious men.

"Thou hast borne the battle, the dust and the heat.
Go down to thy house and wash thy feet!"

Uriah frowned at the words of the king.
His brisk, hard voice had a leaden ring.

"While the hosts of God still camp in the field
My house to me is a garden sealed.

"How shall I rest while the arrow yet flies?
The dust of the war is still in my eyes."

David spoke with his lion's roar:
"If Peace be a bridle that rubs you sore
You shall fill your belly with blood and war!"

Uriah departed, calling him kind.
His eyes were serpents in David's mind.

He summoned a captain, a pliable man,
"Uriah the Hittite shall lead the van.

"In the next assault, when the fight roars high,
And the Lord God is a hostile God,
Retire from Uriah that he may die.
For the Lord is King above all gods."

4

The messenger came while King David played
The friskiest ditty ever made.

"News, O King, from our dubious war!
The Lord of Hosts hath prevailed once more!

"His foes are scattered like chirping sparrows,
Their kings lie breathless, feathered with arrows,

"Many are dead of your captains tall.
Uriah the Hittite was first to fall."

David turned from the frolicsome strings
And rent his clothes for the death of kings.

Yet, as he rent them, he smiled for joy.
The sly, wide smile of a wicked boy.

"The powerful grace of the Lord prevails!
He has cracked Uriah between His nails!

"His blessings are mighty, they shall not cease.
And my days henceforth shall be days of peace!"

His mind grew tranquil, smoother than fleece.
He rubbed his body with scented grease.
And his days thenceforward were days of peace.

His days were fair as the flowering lime
—For a little time, for a little time.

And Bathsheba lay in his breast like a dove,
A vessel of amber, made for love.

5

When Bathsheba was great with child,
(The Lord God is a jealous God!)
Portly and meek as a moon grown mild,
(The Lord is King above all gods!)

Nathan, the prophet, wry and dying,
Preached to the king like a locust crying:

"Hearken awhile to a doleful thing!
There were two men in thy land, O King!

"One was rich as a gilded ram.
One had one treasure, a poor ewe-lamb.

"Rich man wasted his wealth like spittle.
Poor man shared with his lamb spare victual.

"A traveler came to the rich man's door.
'Give me to eat, for I hunger sore!'

"Rich man feasted him fatly, true,
But the meat that he gave him was fiend's meat, too,
Stolen and roasted, the poor man's ewe!

"Hearken, my lord, to a deadly thing!
What shall be done with these men, O King?"

David hearkened, seeing it plain,
His heart grew heavy with angry pain:
"Show me the rich man that he be slain!"

Nathan barked as a jackal can.
"Just, O King! And thou art the man!"

David rose as the thunders rise
When someone in Heaven is telling lies.
But his eyes were weaker than Nathan's eyes.

His huge bulk shivered like quaking sod,
Shoulders bowing to Nathan's rod,
Nathan, the bitter apple of God.

His great voice shook like a runner's, spent,
"My sin has found me! Oh, I repent!"

Answered Nathan, that talkative Jew:
"For many great services, comely and true,
The Lord of Mercy will pardon you.

"But the child in Bathsheba, come of your seed,
Shall sicken and die like a blasted weed."

David groaned when he heard him speak.
The painful tears ran hot on his cheek.

Ashes he cast on his kingly locks.
All night long he lay on the rocks.

Beseeching his Lord with a howling cry:
"O Lord God, O my jealous God,
Be kind to the child that it may not die,
For Thou art King above all gods!"

Seven long nights he lay there, howling,
A lion wounded, moaning and growling.

7

Seven long midnights, sorrowing greatly,
While Sin, like a dead man, embraced him straitly.

Till he was abased from his lust and pride
And the child was born and sickened and died.

He arose at last. It was ruddy Day.
And his sin like water had washed away.

He cleansed and anointed, took fresh apparel,
And worshiped the Lord in a tuneful carol.

His servants, bearing the child to bury,
Marveled greatly to see him so merry.

He spoke to them mildly as mid-May weather:
"The child and my sin are perished together.

"He is dead, my son. Though his whole soul yearn to me,
I must go to him, he may not return to me.

"Why should I sorrow for what was pain?
A cherished grief is an iron chain."

He took up his harp, the sage old chief.
His heart felt clean as a new green leaf.

His soul smelt pleasant as rain-wet clover.
"I have sinned and repented and that's all over.

"In his dealings with heathen, the Lord is hard.
But the humble soul is his spikenard."

His wise thoughts fluttered like doves in the air.
"I wonder is Bathsheba still so fair?

"Does she weep for the child that our sin made perish?
I must comfort my ewe-lamb, comfort and cherish.

"The justice of God is honey and balm.
I will soothe her heart with a little psalm."

He went to her chamber, no longer sad,
Walking as light as a shepherd lad.

He found her weeping, her garments rent,
Trodden like straw by God's punishment.
He solaced her out of his great content.

Being but woman, a while she grieved,
But at last she was comforted, and conceived.

Nine months later she bore him a son.
(The Lord God is a mighty God!)
The name of that child was Solomon.
He was God's tough staff till his days were run!
(And the Lord is King above all gods!)

14:14 For we must needs die, and are as water spilt on the ground, which cannot be gathered up again; neither doth God respect any person: yet doth he devise means, that his banished be not expelled from him.

The Rabbi's Song

Rudyard Kipling

If thought can reach to Heaven,
    On Heaven let it dwell,
For fear thy Thought be given
    Like power to reach Hell.
For fear the desolation
    And darkness of thy mind
Perplex an habitation
    Which thou hast left behind.

Let nothing linger after—
    No whimpering ghost remain,
In wall, or beam, or rafter,
    Of any hate or pain.
Cleanse and call home thy spirit,
    Deny her leave to cast,

On aught thy heirs inherit,
    The shadow of her past.

For think, in all thy sadness,
    What road our griefs may take;
Whose brain reflect our madness,
    Or whom our terrors shake:
For think, lest any languish
    By cause of thy distress—
The arrows of our anguish
    Fly farther than we guess.

Our lives, our tears, as water,
    Are spilled upon the ground;
God giveth no man quarter,
    Yet God a means hath found,
Though Faith and Hope have vanished,
    And even Love grows dim—
A means whereby His banished
    Be not expelled from Him!

15:12–16:14 . . . And when king David came to Bahurim, behold, thence came out a man of the family of the house of Saul, whose name was Shimei, the son of Gera: he came forth, and cursed still as he came. And he cast stones at David, and at all the servants of king David: and all the people and all the mighty men were on his right hand and on his left. . . . And David said, . . . It may be that the LORD will look on mine affliction, and that the LORD will requite me good for his cursing this day. And as David and his men went by the way, Shimei went along on the hill's side over against him, and cursed as he went, and threw stones at him, and cast dust. And the king, and all the people that were with him, came weary, and refreshed themselves there.

ODE XV

Upon the Jealousies raised, and Scandals cast upon the King,* etc.

THOMAS STANLEY

O Lord thou seest my wrongs abound;
Lions enraged my soul surround,
With poisonous words
Their tongues like swords,
Their teeth like arrows wound.

My foes reproach me all the day,
And sworn deceits together lay;
My God! how long
Shall they grow strong,
Who with vain lies inveigh?

The calumnies which they have sown
On every side to thee are known,
Hold not thy peace
Lest they increase,
And bury my renown.

The liar thou wilt ruinate,
The bloody and the false dost hate;
Let my upright
Intents, a light,
Clear as the sun dilate.

My patience let not wrath out-weigh,
Nor silence innocence betray,
That I may tread,
As thou hast led,
Curses with blessings pay.

Shimei, when his envenomed pride
Seemed by thy judgements justified,
Thou didst o'er-throw:
But deal not so
With them that me deride.

* King Charles I of England. This poem is from *Psalterium Carolinum*, 1657, a book of 27 odes dedicated by the author to King Charles II, whose court-in-exile, in France, Stanley served. The dedication reads in part: *The Psalms of* David *have been continued in verse through many Languages; in these your Majesty's Royal Father, (a Person of like Dignity, Sufferings and Piety,) breathes forth, (for so he calls them) the comforts of* David. *The Parallel gave occasion to this attempt. . . .*

My prayer and patience in these wrongs,
Like water, cool, and quench their tongues;
    Inflamed with ire,
    By that black fire
Which unto Hell belongs.

O let my deeds their words refute,
Nor they enjoy the deadly fruit
    Which (dipped in gall)
    Their lips let fall:
But my indulgent suit.

My soul to meek devotion win:
That I thy boundless mercies, in
    Their malice, may
    With joy survey;
Thy justice in their sin.

O let the curses they have thrown
At me, invite thy blessings down.
    What some refuse,
    Be pleased to choose
For the head corner stone.

Look down from thy eternal tower,
Redeem from them that would devour:
    My soul O hide,
    From men's bold pride,
From their invective power.

16:15–23 And Absalom, and all the people the men of Israel, came to Jerusalem, and Ahithophel with him. And it came to pass, when Hushai the Archite, David's friend, was come unto Absalom, that Hushai said unto Absalom, God save the king, God save the king. And Absalom said to Hushai, Is this thy kindness to thy friend? why wentest thou not with thy friend? And Hushai said unto Absalom, Nay; but whom the LORD, and this people, and all the men of Israel, choose, his will I be, and with him will I abide. And again, whom should I serve? should I not serve in the presence of his son? as I have served in thy father's presence, so will I be in thy presence. Then said Absalom to Ahithophel, Give counsel among you what we shall do. And Ahithophel said unto Absalom, Go in unto thy father's concubines, which he hath left to keep the house; and all Israel shall hear that thou art abhorred of thy father: then shall the hands

of all that are with thee be strong. So they spread Absalom a tent upon the top of the house; and Absalom went in unto his father's concubines in the sight of all Israel. And the counsel of Ahithophel, which he counselled in those days, was as if a man had enquired at the oracle of God: so was all the counsel of Ahithophel both with David and with Absalom.

from ABSALOM AND ACHITOPHEL

JOHN DRYDEN

ll. 142–219

Some by their friends, more by themselves thought wise,
Opposed the power, to which they could not rise.
Some had in courts been great, and thrown from thence,
Like fiends, were hardened in impenitence.
Some by their monarch's fatal mercy grown,
From pardoned rebels, kinsmen to the throne;
Were raised in power and public office high:
Strong bands, if bands ungrateful men could tie.
Of these the false Achitophel was first:
A name to all succeeding ages cursed.
For close designs, and crooked counsels fit;
Sagacious, bold, and turbulent of wit:
Restless, unfixed in principles and place;
In power unpleased, impatient of disgrace.
A fiery soul, which working out its way,
Fretted the pigmy body to decay:
And o'er informed the tenement of clay.
A daring pilot in extremity;
Pleased with the danger, when the waves went high
He sought the storms; but for a calm unfit,
Would steer too nigh the sands, to boast his wit.
Great wits are sure to madness near allied;
And thin partitions do their bounds divide:
Else, why should he, with wealth and honor blessed,
Refuse his age the needful hours of rest?
Punish a body which he could not please;
Bankrupt of life, yet prodigal of ease?
And all to leave, what with his toil he won,
To that unfeathered, two-legged thing, a son:
Got, while his soul did huddled notions try;
And born a shapeless lump, like anarchy.
In friendship false, implacable in hate:
Resolved to ruin or to rule the State.
To compass this the triple bond he broke;

The pillars of the public safety shook:
And fitted Israel for a foreign yoke.
Then, seized with fear, yet still affecting fame,
Usurped a patriot's all-atoning name.
So easy still it proves in factious times,
With public zeal to cancel private crimes:
How safe is treason, and how sacred ill,
Where none can sin against the peoples will:
Where crowds can wink; and no offence be known,
Since in anothers guilt they find their own.
Yet, fame deserved, no enemy can grudge;
The statesman we abhor, but praise the judge.
In Israels courts ne'er sat an Abbethdin
With more discerning eyes, or hands more clean:
Unbribed, unsought, the wretched to redress;
Swift of dispatch, and easy of access.
Oh, had he been content to serve the crown,
With virtues only proper to the gown;
Or, had the rankness of the soil been freed
From cockle, that oppressed the noble seed:
David, for him his tuneful harp had strung,
And Heaven had wanted one immortal song.
But wild ambition loves to slide, not stand;
And fortune's ice prefers to virtue's land:
Achitophel, grown weary to possess
A lawful fame, and lazy happiness;
Disdained the golden fruit to gather free,
And lent the crowd his arm to shake the tree.
Now, manifest of crimes, contrived long since,
He stood at bold defiance with his prince:
Held up the buckler of the peoples cause,
Against the crown; and skulked behind the laws.
The wished occasion of the plot he takes,
Some circumstances finds, but more he makes.
By buzzing emissaries, fills the ears
Of listening crowds, with jealousies and fears
Of arbitrary counsels brought to light,
And proves the King himself a Jebusite:
Weak arguments! which yet he knew full well,
Were strong with people easy to rebel.
For, governed by the Moon, the giddy Jews
Tread the same track when she the prime renews:
And once in twenty years, their scribes record,
By natural instinct they change their Lord.

23:8–17 These be the names of the mighty men whom David had: . . . And three of the thirty chief went down, and came to David in the harvest time unto the cave of Adullam: and the troop of the Philistines pitched in the valley of Rephaim. And David was then in an hold, and the garrison of the Philistines was then in Bethlehem. And David longed, and said, Oh that one would give me drink of the water of the well of Bethlehem, which is by the gate! And the three mighty men brake through the host of the Philistines, and drew water out of the well of Bethlehem, that was by the gate, and took it, and brought it to David: nevertheless he would not drink thereof, but poured it out unto the LORD. And he said, Be it far from me, O LORD, that I should do this: is not this the blood of the men that went in jeopardy of their lives? therefore he would not drink it. These things did these three mighty men.

David in the Cave of Adullam

Charles Lamb

David and his three captains bold
Kept ambush once within a hold.
It was in Adullam's cave,
Nigh which no water they could have,
Nor spring, nor running brook was near
To quench the thirst that parched them there.
Then David, king of Israel,
Straight bethought him of a well,
Which stood beside the city gate,
At Bethlem; where, before his state
Of kingly dignity, he had
Oft drunk his fill, a shepherd lad;
But now his fierce Philistine foe
Encamped before it he does know.
Yet ne'er the less, with heat oppressed,
Those three bold captains he addressed;
And wished that one to him would bring
Some water from his native spring.
His valiant captains instantly
To execute his will did fly.
The mighty Three the ranks broke through
Of armed foes, and water drew
For David, their beloved king,
At his own sweet native spring.
Back through their armed foes they haste,
With the hard-earned treasure graced.
But when the good king David found

What they had done, he on the ground
The water poured. "Because," said he,
"That it was at the jeopardy
Of your three lives this thing ye did,
That I should drink it, God forbid."

The First Book of the KINGS

COMMONLY CALLED THE THIRD BOOK OF THE KINGS

COMBINED WITH

The First and Second Books of the CHRONICLES

1 KINGS 1:1–4 Now king David was old and stricken in years; and they covered him with clothes, but he gat no heat. Wherefore his servants said unto him, Let there be sought for my lord the king a young virgin: and let her stand before the king, and let her cherish him, and let her lie in thy bosom, that my lord the king may get heat. So they sought for a fair damsel throughout all the coasts of Israel, and found Abishag a Shunammite, and brought her to the king. And the damsel was very fair, and cherished the king, and ministered to him: but the king knew her not.

Provide, Provide

Robert Frost

The witch that came (the withered hag)
To wash the steps with pail and rag
Was once the beauty Abishag,

The picture pride of Hollywood.
Too many fall from great and good
For you to doubt the likelihood.

Die early and avoid the fate
Or if predestined to die late
Make up your mind to die in state.

Make the whole stock exchange your own!
If need be, occupy a throne,
Where nobody can call *you* crone.

Some have relied on what they knew,
Others on simply being true.
What worked for them might work for you.

No memory of having starred
Atones for later disregard
Or keeps the end from being hard.

Better to go down dignified
With boughten friendship at your side
Than none at all. Provide, provide!

1 KINGS 1:5–31 . . . And Bathsheba went in unto the king into the chamber: and the king was very old; and Abishag the Shunammite ministered unto the king. And Bathsheba bowed, and did obeisance unto the king. And the king said, What wouldest thou? And she said unto him, My lord, thou swarest by the LORD thy God unto thine handmaid, saying, Assuredly Solomon thy son shall reign after me, and he shall sit upon my throne. . . . And the king sware, and said, As the LORD liveth, that hath redeemed my soul out of all distress, Even as I sware unto thee by the LORD God of Israel, saying, Assuredly Solomon thy son shall reign after me, and he shall sit upon my throne in my stead; even so will I certainly do this day. Then Bathsheba bowed with her face to the earth, and did reverence to the king, and said, Let my lord king David live for ever.

DAVID AND BATHSHEBA IN THE PUBLIC GARDEN

ROBERT LOWELL

1. David to Bathsheba

"Worn out of virtue, as the time of year,
The burning City and its bells surround
The Public Garden. What is sound
Past agony is fall:
The children crowding home from school at five,
Punting a football in the bricky air—
You mourn Uriah? If he were alive,
O Love, my age were nothing but the ball
Of leaves inside this lion-fountain, left
For witch and winter." "Yet the leaves' complaint
Is the King's fall . . . whatever suffers theft."
"The Latin labels on the foreign trees are quaint.

The trees, for decades, shook their discontent
On strangers; rustling, rustling the Levant."
"Uriah might have found the want
Of what was never his
A moment, found the falling colors welcome."
"But he was dead before Jehovah sent
Our shadows to the lion's cave. What's come
Is dancing like a leaf for nothing. Kiss:
The leaves are dark and harp." "My Lord, observe
The shedding, park-bound mallards, how they keep
Circling and diving for Uriah's sleep;
Driven, derided, David, and my will a curve.

The fountain's falling waters ring around
The garden." "Love, if you had stayed my hand
Uriah would not understand
The lion's rush, or why
This stone-mouthed fountain laps us like a cat."
"And he is nothing after death but ground,
Anger and anguish, David? When we sat
The nights of summer out, the gravity
Of reaching for the moon. . . . Perhaps it took
Of fall, the Fall?" "Perhaps, I live. I lie
Drinking our likeness from the water. Look:
The Lion's mane and age! Surely, I will not die."

2. Bathsheba's Lament in the Garden

Baring the mares'-nests that the squirrels set
To tangle with the wood-winds of the North,
October blows to wood . . . the fourth
Since David broke our vows
And married Abishag to warm him. Cold!
The pigeons bluer with it, since we met
Beside the lion-fountain, and unrolled
The tackle of our model boats. Our prows
Were sworded as the marlin, and they locked,
Clearing the mallards' grotto, half a mile
Up pond—and foundered; and our splashing mocked
The lion's wrinkled brow. My Love, a little while,

The lion frothed into the basin . . . all,
Water to water—water that begets
A child from water. And the jets
That washed our bodies drowned
The curses of Uriah when he died
For David; still a stranger! *Not-at-all*,
We called him, after the withdrawing tide
Of Joab's armor-bearers slew him, and he found
Jehovah, the whale's belly of the pit.
He is the childless, the unreconciled
Master of darkness. Will Uriah sit
And judge? You nod and babble. But, you are a child;

At last, a child—what we were playing, when
We blew our bubbles at the moon, and fought
Like brothers, and the lion caught
The moonbeams in its jaws.
The harvest moon, earth's friend, that cared so much
For us and cared so little, comes again;
Always a stranger! Farther from my touch,
The mountains of the moon . . . whatever claws
The harp-strings chalks the harper's fingers. Cold
The eyelid drooping on the lion's eye
Of David, child of fortune. I am old;
God is ungirded; open! I must surely die.

1 KINGS 2:1–11 Now the days of David drew nigh that he should die; and he charged Solomon his son, saying, I go the way of all the earth: be thou strong therefore, and shew thyself a man; And keep the charge of the LORD thy God, to walk in his ways, to keep his statutes, and his commandments, and his judgments, and his testimonies, as it is written in the law of Moses, that thou mayest prosper in all that thou doest, and whithersoever thou turnest thyself: That the LORD may continue his word which he spake concerning me, saying, If thy children take heed to their way, to walk before me in truth with all their heart and with all their soul, there shall not fail thee (said he) a man on the throne of Israel. . . .

So David slept with his fathers, and was buried in the city of David. And the days that David reigned over Israel were forty years: seven years reigned he in Hebron, and thirty and three years reigned he in Jerusalem.

In Salem Dwelt a Glorious King

Thomas Traherne

In Salem dwelt a glorious king,
Raised from a shepherd's lowly state,
That did his praises like an angel sing
Who did the world create.
By many great and bloody wars,
He was advanced unto thrones:
But more delighted in the stars,
Than in the splendor of his precious stones.
Nor gold nor silver did his eye regard:
The works of God were his sublime reward.

A warlike champion he had been,
And many feats of chivalry
Had done: in kingly courts his eye had seen
A vast variety
Of earthly joys: Yet he despised
Those fading honors and false pleasures
Which are by mortals so much prized;
And placed his happiness in other treasures.
No state of life which in this world we find
Could yield contentment to his greater mind.

His fingers touched his trembling lyre,
And every quavering string did yield

A sound that filled all the Jewish choir,
And echoed in the field.
No pleasure was so great to him
As in a silent night to see
The moon and stars: a cherubim
Above them even here he seemed to be.
Enflamed with love, it was his great desire
To sing, contemplate, ponder, and admire.

He was a prophet, and foresaw
Things extant in the world to come:
He was a judge, and ruled by a law
That than the honey comb
Was sweeter far: He was a sage,
And all his people could advise;
An oracle, whose every page
Contained in verse the greatest mysteries
But most he then enjoyed himself when he
Did as a poet praise the Deity.

A shepherd, soldier, and divine,
A judge, a courtier, and a king,
Priest, angel, prophet, oracle, did shine
At once; when he did sing.
Philosopher and poet too
Did in his melody appear;
All these in him did please the view
Of those that did his heavenly music hear,
And every drop that from his flowing quill
Came down, did all the world with nectar fill.

He had a deep and perfect sense
Of all the glories and the pleasures
That in God's works are hid, the excellence
Of such transcendent treasures
Made him on Earth an heavenly king,
And filled his solitudes with joy;
He never did more sweetly sing
Than when alone, though that doth mirth destroy:
Sense did his soul with heavenly life inspire
And made him seem in God's celestial choir.

Rich, sacred, deep, and precious things
Did here on Earth the man surround:
With all the glory of the King of Kings
He was most strangely crowned.
His clear soul and open sight
Among the sons of God did see
Things filling angels with delight
His ear did hear their heavenly melody
And when he was alone he all became
That bliss implied, or did increase his fame.

All arts he then did exercise
And as his God he did adore,
By secret ravishments above the skies
He carried was, before
He died. His soul did see and feel
What others know not; and became
While he before his God did kneel,
A constant heavenly pure seraphic flame.
O that I might unto his throne aspire;
And all his joys above the stars admire!

THE HARP THE MONARCH MINSTREL SWEPT

GEORGE NOEL GORDON, LORD BYRON

The harp the monarch minstrel swept,
The king of men, the loved of Heaven,
Which music hallowed while she wept
O'er tones her heart of hearts had given,
Redoubled be her tears, its chords are riven!
It softened men of iron mould,
It gave them virtues not their own;
No ear so dull, no soul so cold,
That felt not, fired not to the tone,
Till David's lyre grew mightier than his throne!

It told the triumphs of our king,
    It wafted glory to our God;
It made our gladdened valleys ring,
    The cedars bow, the mountains nod;
    Its sound aspired to heaven and there abode!
Since then, though heard on earth no more,
    Devotion and her daughter Love
Still bid the bursting spirit soar
    To sounds that seem as from above,
    In dreams that day's broad light can not remove.

1 KINGS 3:5–4:33 In Gibeon the LORD appeared to Solomon in a dream by night: and God said, Ask what I shall give thee.

And Solomon said, . . . O LORD my God, thou hast made thy servant king instead of David my father: and I am but a little child: I know not how to go out or come in. . . . Give therefore thy servant an understanding heart to judge thy people, that I may discern between good and bad: for who is able to judge this thy so great a people?

. . . . And God gave Solomon wisdom and understanding exceeding much, and largeness of heart, even as the sand that is on the sea shore. And Solomon's wisdom excelled the wisdom of all the children of the east country, and all the wisdom of Egypt. . . . And he spake three thousand proverbs: and his songs were a thousand and five. And he spake of trees, from the cedar tree that is in Lebanon even unto the hyssop that springeth out of the wall: he spake also of beasts, and of fowl, and of creeping things, and of fishes.

O to be a Dragon

Marianne Moore

If I, like Solomon, . . .
could have my wish—

my wish . . . O to be a dragon,
a symbol of the power of Heaven—of silkworm
size or immense; at times invisible.
Felicitous phenomenon!

1 KINGS 6:15–7:51 So Solomon built the house, and finished it. And he built the walls of the house within with boards of cedar, . . . and he covered them on the inside with wood, and covered the floor of the house with planks of fir. . . . And the cedar of the house within was carved with knops and open flowers: all was cedar; there was no stone seen. And the oracle he prepared in the house within, to set there the ark of the covenant of the LORD. . . .

So Solomon overlaid the house within with pure gold: and he made a partition by the chains of gold before the oracle; and he overlaid it with gold. And the whole house he overlaid with gold, until he had finished all the house: also the whole altar that was by the oracle he overlaid with gold. . . .

So was ended all the work that king Solomon made for the house of the LORD. And Solomon brought in the things which David his father had dedicated; even the silver, and the gold, and the vessels, did he put among the treasures of the house of the LORD.

Sion

George Herbert

Lord, with what glory wast thou served of old,
When Solomon's temple stood and flourished!
    Where most things were of purest gold;
    The wood was all embellished
With flowers and carvings, mystical and rare:
All showed the builders, craved the seers care.

Yet all this glory, all this pomp and state
Did not affect thee much, was not thy aim;
    Something there was, that sowed debate:
    Wherefore thou quitt'st thy ancient claim
And now thy architecture meets with sin;
For all thy frame and fabric is within.

There thou art struggling with a peevish heart,
Which sometimes crosseth thee, thou sometimes it:
    The fight is hard on either part.
    Great God doth fight, he doth submit.
All Solomon's sea of brass and world of stone
Is not so dear to thee as one good groan.

And truly brass and stones are heavy things,
Tombs for the dead, not temples fit for thee:
    But groans are quick, and full of wings,
    And all their motions upward be;
And ever as they mount, like larks they sing;
The note is sad, yet music for a king.

1 KINGS 10:1–8 And when the queen of Sheba heard of the fame of Solomon concerning the name of the LORD, she came to prove him with hard questions. And she came to Jerusalem with a very great train, with camels that bare spices, and very much gold, and precious stones: and when she was come to Solomon, she communed with him of all that was in her heart. And Solomon told her all her questions: there was not any thing hid from the king, which he told her not. And when the queen of Sheba had seen all Solomon's wisdom. . . she said to the king, It was a true report that I heard in mine own land of thy acts and of thy wisdom. . . . Happy are thy men, happy are these thy servants, which stand continually before thee, and that hear thy wisdom.

King Solomon and the Ants

John Greenleaf Whittier

Out from Jerusalem
    The King rode with his great
    War chiefs and lords of state,
And Sheba's queen with them;

Comely, but black withal,
    To whom, perchance, belongs
    That wondrous Song of songs,
Sensuous and mystical,

Whereto devout souls turn
    In fond, ecstatic dream,
    And through its earth-born theme
The Love of loves discern.

Proud in the Syrian sun,
    In gold and purple sheen,
    The dusky Ethiop queen
Smiled on King Solomon.

Wisest of men, he knew
    The languages of all
    The creatures great or small
That trod the earth or flew.

Across an ant-hill led
    The king's path, and he heard
    Its small folk, and their word
He thus interpreted:

"Here comes the king men greet
    As wise and good and just,
    To crush us in the dust
Under his heedless feet."

The great king bowed his head,
    And saw the wide surprise
    Of the Queen of Sheba's eyes
As he told her what they said.

"O king!" she whispered sweet,
    "Too happy fate have they
    Who perish in thy way
Beneath thy gracious feet!

"Thou of the God-lent crown,
    Shall these vile creatures dare
    Murmur against thee where
The knees of kings kneel down?"

"Nay," Solomon replied,
    "The wise and strong should seek
    The welfare of the weak,"
And turned his horse aside.

His train, with quick alarm
    Curved with their leader round
    The ant-hill's peopled mound
And left it free from harm.

The jewelled head bent low;
    "O king!" she said, "henceforth
    The secret of thy worth
And wisdom I well know.

"Happy must be the state
    Whose ruler heedeth more
    The murmurs of the poor
Than the flatteries of the great."

1 KINGS 10:10–13 And she gave the king an hundred and twenty talents of gold, and of spices very great store, and precious stones: there came no more such abundance of spices as these which the queen of Sheba gave to king Solomon. . . . And king Solomon gave unto the queen of Sheba all her desire, whatsoever she asked, beside that which Solomon gave her of his royal bounty. So she turned and went to her own country, she and her servants.

Solomon and the Witch

William Butler Yeats

And thus declared that Arab lady:
'Last night, where under the wild moon
On grassy mattress I had laid me,
Within my arms great Solomon,
I suddenly cried out in a strange tongue
Not his, not mine.'
                    Who understood
Whatever has been said, sighed, sung,
Howled, miau-d, barked, brayed, belled, yelled, cried, crowed,
Thereon replied: 'A cockerel
Crew from a blossoming apple bough
Three hundred years before the Fall,
And never crew again till now,
And would not now but that he thought,
Chance being at one with Choice at last,
All that the brigand apple brought

And this foul world were dead at last.
He that crowed out eternity
Thought to have crowed it in again.
For though love has a spider's eye
To find out some appropriate pain—
Aye, though all passion's in the glance—
For every nerve, and tests a lover
With cruelties of Choice and Chance;
And when at last that murder's over
Maybe the bride-bed brings despair,
For each an imagined image brings
And finds a real image there;
Yet the world ends when these two things,
Though several, are a single light,
When oil and wick are burned in one;
Therefore a blessed moon last night
Gave Sheba to her Solomon.'

'Yet the world stays.'
'If that be so,
Your cockerel found us in the wrong
Although he thought it worth a crow.
Maybe an image is too strong
Or maybe is not strong enough.'

'The night has fallen; not a sound
In the forbidden sacred grove
Unless a petal hit the ground,
Nor any human sight within it
But the crushed grass where we have lain;
And the moon is wilder every minute.
O! Solomon! let us try again.'

1 KINGS 10:14–19 Now the weight of gold that came to Solomon in one year was six hundred threescore and six talents of gold, Beside that he had of the merchantmen, and of the traffic of the spice merchants, and of all the kings of Arabia, and of the governors of the country. And king Solomon made two hundred targets of beaten gold: six hundred shekels of gold went to one target. And he made three hundred shields of beaten

gold; three pound of gold went to one shield: and the king put them in the house of the forest of Lebanon. Moreover the king made a great throne of ivory, and overlaid it with the best gold. The throne had six steps, and the top of the throne was round behind: and there were stays on either side on the place of the seat, and two lions stood beside the stays.

Solomon and Balkis

Robert Browning

Solomon King of the Jews and the Queen of Sheba, Balkis,
Talk on the ivory throne, and we well may conjecture their talk is
Solely of things sublime: why else has she sought Mount Zion,
Climbed the six golden steps, and sat betwixt lion and lion?

She proves him with hard questions: before she has reached the middle
He smiling supplies the end, straight solves them riddle by riddle;
Until dead-beaten at last, there is left no spirit in her,
And thus she would close the game whereof she was the first beginner:

'O wisest thou of the wise, world's marvel and well-nigh monster,
One crabbèd question more to construe or *vulgo* conster!
Who are those, of all mankind, a monarch of perfect wisdom
Should open to, when they knock at *spheteron do* – that's his dome?'

The King makes tart reply: 'Whom else but the wise his equals
Should he welcome with heart and voice? – since, king though he be,
such weak walls
Of circumstance – power and pomp – divide souls from each other
That whoso proves kingly in craft I must needs acknowledge my
brother.

'Come poet, come painter, come sculptor, come builder – whate'er his
condition,
Is he prime in his art? We are peers! My insight has pierced the partition
And hails – for the poem, the picture, the statue, the building – my
fellow!
Gold's gold though dim in the dust: court-polish soon turns it yellow.

'But tell me in turn, O thou to thy weakling sex superior,
That for knowledge hast travelled so far yet seemest no whit the
wearier, –
Who are those, of all mankind, a queen like thyself, consummate
In wisdom, should call to her side with an affable "Up hither, come,
mate!" '

'The Good are my mates – how else? Why doubt it?' the Queen
upbridled:
'Sure even above the Wise, – or in travel my eyes have idled, –
I see the Good stand plain: be they rich, poor, shrewd or simple,
If Good they only are. . . . Permit me to drop my wimple!'

And in that bashful jerk of her body, she – peace, thou scoffer! –
Jostled the King's right-hand stretched courteously help to proffer,
And so disclosed a portent: all unaware the Prince eyed
The Ring which bore the Name – turned outside now from inside!

The truth-compelling Name! – and at once 'I greet the Wise – Oh,
Certainly welcome such to my court – with this proviso:
The building must be my temple, my person stand forth the statue,
The picture my portrait prove, and the poem my praise – you cat, you!'

But Solomon nonplussed? Nay! 'Be truthful in turn!' so bade he:
'See the Name, obey its hest!' And at once subjoins the lady
– 'Provided the Good are the young, men strong and tall and proper,
Such servants I straightway enlist, – which means . . .' but the blushes
stop her.

'Ah, Soul, the Monarch sighed, 'that wouldst soar yet ever crawlest,
How comes it thou canst discern the greatest yet choose the smallest,
Unless because heaven is far, where wings find fit expansion,
While creeping on all-fours suits, suffices the earthly mansion?

'Aspire to the Best! But which? There are Bests and Bests so many,
With a *habitat* each for each, earth's Best as much Best as any!
On Lebanon roots the cedar – soil lofty, yet stony and sandy –
While hyssop, of worth in its way, on the wall grows low but handy.

'Above may the Soul spread wing, spurn body and sense beneath her;
Below she must condescend to plodding unbuoyed by aether.
In heaven I yearn for knowledge, account all else inanity;
On earth I confess an itch for the praise of fools – that's Vanity.

'It is naught, it will go, it can never presume above to trouble me;
But here, – why, it toys and tickles and teases, howe'er I redouble me
In a doggedest of endeavours to play the indifferent. Therefore,
Suppose we resume discourse? Thou hast travelled thus far: but
wherefore?

'Solely for Solomon's sake, to see whom earth styles Sagest?'
Through her blushes laughed the Queen: 'For the sake of a Sage? The gay jest!
On high, be communion with Mind – there, Body concerns not Balkis:
Down here, – do I make too bold? Sage Solomon, – one fool's small kiss!'

1 KINGS 19:1–13 . . . And he said, Go forth, and stand upon the mount before the LORD. And, behold, the LORD passed by, and a great and strong wind rent the mountains, and brake in pieces the rocks before the LORD; but the LORD was not in the wind: and after the wind an earthquake; but the LORD was not in the earthquake: And after the earthquake a fire; but the LORD was not in the fire: and after the fire a still small voice.

And it was so, when Elijah heard it, that he wrapped his face in his mantle, and went out, and stood in the entering in of the cave. And, behold, there came a voice unto him, and said, What doest thou here, Elijah?

A Successful Summer

DAVID SCHUBERT

The still small voice unto
My still small voice, I listen.
Hardly awake, I breathe, vulnerably,
As in summer trees, the messages
Of telegraphed errands buzz along
July's contour of green.

The Second Book of the
KINGS

COMMONLY CALLED THE THIRD BOOK OF THE KINGS

COMBINED WITH

The First and Second Books of the
CHRONICLES

2 KINGS 2:1–11 . . . And it came to pass, when they were gone over, that Elijah said unto Elisha, Ask what I shall do for thee, before I be taken away from thee. And Elisha said, I pray thee, let a double portion of thy spirit be upon me. And he said, Thou hast asked a hard thing: nevertheless, if thou see me when I am taken from thee, it shall be so unto thee; but if not, it shall not be so. And it came to pass, as they still went on, and talked, that, behold, there appeared a chariot of fire, and horses of fire, and parted them both asunder; and Elijah went up by a whirlwind into heaven.

AND DID THOSE FEET

WILLIAM BLAKE

And did those feet in ancient time
Walk upon England's mountains green?
And was the holy Lamb of God
On England's pleasant pastures seen?

And did the Countenance Divine
Shine forth upon our clouded hills?
And was Jerusalem builded here
Among these dark Satanic Mills?

Bring me my bow of burning gold:
Bring me my Arrows of desire:
Bring me my Spear: O clouds unfold!
Bring me my Chariot of fire.

I will not cease from Mental Fight,
Nor shall my Sword sleep in my hand
Till we have built Jerusalem
In England's green and pleasant Land.

"Would to God that all the Lord's people were Prophets."
Numbers, xi. ch., 29 v.

2 KINGS 2:12–14 And Elisha saw it, and he cried, My father, my father, the chariot of Israel, and the horsemen thereof. And he saw him no more: and he took hold of his own clothes, and rent them in two pieces. He took up also the mantle of Elijah that fell from him, and went back, and stood by the bank of Jordan; And he took the mantle of Elijah that fell from him, and smote the waters, and said, Where is the LORD God of Elijah? and when he also had smitten the waters, they parted hither and thither: and Elisha went over.

Elijah's Wagon knew no thill

EMILY DICKINSON

Elijah's Wagon knew no thill
Was innocent of Wheel
Elijah's horses as unique
As was his vehicle –

Elijah's journey to portray
Expire with him the skill
Who justified Elijah
In feats inscrutable –

2 KINGS 4:8–36 . . . So she went and came unto the man of God to mount Carmel. And it came to pass, when the man of God saw her afar off, that he said to Gehazi his servant, Behold, yonder is that Shunammite: Run now, I pray thee, to meet her, and say unto her, Is it well with thee? is it well with thy husband? is it well with the child? And she answered, It is well: . . . And when Elisha was come into the house,

behold, the child was dead, and laid upon his bed. He went in therefore, and shut the door upon them twain, and prayed unto the LORD. And he went up, and lay upon the child, and put his mouth upon his mouth, and his eyes upon his eyes, and his hands upon his hands: and stretched himself upon the child; and the flesh of the child waxed warm. Then he returned, and walked in the house to and fro; and went up, and stretched himself upon him: and the child sneezed seven times, and the child opened his eyes. And he called Gehazi, and said, Call this Shunammite. So he called her. And when she was come in unto him, he said, Take up thy son.

Another to Urania

On the Death of her First and Only Child

Benjamin Colman

Attend, ye mournful parents, while
I sing, a Mother in Israel;
The famed, the gracious Shunammite,
Whose beauteous story would invite
A saint to yield her only one,
Almost without a tear or groan.
A wondrous son she did embrace,
Heaven's signal work, and special grace;
Nor long embraced, but on her knees
Arrested by a fierce disease,
Scarce could he cry, *My Head, My Head!*
E'er the dear parent saw him dead:
She laid him breathless on the bed.
Deep was her anguish, yet her peace
She held, and went to God for ease.
No signs of grief distort her face,
Nor cloud its wonted beams of grace.
No moans, no shrieks, no piercing cries;
No wringed hands, or flowing eyes
Distressed the house in that surprise.
She hastes her to the Man of God,
Hastes to the place of his abode:
Mildly denies the cause to tell
To her dear spouse; all would be well
She trusts: so did her faith excel.
Elisha, with a tender fear,
Saw his illustrious friend draw near:

'Twas not one of the Holy Days
Sacred to public prayer and praise;
Why then the Shunammite from home?
On what great errand was she come?
Her speed bespoke some weighty care,
Which generous friendship longed to share.
It struck him, something had befell
The husband, child,—*All was not well*—
Go, run Gehazi, said the Seer,
Enquire, with earnestness sincere;
"Say, generous host, if all be well?—
"*All's well;* my Lord! she said, and fell
At her great intercessor's feet:
There vents her grief in accents sweet,
Mild in her anguish, in her plaints discreet.
Such dear Urania, you to me!
O might I be but such to thee!
Mind, gracious friend, the word she said,
All well, and yet the child was dead.
What God ordains is well and best.
Well 'tis with ours, when gone to rest.
It's well with us, who stay behind,
If more from earth and sense refined
We're patient, prayerful, meek, resigned.

2 KINGS 5:9–14 So Naaman came with his horses and with his chariot, and stood at the door of the house of Elisha. And Elisha sent a messenger unto him, saying, Go and wash in Jordan seven times, and thy flesh shall come again to thee, and thou shalt be clean. But Naaman was wroth, and went away, and said, Behold, I thought, He will surely come out to me, and stand, and call on the name of the LORD his God, and strike his hand over the place, and recover the leper. Are not Abana and Pharpar, rivers of Damascus, better than all the waters of Israel? may I not wash in them, and be clean? So he turned and went away in a rage. And his servants came near, and spake unto him, and said, My father, if the prophet had bid thee do some great thing, wouldest thou not have done it? how much rather then, when he saith to thee, Wash, and be clean? Then went he down, and dipped himself seven times in Jordan, according to the saying of the man of God: and his flesh came again like unto the flesh of a little child, and he was clean.

Naaman's Song

RUDYARD KIPLING

"Go wash thyself in Jordan—go, wash thee and be clean!"
Nay, not for any Prophet will I plunge a toe therein!
For the banks of curious Jordan are parcelled into sites,
Commanded and embellished and patrolled by Israelites.

There rise her timeless capitals of Empires daily born,
Whose plinths are laid at midnight, and whose streets are packed at
morn;
And here come hired youths and maids that feign to love or sin
In tones like rusty razor-blades to tunes like smitten tin.

And here be merry murtherings, and steeds with fiery hooves;
And furious hordes with guns and swords, and clamberings over rooves;
And horrid tumblings down from Heaven, and flights with wheels and
wings;
And always one weak virgin who is chased through all these things.

And here is mock of faith and truth, for children to behold;
And every door of ancient dirt reopened to the old;
With every word that taints the speech, and show that weakens thought;
And Israel watcheth over each, and —doth not watch for nought. . . .

But Pharpar — but Abana —which Hermon launcheth down—
They perish fighting desert sands beyond Damascus-town.
But yet their pulse is of the snows—their strength is from on high—
And, if they cannot cure my woes, a leper will I die!

2 KINGS 6:8–16 Then the king of Syria warred against Israel, and took counsel with his servants, saying, In such and such a place shall be my camp. And the man of God sent unto the king of Israel, saying, Beware that thou pass not such a place; for thither the Syrians are come down. And the king of Israel sent to the place which the man of God told him and warned him of, and saved himself there, not once nor twice. Therefore the heart of the king of Syria was sore troubled for this thing; and he called his servants, and said unto them, Will ye not shew me which of us is for the king of Israel? And one of his servants said, None, my lord, O king: but Elisha, the prophet that is in Israel, telleth the king of Israel the words that thou speakest in thy bedchamber. And he said, Go and spy

where he is, that I may send and fetch him. And it was told him, saying, Behold, he is in Dothan.

Therefore sent he thither horses, and chariots, and a great host: and they came by night, and compassed the city about. And when the servant of the man of God was risen early, and gone forth, behold, an host compassed the city both with horses and chariots. And his servant said unto him, Alas, my master! how shall we do? And he answered, Fear not: for they that be with us are more than they that be with them.

FEAR NOT: FOR THEY THAT BE WITH US

JONES VERY

The wicked and the base do compass round
The meek and humble in their righteous way,
And with fierce onset and the trumpet's sound
They seek the servants of the Lord to slay;
They trust in wealth, or in the cruel sword,
Vain idols that cannot defend, or save!
They fear no threatenings of God's holy Word,
But, trusting in themselves alone, are brave.
But though no human help the righteous know,
They fear not in the last, the trying hour;
God, through His gracious love, to them doth
The unseen hosts and ensigns of His power,
Who compass them about on every side,
In whose protection they may safe confide.

2 KINGS 9:30–37 **And in the eleventh year of Joram the son of Ahab began Ahaziah to reign over Judah. And when Jehu was come to Jezreel, Jezebel heard of it; and she painted her face, and tired her head, and looked out at a window. And as Jehu entered in at the gate, she said, Had Zimri peace, who slew his master? And he lifted up his face to the window, and said, Who is on my side? who? And there looked out to him two or three eunuchs. And he said, Throw her down. So they threw her down: and some of her blood was sprinkled on the wall, and on the horses: and he trode her under foot. And when he was come in, he did eat and drink, and said, Go, see now this cursed woman, and bury her: for she is a king's daughter. And they went to bury her: but they found no more of her than the skull, and the feet, and the palms of her hands. Wherefore they came again, and told him. And he said, This is the word of the LORD, which he spake by his servant Elijah the Tishbite, saying, In the portion of Jezreel shall dogs eat the flesh of Jezebel: And the carcase of**

Jezebel shall be as dung upon the face of the field in the portion of Jezreel; so that they shall not say, This is Jezebel.

Song for the Clatter-bones

F. R. Higgins

God rest that Jewy woman,
Queen Jezebel, the bitch
Who peeled the clothes from her shoulder-bones
Down to her spent teats
As she stretched out of the window
Among the geraniums, where
She chaffed and laughed like one half daft
Titivating her painted hair—

King Jehu he drove to her,
She tipped him a fancy beck;
But he from his knacky side-car spoke,
"Who will break that dewlapped neck?"
And so she was thrown from the window;
Like Lucifer she fell
Beneath the feet of the horses and they beat
The light out of Jezebel.

That corpse wasn't planted in clover;
Ah, nothing of her was found
Save those grey bones that Hare-foot Mike
Gave me for their lovely sound;
And as once her dancing body
Made star-lit princes sweat,
So I'll just clack: though her ghost lacks a back
There's music in the old bones yet.

2 CHRONICLES 29:1–25 Hezekiah began to reign when he was five and twenty years old, and he reigned nine and twenty years in Jerusalem. . . . And he did that which was right in the sight of the LORD, according to all that David his father had done. He in the first year of his reign, in the first month, opened the doors of the house of the LORD, and repaired them. And he brought in the priests and the Levites, and gathered them together into the east street, And said unto them, Hear me, ye Levites, sanctify now yourselves, and sanctify the house of the LORD God of your

fathers, and carry forth the filthiness out of the holy place. . . .

Then Hezekiah the king rose early, and gathered the rulers of the city, and went up to the house of the LORD. And the priests . . . made . . . an atonement for all Israel: for the king commanded that the burnt offering and the sin offering should be made for all Israel. And he set the Levites in the house of the LORD with cymbals, with psalteries, and with harps, according to the commandment of David, and of Gad the king's seer, and Nathan the prophet.

from HEZEKIAH

THOMAS PARNELL

From the bleak beach and broad expanse of sea,
To lofty Salem, thought direct thy way;
Mount thy light chariot, move along the plains,
And end thy flight where Hezekiah reigns.
How swiftly thought has passed from land to land,
And quite outrun time's measuring glass of sand,
Great Salem's walls appear and I resort
To view the state of Hezekiah's court.
Well may that king a pious verse inspire,
Who cleansed the temple, who revived the choir,
Pleased with the service David fixed before,
That heavenly music might on earth adore.
Deep-robed in white, he made the Levites stand
With cymbals, harps, and psalteries in their hand;
He gave the priests their trumpets, prompt to raise
The tuneful soul, by force of sound to praise.
A skillful master for the song he chose,
The songs were David's these, and Asaph's those.
Then burns their offering, all around rejoice,
Each tunes his instrument to join the voice;
The trumpets sounded, and the singers sung,
The people worshipped and the temple rung.
Each while the victim burns presents his heart,
Then the priest blesses, and the people part.
Hail sacred music! since you know to draw
The soul to Heaven, the spirit to the law,
I come to prove thy force, thy warbling string
May tune my soul to write what others sing.

1 CHRONICLES 4:9–10 And Jabez was more honourable than his brethren: and his mother called his name Jabez, saying, Because I bare him with sorrow. And Jabez called on the God of Israel, saying, Oh that thou wouldest bless me indeed, and enlarge my coast, and that thine hand might be with me, and that thou wouldest keep me from evil, that it may not grieve me! And God granted him that which he requested.

The Prayer of Jabez

JONES VERY

The prayer of Jabez, too, should be our prayer:
"Keep me from evil, that it may not grieve."
How hard the sight of wrong and ill to bear,
When we cannot the sufferers relieve!
The child of sorrow, he for others' woe,
As if it were his own, did deeply feel;
Though he had naught of riches to bestow,
Nor power their wrongs and miseries to heal.
God heard his prayer, and answered his request;
And by his sympathy did help impart
Unto the poor, the suffering, and oppressed,
That healed their wounds and robbed them of their smart;
Nor suffered cruel deeds, nor words unkind,
To grieve his heart, or rankle in his mind.

2 CHRONICLES 32:1–8 After these things, and the establishment thereof, Sennacherib king of Assyria came, and entered into Judah, and encamped against the fenced cities, and thought to win them for himself. And when Hezekiah saw that Sennacherib was come, and that he was purposed to fight against Jerusalem, . . . 2 KINGS 19:15–36 Hezekiah prayed before the LORD. . . . Then Isaiah the son of Amoz sent to Hezekiah, saying, Thus saith the LORD God of Israel, That which thou hast prayed to me against Sennacherib king of Assyria I have heard. . . .

And it came to pass that night, that the angel of the LORD went out, and smote in the camp of the Assyrians an hundred fourscore and five thousand: and when they arose early in the morning, behold, they were all dead corpses.

So Sennacherib king of Assyria departed, and went and returned, and dwelt at Nineveh.

The Destruction of Sennacherib

George Noel Gordon, Lord Byron

The Assyrian came down like the wolf on the fold,
And his cohorts were gleaming in purple and gold;
And the sheen of their spears was like stars on the sea,
When the blue wave rolls nightly on deep Galilee.

Like the leaves of the forest when summer is green,
That host with their banners at sunset were seen:
Like the leaves of the forest when autumn hath blown,
That host on the morrow lay withered and strown.

For the Angel of Death spread his wings on the blast,
And breathed in the face of the foe as he passed;
And the eyes of the sleepers waxed deadly and chill,
And their hearts but once heaved—and for ever grew still!

And there lay the steed with his nostril all wide,
But through it there rolled not the breath of his pride;
And the foam of his gasping lay white on the turf,
And cold as the spray of the rock-beating surf.

And there lay the rider distorted and pale,
With the dew on his brow, and the rust on his mail;
And the tents were all silent, the banners alone,
The lances unlifted, the trumpet unblown.

And the widows of Ashur are loud in their wail,
And the idols are broke in the temples of Baal;
And the might of the Gentile, unsmote by the sword,
Hath melted like snow in the glance of the Lord!

2 KINGS 20:1–11 In those days was Hezekiah sick unto death. And the prophet Isaiah the son of Amoz came to him, and said unto him, Thus saith the LORD, Set thine house in order; for thou shalt die, and not live.

Then he turned his face to the wall, and prayed unto the LORD, saying, I beseech thee, O LORD, remember now how I have walked before thee in truth and with a perfect heart, and have done that which is good in thy sight. And Hezekiah wept sore.

And it came to pass, afore Isaiah was gone out into the middle court, that the word of the LORD came to him, saying, Turn again, and tell Hezekiah the captain of my people, Thus saith the LORD, the God of David thy father, I have heard thy prayer, I have seen thy tears: behold, I will heal thee: on the third day thou shalt go up unto the house of the LORD. . . .

And Hezekiah said unto Isaiah, What shall be the sign that the LORD will heal me, and that I shall go up into the house of the LORD the third day? And Isaiah said, This sign shalt thou have of the LORD, that the LORD will do the thing that he hath spoken: shall the shadow go forward ten degrees, or go back ten degrees?

And Hezekiah answered, It is a light thing for the shadow to go down ten degrees: nay, but let the shadow return backward ten degrees. And Isaiah the prophet cried unto the LORD: and he brought the shadow ten degrees backward, by which it had gone down in the dial of Ahaz.

Hymn to the Supreme Being

Christopher Smart

On recovery from a dangerous fit of illness.

When Israel's ruler on the royal bed
In anguish and in perturbation lay,
The down relieved not his anointed head,
And rest gave place to horror and dismay.
Fast flowed the tears, high heaved each gasping sigh
When God's own prophet thundered—MONARCH, THOU MUST DIE.

'And must I go,' th' illustrious mourner cried,
'I who have served thee still in faith and truth,
Whose snow-white conscience no foul crime has died
From youth to manhood, infancy to youth,
Like David, who have still revered thy word
The sovereign of myself and servant of the Lord!'

The judge Almighty heard his suppliant's moan,
  Repealed his sentence, and his health restored;
The beams of mercy on his temples shone,
  Shot from that heaven to which his sighs had soared;
The sun retreated at his maker's nod
And miracles confirm the genuine work of God.

But, O immortals! What had I to plead
  When death stood o'er me with his threatening lance,
When reason left me in the time of need,
  And sense was lost in terror or in trance,
My sickening soul was with my blood inflamed,
And the celestial image sunk, defaced and maimed.

I sent back memory, in heedful guise,
  To search the records of preceding years;
Home, like the raven to the ark, she flies,
  Croaking bad tidings to my trembling ears.
O Sun, again that thy retreat was made,
And threw my follies back into the friendly shade!

But who are they, that bid affliction cease!—
  Redemption and forgiveness, heavenly sounds!
Behold the dove that brings the branch of peace,
  Behold the balm that heals the gaping wounds—
Vengeance divine's by penitence suppressed—
She struggles with the angel, conquers, and is blessed.

Yet hold, presumption, nor too fondly climb,
  And thou too hold, O horrible despair!
In man humility's alone sublime,
  Who diffidently hopes he's Christ's own care—
O all-sufficient Lamb! in death's dread hour
Thy merits who shall slight, or who can doubt thy power?

But soul-rejoicing health again returns,
  The blood meanders gentle in each vein,
The lamp of life renewed with vigour burns,
  And exiled reason takes her seat again—
Brisk leaps the heart, the mind's at large once more,
To love, to praise, to bless, to wonder and adore.

The virtuous partner of my nuptial bands,
    Appeared a widow to my frantic sight;
My little prattlers lifting up their hands,
    Beckon me back to them, to life, and light;
I come, ye spotless sweets! I come again,
Nor have your tears been shed, nor have ye knelt in vain.

All glory to th' Eternal, to th' Immense,
    All glory to th' Omniscient and Good,
Whose power's uncircumscribed, whose love's intense,
    But yet whose justice ne'er could be withstood.
Except through him—through him, who stands alone,
Of worth, of weight allowed for all Mankind t' atone!

He raised the lame, the lepers he made whole,
    He fixed the palsied nerves of weak decay,
He drove out Satan from the tortured soul,
    And to the blind gave or restored the day,—
Nay more,—far more unequaled pangs sustained,
Till his lost fallen flock his taintless blood regained.

My feeble feet refused my body's weight,
    Nor would my eyes admit the glorious light,
My nerves convulsed shook fearful of their fate,
    My mind lay open to the powers of night.
He pitying did a second birth bestow
A birth of joy—not like the first of tears and woe.

Ye strengthened feet, forth to his altar move;
    Quicken, ye new-strung nerves, th' enraptured lyre;
Ye heaven-directed eyes, o'erflow with love;
    Glow, glow, my soul, with pure seraphic fire;
Deeds, thoughts, and words no more his mandates break,
But to his endless glory work, conceive, and speak.

O! penitence, to virtue near allied,
    Thou canst new joys e'en to the blessed impart;
The listening angels lay their harps aside
    To hear the music of thy contrite heart;
And heaven itself wears a more radiant face,
When charity presents thee to the throne of grace.

Chief of metallic forms is regal gold;
    Of elements, the limpid fount that flows;
Give me 'mongst gems the brilliant to behold;
    O'er Flora's flock imperial is the rose;
Above all birds the sovereign eagle soars;
And monarch of the field the lordly lion roars.

What can with great Leviathan compare,
    Who takes his pastime in the mighty main?
What, like the sun, shines through the realms of air,
    And gilds and glorifies th' ethereal plain—
Yet what are these to man, who bears the sway;
For all was made for him—to serve and to obey.

Thus in high heaven charity is great,
    Faith, hope, devotion hold a lower place;
On her the cherubs and the seraphs wait,
    Her, every virtue courts, and every grace;
See! on the right, close by th' Almighty's throne,
In him she shines confessed, who came to make her known.

Deep-rooted in my heart then let her grow,
    That for the past the future may atone;
That I may act what thou hast given to know,
    That I may live for Thee and Thee alone,
And justify those sweetest words from Heaven,
'THAT HE SHALL LOVE THEE MOST TO WHOM THOU'ST MOST FORGIVEN.'

2 KINGS 20:12–19 At that time Berodachbaladan, the son of Baladan, king of Babylon, sent letters and a present unto Hezekiah: for he had heard that Hezekiah had been sick. And Hezekiah hearkened unto them, and shewed them all the house of his precious things. . . .

Then came Isaiah the prophet unto king Hezekiah, and said unto him, What said these men? and from whence came they unto thee? And Hezekiah said, They are come from a far country, even from Babylon. And he said, What have they seen in thine house? And Hezekiah answered, All the things that are in mine house have they seen: there is nothing among my treasures that I have not shewed them.

And Isaiah said unto Hezekiah, Hear the word of the LORD. Behold, the days come, that all that is in thine house, and that which thy fathers

have laid up in store unto this day, shall be carried into Babylon: nothing shall be left, saith the LORD. And of thy sons that shall issue from thee, which thou shalt beget, shall they take away; and they shall be eunuchs in the palace of the king of Babylon.

Then said Hezekiah unto Isaiah, Good is the word of the LORD which thou hast spoken. And he said, Is it not good, if peace and truth be in my days?

Hezekiah's Display

John Keble

When Heaven in mercy gives thy prayers return,
And Angels bring thee treasures from on high,
Shut fast the door, nor let the world discern,
And offer thee fond praise when God is nigh.

In friendly guise, perchance with friendly heart,
From Babel, see, they haste with words of love:
But if thou lightly all thy wealth impart,
Their race will come again, and all remove.

Ill thoughts, the children of that King of Pride,
O'er richest halls will swarm, and holiest bowers,
Profaning first, then spoiling far and wide:—
Voluptuous sloth make free with Sharon's flowers.

Close thou the garden-gate, and keep the key,
There chiefly, where the tender seedlings fold
Their dainty leaves—a treasure even to thee
Unknown, till airs celestial make them bold.

When sun and shower give token, freely then
The fragrance will steal out, the flower unclose:
But busy hands, and an admiring ken,
Have blighted ere its hour full many a rose.

Then rest thee, bright one, in thy tranquil nook,
Fond eyes to cherish thee, true arms to keep,
Nor wistful for the world's gay sunshine look;—
In its own time the light will o'er thee sweep.

Think of the babes of Judah's royal line:—
    Display but touched them with her parching glare
Once, and for ages four they bare the sign,
    The fifth beheld them chained in Babel's lair.

2 KINGS 25:1–7 And it came to pass in the ninth year of his reign, in the tenth month, in the tenth day of the month, that Nebuchadnezzar king of Babylon came, he, and all his host, against Jerusalem, and pitched against it; and they built forts against it round about. And the city was besieged unto the eleventh year of king Zedekiah. . . . So they took the king, and brought him up to the king of Babylon to Riblah; and they gave judgment upon him. And they slew the sons of Zedekiah before his eyes, and put out the eyes of Zedekiah, and bound him with fetters of brass, and carried him to Babylon. 2 CHRONICLES 36:17–20 . . . And all the vessels of the house of God, great and small, and the treasures of the house of the LORD, and the treasures of the king, and of his princes; all these he brought to Babylon. And they burnt the house of God, and brake down the wall of Jerusalem, and burnt all the palaces thereof with fire, and destroyed all the goodly vessels thereof. And them that had escaped from the sword carried he away to Babylon; where they were servants to him and his sons until the reign of the kingdom of Persia:

Oh! Weep for Those

George Noel Gordon, Lord Byron

Oh! weep for those that wept by Babel's stream,
Whose shrines are desolate, whose land a dream;
Weep for the harp of Judah's broken shell;
Mourn—where their god hath dwelt the godless dwell!

And where shall Israel lave her bleeding feet?
And when shall Zion's songs again seem sweet?
And Judah's melody once more rejoice
The hearts that leaped before its heavenly voice?

Tribes of the wandering foot and weary breast,
How shall ye flee away and be at rest!
The wild-dove hath her nest, the fox his cave,
Mankind their country—Israel but the grave!

2 CHRONICLES 36:21 To fulfil the word of the LORD by the mouth of Jeremiah, until the land had enjoyed her sabbaths: for as long as she lay desolate she kept sabbath, to fulfil threescore and ten years.

Sion Lies Waste

Fulke Greville, Lord Brooke

Sion lies waste, and thy Jerusalem
O Lord, is fallen to utter desolation.
Against thy prophets and thy holy men
The sin hath wrought a fatal combination:
  Profaned thy name, thy worship overthrown,
  And made thee, living Lord, a God unknown.

Thy powerful laws, thy wonders of creation,
Thy word incarnate, glorious heaven, dark hell,
Lie shadowed under man's degeneration,
Thy Christ still crucified for doing well.
  Impiety, O Lord, sits on thy throne,
  Which makes thee, living light, a God unknown.

Man's superstition hath thy truths entombed,
His atheism again her pomps defaceth;
That sensual unsatiable vast womb
Of thy seen church thy unseen church disgraceth.
  There lives no truth with them that seem thine own,
  Which makes thee, living Lord, a God unknown.

Yet unto thee, Lord, mirror of transgression,
We who for earthly idols have forsaken
Thy heavenly image, sinless, pure impression,
And so in nets of vanity lie taken
  All desolate implore that to thine own,
  Lord, thou no longer live a God unknown.

Yet, Lord, let Israel's plagues not be eternal,
Nor sin forever cloud thy sacred mountains,
Nor with false flames, spiritual but infernal,
Dry up thy mercy's ever springing fountains.
  Rather, sweet Jesus, fill up time and come
  To yield the sin her everlasting doom.

1 CHRONICLES 1:1–3:16 Adam, Sheth, Enosh, Kenan, Mahalaleel, Jered, Henoch, Methuselah, Lamech, Noah, Shem, Ham, and Japheth. . . . the sons of David, which were born unto him in Hebron; the firstborn Amnon, of Ahinoam the Jezreelitess; the second Daniel, of Abigail the Carmelitess: The third, Absalom the son of Maachah the daughter of Talmai king of Geshur: the fourth, Adonijah the son of Haggith: The fifth, Shephatiah of Abital: the sixth, Ithream by Eglah his wife. These six were born unto him in Hebron; and there he reigned seven years and six months: and in Jerusalem he reigned thirty and three years. And these were born unto him in Jerusalem; Shimea, and Shobab, and Nathan, and Solomon, four, of Bathshua the daughter of Ammiel: . . . And Solomon's son was Rehoboam, Abia his son, Asa his son, Jehoshaphat his son, Joram his son, Ahaziah his son, Joash his son, Amaziah his son, Azariah his son, Jotham his son, Ahaz his son, Hezekiah his son, Manasseh his son, Amon his son, Josiah his son. And the sons of Josiah were, the firstborn Johanan, the second Jehoiakim, the third Zedekiah, the fourth Shallum. And the sons of Jehoiakim: Jeconiah his son, Zedekiah his son.

from *JUBILATE AGNO*

CHRISTOPHER SMART

For man is between the pinchers while his soul is shaping and purifying.
For the English are the seed of Abraham and work up to him by Joab,
    David, and Naphtali. God be gracious to us this day. General Fast
    March 14th 1760.
For the Romans and the English are one people the children of the
    brave man who died at the altar praying for his posterity, whose
    death was the type of our Saviour's.
For the Welsh are the children of Mephibosheth and Ziba with a
    mixture of David in the Jones's.
For the Scotch are the children of Doeg with a mixture of Cush the
    Benjamite, whence their innate antipathy to the English.
For the Irish are the children of Shimei and Cush with a mixture of
    something lower – the Lord raise them!
For the French are Moabites even the children of Lot.
For the Dutch are the children of Gog.

For the Poles are the children of Magog.
For the Italians are the children of Samuel and are the same as the Grecians.
For the Spaniards are the children of Abishai Joab's brother, hence is the goodwill between the two nations.
For the Portuguese are the children of Ammon – God be gracious to Lisbon and send good angels amongst them!
For the Hottentots are the children of Gog, with a Black mixture.
For the Russians are the children of Ishmael.
For the Turks are the children of Esau, which is Edom.
For the Wallachians are the children of Huz. God be gracious to Elizabeth Hughes, as she was.
For the Germans are the children of the Philistines even the seed of Anak.
For the Prussians are the children of Goliah – but the present, whom God bless this hour, is a Campbell of the seed of Phinees.
For the Hanoverians are Hittites of the seed of Uriah. God save the King.
For the Hessians are Philistines with a mixture of Judah.
For the Saxons are Benjamites, men of great subtlety and Marshal Saxe was direct from Benjamin.
For the Danes are of the children of Zabulon.
For the Venetians are the children of Mark and Romans.
For the Swiss are Philistines of a particular family. God be gracious to Jonathan Tyers his family and to all the people at Vaux Hall.
For the Sardinians are of the seed of David – The Lord forward the Reformation amongst the good seed first.
For the Mogul's people are the children of Phut.
For the old Greeks and the Italians are one people, which are blessed in the gift of music by reason of the song of Hannah and the care of Samuel with regard to divine melody.
For the Germans and the Dutch are the children of the Goths and Vandals who did a good in destruction of books written by heathen Free Thinkers against God.
For there are Americans of the children of Toi.
For the Laplanders are the children of Gomer.

EZRA

1:1–8 Now in the first year of Cyrus king of Persia, that the word of the LORD by the mouth of Jeremiah might be fulfilled, the LORD stirred up the spirit of Cyrus king of Persia, that he made a proclamation throughout all his kingdom, and put it also in writing, saying, Thus saith Cyrus king of Persia, The LORD God of heaven hath given me all the kingdoms of the earth; and he hath charged me to build him an house at Jerusalem, which is in Judah. Who is there among you of all his people? his God be with him, and let him go up to Jerusalem, which is in Judah, and build the house of the LORD God of Israel, (he is the God,) which is in Jerusalem. And whosoever remaineth in any place where he sojourneth, let the men of his place help him with silver, and with gold, and with goods, and with beasts, beside the freewill offering for the house of God that is in Jerusalem.

Then rose up the chief of the fathers of Judah and Benjamin, and the priests, and the Levites, with all them whose spirit God had raised, to go up to build the house of the LORD which is in Jerusalem. And all they that were about them strengthened their hands with vessels of silver, with gold, with goods, and with beasts, and with precious things, beside all that was willingly offered. Also Cyrus the king brought forth the vessels of the house of the LORD, which Nebuchadnezzar had brought forth out of Jerusalem, and had put them in the house of his gods; Even those did Cyrus king of Persia bring forth by the hand of Mithredath the treasurer, and numbered them unto Sheshbazzar, the prince of Judah.

BABYLON: 539 B.C.E.

CHARLES REZNIKOFF

An Elder. Our fathers were saved from the deaths
others died by hunger, plague, or sword,
when the cities of Judah and Jerusalem itself were taken,
and from the deaths so many died
along the journey that left our fathers
—the hills of Judah and the sea
out of sight many months and years—
exiles by the quiet waters and willows of Babylon;
but for us the noise of battle, not the battle itself,
is over; there is no shouting of soldiers
to warn us; no arrows; no shrieks
of the wounded;

only the suction
of this city
to pull us off our feet
until the remnant of Judah—Jerusalem and our God forgotten—
are particles in the dust of Babylon,
like other thousands and tens of thousands
Babylon has taken.
Another Elder. Did the Lord, whom our fathers served,
come from the sky to stand beside them,
or even from the safety of the clouds with His lightnings
save His citadel?—
an aloof God, saving a few alive
of all Judah's thousands and tens of thousands.
Is there another people who, their cities taken,
the temple of their God become the stones it had been,
and they themselves scattered from the land,
are still worshippers of its God?
Nor, as it might have happened, are we captives among a savage people,
a brutish people, living in tents or caves:
these Babylonians are a great people,
living in palaces and gardens—
but we were only shepherds and herdsmen,
tenders of vineyards and of trees, ploughmen;
this is a nation of merchants and warriors,
priests of triumphant gods.
It was meant for ill to us,
but it has been for good, as to Joseph
who was brought to Egypt among slaves.
to be second in his master's and in the king's house.
Messenger. To all you Jews,
captives of Babylon,
Cyrus the Persian, worshipper of one god and hater of idols,
proclaims,
Joy and rejoicing!
Your enemy is about to fall
and Babylon become a proverb among the nations!
Return to Judah,
rebuild Jerusalem
and the temple of your God;
your captivity is ended!
The First Elder. Surely the sun rises in the east!
Let it not be said that God has forgotten Judah,
or that the Lord was aloof
when puddles of blood stood in the streets of Jerusalem;

we looked for one of us—
and our deliverer is a stranger;
now let us hear no more of the God of Judah,
but tell us of the Lord of the Universe and of Eternity,
before whom the multitudes of Babylonia
are as powerless
as when their cities,
the great angels of granite before their palaces,
the great gods and the lesser gods,
will be looked for with spoons in the desert
and remembered
only because Judah has remembered them for evil.

An Elder. It was hard for our fathers when they were slaves in Egypt,
building a mountain range of granite
along the flat banks of the Nile,
under the quick fists and staffs of taskmasters,
to leave the pots of fish that were theirs for the taking
and the plentiful sweet water
for the wilderness
and the knives of its tribes;
how much harder will it be for you, Judah,
to leave the gardens of Babylon,
the suits of linen and the cloaks of wool,
the meats and the cool fruits and wine
to become again dusty shepherds and herdsmen
on your barren hills, Judah;
to toil in your fields
eating only of what they shall plant,
if locusts and grasshoppers
leave what is saved from drouth and the storm,
and thieves and armed bands
what is spared by the locusts and worms.
Now shall the longings of your heart
and the words of your mouth, Jacob,
the sighs and groans, the cries and outcries of fifty years,
be put to the proof;
for the time is come of choosing and refusing:
your deliverer
calls upon Judah with the crash of thunder,
speaking your name with the voice of the earthquake.

The Prince of the Captivity. Servant of Cyrus,
who hates even as we do,
the vanity of idols,

in a world where their worshippers are like the sands for number,
those who love the truth are drawn to each other
like particles of iron that have known the loadstone;
build on each other like coral in the sea
against the waves, the tides and spring tides, tempests and typhoons,
that would sweep us all away!
The Jews are few; Judah is small among the nations,
without cities and land,
and you Persians have become a mighty people;
but in the battle we have known a pebble in a sling
to do as much
as a spear weighing many shekels of brass,
and Judah will not forget the friendliness of Cyrus.
Now let the young men who are ill at ease
where all the ground is field and garden, street and square,
and all the water is canals,
or the smooth river flowing between steps,
men who like the taste of salt better than that of honey,
try their strength against the hills
and from the rubbish heaps that are Jerusalem
rebuild the city;
replant the land
with olive trees and fig trees, with vineyards and fields of barley,
    fields of wheat:
so shall Judah like a tree that has seen many tribes—
many cities become mounds and heaps—
flourish and renew itself;
for here we are only so much timber,
although smoothed and polished.
And there is other work to do in Babylon—
in courtyards, where flowers and leaves are brilliant
against a white-washed wall, the only noise
that of the fountain and the long leaves of the palms;
in cool rooms
where one need only put out his hand
to take food from the dish
or lift the cup to his lips
while the noise of the street
touches the listener no more than rain;
here others have their work,
like the stars in their orbits, seemingly
motionless,
but shining, not without influence,
upon the action of the world.

Let hands build the walls
hands more numerous
may pull down again,
but we must build in Babylon
another Zion
of precepts, laws, ordinances and commandments
to outlast stone or metal,
between every Jew and the fury or blandishment of any land—
that shall keep up a man as much as bread
and swallows of water in his belly, strengthen him
like links of armor on his body.
Let other people come as streams
that overflow a valley
and leave dead bodies, uprooted trees and fields of sand;
we Jews are as the dew,
on every blade of grass,
trodden under foot today
and here tomorrow morning.

The Book of NEHEMIAH

1:1–11 The words of Nehemiah the son of Hachaliah. And it came to pass in the month Chisleu, in the twentieth year, as I was in Shushan the palace, That Hanani, one of my brethren, came, he and certain men of Judah; and I asked them concerning the Jews that had escaped, which were left of the captivity, and concerning Jerusalem. And they said unto me, The remnant that are left of the captivity there in the province are in great affliction and reproach: the wall of Jerusalem also is broken down, and the gates thereof are burned with fire. And it came to pass, when I heard these words, that I sat down and wept, and mourned certain days, and fasted, and prayed before the God of heaven, And said, I beseech thee, O LORD God of heaven, the great and terrible God, that keepeth covenant and mercy for them that love him and observe his commandments: . . . O Lord, I beseech thee, let now thine ear be attentive to the prayer of thy servant, and to the prayer of thy servants, who desire to fear thy name: and prosper, I pray thee, thy servant this day, and grant him mercy in the sight of this man. For I was the king's cupbearer.

The Prayer of Nehemiah

George Wither

Lord God of Heaven, who only are
The mighty God, and full of fear;
Who never promise-breaker wert,
But ever shewing mercy there,
    Where men affection bear to thee
    And of thy Laws observers be.

Give ear, and ope thine eyes, I pray,
That heard thy servant's suit may be,
Made in thy presence, night and day,
For Israel's seed, that serveth thee:
    For Israel's seed, who (I confess)
    Against thee grievously transgress.

I, and my father's house did sin,
Corrupted all our actions be:
And disrespective we have been
Of statutes, judgments, and decree;
    Of those, which to retain so fast,
    Thy servant Moses charged thou hast.

Oh yet, remember thou, I pray,
These words, which thou didst heretofore
Unto thy servant Moses say:
If e'er (saidst thou) they vex me more,
    I will disperse them every where,
    Among the nations here and there.

But, if to me they shalt convert,
To do those things my laws contain;
Though spread to heavens extremest part,
I would collect them thence again,
    And bring them there to make repose,
    Where I to place my name have chose.

Now, these thy people are (of right)
Thy servants, who to thee belong;
Whom thou hast purchased by thy might,
And by thine arm, exceeding strong:
    Oh let thine ear, Lord, I thee pray,
    Attentive be to what I say.

The prayer of thy servant hear;
Oh, hear thy servants, when they pray,
(Who willing are thy name to fear)
Thy servant prosper thou today:
    And be thou pleased to grant, that he
    May favored in thy presence be.

8:13–9:7 And on the second day were gathered together the chief of the fathers of all the people, the priests, and the Levites, unto Ezra the scribe, even to understand the words of the law. And they found written in the law which the LORD had commanded by Moses, . . .

Now in the twenty and fourth day of this month the children of Israel were assembled with fasting, and with sackclothes, and earth upon them. And the seed of Israel separated themselves from all strangers, and stood and confessed their sins, and the iniquities of their fathers. And they stood up in their place, and read in the book of the law of the LORD their God one fourth part of the day; and another fourth part they confessed, and worshipped the LORD their God. . . .

Then the Levites, Jeshua, and Kadmiel, Bani, Hashabniah, Sherebiah, Hodijah, Shebaniah, and Pethahiah, said, Stand up and bless the LORD your God for ever and ever: and blessed be thy glorious name, which is exalted above all blessing and praise. Thou, even thou, art LORD alone; thou hast made heaven, the heaven of heavens, with all their host, the earth, and all things that are therein, the seas, and all that is therein, and thou preservest them all; and the host of heaven worshippeth thee. Thou art the LORD the God, who didst choose Abram, and broughtest him forth out of Ur of the Chaldees, and gavest him the name of Abraham;

SERVICES

CARL RAKOSI

There was a man in the land of Ur.

Who's that at my coattails?
A pale cocksman.

Hush!
The rabbi walks in thought
                    as in an ordained measure
to the Ark
          and slowly opens its great doors.
The congregation rises
                    and faces the six torahs

and the covenant
                    and all beyond.
The Ark glows.
          Hear, O Israel!

The rabbi stands before the light
inside, alone, and prays.
It is a modest prayer
for the responsibilities of his office.
The congregation is silent.

I too pray:
Let Leah my wife be recompensed for her sweet smile
and our many years of companionship
and not stick me when she cuts my hair.
And let her stay at my side at large gatherings.
And let my son George and his wife Leanna
and my daughter Barbara be close,
and let their children, Jennifer, Julie and Joanna
be my sheep
             and I their old shepherd.
Let them remain as they are.

And let not my white hair frighten me.

The tiger leaps,
the baboon cries,
Pity, pity.
The rabbi prays.

I, son of Leopold and Flora,
also pray:
I pray for meaning.
I pray for the physical,
for my soul needs no suppliant.
I pray for man.

And may a special providence look out
for those who feel deeply.

ESTHER

1:1–3:6 Now it came to pass in the days of Ahasuerus, (this is Ahasuerus which reigned, from India even unto Ethiopia, over an hundred and seven and twenty provinces:) That in those days, when the king Ahasuerus sat on the throne of his kingdom, which was in Shushan the palace, In the third year of his reign, . . . did king Ahasuerus promote Haman the son of Hammedatha the Agagite, and advanced him, and set his seat above all the princes that were with him. And all the king's servants, that were in the king's gate, bowed, and reverenced Haman: for the king had so commanded concerning him. But Mordecai bowed not, nor did him reverence. Then the king's servants, which were in the king's gate, said unto Mordecai, Why transgressest thou the king's commandment?

Now it came to pass, when they spake daily unto him, and he hearkened not unto them, that they told Haman, to see whether Mordecai's matters would stand: for he had told them that he was a Jew. And when Haman saw that Mordecai bowed not, nor did him reverence, then was Haman full of wrath. And he thought scorn to lay hands on Mordecai alone; for they had shewed him the people of Mordecai: wherefore Haman sought to destroy all the Jews that were throughout the whole kingdom of Ahasuerus, even the people of Mordecai.

Meditatio Septima

FRANCIS QUARLES

Fights God for cursed Amalek? That hand
That once did curse, doth now the curse withstand:
Is God unjust? Is justice fled from heaven;
Or are the righteous balances uneven?
Is this that just Jehovah's sacred word,
Firmly enrolled within the law's record,
I'll fight with Amalek, destroy his Nation,
And from remembrance blur his Generation?
What, shall his curse to Amalek be void?
And with those plagues shall Israel be destroyed?
Ah, sooner shall the sprightly flames of fire
Descend, and moisten: and dull earth aspire,
And with her dryness quench fair Titan's heat,

Then shall thy words, and just decrees retreat:
The day (as weary of his burden) tires;
The year (full laden with her months) expires:
The heavens (grown great with age) must soon decay,
The ponderous earth in time shall pass away;
But yet thy sacred words shall always flourish,
Though days, and years, and heaven, and earth do perish.
    How perks proud Haman then? What prosperous fate
Exalts his pagan head? How fortunate
Hath favor crowned his times? Hath God decreed
No other curse upon that cursed seed?
    The mortal eye of man can but perceive
Things present; when his heart cannot conceive,
He's either by his outward senses guided,
Or else (like riddles) leaves it undecided:
The fleshly eye that lends a feeble sight,
Fails in extent, and hath no further might
Than to attain the object: and there ends
His office; and of what it apprehends,
Acquaints the understanding, which conceives,
And descants on that thing the sight perceives,
Or good, or bad; unable to project
The just occasion, or the true effect:
Man sees like man, and can but comprehend
Things as they seeming are, not as they end;
God sees a king's heart, in a shepherd's breast,
And in a mighty king, he sees a beast:
'Tis not the spring-tide of an high estate
Creates a man (though seeming) fortunate:
The blaze of honor, fortune's sweet excess,
Do undeserve the name of happiness:
The frowns of indisposëd fortune makes
Man poor, but not unhappy. He that takes
Her checks with patience, leaves the name of poor,
And lets in fortune at a backer door.
Lord, let my fortunes be or rich, or poor:
If small, the less account; if great, the more.

7:1–6 So the king and Haman came to banquet with Esther the queen. And the king said again unto Esther on the second day at the banquet of wine, What is thy petition, queen Esther? and it shall be granted thee: and what is thy request? and it shall be performed, even to the half of the kingdom.

Then Esther the queen answered and said, If I have found favour in thy sight, O king, and if it please the king, let my life be given me at my petition, and my people at my request: For we are sold, I and my people, to be destroyed, to be slain, and to perish. But if we had been sold for bondmen and bondwomen, I had held my tongue, although the enemy could not countervail the king's damage.

Then the king Ahasuerus answered and said unto Esther the queen, Who is he, and where is he, that durst presume in his heart to do so?

And Esther said, The adversary and enemy is this wicked Haman.

From Life to Love

Countee Cullen

Four winds and seven seas have called me friend,
And countless roads have known my restless feet;
Deep crystal springs and pollened buds were sweet
For sustenance their princely fare to lend,
While nameless birds from grove and blossomed bend
Deluged my soul with song; if it were meet
To love Life so, then Love will but complete
My joy, for Life with Love can never end.
Love, I have heard the sweet of your voice, have seen
You pass the dawn-flushed singing hills between;
Now suppliant I kneel and pray you show
The mercied sceptre favored Esther saw;
The dawn in me has broke, and well I know
That Love is king and creed and Persian law.

The Book of
JOB

1:1–7 There was a man in the land of Uz, whose name was Job; and that man was perfect and upright, and one that feared God, and eschewed evil. And there were born unto him seven sons and three daughters. His substance also was seven thousand sheep, and three thousand camels, and five hundred yoke of oxen, and five hundred she asses, and a very great household; so that this man was the greatest of all the men of the east. And his sons went and feasted in their houses, every one his day; and sent and called for their three sisters to eat and to drink with them. And it was so, when the days of their feasting were gone about, that Job sent and sanctified them, and rose up early in the morning, and offered burnt offerings according to the number of them all: for Job said, It may be that my sons have sinned, and cursed God in their hearts. Thus did Job continually.

Now there was a day when the sons of God came to present themselves before the LORD, and Satan came also among them. And the LORD said unto Satan, Whence comest thou? Then Satan answered the LORD, and said, From going to and fro in the earth, and from walking up and down in it.

To Brooklyn Bridge

Hart Crane

From going to and fro in the earth,
and from walking up and down in it.

How many dawns, chill from his rippling rest
The seagull's wings shall dip and pivot him,
Shedding white rings of tumult, building high
Over the chained bay waters Liberty—

Then with inviolate curve, forsake our eyes
As apparitional as sails that cross
Some page of figures to be filed away;
—Till elevators drop us from our day . . .

I think of cinemas, panoramic sleights
With multitudes bent toward some flashing scene
Never disclosed, but hastened to again,
Foretold to other eyes on the same screen;

And Thee, across the harbor, silver-paced
As though the sun took step of thee, yet left
Some motion ever unspent in thy stride,—
Implicitly thy freedom staying thee!

Out of some subway scuttle, cell or loft
A bedlamite speeds to thy parapets,
Tilting there momently, shrill shirt ballooning,
A jest falls from the speechless caravan.

Down Wall, from girder into street noon leaks,
A rip-tooth of the sky's acetylene;
All afternoon the cloud-flown derricks turn . . .
Thy cables breathe the North Atlantic still.

And obscure as that heaven of the Jews,
Thy guerdon . . . Accolade thou dost bestow
Of anonymity time cannot raise:
Vibrant reprieve and pardon thou dost show.

O harp and altar, of the fury fused,
(How could mere toil align thy choiring strings!)
Terrific threshold of the prophet's pledge,
Prayer of pariah, and the lover's cry,—

Again the traffic lights that skim thy swift
Unfractioned idiom, immaculate sigh of stars,
Beading thy path—condense eternity:
And we have seen night lifted in thine arms.

Under thy shadow by the piers I waited;
Only in darkness is thy shadow clear.
The City's fiery parcels all undone,
Already snow submerges an iron year . . .

O Sleepless as the river under thee,
Vaulting the sea, the prairies' dreaming sod,
Unto us lowliest sometime sweep, descend
And of the curveship lend a myth to God.

1:8–21 And the LORD said unto Satan, Hast thou considered my servant Job, that there is none like him in the earth, a perfect and an upright man, one that feareth God, and escheweth evil?

Then Satan answered the LORD, and said, Doth Job fear God for nought? Hast not thou made an hedge about him, and about his house, and about all that he hath on every side? thou hast blessed the work of his hands, and his substance is increased in the land. But put forth thine hand now, and touch all that he hath, and he will curse thee to thy face.

And the LORD said unto Satan, Behold, all that he hath is in thy power; only upon himself put not forth thine hand. So Satan went forth from the presence of the LORD. . . .

Then Job arose, and rent his mantle, and shaved his head, and fell down upon the ground, and worshipped, And said, Naked came I out of my mother's womb, and naked shall I return thither: the LORD gave, and the LORD hath taken away; blessed be the name of the LORD.

JOB. I

JOHN HALL

Out of my mother's womb
All naked came I lo:
And naked shall I turn again,
To earth that I came fro.

The Lord gave at the first,
As his good pleasure was,
And at his will did take again,
As it is come to pass.

The Lord his holy name
Be praised now therefore,
As it hath been, as it is now,
And shall be evermore.

1:22–2:12 In all this Job sinned not, nor charged God foolishly.

Again there was a day when the sons of God came to present themselves before the LORD, and Satan came also among them to present himself before the LORD. And the LORD said unto Satan, From whence comest thou? And Satan answered the LORD, and said, From going to and fro in the earth, and from walking up and down in it. And the LORD said unto Satan, Hast thou considered my servant Job, that there is none like him in the earth, a perfect and an upright man, one that feareth God, and escheweth evil? and still he holdeth fast his integrity, although thou movedst me against him, to destroy him without cause. And Satan answered the LORD, and said, Skin for skin, yea, all that a man hath will he give for his life. But put forth thine hand now, and touch his bone and his flesh, and he will curse thee to thy face. And the LORD said unto Satan, Behold, he is in thine hand; but save his life.

So went Satan forth from the presence of the LORD, and smote Job with sore boils from the sole of his foot unto his crown. And he took him a potsherd to scrape himself withal; and he sat down among the ashes.

Then said his wife unto him, Dost thou still retain thine integrity? curse God, and die. But he said unto her, Thou speakest as one of the foolish women speaketh. What? shall we receive good at the hand of God, and shall we not receive evil? In all this did not Job sin with his lips.

Now when Job's three friends heard of all this evil that was come upon him, they came every one from his own place; Eliphaz the Temanite, and Bildad the Shuhite, and Zophar the Naamathite: for they had made an appointment together to come to mourn with him and to comfort him. And when they lifted up their eyes afar off, and knew him not, they lifted up their voice, and wept; and they rent every one his mantle, and sprinkled dust upon their heads toward heaven.

JOB

ELIZABETH SEWELL

They did not know this face
Where the chin rested on the sunken breastbone,
So changed it was, emptied, rinsed out and dried,
And for some future purpose put aside.
Expecting torment, they were much perplexed.

His world had gone
And he sat isolated, foul and flyblown,
Without a world, with nothing but a mind
Staggered to silence since it could not find
Language to utter its amazing text.

For where was Job?
In some strange state, unknown and yet well-known,
A mask that stared hollowly in God's breath,
Mind that perceived the irrelevance of death,
And the astonished heart unmoved, unvexed.

They did not see his soul
Perched like a bird upon the broken hearthstone,
Piping incessantly above the ashes
What next what next what next what next what next

2:13 So they sat down with him upon the ground seven days and seven nights, and none spake a word unto him: for they saw that his grief was very great.

CÆSURA

JOHN ASHBERY

Job sat in a corner of the dump eating asparagus
With one hand and scratching his unsightly eruptions
With the other. Pshaw, it'd blow over. In the office
They'd like discussing it. His thoughts

Were with the office now: how protected it was,
Though still a place to work. Sit up straight, the
Monitor inside said. It worked for a second
But didn't improve the posture of his days, taken

As a cross section of the times. Correction: of our time.
And it was (it was again): "Have you made your list up?
I have one ambulance three nuns two (black-
And-white list) cops dressed as Keystone Kops lists, a red light

At leafy intersection list." Then it goes blank, pulp-color.
Until at the end where they give out the list
Of awardees. The darkness and light have returned. It was still
The weather of the soul, vandalized, out-at-elbow. A blight. Spared,
though.

4:12–21 Now a thing was secretly brought to me, and mine ear received a little thereof. In thoughts from the visions of the night, when deep sleep falleth on men, Fear came upon me, and trembling, which made all my bones to shake. Then a spirit passed before my face; the hair of my flesh stood up: It stood still, but I could not discern the form thereof: an image was before mine eyes, there was silence, and I heard a voice, saying, Shall mortal man be more just than God? shall a man be more pure than his maker? Behold, he put no trust in his servants; and his angels he charged with folly: How much less in them that dwell in houses of clay, whose foundation is in the dust, which are crushed before the moth? They are destroyed from morning to evening: they perish for ever without any regarding it. Doth not their excellency which is in them go away? they die, even without wisdom.

A Spirit Passed Before Me

George Noel Gordon, Lord Byron

A spirit passed before me: I beheld
The face of immortality unveiled—
Deep sleep came down on every eye save mine—
And there it stood,—all formless—but divine;
Along my bones the creeping flesh did quake;
And as my damp hair stiffened, thus it spake:

'Is man more just than God? Is man more pure
Than he who deems even seraphs insecure?
Creatures of clay—vain dwellers in the dust!
The moth survives you, and are ye more just?
Things of a day! you wither ere the night,
Heedless and blind to wisdom's wasted light!'

7:17–10:22 What is man, that thou shouldest magnify him? and that thou shouldest set thine heart upon him? And that thou shouldest visit him every morning, and try him every moment? How long wilt thou not depart from me, nor let me alone till I swallow down my spittle? I have sinned; what shall I do unto thee, O thou preserver of men? why hast thou set me as a mark against thee, so that I am a burden to myself? And why dost thou not pardon my transgression, and take away my iniquity? for now shall I sleep in the dust; and thou shalt seek me in the morning, but I shall not be. . . .

Wherefore then hast thou brought me forth out of the womb? Oh that I had given up the ghost, and no eye had seen me! I should have been as though I had not been; I should have been carried from the womb to the grave. Are not my days few? cease then, and let me alone, that I may take comfort a little, Before I go whence I shall not return, even to the land of darkness and the shadow of death; A land of darkness, as darkness itself; and of the shadow of death, without any order, and where the light is as darkness.

Death

A Dialogue

HENRY VAUGHAN

Soul.

'Tis a sad Land, that in one day
Hath dulled thee thus, when death shall freeze
Thy blood to ice, and thou must stay
Tenant for years, and centuries,
How wilt thou brook't?—

Body.

I cannot tell,—
But if all sense wings not with thee,
And something still be left the dead,
I'll wish my curtains off to free
Me from so dark, and sad a bed;

A nest of nights, a gloomy sphere,
Where shadows thicken, and the cloud
Sits on the sun's brow all the year,
And nothing moves without a shroud;

Soul.

'Tis so: But as thou sawest that night
We travelled in, our first attempts
Were dull, and blind, but custom straight
Our fears, and falls brought to contempt,

Then, when the ghastly *twelve* was past
We breathed still for a blushing *East,*
And bad the lazy sun make haste,
And on sure hopes, though long, did feast;

But when we saw the clouds to crack
And in those crannies light appeared,
We thought the day then was not slack,
And pleased our selves with what we feared;

Just so it is in death. But thou
Shalt in thy mothers bosom sleep
Whilst I each minute groan to know
How near Redemption creeps.

Then shall we meet to mix again, and met,
'Tis last good-night, our sun shall never set.

13:14–18 Wherefore do I take my flesh in my teeth, and put my life in mine hand? Though he slay me, yet will I trust in him: but I will maintain mine own ways before him. He also shall be my salvation: for an hypocrite shall not come before him. Hear diligently my speech, and my declaration with your ears.

Behold now, I have ordered my cause; I know that I shall be justified.

THE ENTHUSIAST

HERMAN MELVILLE

Shall hearts that beat no base retreat
In youth's magnanimous years—
Ignoble hold it, if discreet
When interest tames to fears;
Shall spirits that worship light
Perfidious deem its sacred glow,
Recant, and trudge where worldlings go,
Conform and own them right?

Shall time with creeping influence cold
Unnerve and cow? the heart
Pine for the heartless ones enrolled
With palterers of the mart?
Shall faith abjure her skies,
Or pale probation blench her down
To shrink from truth so still, so lone
Mid loud gregarious lies?

Each burning boat in Caesar's rear,
    Flames—No return through me!
So put the torch to ties though dear,
    If ties but tempters be.
Nor cringe if come the night:
    Walk through the cloud to meet the pall,
    Though light forsake thee, never fall
From fealty to light.

14:1–10 Man that is born of a woman is of few days and full of trouble. He cometh forth like a flower, and is cut down: he fleeth also as a shadow, and continueth not. And dost thou open thine eyes upon such an one, and bringest me into judgment with thee? Who can bring a clean thing out of an unclean? not one. Seeing his days are determined, the number of his months are with thee, thou hast appointed his bounds that he cannot pass; Turn from him, that he may rest, till he shall accomplish, as an hireling, his day. For there is hope of a tree, if it be cut down, that it will sprout again, and that the tender branch thereof will not cease. Though the root thereof wax old in the earth, and the stock thereof die in the ground; Yet through the scent of water it will bud, and bring forth boughs like a plant. But man dieth, and wasteth away: yea, man giveth up the ghost, and where is he?

Grace

George Herbert

My stock lies dead, and no increase
Doth my dull husbandry improve:
O let thy graces without cease
        Drop from above!

If still the sun should hide his face,
Thy house would but a dungeon prove,
Thy works nights captives: O let grace
        Drop from above!

The dew doth every morning fall;
And shall the dew out-strip thy dove?
The dew, for which grass cannot call,
        Drop from above.

Death is still working like a mole,
And digs my grave at each remove:
Let grace work too, and on my soul
Drop from above.

Sin is still hammering my heart
Unto a hardness, void of love:
Let suppling grace, to cross his art,
Drop from above.

O come! for thou dost know the way.
Or if to me thou wilt not move,
Remove me, where I need not say,
Drop from above.

17:1–13 My breath is corrupt, my days are extinct, the graves are ready for me. . . . But as for you all, do ye return, and come now: for I cannot find one wise man among you. My days are past, my purposes are broken off, even the thoughts of my heart. They change the night into day: the light is short because of darkness. If I wait, the grave is mine house: I have made my bed in the darkness.

Solum Mihi Superest Sepulchrum

William Habington

Welcome thou safe retreat!
Where th' injured man may fortify
'Gainst the invasions of the great:
Where the lean slave, who th' oar doth ply,
Soft as his admiral may lie.

Great Statist! 'tis your doom
Though your designs swell high, and wide
To be contracted in a tomb!
And all your happy cares provide
But for your heir authorized pride.

Nor shall your shade delight
I'th' pomp of your proud obsequies.
And should the present flattery write
A glorious epitaph, the wise
Will say, The poet's wit here lies.

How reconciled to fate
Will grow the aged villager,
When he shall see your funeral state?
Since death will him as warm inter
As you in your gay sepulcher.

The great decree of God
Makes every path of mortals lead
To this dark common period.
For what by ways so e'er we tread,
We end our journey 'mong the dead.

Even I, while humble zeal
Makes fancy a sad truth indite,
Insensible away do steal:
And when I'm lost in death's cold night,
Who will remember, now I write?

24:1–25 Why, seeing times are not hidden from the Almighty, do they that know him not see his days? . . . He draweth also the mighty with his power: he riseth up, and no man is sure of life. Though it be given him to be in safety, whereon he resteth; yet his eyes are upon their ways. They are exalted for a little while, but are gone and brought low; they are taken out of the way as all other, and cut off as the tops of the ears of corn. And if it be not so now, who will make me a liar, and make my speech nothing worth?

from Job Militant

Meditatio tertia decima

Francis Quarles

The wisest men that Nature e'er could boast,
For secret knowledge of her power, were lost
Confounded, and in deep amazement stood,
In the discovery of the chiefest good:
Keenly they hunted, beat in every brack,
Forwards they went, on either hand, and back
Returned they counter; but their deep-mouthed art,
(Though often challenged scent, yet) ne'er could start,

In all th' enclosures of philosophy,
That game, from squat, they term, felicity:
They jangle, and their maxims disagree;
As many men, so many minds there be.
One digs to Pluto's throne, thinks there to find
Her grace, raked up in gold: Another's mind
Mounts to the courts of kings, with plumes of honor
And feathered hopes, hopes there to seize upon her;
A third, unlocks the painted gates of pleasure,
And ransacks there, to find this peerless treasure.
A fourth, more sage, more wisely melancholy,
Persuades himself, her deity's too holy,
For common hands to touch; he rather chooses
To make a long day's journey to the Muses:
To Athens (gowned) he goes, and from that school
Returns unsped, a more instructed fool.
Where lies she then? Or lies she any where?
Honors are bought and sold, she rests not there;
Much less in pleasures hath she her abiding,
For they are shared to beasts, and ever sliding;
Nor yet in virtue, virtue's often poor,
And (crushed with fortune) begs from door to door;
Nor is she sainted in the shrine of wealth;
That makes men slaves, is unsecured from stealth;
Conclude we then, Felicity consists
Not in exterior fortunes, but her lists
Are boundless, and her large extension
Outruns the pace of human apprehension;
Fortunes are seldom measured by desert,
The fairer face, hath oft the fouler heart;
Sacred felicity doth ne'er extend
Beyond itself: In it all wishes end:
The swelling of an outward fortune can
Create a prosperous, not a happy man;
A peaceful conscience is the true content,
And wealth is but her golden ornament.
I care not, so my kernel relish well,
How slender be the substance of my shell;
My heart being virtuous, let my face be wan,
I am to God, I only seem to man.

38:1–30 Then the LORD answered Job out of the whirlwind, and said, Who is this that darkeneth counsel by words without knowledge? Gird up now thy loins like a man; for I will demand of thee, and answer thou me. . . . Where wast thou when I laid the foundations of the earth? declare, if thou hast understanding. . . . Who hath divided a watercourse for the overflowing of waters, or a way for the lightning of thunder; To cause it to rain on the earth, where no man is; on the wilderness, wherein there is no man; To satisfy the desolate and waste ground; and to cause the bud of the tender herb to spring forth? Hath the rain a father? or who hath begotten the drops of dew? Out of whose womb came the ice? and the hoary frost of heaven, who hath gendered it? The waters are hid as with a stone, and the face of the deep is frozen.

HATH THE RAIN A FATHER?

JONES VERY

We say, "It rains." An unbelieving age!
Its very words its unbelief doth show;
Forgot the lessons of the sacred page,
Spoken by men of faith so long ago!
No farther than they see men's faith extends;
The mighty changes of the earth and sky
To them are causeless all, where Science ends;
An Unseen Cause they know not or deny.
They hear not in the whirlwind, or the storm,
The mighty Voice which spake to man of old;
They see not in the clouds of heaven His form,
Nor in His ceaseless works his power behold;
Who maketh small the countless drops of rain,
And sendeth showers upon the springing grain.

41:1–34 Canst thou draw out leviathan with an hook? or his tongue with a cord which thou lettest down? Canst thou put an hook into his nose? or bore his jaw through with a thorn? . . . By his neesings a light doth shine, and his eyes are like the eyelids of the morning. Out of his mouth go burning lamps, and sparks of fire leap out. Out of his nostrils goeth smoke, as out of a seething pot or caldron. His breath kindleth coals, and a flame goeth out of his mouth. In his neck remaineth strength, and sorrow is turned into joy before him. The flakes of his flesh are joined together: they are firm in themselves; they cannot be moved. His heart is as firm as a stone; yea, as hard as a piece of the nether millstone. When he raiseth up himself, the mighty are afraid: by reason of breakings they

purify themselves. The sword of him that layeth at him cannot hold: the spear, the dart, nor the habergeon. He esteemeth iron as straw, and brass as rotten wood. The arrow cannot make him flee: slingstones are turned with him into stubble. Darts are counted as stubble: he laugheth at the shaking of a spear. Sharp stones are under him: he spreadeth sharp pointed things upon the mire. He maketh the deep to boil like a pot: he maketh the sea like a pot of ointment. He maketh a path to shine after him; one would think the deep to be hoary. Upon earth there is not his like, who is made without fear. He beholdeth all high things: he is a king over all the children of pride.

Leviathan

W. S. Merwin

This is the black sea-brute bulling through wave-wrack,
Ancient as ocean's shifting hills, who in sea-toils
Travelling, who furrowing the salt acres
Heavily, his wake hoary behind him,
Shoulders spouting, the fist of his forehead
Over wastes gray-green crashing, among horses unbroken
From bellowing fields, past bone-wreck of vessels,
Tide-ruin, wash of lost bodies bobbing
No longer sought for, and islands of ice gleaming,
Who ravening the rank flood, wave-marshalling,
Overmastering the dark sea-marches, finds home
And harvest. Frightening to foolhardiest
Mariners, his size were difficult to describe:
The hulk of him is like hills heaving,
Dark, yet as crags of drift-ice, crowns cracking in thunder,
Like land's self by night black-looming, surf churning and trailing
Along his shores' rushing, shoal-water boding
About the dark of his jaws; and who should moor at his edge
And fare on afoot would find gates of no gardens,
But the hill of dark underfoot diving,
Closing overhead, the cold deep, and drowning.
He is called Leviathan, and named for rolling,
First created he was of all creatures,
He has held Jonah three days and nights,
He is that curling serpent that in ocean is,
Sea-fright he is, and the shadow under the earth.

Days there are, nonetheless, when he lies
Like an angel, although a lost angel
On the waste's unease, no eye of man moving,
Bird hovering, fish flashing, creature whatever
Who after him came to herit earth's emptiness.
Froth at flanks seething soothes to stillness,
Waits; with one eye he watches
Dark of night sinking last, with one eye dayrise
As at first over foaming pastures. He makes no cry
Though that light is a breath. The sea curling
Star-climbed, wind-combed, cumbered with itself still
As at first it was, is the hand not yet contented
Of the Creator. And he waits for the world to begin.

42:10–16 And the LORD turned the captivity of Job, when he prayed for his friends: also the LORD gave Job twice as much as he had before. Then came there unto him all his brethren, and all his sisters, and all they that had been of his acquaintance before, and did eat bread with him in his house: and they bemoaned him, and comforted him over all the evil that the LORD had brought upon him: every man also gave him a piece of money, and every one an earring of gold.

So the LORD blessed the latter end of Job more than his beginning: for he had fourteen thousand sheep, and six thousand camels, and a thousand yoke of oxen, and a thousand she asses. He had also seven sons and three daughters. And he called the name of the first, Jemima; and the name of the second, Kezia; and the name of the third, Kerenhappuch. And in all the land were no women found so fair as the daughters of Job: and their father gave them inheritance among their brethren.

After this lived Job an hundred and forty years, and saw his sons, and his sons' sons, even four generations.

The Beauty of Job's Daughters

Jay MacPherson

The old, the mad, the blind have fairest daughters.
Take Job: the beasts the accuser sends at evening
Shoulder his house and shake it; he's not there,
Attained in age to inwardness of daughters,
In all the land no women found so fair.

Angels and sons of God are nearest neighbours,
And even the accuser may repair
To walk with Job in pleasures of his daughters:
Wide shining rooms more warmly lit at evening,
Gardens beyond whose secrets scent the air.

Not wiles of men nor envy of the neighbours,
Riches of earth, nor what heaven holds more rare,
Can take from Job the beauty of his daughters,
The gardens in the rock, music at evening,
And cup so full that all who come must share.

Perhaps we passed them? it was late, or evening,
And surely those were desert stumps, not daughters,
In fact we doubt that they were ever there.
The old, the mad, the blind have fairest daughters.
In all the land no women found so fair.

42:17 So Job died, being old and full of days.

from A PARAPHRASE UPON JOB

Chapter XLII

GEORGE SANDYS

"O Father, I acknowledge," Job replied,
"Thy all-effecting power. O who can hide
His thoughts from Thee? who can reverse or shun
Thy just decree? What Thou wouldst do, is done.
I heard thee say; 'Dare brutish man profane
My darkened counsels, and of God complain?'
Great Judge, I in Thy mirror see my shame:
Those lips that justified, my guilt proclaim.
Our knowledge is but ignorance, and we
The sons of folly, if compared with Thee.
Thy ways and sacred mysteries transcend
Their apprehensions, who in death must end.
O to my prayers afford a gracious ear!
Instruct thy servant, and his darkness clear!
I of Thy excellence have oft been told,
But now my ravished eyes Thy face behold.

Who, therefore, in this weeping palinode
Abhor myself, that have displeased my God,
In dust and ashes mourn. Nor will my fears
Forsake me, till I cleanse my soul with tears."
When contrite Job had this submission made,
The Lord to Eliphaz of Teman said:
"Against thee, and thy two associates,
My anger burns, and hastens to your fates;
Since you, unlike my servant Job, have erred,
And victory before the truth preferred.
Seven spotless rams, seven bulls that never bare
The yoke, select; with these to Job repair;
Their bleeding limbs upon my altar lay,
His ready charity for you shall pray,
And reconcile my wrath: else merited
Revenge should forthwith send you to the dead,
Who have my rule and providence profaned,
Nor, like my servant Job, the truth maintained."
Then Bildad, Eliphaz, and Zophar came
To their old friend; the feasted altars flame;
For whom that injured servant devoutly prayed;
And with the incense their atonement made.
Even in that piteous duty the Most High
Beheld his patience with a tender eye;
From envious Satan's tyranny released;
Dried up his tears, and with abundance blessed.
His brothers and his sisters, all the train
That followed his prosperity, again
Present their visits; at his table feed,
Bemoan and comfort. Joys his grief succeed.
With gold and silver they increase his store;
And gave the precious earrings which they wore.
So that Jehovah blessed his latter days
More than the first; his loss with interest pays.
His droves of asses, camels, herds of neat,
And flocks of sheep, grew shortly twice as great.
Blessed with seven sons; three daughters, who for fair
Might with the beauties of the earth compare;
One called Jemima, of the rising light;
A second, for her sweetness, Cassia hight;
The youngest Kerenhappa, of the power
And rays of beauty. Rich in nature's dower,
As in their father's love; who gave them shares
Among his sons, and joined them with his heirs.

Job seven-score years his miseries survived;
His children's children saw; those who derived
From them their birth, even to the fourth descent;
And in tranquillity his old age spent.
Then, full of days and deathless honor, gave
His soul to God; his body to the grave.

Job's Epitaph

Joshua Sylvester

*	*	*	*
**	**	**	**
Who	*Who*	*Who*	*Heaven's*
SELF,	*Wealth's*	*Friends'*	*Frown,*
The World,	*& Health's*	*Rebuke,*	*Earth's Force*
&	*&*	*Foes'*	*Hell's*
Satan,	*Children's*	*Rage, Wife's*	*Fury,*
triumphed	*rueful*	*cursing*	*calmly*
o'er;	*Loss;*	*Cross;*	*bore;*

Th' Invincible *in Virtue, JOB, Her* Fere,
The Virgin Patience (*Widow now*) *tombed Here*

The Book of PSALMS

Stanzas on the Psalms

Thomas Warton the Elder

Not the songs that nobly tell,
How Troy was sacked, and Rome began,
Not the numbers that reveal
The wars of Heaven to falling man;

Can boast that true celestial fire,
That equal strength and ease,
Or with such various charms conspire,
To move, to teach, to please.

Those complaints how sadly sweet,
Which weeping seraphim repeat;
Those prayers how happily preferred,
Which God himself inspired and heard.

Ye partial wits no longer boast
Of Pindar's fire in David's lost!
Who to the Hebrew harp must yield,
As Jove by great Jehovah is excelled.

1:1–2 Blessed is the man that walketh not in the counsel of the ungodly, nor standeth in the way of sinners, nor sitteth in the seat of the scornful. But his delight is in the law of the LORD; and in his law doth he meditate day and night.

Blessed is the Man

Marianne Moore

who does not sit in the seat of the scoffer—
the man who does not denigrate, depreciate, denunciate;
who is not "characteristically intemperate,"
who does not "excuse, retreat, equivocate; and will be heard."

(Ah, Giorgione! there are those who mongrelize
and those who heighten anything they touch; although it may well be
that if Giorgione's self-portrait were not said to be he,
it might not take my fancy. Blessed the geniuses who know

that egomania is not a duty.)
"Diversity, controversy; tolerance"—in that "citadel
of learning" we have a fort that ought to armor us well.
Blessed is the man who "takes the risk of decision"—asks

himself the question: "Would it solve the problem?
Is it right as I see it? Is it in the best interests of all?"
Alas. Ulysses' companions are now political—
living self-indulgently until the moral sense is drowned,

having lost all power of comparison,
thinking license emancipates one, "slaves whom they themselves have bound."
Brazen authors, downright soiled and downright spoiled, as if sound
and exceptional, are the old quasi-modish counterfeit,

mitin-proofing conscience against character.
Affronted by "private lies and public shame," blessed is the author
Who favors what the supercilious do not favor—
who will not comply. Blessed, the unaccommodating man.

Blessed the man whose faith is different
from possessiveness—of a kind not framed by "things which do appear"—
who will not visualize defeat, too intent to cower;
whose illumined eye has seen the shaft that gilds the sultan's tower.*

* M.M.'s notes:

Line 4: "*characteristically intemperate.*" Campaign manager's evaluation of an attack on the Eisenhower Administration.

Line 5: "*excuse...heard.*" Charles Poore reviewing James B. Conant's *The Citadel of Learning* (New Haven, Yale University Press)—quoting Lincoln. *New York Times*, April 7, 1956.

Line 8: *Giorgione's self-portrait.* Reproduced in *Life*, October 24, 1955.

Lines 11-12: "*Diversity...learning.*" James B. Conant, *The Citadel of Learning*.

Line 13: "*takes...decision.*" Louis Dudek: "poetry...must...take the risk of a decision"; "to say what we know, loud and clear—and if necessary ugly—that would be better than to say nothing with great skill." "The New Laocoön," *Origin*, Winter-Spring 1956.

Lines 14-15: "*Would...*" "President Eisenhower Vetoes Farm Compromise [Agricultural Act of 1956]," *New York Times*, April 17, 1956: "We would produce more of certain crops at a time when we need less of them...If natural resources are squandered on crops that we cannot eat or sell, all Americans lose."

Line 19: *Ulysses' companions.* "The Companions of Ulysses," Book Twelve, Fable I, *The Fables of La Fontaine* (The Viking Press, 1954).

Line 22: Mitin (From *la mite*, moth). Odorless, non-toxic product of Geigy Chemical Corporation research scientists (Swiss). *New York Times*, April 7, 1956.

Line 23: "*private...shame.*" See note for line 13.

Line 27: "*things which...appear.*" Hebrews 11:3.

12:1–8 Help, LORD; for the godly man ceaseth; for the faithful fail from among the children of men. They speak vanity every one with his neighbour: with flattering lips and with a double heart do they speak. The LORD shall cut off all flattering lips, and the tongue that speaketh proud things: Who have said, With our tongue will we prevail; our lips are our own: who is lord over us? For the oppression of the poor, for the sighing of the needy, now will I arise, saith the LORD; I will set him in safety from him that puffeth at him. The words of the LORD are pure words: as silver tried in a furnace of earth, purified seven times. Thou shalt keep them, O LORD, thou shalt preserve them from this generation for ever. The wicked walk on every side, when the vilest men are exalted.

ROCHESTER *EXTEMPORE*

JOHN WILMOT, EARL OF ROCHESTER

And after singing Psalm the Twelfth,
He laid his book upon the shelf
And looked much simply like himself;
With eyes turned up, as white as ghost,
He cried, "Ah, Lard! ah, Lard of Hosts!
I am a rascal, that thou knowst!"

13:1–6 How long wilt thou forget me, O LORD? for ever? how long wilt thou hide thy face from me? How long shall I take counsel in my soul, having sorrow in my heart daily? how long shall mine enemy be exalted over me? Consider and hear me, O LORD my God: lighten mine eyes, lest I sleep the sleep of death; Lest mine enemy say, I have prevailed against him; and those that trouble me rejoice when I am moved. But I have trusted in thy mercy; my heart shall rejoice in thy salvation. I will sing unto the LORD, because he hath dealt bountifully with me.

from ANE GODLY DREAM

ELIZABETH MELVILLE, LADY CULROSS

Upon one day as I did mourn full sore
With sundry things wherewith my soul was grieved,
My grief increased and grew more and more
My comfort fled and could not be relieved,
With heaviness my heart was so mischieved,
I loathed my life, I could not eat nor drink,

I might not speak nor look to none that lived,
But mused alone and diverse things did think.

The wretched world did so molest my mind,
I thought upon this false and iron age.
And how our hearts were so to vice inclined,
That Satan seemed most fearfully to rage.
Nothing in earth my sorrow could assuage,
I felt my sin most strangely to increase,
I grieved my sprite that wont to be my pledge,
My soul was drowned into most deep distress.

All merriness did aggravate my pain,
And earthly joys did still increase my woe:
In company I no ways could remain,
But fled resort and so alone did go.
My silly soul was tossëd to and fro,
With sundry thoughts which troubled me full sore:
I pressed to pray, but sighs overset me so,
I could do nought but sigh and say no more.

The twinkling tears abundantly ran down,
My heart was eased when I had mourned my fill:
Than I began my lamentation,
And said, O Lord, how long it is thy will,
That thy poor saints shall be afflicted still?
Alas, how long shall subtle Satan rage?
Make haste O Lord, thy promise to fulfill,
Make haste to end our painful pilgrimage.

Thy silly saints are tossëd to and fro,
Awake, O Lord, why sleepest thou so long?
We have no strength against our cruel foe,
In sighs and sobs now changëd is our song.
The world prevails, our enemies are strong,
The wicked rage, but we are poor and weak:
O show thy self, with speed revenge our wrong,
Make short their days, even for thy chosen's sake. . . .

23:1–6 The LORD is my shepherd; I shall not want. He maketh me to lie down in green pastures: he leadeth me beside the still waters. He restoreth my soul: he leadeth me in the paths of righteousness for his

name's sake. Yea, though I walk through the valley of the shadow of death, I will fear no evil: for thou art with me; thy rod and thy staff they comfort me. Thou preparest a table before me in the presence of mine enemies: thou anointest my head with oil; my cup runneth over. Surely goodness and mercy shall follow me all the days of my life: and I will dwell in the house of the LORD for ever.

Psalm 23

Richard Crashaw

Happy me! o happy sheep!
Whom my God vouchsafes to keep;
Even my God, even he it is,
That points me to these ways of bliss;
On whose pastures cheerful spring,
All the year doth sit and sing,
And rejoicing smiles to see
Their green backs were his livery:
Pleasure sings my soul to rest,
Plenty wears me at her breast,
Whose sweet temper teaches me
Nor wanton, nor in want to be.
At my feet the blubbering mountain
Weeping, melts into a fountain,
Whose soft silver-sweating streams
Make high noon forget his beams:
When my wayward breath is flying,
He calls home my soul from dying,
Strokes and tames my rabid grief,
And does woo me into life:
When my simple weakness strays,
(Tangled in forbidden ways)
He (my Shepherd) is my guide,
He's before me, on my side,
And behind me, he beguiles
Craft in all her knotty wiles;
He expounds the giddy wonder
Of my weary steps, and under
Spreads a path clear as the day,
Where no churlish rub says nay
To my joy-conducted feet,
Whilst they gladly go to meet
Grace and peace, to meet new lays

Tuned to my great Shepherd's praise.
Come now all ye terrors, sally
Muster forth into the valley,
Where triumphant darkness hovers
With a sable wing, that covers
Brooding horror. Come thou Death,
Let the damps of thy dull breath
Overshadow even the shade,
And make darkness self afraid;
There my feet, even there shall find
Way for a resolved mind.
Still my Shepherd, still my God,
Thou art with me, still thy rod,
And thy staff, whose influence
Gives direction, gives defence.
At the whisper of thy Word
Crowned abundance spreads my board:
While I feast, my foes do feed
Their rank malice not their need,
So that with the self-same bread
They are starved, and I am fed.
How my head in ointment swims!
How my cup o'erlooks her brims!
So, even so still may I move
By the line of thy dear love;
Still may thy sweet mercy spread
A shady arm above my head,
About my paths, so shall I find
The fair center of my mind
Thy temple, and those lovely walls
Bright ever with a beam that falls
Fresh from the pure glance of thine eye,
Lighting to Eternity.
There I'll dwell forever, there
Will I find a purer air
To feed my life with, there I'll sup
Balm and nectar in my cup,
And thence my ripe soul will I breath
Warm into the arms of Death.

Psalm XXIII

P. Hately Waddell

The sheep-keepin o' the Lord's kind an' canny, wi' a braw howff at lang last: David keeps his sheep; the Lord keeps David.

An heigh-lilt o' David's.

The Lord is my herd, nae want sal fa' me:
He luts me till lie amang green howes; he airts me atowre by the lown watirs:
He waukens my wa'-gen saul; he weises me roun, for his ain name's sake, intil right roddins.
Na!, tho' I gang thro' the dead-mirk-dail; e'en thar, sal I dread ane skaithin:
for yersel are nar-by me; yer stok an' yer stay haud me baith fu' cheerie.
My buird ye hae hansell'd in face o' my faes; ye hae drookit my head wi' oyle;
my bicker is fu' an' skailin.
E'en sae, sal gude-guidin' an' gude-gree gang wi' me, ilk day o' my livin;
an' evir mair syne, i' the Lord's ain howff, at lang last, sal I mak bydan.

Whitmonday

Louis MacNeice

Their feet on London, their heads in the gray clouds,
The Bank (if you call it a holiday) Holiday crowds
Stroll from street to street, cocking an eye
For where the angel used to be in the sky;
But the Happy Future is a thing of the past, and the street
Echoes to nothing but their dawdling feet
The Lord's my shepherd—familiar words of myth
Stand up better to bombs than a granite monolith.
Perhaps there is something in them. *I'll not want*—
Not when I'm dead. *He makes me down to lie*—
Death my christening and fire my font—
The quiet (Thames' or Don's or Salween's) *waters by.*

27:1 The LORD is my light and my salvation; whom shall I fear? the LORD is the strength of my life; of whom shall I be afraid?

Psalm III

Allen Ginsberg

To God: to illuminate all men. Beginning with Skid Road.
Let Occidental and Washington be transformed into a higher place,
the plaza of eternity,
Illuminate the welders in shipyards with the brilliance of their
torches.
Let the crane operator lift up his arm for joy.
Let elevators creak and speak, ascending and descending in awe.
Let the mercy of the flower's direction beckon in the eye.
Let the straight flower bespeak its purpose in straightness—to seek
the light.
Let the crooked flower bespeak its purpose in crookedness—to seek
the light.
Let the crookedness and straightness bespeak the light.
Let Puget Sound be a blast of light.
I feed on your Name like a cockroach on a crumb—this cockroach
is holy.

Seattle 1956

34:8 O taste and see that the LORD is good: blessed is the man that trusteth in him.

O Taste and See

Denise Levertov

The world is
not with us enough.
O taste and see

the subway Bible poster said,
meaning The Lord, meaning
if anything all that lives
to the imagination's tongue,

grief, mercy, language,
tangerine, weather, to
breathe them, bite
savor, chew, swallow, transform

into our flesh our
deaths, crossing the street, plum, quince,
living in the orchard and being

hungry, and plucking
the fruit.

38:1–18 O LORD, rebuke me not in thy wrath: neither chasten me in thy hot displeasure. For thine arrows stick fast in me, and thy hand presseth me sore. There is no soundness in my flesh because of thine anger; neither is there any rest in my bones because of my sin. For mine iniquities are gone over mine head: as an heavy burden they are too heavy for me. My wounds stink and are corrupt because of my foolishness. I am troubled; I am bowed down greatly; I go mourning all the day long. For my loins are filled with a loathsome disease: and there is no soundness in my flesh. I am feeble and sore broken: I have roared by reason of the disquietness of my heart. Lord, all my desire is before thee; and my groaning is not hid from thee. My heart panteth, my strength faileth me: as for the light of mine eyes, it also is gone from me. My lovers and my friends stand aloof from my sore; and my kinsmen stand afar off. They also that seek after my life lay snares for me: and they that seek my hurt speak mischievous things, and imagine deceits all the day long. But I, as a deaf man, heard not; and I was as a dumb man that openeth not his mouth. Thus I was as a man that heareth not, and in whose mouth are no reproofs. For in thee, O LORD, do I hope: thou wilt hear, O Lord my God. For I said, Hear me, lest otherwise they should rejoice over me: when my foot slippeth, they magnify themselves against me. For I am ready to halt, and my sorrow is continually before me. For I will declare mine iniquity; I will be sorry for my sin.

COGITABO PRO PECCATO MEO

WILLIAM HABINGTON

In what dark silent grove
Profaned by no unholy love,
Where witty melancholy ne'er
Did carve the trees or wound the air,
Shall I religious leisure win
To weep away my sin?

How fondly have I spent
My youth's unvalued treasure, lent
To traffic for celestial joys?
My unripe years pursuing toys;
Judging things best that were most gay
Fled unobserved away.

Grown elder I admired
Our poets as from heaven inspired.
What obelisks decreed I fit
For Spenser's Art, and Sydney's wit?
But waxing sober soon I found
Fame but an idle sound.

Then I my blood obeyed
And each bright face an idol made:
Verse in an humble sacrifice,
I offered to my mistress' eyes.
But I no sooner grace did win
But met the devil within.

But grown more politic
I took account of each state trick:
Observed each motion, judged him wise,
Who had a conscience fit to rise.
Whom soon I found but form and rule
And the more serious fool.

But now my soul prepare
To ponder what and where we are:
How frail is life, how vain a breath
Opinion, how uncertain death:
How only a poor stone shall bear
Witness that once we were.

How a shrill trumpet shall
Us to the bar as traitors call.
Then shall we see too late that pride
Hath hope with flattery belied
And that the mighty in command
Pale cowards there must stand.

38:19–22 But mine enemies are lively, and they are strong: and they that hate me wrongfully are multiplied. They also that render evil for good are mine adversaries; because I follow the thing that good is. Forsake me not, O LORD: O my God, be not far from me. Make haste to help me, O Lord my salvation.

Complaining

George Herbert

Do not beguile my heart,
Because thou art
My power and wisdom. Put me not to shame,
Because I am
Thy clay that weeps, thy dust that calls.

Thou art the Lord of glory:
The deed and story
Are both thy due: but I a silly fly
That live or die
According as the weather falls.

Art thou all justice, Lord?
Shows not thy word
More attributes? Am I all throat or eye,
To weep or cry?
Have I no parts but those of grief?

Let not thy wrathful power
Afflict my hour,
My inch of life: or let thy gracious power
Contract my hour,
That I may climb and find relief.

39:1–5 I said, I will take heed to my ways, that I sin not with my tongue: I will keep my mouth with a bridle, while the wicked is before me. I was dumb with silence, I held my peace, even from good; and my sorrow was stirred. My heart was hot within me, while I was musing the fire burned: then spake I with my tongue, LORD, make me to know mine end, and the measure of my days, what it is: that I may know how frail I am. Behold, thou hast made my days as an handbreadth; and mine age is as nothing before thee: verily every man at his best state is altogether vanity. Selah.

AWAKE, AWAKE, THOU HEAVY SPRITE

THOMAS CAMPION

Awake, awake, thou heavy sprite,
That sleepst the deadly sleep of sin;
Rise now, and walk the ways of light:
'Tis not too late yet to begin.
Seek heaven early, seek it late,
True faith still finds an open gate.

Get up, get up, thou leaden man:
Thy tracks to endless joy or pain
Yields but the model of a span;
Yet burns out thy life's lamp in vain.
One minute bounds thy bane, or bliss,
Then watch, and labor while time is.

39:6–13 Surely every man walketh in a vain shew: surely they are disquieted in vain: he heapeth up riches, and knoweth not who shall gather them. And now, Lord, what wait I for? my hope is in thee. Deliver me from all my transgressions: make me not the reproach of the foolish. I was dumb, I opened not my mouth; because thou didst it. Remove thy stroke away from me: I am consumed by the blow of thine hand. When thou with rebukes dost correct man for iniquity, thou makest his beauty to consume away like a moth: surely every man is vanity. Selah. Hear my prayer, O LORD, and give ear unto my cry; hold not thy peace at my tears: for I am a stranger with thee, and a sojourner, as all my fathers were. O spare me, that I may recover strength, before I go hence, and be no more.

FIRE IN MY MEDITATION BURNED

HENRY AINSWORTH

Fire in my meditation burned;
I with my tongue did speak.
Jehovah, make me know my end,
What my days' measure eke,
Know let me how short lived I am.
Lo, thou hast given my days
As handbreadths, and my worldly time
'Fore thee as nothing weighs.

Sure wholly vain is every man
Though settled fast, Selah.
Sure in an image walk doth man;
Surely vain stir make they.
One heaps up goods, and knoweth not
Who shall their gatherer be;
And now, what do I look for, Lord?
My longing is for thee.

Free me from all my trespasses;
Fools' mockage make not me.
I dumb am, open not my mouth,
For it is done of thee.
A pilgrim as my fathers all,
Stay from me, and let me
Refresh myself; ere that I go
And I no more shall be.

40:1–6 I waited patiently for the LORD; and he inclined unto me, and heard my cry. He brought me up also out of an horrible pit, out of the miry clay, and set my feet upon a rock, and established my goings. And he hath put a new song in my mouth, even praise unto our God: many shall see it, and fear, and shall trust in the LORD. Blessed is that man that maketh the LORD his trust, and respecteth not the proud, nor such as turn aside to lies. Many, O LORD my God, are thy wonderful works which thou hast done, and thy thoughts which are to us-ward: they cannot be reckoned up in order unto thee: if I would declare and speak of them, they are more than can be numbered. Sacrifice and offering thou didst not desire; mine ears hast thou opened: burnt offering and sin offering hast thou not required.

When Israel, of the Lord beloved

Sir Walter Scott

When Israel, of the Lord beloved,
        Out from the land of bondage came,
Her fathers' God before her moved,
        An awful guide in smoke and flame.
By day, along the astonished lands
        The cloudy pillar glided slow;
By night, Arabia's crimsoned sands
        Returned the fiery column's glow.

There rose the choral hymn of praise,
And trump and timbrel answered keen,
And Zion's daughters poured their lays,
With priest's and warrior's voice between.
No portents now our foes amaze,
Forsaken Israel wanders lone;
Our fathers would not know Thy ways,
And Thou hast left them to their own.

But present still, though now unseen!
When brightly shines the prosperous day,
Be thoughts of Thee a cloudy screen
To temper the deceitful ray.
And oh, when stoops on Judah's path
In shade and storm the frequent night,
Be Thou, long-suffering, slow to wrath,
A burning and a shining light!

Our harps we left by Babel's streams,
The tyrant's jest, the Gentile's scorn;
No censer round our altar beams,
And mute are timbrel, harp, and horn.
But Thou hast said, The blood of goat,
The flesh of rams I will not prize;
A contrite heart, a humble thought,
Are mine accepted sacrifice.

45:1–2 My heart is inditing a good matter: I speak of the things which I have made touching the king: my tongue is the pen of a ready writer. Thou art fairer than the children of men: grace is poured into thy lips: therefore God hath blessed thee for ever.

Meditation Seven

Edward Taylor

Thy human frame, my glorious Lord, I spy.
A golden still with heavenly choice drugs filled:
Thy holy love, the glowing heat whereby

The spirit of grace is graciously distilled.
Thy mouth the neck through which these spirits still;
My soul thy vial make, and therewith fill.

Thy speech the liquour in thy vessel stands,
Well tinged with grace, a blessed tincture, lo,
Thy words distilled grace in thy lips poured, and
Give graces tincture in them where they go.
Thy words in graces tincture stilled, Lord, may
The tincture of thy grace in me convey.

That golden mint of words thy mouth divine
Doth tip these words, which by my fall were spoiled:
And dub with gold dug out of graces mine,
That they thine image might have in them foiled.
Grace in thy lips poured out's as liquid gold:
Thy bottle make my soul, Lord, it to hold.

46:1–11 God is our refuge and strength, a very present help in trouble. Therefore will not we fear, though the earth be removed, and though the mountains be carried into the midst of the sea; Though the waters thereof roar and be troubled, though the mountains shake with the swelling thereof. Selah. There is a river, the streams whereof shall make glad the city of God, the holy place of the tabernacles of the most High. God is in the midst of her; she shall not be moved: God shall help her, and that right early. The heathen raged, the kingdoms were moved: he uttered his voice, the earth melted. The LORD of hosts is with us; the God of Jacob is our refuge. Selah. Come, behold the works of the LORD, what desolations he hath made in the earth. He maketh wars to cease unto the end of the earth; he breaketh the bow, and cutteth the spear in sunder; he burneth the chariot in the fire. Be still, and know that I am God: I will be exalted among the heathen, I will be exalted in the earth.The LORD of hosts is with us; the God of Jacob is our refuge. Selah.

HEXAMETERS

SAMUEL TAYLOR COLERIDGE

God is our strength and our refuge: therefore will we not tremble,
Though the Earth be removed and though the perpetual mountains
Sink in the swell of the ocean! God is our strength and our refuge.

There is a river the flowing whereof shall gladden the city,
Hallelujah! the City of God! Jehova shall help her.
The idolaters raged, the kingdoms were moving in fury;
But he uttered his voice: Earth melted away from beneath them.
Hallelujah! th' Eternal is with us, Almighty Jehova!
Fearful the works of the Lord, yea fearful his desolations;
But He maketh the battle to cease, he burneth the spear and the chariot.
Hallelujah! th' Eternal is with us, the God of our Fathers!

64:1–6 Hear my voice, O God, in my prayer: preserve my life from fear of the enemy. Hide me from the secret counsel of the wicked; from the insurrection of the workers of iniquity: Who whet their tongue like a sword, and bend their bows to shoot their arrows, even bitter words: That they may shoot in secret at the perfect: suddenly do they shoot at him, and fear not. They encourage themselves in an evil matter: they commune of laying snares privily; they say, Who shall see them? They search out iniquities; they accomplish a diligent search: both the inward thought of every one of them, and the heart, is deep.

The Heart is Deep

Roger Wolcott

He that can trace a ship making her way,
Amidst the threatening surges on the sea;
Or track a towering eagle in the air,
Or on a rock find the impressions there
Made by a serpent's footsteps; who surveys
The subtle intrigues that a young man lays,
In his sly courtship of an harmless maid,
Whereby his wanton amours are conveyed
Into her breast; 'tis he alone that can
Find out cursed policies of man.

73:2–3 But as for me, my feet were almost gone; my steps had well nigh slipped. For I was envious at the foolish, when I saw the prosperity of the wicked.

Some Reflections

In a Dialogue Between Teresa and Ardelia On the 2nd and 3rd Verses of the 73rd Psalm

Anne Finch, Countess of Winchilsea

Teresa

Hither, Ardelia, I your steps pursue,
No solitude should e'er exclude a friend,
Your griefs I see, and as to friendship due,
Demand the cause, to which these sorrows tend,
What their beginnings were, and what may be their end?

Ardelia

Alas! Ardelia is not vainly sad,
Nor to the clouds, that shade my careful brow,
Can fancies, dark and false suggestions add,
But my Teresa, since you wish to know,
I all my cares will tell, and all my griefs will show.

How, I my God, and his just laws adore,
How I have served him, with my early years,
How I have loved his name, and feared his power,
Witness his temples, where my falling tears,
Have followed still my faults, and ushered in my fears.

But oh! this God, the glorious architect
Of this fair world, of this large globe we see,
Seems those who trust him most, most to neglect,
Else my Teresa, else, how could it be,
That all his storms attend, and tempests fall on me.

The proud he hates, yet me he does expose
Empty of all things, naked to their scorn.
His world, on them he liberally bestows,
Theirs are his vines, his fields, his flocks, his corn,
And all that can sustain, and all that can adorn.

These are the men, possess the mighty store,
Compass the Earth, and with the boundless deep
All they bestow, receive again, with more;
Whilst I, in fears to lose, and cares to keep,
Obtain but daily bread, with interrupted sleep.

Teresa

Ardelia hold, if more thou hast to say
 On this pernicious subject, let it die;
The subtle Fiend, that leads thy soul astray,
 Thou dost not in this hour of sin, descry,
 Oh! if we wander once, how soon the serpent's nigh.

Art thou content, to have thy portion here,
 The Tyrian purple, and the costly fare,
The purchase waits thee, but will cost thee dear,
 For mighty sums of vice, thou must not spare,
 Do, as the wicked does, and thou, with him mayst share?

Canst thou repine, that Earth is not thy lot,
 And in that want, thy bounteous God distrust,
Confining all his mercies to that spot?
 Others of weight, acknowledge sure, we must,
 Or be to truth opposed, and providence unjust.

Who seals thy forehead, when the plague is nigh,
 Ere the destroying angel can descend?
Who guides th' avenging shafts, that o'er thee fly?
 When thou didst yet upon the breast depend,
 Who was thy father then, and who was then thy friend?

Who gave his blood, when thine could not suffice
 To pay thy debt, who for thee sighed and wept,
And bought that glory, at a wondrous price,
 Which is to future ages for thee kept,
 Unless thou choose this world, and that to come, neglect?

Who leads thee through this vale of tears below,
 To bring thee to thy country, safe at last?
Who in the way, does all thou wantst below,
 For more than this, his sacred word ne'er passed,
 And all thou truly wantst, assuredly thou hast?

What if to prove thee, when the billows rise,
 He from thy danger turns, and seems to sleep,
Wilt thou to murmurs, straight convert thy cries,
 The crowd we see, the shore may safely keep,
 Whilst the distinguished twelve are threatened by the deep?

Ardelia

Teresa, from my guilty dream, I wake,
The truth has reached me, and my fault I find,
Forgive me God, forgive the short mistake,
How could it enter my deluded mind,
That all, both worlds could give, was for one wretch designed?

I saw the Mighty, and began to slide,
My feet were gone, but I return again,
And would not with them here, the spoils divide;
Nor looked I at the end of glorious men,
Nor thought how lost they were, nor how abandoned then.

A while, the servant of Elisha, so
Although his master's power with Heaven he knew,
His faith forgoes, surrounded with the foe,
Till by the prophet's prayer, the veil withdrew
And showed the doubted aid of providence in view.

76:4–9 Thou art more glorious and excellent than the mountains of prey. The stouthearted are spoiled, they have slept their sleep: and none of the men of might have found their hands. At thy rebuke, O God of Jacob, both the chariot and horse are cast into a dead sleep. Thou, even thou, art to be feared: and who may stand in thy sight when once thou art angry? Thou didst cause judgment to be heard from heaven; the earth feared, and was still, When God arose to judgment, to save all the meek of the earth. Selah.

Lord I Sleep and I Sleep

David Shapiro

Lord I sleep and I sleep

I am haunted all night by the look of cars

When I sleep they can speak, they say: Ride me,
David. I am fast as death

Well who lighted this road up? Who made me this clear?

You know I am soft as plasma

I am haunted by all these things

I am crushed instantly

79:1–8 O god, the heathen are come into thine inheritance; thy holy temple have they defiled; they have laid Jerusalem on heaps. The dead bodies of thy servants have they given to be meat unto the fowls of the heaven, the flesh of thy saints unto the beasts of the earth. Their blood have they shed like water round about Jerusalem; and there was none to bury them. We are become a reproach to our neighbours, a scorn and derision to them that are round about us. How long, LORD? wilt thou be angry for ever? shall thy jealousy burn like fire? Pour out thy wrath upon the heathen that have not known thee, and upon the kingdoms that have not called upon thy name. For they have devoured Jacob, and laid waste his dwelling place. O remember not against us former iniquities: let thy tender mercies speedily prevent us: for we are brought very low.

On Jordan's Banks

George Noel Gordon, Lord Byron

On Jordan's banks the Arab's camels stray,
On Sion's hill the False One's votaries pray,
The Baal-adorer bows on Sinai's steep—
Yet there—even there—Oh God! thy thunders sleep:

There—where thy finger scorched the tablet stone!
There—where thy shadow to thy people shone!
Thy glory shrouded in its garb of fire:
Thyself—none living see and not expire!

Oh! in the lightning let thy glance appear;
Sweep from his shivered hand the oppressor's spear!
How long by tyrants shall thy land be trod?
How long thy temples worshipless, Oh God?

90:1–6 Lord, thou hast been our dwelling place in all generations. Before the mountains were brought forth, or ever thou hadst formed the earth and the world, even from everlasting to everlasting, thou art God. Thou turnest

man to destruction; and sayest, Return, ye children of men. For a thousand years in thy sight are but as yesterday when it is past, and as a watch in the night. Thou carriest them away as with a flood; they are as a sleep: in the morning they are like grass which groweth up. In the morning it flourisheth, and groweth up; in the evening it is cut down, and withereth.

The First Six Verses of the Ninetieth Psalm

Robert Burns

O Thou, the first, the greatest friend
Of all the human race!
Whose strong right hand has ever been
Their stay and dwelling-place!

Before the mountains heaved their heads
Beneath thy forming hand,
Before this ponderous globe itself
Arose at thy command:

That power which raised and still upholds
This universal frame,
From countless, unbeginning time
Was ever still the same.

Those mighty periods of years
Which seem to us so vast,
Appear no more before thy sight
Than yesterday that's past.

Thou giv'st the word; thy creature, man,
Is to existence brought;
Again thou sayst, 'Ye sons of men,
'Return ye into nought!'

Thou layest them with all their cares
In everlasting sleep;
As with a flood thou tak'st them off
With overwhelming sweep.

They flourish like the morning flower,
In beauty's pride arrayed;
But long ere night cut down it lies
All withered and decayed.

90:7–17 For we are consumed by thine anger, and by thy wrath are we troubled. Thou hast set our iniquities before thee, our secret sins in the light of thy countenance. For all our days are passed away in thy wrath: we spend our years as a tale that is told. The days of our years are threescore years and ten; and if by reason of strength they be fourscore years, yet is their strength labour and sorrow; for it is soon cut off, and we fly away. Who knoweth the power of thine anger? even according to thy fear, so is thy wrath. So teach us to number our days, that we may apply our hearts unto wisdom. Return, O LORD, how long? and let it repent thee concerning thy servants. O satisfy us early with thy mercy; that we may rejoice and be glad all our days. Make us glad according to the days wherein thou hast afflicted us, and the years wherein we have seen evil. Let thy work appear unto thy servants, and thy glory unto their children. And let the beauty of the LORD our God be upon us: and establish thou the work of our hands upon us; yea, the work of our hands establish thou it.

In Pilgrim Life our Rest

Edwin Sandys

In pilgrim life our rest,
In thralled estate our stay;
From age to age thou, Lord, hast been
And saved us from decay.
Thyself, ere birth to hills,
To earth ere form didst give;
Ere world hadst framed; from aye to aye
All glorious God dost live.
But man, thy creature fallen,
Thy justice doth pursue
To dust, and saith, "Ye Adam's sons,
Return whence first ye grew."

When thousand years we lived,
Those thousand in thy sight
Not more appeared than one day past,
Than watch in shortest night.
Since when our dream-like life,
As weakest herb, soon dies;
Which morn makes flower, hot noon bids fade,
Sad even mows down and dries.
What have our toils achieved?
Through anger thine, our day
Black night devours; our fruitless years
As thought fly vain away.

And comfort, cheer us, Lord,
As chastised long by thee;
Much ill our woeful eyes have seen;
Like joy so cause us see.
This joy with life shall last.
Then let thy work grow clear
Toward servants thine; on children there
Thy glory make appear.
And let God's pleasèd face,
Us with is beauties bless
And from our works; O Thou, our works
To happiest end address.

98:1 O sing unto the LORD a new song; for he hath done marvellous things: his right hand, and his holy arm, hath gotten him the victory.

Te Deum

Charles Reznikoff

Not because of victories
I sing,
having none,
but for the common sunshine,
the breeze,
the largess of the spring.

Not for victory
but for the day's work done
as well as I was able;
not for a seat upon the dais
but at the common table.

102:1–17 Hear my prayer, O LORD, and let my cry come unto thee. Hide not thy face from me in the day when I am in trouble; incline thine ear unto me: in the day when I call answer me speedily. For my days are consumed like smoke, and my bones are burned as an hearth. My heart is smitten, and withered like grass; so that I forget to eat my bread. By reason of the voice of my groaning my bones cleave to my skin. I am like a

pelican of the wilderness: I am like an owl of the desert. I watch, and am as a sparrow alone upon the house top. Mine enemies reproach me all the day; and they that are mad against me are sworn against me. For I have eaten ashes like bread, and mingled my drink with weeping. Because of thine indignation and thy wrath: for thou hast lifted me up, and cast me down. My days are like a shadow that declineth; and I am withered like grass. But thou, O LORD, shall endure for ever; and thy remembrance unto all generations. Thou shalt arise, and have mercy upon Zion: for the time to favour her, yea, the set time, is come. For thy servants take pleasure in her stones, and favour the dust thereof. So the heathen shall fear the name of the LORD, and all the kings of the earth thy glory. When the LORD shall build up Zion, he shall appear in his glory. He will regard the prayer of the destitute, and not despise their prayer.

Lord, Hear My Prayer

John Clare

Lord, hear my prayer when trouble glooms,
Let sorrow find a way,
And when the day of trouble comes,
Turn not thy face away:
My bones like hearthstones burn away,
My life like vapoury smoke decays.

My heart is smitten like the grass,
That withered lies and dead,
And I, so lost to what I was
Forget to eat my bread.
My voice is groaning all the day,
My bones prick through this skin of clay.

The wilderness's pelican,
The desert's lonely owl—
I am their like, a desert man
In ways as lone and foul.
As sparrows on the cottage top
I wait till I with fainting drop.

I hear my enemies reproach,
All silently I mourn;
They on my private peace encroach,
Against me they are sworn.
Ashes as bread my trouble shares,
And mix my food with weeping cares.

Yet not for them is sorrow's toil,
I fear no mortal's frowns—
But thou hast held me up awhile
And thou has cast me down.
My days like shadows waste from view,
I mourn like withered grass in dew.

But thou, Lord, shalt endure for ever,
All generations through;
Thou shalt to Zion be the giver
Of joy and mercy too.
Her very stones are in thy trust,
Thy servants reverence her dust.

Heathens shall hear and fear thy name,
All kings of earth thy glory know
When thou shalt build up Zion's fame
And live in glory there below.
He'll not despise their prayers, though mute,
But still regard the destitute.

104:24–31 O LORD, how manifold are thy works! in wisdom hast thou made them all: the earth is full of thy riches. So is this great and wide sea, wherein are things creeping innumerable, both small and great beasts. There go the ships: there is that leviathan, whom thou hast made to play therein. These wait all upon thee; that thou mayest give them their meat in due season. That thou givest them they gather: thou openest thine hand, they are filled with good. Thou hidest thy face, they are troubled: thou takest away their breath, they die, and return to their dust. Thou sendest forth thy spirit, they are created: and thou renewest the face of the earth. The glory of the LORD shall endure for ever: the LORD shall rejoice in his works.

Praise Ye the Lord, O Celebrate His Fame

Peleg Folger

Praise ye the Lord, O celebrate his fame
Praise the eternal God that dwells above;
His power will forever be the same,
The same forever his eternal love.

Ye sailors speak that plow the watery main,
Where raging seas and foaming billows roar,
Praise ye the Lord, and in a lofty strain,
Sing of his wonder-working love and power.

Thou didst, O Lord, create the mighty whale
That wondrous monster of a mighty length;
Vast is his head and body, vast his tail,
Beyond conception his unmeasured strength.

But, everlasting God, thou dost ordain,
That we poor feeble mortals should engage
(Ourselves, our wives and children to maintain)
This dreadful monster with a martial rage.

And, though he furiously doth us assail,
Thou dost preserve us from all dangers free;
He cuts our boat in pieces with his tail,
And spills us all at once into the sea.

I twice into the dark abyss was cast,
Straining and struggling to retain my breath,
Thy waves and billows over me were past,
Thou didst, O Lord, deliver me from death.

Thou savedst me from the dangers of the sea,
That I might bless thy name for ever more.
Thy love and power the same will ever be
Thy mercy is an inexhausted store.

And when I shall this earthly ball forsake,
And leave behind me frail mortality,
Then may my soul her nimble journey take
Into the regions of eternity.

116:1–19 I love the LORD, because he hath heard my voice and my supplications. Because he hath inclined his ear unto me, therefore will I call upon him as long as I live. The sorrows of death compassed me, and the pains of hell gat hold upon me: I found trouble and sorrow. Then called I upon the name of the LORD; O LORD, I beseech thee, deliver my soul. Gracious is the LORD, and righteous; yea, our God is merciful. The

LORD preserveth the simple: I was brought low, and he helped me. Return unto thy rest, O my soul; for the LORD hath dealt bountifully with thee. For thou hast delivered my soul from death, mine eyes from tears, and my feet from falling. I will walk before the LORD in the land of the living. I believed, therefore have I spoken: I was greatly afflicted: I said in my haste, All men are liars. What shall I render unto the LORD for all his benefits toward me? I will take the cup of salvation, and call upon the name of the LORD. I will pay my vows unto the LORD now in the presence of all his people. Precious in the sight of the LORD is the death of his saints. O LORD, truly I am thy servant; I am thy servant, and the son of thine handmaid: thou hast loosed my bonds. I will offer to thee the sacrifice of thanksgiving, and will call upon the name of the LORD. I will pay my vows unto the LORD now in the presence of all his people. In the courts of the LORD'S house, in the midst of thee, O Jerusalem. Praise ye the LORD.

Praise II

George Herbert

King of Glory, King of Peace,
I will love thee;
And that love may never cease,
I will move thee.

Thou has granted my request,
Thou hast heard me:
Thou didst note my working breast,
Thou hast spared me.

Wherefore with my utmost art
I will sing thee,
And the cream of all my heart
I will bring thee.

Though my sins against me cried,
Thou didst clear me;
And alone, when they replied,
Thou didst hear me.

Seven whole days, not one in seven,
I will praise thee.
In my heart, though not in heaven,
I can raise thee.

Thou grewst soft and moist with tears,
Thou relentedst:
And when Justice called for fears,
Thou dissentedst.

Small it is, in this poor sort
To enrol thee:
Even eternity is too short
To extol thee.

117:1–2 O praise the LORD, all ye nations: praise him, all ye people. For his merciful kindness is great toward us: and the truth of the LORD endureth for ever. Praise ye the LORD.

Laudate Dominum

Mary Herbert, Countess of Pembroke

P raise him that aye
R emains the same:
A ll tongues display
I ehovas fame.
S ing all that share
T his earthly ball:
H is mercies are
E xposed to all:
L ike as the word
O nce he doth give,
R olled in record,
D oth time outlive.

119:9–16 Wherewithal shall a young man cleanse his way? by taking heed thereto according to thy word. With my whole heart have I sought thee: O let me not wander from thy commandments. Thy word have I hid in mine heart, that I might not sin against thee. Blessed art thou, O LORD: teach me thy statutes. With my lips have I declared all the judgments of thy mouth. I have rejoiced in the way of thy testimonies, as much as in all riches. I will meditate in thy precepts, and have respect unto thy ways. I will delight myself in thy statutes: I will not forget thy word.

Stanzas Imitated from Psalm CXIX

Thomas Warton the Elder

Say, how shall thoughtless, easy-natured youth,
Be pure from all the stains their follies give?
O let them learn the sober law of truth,
Know thy rewards, and answerably live.

Full of this hope I seek thee, dearest Lord,
And lest the foe once more my soul should win,
Deep in my heart I treasure up thy Word,
A constant guard against the charms of sin.

How am I pleased when joy, and faith, and awe,
Strive which shall most employ my various tongue,
That loves to dwell on all thy wondrous Law,
Guide of my life, and subject of my song!

Now fame or pleasure, or the wealthy East,
May tempt indeed—but never shall remove,
The lively zeal that burns within my breast,
Thy Name to honor, and thy Law to love.

119:24–25 Thy testimonies also are my delight and my counsellors. My soul cleaveth unto the dust: quicken thou me according to thy word.

On the Spirit Adulterated by the Flesh

Henry Colman

How do I spin my time away
In caring how to get
Ungodly wealth, and fret
My self to sweat,
As if thou Lord hadst meant this clay
No after life, no reckoning day.

What graceless fool would love his earth
    So, as with all his might
    To pamper with delight
        The same 'gainst right,
Forgetting his divine soul's birth
Was nobler, and of greater worth?

Thou Lord didst frame this soul of mine
    Only to honor thee,
    Not basely fond to be
        Of vanity,
Unflesh it then, and so refine
It Lord it may be all divine.

Quicken my dull-drooping spirit
    That it may praise thy name,
    Cleanse it from sin and blame,
        Take from it shame.
Grant that by my Savior's merit
Eternity it may inherit.

Let it not grovelling lie pressed down
    With earth, but mount, and gain
    An everlasting reign,
        Let it retain
No dross, and when it shall have thrown
Its cover off, grant it a crown.

119:33–40 Teach me, O LORD, the way of thy statutes; and I shall keep it unto the end. Give me understanding, and I shall keep thy law; yea, I shall observe it with my whole heart. Make me to go in the path of thy commandments; for therein do I delight. Incline my heart unto thy testimonies, and not to covetousness. Turn away mine eyes from beholding vanity; and quicken thou me in thy way. Stablish thy word unto thy servant, who is devoted to thy fear. Turn away my reproach which I fear: for thy judgments are good. Behold, I have longed after thy precepts: quicken me in thy righteousness.

Psalm 119. 37

Francis Quarles

How like to threads of flax
That touch the flame, are my inflamed desires!
How like to yielding wax
My soul dissolves before these wanton fires!
The fire, but touched, the flame but felt,
Like flax, I burn; like wax, I melt.

O how this flesh doth draw
My fettered soul to that deceitful fire!
And how th' eternal Law
Is baffled by the law of my desire!
How truly bad, how seeming good
Are all the laws of flesh and blood!

O wretched state of men,
The height of whose ambition is to borrow
What must be paid again
With griping interest, of the next days sorrow!
How wild his thoughts! How apt to range!
How apt to vary! Apt to change!

How intricate and nice
Is man's perplexed way to man's desire!
Sometimes upon the ice
He slips, and sometimes falls into the fire;
His progress is extreme and bold,
Or very hot, or very cold.

The common food he doth
Sustain his soul-tormenting thoughts withal,
Is honey in his mouth
To-night, and in his heart, to-morrow, gall;
'T is oftentimes, within an hour,
Both very sweet and very sour.

If sweet Corinna smile,
A heaven of joy breaks down into his heart:
Corinna frowns awhile,

Hell's torments are but copies of his smart:
    Within a lustful heart doth dwell
    A seeming Heaven, a very Hell.

    Thus worthless, vain, and void
Of comfort, are the fruits of earth's employment;
    Which ere they be enjoyed
Distract us, and destroy us in th' enjoyment;
    These be the pleasures that are prized
    When Heaven's cheap pen'worth stands despised.

    Lord, quench these hasty flashes,
Which dart as lightning from the thundering skies,
    And every minute, dashes
Against the wanton windows of mine eyes:
    Lord, close the casement, whilst I stand
    Behind the curtain of thy hand.

121:1 I will lift up mine eyes unto the hills, from whence cometh my help.

The Hills

D. H. Lawrence

I lift up mine eyes unto the hills
and there they are, but no strength comes from them to me.

Only from darkness
and ceasing to see
strength comes.

127:1–2 Except the LORD build the house, they labour in vain that build it: except the LORD keep the city, the watchman waketh but in vain. It is vain for you to rise up early, to sit up late, to eat the bread of sorrows: for so he giveth his beloved sleep.

The Sleep

Elizabeth Barrett Browning

Of all the thoughts of God that are
Borne inward unto souls afar,
Along the Psalmist's music deep,
Now tell me if that any is,
For gift or grace, surpassing this:
"He giveth his belovèd—sleep?"

What would we give to our beloved?
The hero's heart to be unmoved,
The poet's star-tuned harp to sweep,
The patriot's voice to teach and rouse,
The monarch's crown to light the brows?
He giveth his belovèd—sleep.

What do we give to our beloved?
A little faith all undisproved,
A little dust to overweep,
And bitter memories to make
The whole earth blasted for our sake:
He giveth his belovèd—sleep.

"Sleep soft, beloved!" we sometimes say,
Who have no tune to charm away
Sad dreams that through the eyelids creep:
But never doleful dream again
Shall break the happy slumber when
He giveth his belovèd—sleep.

O earth, so full of dreary noises!
O men, with wailing in your voices!
O delved gold, the wailers heap!
O strife, O curse, that o'er it fall!
God strikes a silence through you all,
And giveth his beloved—sleep.

His dews drop mutely on the hill,
His cloud above it saileth still,
Though on its slope men sow and reap:
More softly than the dew is shed,
Or cloud is floated overhead,
He giveth his belovèd—sleep.

Aye, men may wonder while they scan
A living, thinking, feeling man
Confirmed in such a rest to keep;
But angels say,—and through the word
I think their happy smile is heard—
"He giveth his belovèd—sleep."

For me, my heart that erst did go
Most like a tired child at a show,
That sees through tears the mummers leap,
Would now its wearied vision close,
Would childlike on his love repose
Who giveth his belovèd—sleep.

And friends, dear friends, when it shall be
That this low breath is gone from me,
And round my bier ye come to weep,
Let One, most loving of you all,
Say, "Not a tear must o'er her fall!
He giveth his belovèd—sleep."

130:1–8 Out of the depths have I cried unto thee, O LORD. Lord, hear my voice: let thine ears be attentive to the voice of my supplications. If thou, LORD, shouldest mark iniquities, O Lord, who shall stand? But there is forgiveness with thee, that thou mayest be feared. I wait for the LORD, my soul doth wait, and in his word do I hope. My soul waiteth for the Lord more than they that watch for the morning: I say, more than they that watch for the morning. Let Israel hope in the LORD: for with the LORD there is mercy, and with him is plenteous redemption. And he shall redeem Israel from all his iniquities.

THE INTRODUCTION TO THE PSALM OF *DE PROFUNDIS*

GEORGE GASCOIGNE

The skies gan scowl, o'ercast with misty clouds,
When (as I rode alone by London way,

Cloakless, unclad) thus did I sing and say:
Behold, quoth I, bright Titan how he shrouds
His head aback, and yields the rain his reach,
'Til in his wrath, Dan Jove have soused the soil,
And washed me, wretch, which in his travail toil.
But holla (here) doth rudeness me appeach,
Since Jove is Lord and king of mighty power,
Which can command the sun to show his face,
And (when him list) to give the rain his place.
Why do not I my weary muses frame,
(Although I be well soused in this shower,)
To write some verse in honor of his name?

GASCOIGNE'S *DE PROFUNDIS*

From depth of dole wherein my soul doth dwell,
From heavy heart which harbors in my breast,
From troubled sprite which seldom taketh rest,
From hope of heaven, from dread of darksome hell,
O gracious God, to thee I cry and yell.
My God, my Lord, my lovely Lord alone,
To thee I call, to thee I make my moan.
And thou (good God) vouchsafe in gree to take,
This woeful plaint,
Wherein I faint.
Oh hear me then for thy great mercy's sake.

Oh bend thine ears attentively to hear,
Oh turn thine eyes, behold me how I wail,
Oh hearken Lord, give ear for mine avail,
Oh mark in mind the burdens that I bear:
See how I sink in sorrows everywhere.
Behold and see what dolors I endure,
Give ear and hark what plaints I put in ure.
Bend willing ear: and pity therewithall,
My wailing voice,
Which hath no choice.
But evermore upon thy name to call.

If thou good Lord shouldst take thy rod in hand,
If thou regard what sins are daily done,
If thou take hold where we our works begun,

If thou decree in judgement for to stand,
And be extreme to see our scuses scanned,
If thou take note of every thing amiss,
And write in roles how frail our nature is,
O glorious God, O King, O Prince of power,
What mortal wight,
May then have light,
To feel thy frown, if thou have list to lower?

But thou art good, and hast of mercy store,
Thou not delightst to see a sinner fall,
Thou heark'nest first, before we come to call.
Thine ears are set wide open evermore,
Before we knock thou comest to the door.
Thou art more pressed to hear a sinner cry,
Than he is quick to climb to thee on high.
Thy mighty name be praised then alway,
Let faith and fear,
True witness bear.
How fast they stand which on thy mercy stay.

I look for thee (my lovely Lord) therefore.
For thee I wait, for thee I tarry still,
Mine eyes do long to gaze on thee my fill.
For thee I watch, for thee I pry and pore.
My soul for thee attendeth evermore.
My soul doth thirst to take of thee a taste,
My soul desires with thee for to be placed.
And to thy word (which can no man deceive)
Mine only trust,
My love and lust
In confidence continually shall cleave.

Before the break or dawning of the day,
Before the light be seen in lofty skies,
Before the sun appear in pleasant wise,
Before the watch (before the watch I say)
Before the ward that waits therefore alway:
My soul, my sense, my secret thought, my sprite,
My will, my wish, my joy, and my delight:
Unto the Lord that sits in heaven on high,
With hasty wing,
From me doth fling,
And striveth still, unto the Lord to fly.

O Israel, O household of the Lord,
O Abraham's Brats, O brood of blessed seed,
O chosen sheep that love the Lord in deed:
O hungry hearts, feed still upon his word,
And put your trust in him with one accord.
For he hath mercy evermore at hand,
His fountains flow, his springs do never stand.
And plenteously he loveth to redeem,
Such sinners all,
As on him call,
And faithfully his mercies most esteem.

He will redeem our deadly drooping state,
He will bring home the sheep that go astray,
He will help them that hope in him alway:
He will appease our discord and debate,
He will soon save, though we repent us late.
He will be ours if we continue his,
He will bring bale to joy and perfect bliss.
He will redeem the flock of his elect,
From all that is,
Or was amiss.
Since Abraham's heirs did first his Laws reject.

Ever or never.

137:1–9 By the rivers of Babylon, there we sat down, yea, we wept, when we remembered Zion. We hanged our harps upon the willows in the midst thereof. For there they that carried us away captive required of us a song; and they that wasted us required of us mirth, saying, Sing us one of the songs of Zion. How shall we sing the LORD'S song in a strange land? If I forget thee, O Jerusalem, let my right hand forget her cunning. If I do not remember thee, let my tongue cleave to the roof of my mouth; if I prefer not Jerusalem above my chief joy. Remember, O LORD, the children of Edom in the day of Jerusalem; who said, Rase it, rase it, even to the foundation thereof. O daughter of Babylon, who art to be destroyed; happy shall he be, that rewardeth thee as thou hast served us. Happy shall he be, that taketh and dasheth thy little ones against the stones.

PSALM 137

THOMAS CAREW

Sitting by the streams that glide
    Down by Babel's towering wall,
With our tears we filled the tide
    Whilst our mindful thoughts recall
    Thee Oh Sion, and thy fall.

Our neglected harps unstrung,
    Not acquainted with the hand
Of the skillful tuner, hung
    On the willow trees that stand
    Planted in the neighbour land.

Yet the spiteful foe commands
    Songs of mirth, and bids us lay
To dumb harps, our captive hands,
    And, (to scoff our sorrows) say
    Sing us some sweet Hebrew lay.

But say we, our holy strain
    Is too pure for heathen land,
Nor may we God's hymns profane,
    Or move either voice or hand
    To delight a savage band.

Holy Salem if thy love
    Fall from my forgetful heart,
May the skill by which I move
    Strings of music tuned with art,
    From my withered hand depart!

May my speechless tongue give sound
    To no accents, but remain
To my prison roof fast bound,
    If my sad soul entertain
    Mirth, till thou rejoice again!

In that day remember, Lord
    Edom's brood, that in our groans
They triumph; with fire and sword
    Burn their city, hew their bones
    And make all one heap of stones.

Cruel Babel, thou shalt feel
    The revenger of our groans,
When the happy victor's steel
    As thine, ours, shall hew thy bones,
    And make thee one heap of stones.

Men shall bless the hand that tears
    From the mother's soft embraces
Sucking infants, and besmears
    With their brains, the rugged faces
    Of the rocks and stony places.

Along the Banks

JOEL BARLOW

Along the banks where Babel's current flows,
Our captive bands in deep despondence strayed,
While Zion's fall in sad remembrance rose,
Her friends, her children, mingled with the dead.

The tuneless harp that once with joy we strung,
When praise employed and mirth inspired the lay,
In mournful silence on the willows hung,
And growing grief prolonged the tedious day.

The barbarous tyrants, to increase the woe,
With taunting smiles a song of Zion claim;
Bid sacred praise in strains melodious flow,
While they blaspheme the great Jehovah's name.

But how, in heathen chains and lands unknown,
Shall Israel's sons, a song of Zion raise?
O hapless Salem, God's terrestial throne,
Thou land of glory, sacred mount of praise.

If e'er my memory lose thy lovely name,
If my cold heart neglect my kindred race,
Let dire destructions seize this guilty frame;
My hand shall perish and my voice shall cease.

Yet shall the Lord, who hears when Zion calls,
O'ertake her foes, with terror and dismay,
His arm avenge her desolated walls,
And raise her children to eternal day.

By the Rivers of Babylon We Sat Down and Wept

George Noel Gordon, Lord Byron

We sat down and wept by the waters
Of Babel, and thought of the day
When our foe, in the hue of his slaughters,
Made Salem's high places his prey;
And ye, oh her desolate daughters!
Were scattered all weeping away.

While sadly we gazed on the river
Which rolled on in freedom below.
They demanded the song: but, oh never
That triumph the stranger shall know!
May this right hand be withered forever,
Ere it string our high harp for the foe!

On the willow that harp is suspended,
Oh, Salem! its sound should be free;
And the hour when thy glories were ended
But left me that token of thee:
And ne'er shall its soft tones be blended
With the voice of the spoiler by me!

139:1–18 O LORD, thou hast searched me, and known me. Thou knowest my downsitting and mine uprising, thou understandest my thought afar off. Thou compassest my path and my lying down, and art acquainted with all my ways. For there is not a word in my tongue, but, lo, O LORD, thou knowest it altogether. Thou hast beset me behind and before, and laid thine hand upon me. Such knowledge is too wonderful

for me; it is high, I cannot attain unto it. Whither shall I go from thy spirit? or whither shall I flee from thy presence? If I ascend up into heaven, thou art there: if I make my bed in hell, behold, thou art there. If I take the wings of the morning, and dwell in the uttermost parts of the sea; Even there shall thy hand lead me, and thy right hand shall hold me. If I say, Surely the darkness shall cover me; even the night shall be light about me. Yea, the darkness hideth not from thee; but the night shineth as the day: the darkness and the light are both alike to thee. For thou hast possessed my reins: thou hast covered me in my mother's womb. I will praise thee; for I am fearfully and wonderfully made: marvellous are thy works; and that my soul knoweth right well. My substance was not hid from thee, when I was made in secret, and curiously wrought in the lowest parts of the earth. Thine eyes did see my substance, yet being unperfect; and in thy book all my members were written, which in continuance were fashioned, when as yet there was none of them. How precious also are thy thoughts unto me, O God! how great is the sum of them! If I should count them, they are more in number than the sand: when I awake, I am still with thee.

A Paraphrase upon Part of the CXXXIX Psalm

THOMAS STANLEY

Great Monarch, whose feared hands the thunder fling,
And whose quick eyes, all darkness vanquishing,
Pierce in a moment earth's remotest parts,
The night of futures, and abyss of hearts;
My breast, the closest thoughts which there reside,
From thy all-seeing knowledge cannot hide;
The number of my steps before thee lies,
And my intents (ere mine) before thy eyes.
Thou knowest me, when my self I cannot know,
And without error seest what is not so.

Speech, that light garment, which our thoughts attires,
The image of our wishes and desires,
Daughter of air, from soul to soul which flies,
And in her mother's bosom melting dies:
By higher flight appears before thee, long
Before she birth receiveth from my tongue,

Before she from my lips had learnt to frame
Those accents, which my heart did first enflame,
And this invisible body flying hence,
Assumes, by which she is betrayed to sense.

The past and future still with thee abide,
The present, which from us like streams doth slide,
With a firm constant foot before thee stays,
To thee nought young is, nought oppressed with days;
Man (as if that bright fire thine eye reflects,
Consumed of mortal objects the defects,
And changed the changing laws of his frail breath)
A heap of scattered dust, a mass of earth,
A work almost below mortality,
Immortal in thy knowledge is like thee.

But if thy anger's dreadful storm break forth,
The Orient, or the West, the South, or North,
Can no profound abyss or exile lend,
Whose depth may hide, or strength my life defend;
Though swifter than the morning I could fly,
Thy thunder, which that speed doth far outvie,
Outstripping me, my flight would soon restrain:
Though I could dive into th'unsounded main,
Which nightly quencheth the bright light o'th'skies,
I should lie open to thy brighter eyes.

Yet I not wonder, if unveiled thou find
The darkest secrets of my naked mind;
As a learned artist thou mayst well foresee
The motions of that work is framed by thee:
Thou first into this dust a soul didst send,
Thy hand my skin did o'er my bones extend,
Which greater masterpiece, whilst I admire,
I fall down lost, in seeking to rise higher:
And finding 'bove my self, my self to be,
Turn to that nothing, from whence raised by thee.

141:1–7 LORD, I cry unto thee: make haste unto me; give ear unto my voice, when I cry unto thee. Let my prayer be set forth before thee as incense; and the lifting up of my hands as the evening sacrifice. Set a watch, O LORD, before my mouth; keep the door of my lips. Incline not my heart to any evil thing, to practice wicked works with men that work iniquity: and let me not eat of their dainties. Let the righteous smite me; it shall be a kindness: and let him reprove me; it shall be an excellent oil, which shall not break my head: for yet my prayer also shall be in their calamities. When their judges are overthrown in stony places, they shall hear my words; for they are sweet. Our bones are scattered at the grave's mouth, as when one cutteth and cleaveth wood upon the earth. But mine eyes are unto thee, O GOD the Lord: in thee is my trust; leave not my soul destitute. Keep me from the snares which they have laid for me, and the gins of the workers of iniquity. Let the wicked fall into their own nets, whilst that I withal escape.

142:1–4 I cried unto the LORD with my voice; with my voice unto the LORD did I make my supplication. I poured out my complaint before him; I shewed before him my trouble. When my spirit was overwhelmed within me, then thou knewest my path.

In the way wherein I walked have they privily laid a snare for me. I looked on my right hand, and beheld, but there was no man that would know me: refuge failed me; no man cared for my soul.

In Tenebris

Thomas Hardy

When the clouds' swoln bosoms echo back the shouts of the many and
strong
That things are all as they best may be, save a few to be right ere long,
And my eyes have not the vision in them to discern what to these is so
clear,
The blot seems straightway in me alone; one better he were not here.

The stout upstanders say, All's well with us: ruers have nought to rue!
And what the potent say so oft, can it fail to be somewhat true?
Breezily go they, breezily come; their dust smokes around their career,
Till I think I am one born out of due time, who has no calling here.

Their dawns bring lusty joys, it seems; their evenings all that is sweet;
Our times are blessed times, they cry: Life shapes it as is most meet,
And nothing is much the matter; there are many smiles to a tear;
Then what is the matter is I, I say. Why should such an one be here? . . .

Let him in whose ears the low-voiced Best is killed by the clash of the First,
Who holds that if way to the Better there be, it exacts a full look at the Worst,
Who feels that delight is a delicate growth cramped by crookedness, custom, and fear,
Get him up and be gone as one shaped awry; he disturbs the order here.

Evening Prayer

THOMAS MERTON

Lord, receive my prayer
Sweet as incense smoke
Rising from my heart
Full of care
I lift up my hands
In evening sacrifice
Lord, receive my prayer.

When I meet the man
On my way
When he starts to curse
And threatens me,
Lord, guard my lips
I will not reply
Guide my steps in the night
As I go my way.

Maybe he belongs
To some other Lord
Who is not so wise and good
Maybe that is why those bones
Lie scattered on his road.

When I look to right and left
No one cares to know
Who I am, where I go.

Hear my prayer
I will trust in you
If they set their traps

On my way
If they aim their guns at me
You will guide my steps
I will pass them by
In the dark
They will never see.

Lord, to you I raise
Wide and bright
Faith-filled eyes
In the night
You are my protection
Bring me home.

And receive my prayer
Sweet as incense smoke
Rising from my heart
Free of care.

148:1–8 Praise ye the LORD. Praise ye the LORD from the heavens: praise him in the heights. Praise ye him, all his angels: praise ye him, all his hosts. Praise ye him, sun and moon: praise him, all ye stars of light. Praise him, ye heavens of heavens, and ye waters that be above the heavens. Let them praise the name of the LORD: for he commanded, and they were created. He hath also stablished them for ever and ever: he hath made a decree which shall not pass. Praise the LORD from the earth, ye dragons, and all deeps: Fire, and hail; snow, and vapours; stormy wind fulfilling his word:

from A PINDARIC POEM

Upon the Hurricaine in November 1703, referring to Psalm 148. ver. 8. With a Hymn composed of the 148th Psalm Paraphrased

ANNE FINCH, COUNTESS OF WINCHILSEA

The Hymn

To the Almighty on his radiant throne,
Let endless hallelujas rise!
Praise Him, ye wondrous heights to us unknown,
Praise Him, ye heavens unreached by mortal eyes,
Praise Him, in your degree, ye sublunary skies!

Praise Him, you angels that before him bow,
You creatures of celestial frame,
Our guests of old, our wakeful guardians now,
Praise Him, and with like zeal our hearts enflame,
Transporting then our praise to seats from whence you came!

Praise Him, thou Sun in thy meridian force;
Exalt Him, all ye stars and light!
Praise Him, thou Moon in thy revolving course,
Praise Him, thou gentler guide of silent night,
Which does to solemn praise, and serious thoughts invite.

Praise Him, ye humid vapors, which remain
Unfrozen by the sharper air;
Praise Him, as you return in showers again,
To bless the Earth and make her pastures fair:
Praise Him, ye climbing fires, the emblems of our prayer.

Praise Him, ye waters petrified above,
Ye shredded clouds that fall in snow,
Praise Him, for that you so divided move;
Ye hailstones, that you do no larger grow,
Nor, in one solid mass, oppress the world below.

Praise Him, ye soaring fowls, still as you fly,
And on gay plumes your bodies raise;
You insects, which in dark recesses lie,
Although th' extremest distances you try,
Be reconciled in this, to offer mutual praise.

Praise Him, thou Earth, with thy unbounded store;
Ye depths which to the center tend;
Praise Him, ye beasts which in the forests roar;
Praise Him ye serpents, though you downwards bend,
Who made your bruised head our ladder to ascend.

Praise Him, ye men whom youthful vigor warms;
Ye children hastening to your prime;
Praise Him, ye virgins of unsullied charms,
With beauteous lips becoming sacred rhyme:
You aged, give Him praise for your increase of time.

Praise Him, ye monarchs in supreme command,
By anthems, like the Hebrew kings;
Then with enlarged zeal throughout the land
Reform the numbers and reclaim the strings,
Converting to His praise, the most harmonious things.

Ye senators presiding by our choice,
And you hereditary peers!
Praise Him by union, both in heart and voice;
Praise Him, who your agreeing council steers,
Producing sweeter sounds than the according spheres.

Praise Him, ye native altars of the Earth!
Ye mountains of stupendous size!
Praise Him, ye trees and fruits which there have birth,
Praise Him, ye flames that from their bowels rise,
All fitted for the use of grateful sacrifice.

He spake the Word; and from the chaos rose
The forms and species of each kind:
He spake the Word, which did their law compose,
And all, with never ceasing order joined,
Till ruffled for our sins by his chastising wind.

But now, you storms, that have your fury spent,
As you his dictates did obey,
Let now your loud and threatening notes relent,
Tune all your murmurs to a softer key,
And bless that Gracious Hand, that did your progress stay.

From my contemned retreat, obscure and low,
As grots from whence the winds disperse,
May this His praise as far extended flow;
And if that future times shall read my verse,
Though worthless in itself, let them His praise rehearse.

148:9–10 Mountains, and all hills; fruitful trees, and all cedars: Beasts, and all cattle; creeping things, and flying fowl:

Flying Fowl, and Creeping Things, Praise Ye the Lord

Isaac Watts

Sweet flocks, whose soft enamel's wing
Swift and gently cleaves the sky;
Whose charming notes address the spring
With an artless harmony.
Lovely minstrels of the field,
Who in leafy shadows sit,
And your wondrous structures build,
Awake your tuneful voices with the dawning light;
To nature's God your first devotions pay,
E'er you salute the rising day,
'Tis he calls up the sun, and gives him every ray.

Serpents, who o'er the meadows slide,
And wear upon your shining back
Numerous ranks of gaudy pride,
Which thousand mingling colors make:
Let the fierce glances of your eyes
Rebate their baleful fire;
In harmless play twist and unfold
The volumes of your scaly gold:
That rich embroidery of your gay attire,
Proclaims your Maker kind and wise.

Insects and mites, of mean degree,
That swarm in myriads o'er the land,
Moulded by wisdom's artful hand,
And curled and painted with a various die;
In your innumerable forms
Praise him that wears th' ethereal crown,
And bends his lofty counsels down
To despicable worms.

THE PROVERBS

6:6–8 Go to the ant, thou sluggard; consider her ways, and be wise: Which having no guide, overseer, or ruler, Provideth her meat in the summer, and gathereth her food in the harvest.

PROVERBS 6:6

DAVID CURZON

Go to the ant, you sluggard,

and watch it lug an object
forward single file
with no short breaks for
coffee, gossip, a croissant,

and no stopping to apostrophize
blossom, by-passed because
pollen is not its job,
no pause for trampled companions:

consider her ways—and be content.

6:9–11 How long wilt thou sleep, O sluggard? when wilt thou arise out of thy sleep? Yet a little sleep, a little slumber, a little folding of the hands to sleep: So shall thy poverty come as one that travelleth, and thy want as an armed man.

PARAPHRASE

SAMUEL JOHNSON

Turn on the prudent ant thy heedless eyes,
Observe her labours, sluggard, and be wise;
No stern command, no monitory voice,
Prescribes her duties, or directs her choice;
Yet, timely provident, she hastes away

To snatch the blessings of a plenteous day;
When fruitful summer loads the teeming plain,
She crops the harvest and she stores the grain.
How long shall sloth usurp thy useless hours,
Unnerve thy vigor, and enchain thy powers?
While artful shades thy downy couch enclose,
And soft solicitation courts repose,
Amidst the drowsy charms of dull delight,
Year chases year with unremitted flight,
Till want now following, fraudulent and slow,
Shall spring to seize thee, like an ambushed foe.

8:2–31 She standeth in the top of high places, by the way in the places of the paths. She crieth at the gates, at the entry of the city, at the coming in at the doors. Unto you, O men, I call; and my voice is to the sons of man. . . .

The LORD possessed me in the beginning of his way, before his works of old. I was set up from everlasting, from the beginning, or ever the earth was. When there were no depths, I was brought forth; when there were no fountains abounding with water. Before the mountains were settled, before the hills was I brought forth: While as yet he had not made the earth, nor the fields, nor the highest part of the dust of the world. When he prepared the heavens, I was there: when he set a compass upon the face of the depth: When he established the clouds above: when he strengthened the fountains of the deep: When he gave to the sea his decree, that the waters should not pass his commandment: when he appointed the foundations of the earth: Then I was by him, as one brought up with him: and I was daily his delight, rejoicing always before him; Rejoicing in the habitable part of his earth; and my delights were with the sons of men.

Wisdom

William Cowper

Ere God had built the mountains,
    Or raised the fruitful hills;
Before he filled the fountains
    That feed the running rills;
In me, from everlasting,
    The wonderful I AM,
Found pleasures never-wasting,
    And Wisdom is my name.

When, like a tent to dwell in,
He spread the skies abroad,
And swathed about the swelling
Of Ocean's mighty flood;
He wrought by weight and measure,
And I was with him then:
Myself the Father's pleasure,
And mine, the sons of men.

Thus Wisdom's words discover
Thy glory and thy grace,
Thou everlasting lover
Of our unworthy race!
Thy gracious eye surveyed us
Ere stars were seen above;
In wisdom thou hast made us,
And died for us in love.

And couldst thou be delighted
With creatures such as we,
Who, when we saw thee, slighted
And nailed thee to a tree?
Unfathomable wonder,
And mystery divine!
The voice that speaks in thunder,
Says, "Sinner, I am thine!"

25:24 It is better to dwell in the corner of the housetop, than with a brawling woman and in a wide house.

For a Mouthy Woman

Countee Cullen

God and the devil still are wrangling
Which should have her, which repel;
God wants no discord in his heaven;
Satan has enough in hell.

27:17–19 Iron sharpeneth iron; so a man sharpeneth the countenance of his friend. Whoso keepeth the fig tree shall eat the fruit thereof: so he that waiteth on his master shall be honoured. As in water face answereth to face, so the heart of man to man.

Do the Others Speak of Me Mockingly, Maliciously?

Delmore Schwartz

Do they whisper behind my back? Do they speak
Of my clumsiness? Do they laugh at me,
Mimicking my gestures, retailing my shame?
I'll whirl about, denounce them, saying
That they are shameless, they are treacherous,
No more my friends, nor will I once again
Never, amid a thousand meetings in the street,
Recognize their faces, take their hands,
Not for our common love or old times' sake:
They whispered behind my back, they mimicked me.

I know the reason why, I too have done this,
Cruel for wit's sake, behind my dear friend's back,
And to amuse betrayed his private love,
His nervous shame, her habit, and their weaknesses;
I have mimicked them, I have been treacherous,
For wit's sake, to amuse, because their being weighed
Too grossly for a time, to be superior,
To flatter the listeners by this, the intimate,
Betraying the intimate, but for the intimate,
To free myself of friendship's necessity,
Fearing from time to time that they would hear,
Denounce me and reject me, say once for all
That they would never meet me, take my hands,
Speaking for old times' sake and our common love.

What an unheard-of thing it is, in fine,
To love another and equally be loved!
What sadness and what joy! How cruel it is
That pride and wit distort the heart of man,
How vain, how sad, what cruelty, what need,
For this is true and sad, that I need them
And they need me. What can we do? We need
Each other's clumsiness, each other's wit,

Each other's company and our own pride. I need
My face unshamed, I need my wit, I cannot
Turn away. We know our clumsiness,
Our weakness, our necessities, we cannot
Forget our pride, our faces, our common love.

30:5–9 Every word of God is pure: he is a shield unto them that put their trust in him. Add thou not unto his words, lest he reprove thee, and thou be found a liar. Two things have I required of thee; deny me them not before I die: Remove far from me vanity and lies: give me neither poverty nor riches; feed me with food convenient for me: Lest I be full, and deny thee, and say, Who is the LORD? or lest I be poor, and steal, and take the name of my God in vain.

PROVERB. XXX

JOHN HALL

O Lord two things I thee require,
That thou me not deny,
But that I may the fruit thereof
Receive before I die.

The first shall be that vanity
Thou wilt from me restrain,
And eke the lips that lust to lie,
To flatter, glose and feign.

The second that thou make me not
Too poor in any wise,
Ne yet too rich: but mean living,
Of necessary size.

Lest when I am too full of wealth
I thee forget and say:
What fellow is the Lord? when I
Forgotten have thy way.

And likewise lest that poverty
Constrain me out of frame,
And me provoke to steal O God
And to forswear thy name.

30:21–23 For three things the earth is disquieted, and for four which it cannot bear: For a servant when he reigneth; and a fool when he is filled with meat; For an odious woman when she is married; and an handmaid that is heir to her mistress.

'A Servant when He Reigneth'

Rudyard Kipling

Three things make earth unquiet
And four she cannot brook
The godly Agur counted them
And put them in a book—
Those Four Tremendous Curses
With which mankind is cursed;
But a Servant when He Reigneth
Old Agur entered first.

An Handmaid that is Mistress
We need not call upon.
A Fool when he is full of Meat
Will fall asleep anon.
An Odious Woman Married
May bear a babe and mend;
But a Servant when He Reigneth
Is Confusion to the end.

His feet are swift to tumult,
His hands are slow to toil,
His ears are deaf to reason,
His lips are loud in broil.
He knows no use for power
Except to show his might.
He gives no heed to judgment
Unless it prove him right.

Because he served a master
Before his Kingship came,
And hid in all disaster
Behind his master's name,
So, when his Folly opens
The unnecessary hells,
A Servant when He Reigneth
Throws the blame on some one else.

His vows are lightly spoken,
His faith is hard to bind,
His trust is easy broken,
He fears his fellow-kind.
The nearest mob will move him
To break the pledge he gave—
Oh, a Servant when He Reigneth
Is more than ever slave!

31:6–7 Give strong drink unto him that is ready to perish, and wine unto those that be of heavy hearts. Let him drink, and forget his poverty, and remember his misery no more.

Scotch Drink

Robert Burns

Gie him strong Drink *until he wink,*
That's sinking in despair;
An' liquor *guid, to fire his bluid,*
That's prest wi' grief an' care:
There let him bowse an' deep carouse,
Wi' bumpers flowing o'er,
Till he forgets his loves *or* debts,
An' minds his griefs no more.
Solomon's Proverbs, Ch. 31st V. 6, 7.

Let other Poets raise a fracas
'Bout vines, an' wines, an' druken Bacchus,
An' crabbed names an' stories wrack us,
An' grate our lug,
I sing the juice Scotch bear can mak us,
In glass or jug.

O thou, my Muse! guid, auld Scotch Drink!
Whether thro' wimplin worms thou jink,
Or, richly brown, ream owre the brink,
In glorious faem,
Inspire me, till I lisp an' wink,
To sing thy name!

Let husky Wheat the haughs adorn,
And Aits set up their awnie horn,
An' Pease an' Beans, at een or morn,
Perfumes the plain,
Leeze me on thee John Barleycorn,
Thou king o' grain!

On the thee aft Scotland chows her cood,
In souple scones, the wale o' food!
Or tumbling in the boiling flood
        Wi' kail an' beef;
But when thou pours thy strong heart's blood,
        There thou shines chief.

Food fills the wame, an' keeps us livin:
Tho' life's a gift no worth receivin,
When heavy-dragg'd wi' pine an' grievin;
        But oil'd by thee,
The wheels o' life gae down-hill, scrievin,
        Wi' rattlin glee.

Thou clears the head o' doited Lear;
Thou chears the heart o' drooping Care;
Thou strings the nerves o' Labor-sair,
        At 's weary toil;
Thou ev'n brightens dark Despair,
        Wi' gloomy smile.

Aft, clad in massy, siller weed,
Wi' Gentles thou erects thy head;
Yet, humbly kind, in time o' need,
        The poorman's wine,
His wee drap pirratch, or his bread,
        Thou kitchens fine.

Thou art the life o' public haunts;
But thee, what were our fairs an' rants?
Ev'n goodly meetings o' the saunts,
        By thee inspir'd,
When gaping they besiege the tents,
        Are doubly fir'd.

That merry night we get the corn in
O sweetly, then, thou reams the horn in!
Or reekan on a New-year-mornin
        In cog or bicker,
An' just a wee drap sp'ritual burn in,
        An' gusty sucker!

When Vulcan gies his bellys breath,
An' Ploughmen gather wi' their graith,
O rare! to see thee fiz an' fraeth
  I' the lugget caup!
Then Burnewin comes on like Death,
  At ev'ry chap.

Nae mercy, then, for airn or steel;
The brawnie, banie, Ploughman-chiel
Brings hard owrehip, wi' sturdy wheel,
  The strong forehammer,
Till block an' studdie ring an' reel
  Wi' dinsome clamour.

When skirlin weanies see the light,
Thou maks the gossips clatter bright,
How fumbling coofs their dearies slight,
  Wae worth the name!
Nae Howdie gets a social night,
  Or plack frae them.

When neebors anger at a plea,
An just as wud as wud can be,
How easy can the barley-bree
  Cement the quarrel!
It's ay the cheapest Lawyer's fee
  To taste the barrel.

Alake! that e'er my Muse has reason
To wyte her countrymen wi' treason!
But mony daily weet their weason
  Wi' liquors nice,
An' hardly, in a winter season,
  E'er spier her price.

Wae worth that Brandy, burnan trash!
Fell source o' monie a pain an' brash!
Twins mony a poor, doylt, druken hash
  O' half his days;
An' sends, beside, auld Scotland's cash
  To her warst faes.

Ye Scots wha wish auld Scotland well,
Ye chief, to you my tale I tell,
Poor, plackless devils like mysel,

It sets you ill,
Wi' bitter, dearthfu' wines to mell
Or foreign gill.

May Gravels round his blather wrench,
An' Gouts torment him, inch by inch,
Wha twists his gruntle wi' a glunch
O' sour disdain,
Out owre a glass o' Whisky-punch
Wi' honest men!

O Whisky! soul o' plays an' pranks!
Accept a Bardie's gratefu' thanks!
When wanting thee, what tuneless cranks
Are my poor Verses!
Thou comes—they rattle i' their ranks
At ither's arses!

Thee, Ferintosh! O sadly lost!
Scotland lament frae coast to coast!
Now colic-grips, an' barkin hoast,
May kill us a';
For loyal Forbes' Charter'd boast
Is taen awa!

Thae curst horse-leeches o' th' Excise,
Wha mak the Whisky stills their prize!
Haud up thy han' Deil! ance, twice, thrice!
There, sieze the blinkers!
An' bake them up in brunstane pies
For poor damn'd Drinkers.

Fortune, if thou'll but gie me still
Hale breeks, a scone, an' Whisky gill,
An' rowth o' rhyme to rave at will,
Tak a' the rest,
An' deal 't about as thy blind skill
Directs thee best.

31:10–31 Who can find a virtuous woman? for her price is far above rubies. The heart of her husband doth safely trust in her, so that he shall have no need of spoil. . . . Give her of the fruit of her hands; and let her own works praise her in the gates.

On Woman

William Butler Yeats

May God be praised for woman
That gives up all her mind,
A man may find in no man
A friendship of her kind
That covers all he has brought
As with her flesh and bone,
Nor quarrels with a thought
Because it is not her own.

Though pedantry denies,
It's plain the Bible means
That Solomon grew wise
While talking with his queens,
Yet never could, although
They say he counted grass,
Count all the praises due
When Sheba was his lass,
When she the iron wrought, or
When from the smithy fire
It shuddered in the water:
Harshness of their desire
That made them stretch and yawn,
Pleasure that comes with sleep,
Shudder that made them one.
What else He give or keep
God grant me—no, not here,
For I am not so bold
To hope a thing so dear
Now I am growing old,
But when, if the tale's true,
The Pestle of the moon
That pounds up all anew
Brings me to birth again—
To find what once I had
And know what once I have known,
Until I am driven mad,
Sleep driven from my bed,
By tenderness and care,
Pity, an aching head,

Gnashing of teeth, despair;
And all because of some one
Perverse creature of chance,
And live like Solomon
That Sheba led a dance.

ECCLESIASTES

OR, THE PREACHER

1:1–3 The words of the Preacher, the son of David, king in Jerusalem. Vanity of vanities, saith the Preacher, vanity of vanities; all is vanity. What profit hath a man of all his labour which he taketh under the sun?

EVEN AS THE WANDERING TRAVELER

JOHN HALL THE LATTER

Even as the wandering traveler doth stray,
    Led from his way
By a false fire, whose flame to cheated sight
    Doth lead aright,
All paths are footed over but that one
    Which should be gone;
Even so my foolish wishes are in chase
Of everything but what they should embrace.

We laugh at children, that can when they please
    A bubble raise,
And when their fond ambition sated is,
    Again dismiss
The fleeting toy into its former air;
    What do we here
But act such tricks? Yet thus we differ: they
Destroy, so do not we; we sweat, they play.

Ambition's towerings do some gallants keep
From calmer sleep;
Yet when their thoughts the most possessëd are,
They grope but air,
And when they're highest, in an instant fade
Into a shade;
Or like a stone, that more forced upwards, shall
With greater violence to its center fall.

Another, whose conceptions only dream
Monsters of fame,
The vain applause of other madmen buys
With his own sighs,
Yet his enlargëd name shall never crawl
Over this ball,
But soon consume; thus doth a trumpet's sound
Rush bravely on a little, then's not found.

But we as soon may tell how often shapes
Are changed by apes,
As know how oft man's childish thoughts do vary,
And still miscarry.
So a weak eye in twilight thinks it sees
New species,
While it sees nought; so men in dreams conceive
Of specters, till that waking undeceive.

1:4 One generation passeth away, and another generation cometh: but the earth abideth for ever.

ONE GENERATION PASSETH AWAY

JONES VERY

As is the sand upon the ocean's shore,
So without number seems the human race;
And to that number still are added more,
As wave on wave each other onward chase.

As are the drops of rain, that countless fall
Upon the earth, or on the briny sea,
So seem man's generations great and small,
Those that have been, and those who yet shall be.

As are the snowflakes, fluttering on the air,
Succeeded still by others thick and fast,
So many souls the mortal image bear,
That stand within the present, or the past.

More than the ancient Preacher now we know,
Though wiser he than all the sons of men;
God through his Son the promise doth bestow,
That all the sons of earth shall live again.

Nor countless forms alone the earth doth hold,
Which on it move or in its bosom lie;
As numberless the stars, which we behold,
Which fill the spaces of the azure sky,

So, we believe, unnumbered still in heaven
Will be the forms that meet our new-born,
When to each soul a spotless robe is given,
To dwell forever in its cloudless light.

1:5–11 The sun also ariseth, and the sun goeth down, and hasteth to his place where he arose. The wind goeth toward the south, and turneth about unto the north; it whirleth about continually, and the wind returneth again according to his circuits. All the rivers run into the sea; yet the sea is not full; unto the place from whence the rivers come, thither they return again.

All things are full of labour; man cannot utter it: the eye is not satisfied with seeing, nor the ear filled with hearing. The thing that hath been, it is that which shall be; and that which is done is that which shall be done: and there is no new thing under the sun. Is there any thing whereof it may be said, See, this is new? it hath been already of old time, which was before us. There is no remembrance of former things; neither shall there be any remembrance of things that are to come with those that shall come after.

The Vanity of All Worldly Things

Anne Bradstreet

As he said vanity, so vain say I,
Oh! vanity, O vain all under sky;
Where is the man can say, "Lo, I have found

On brittle earth a consolation sound"?
What is't in honor to be set on high?
No, they like beasts and sons of men shall die,
And whilst they live, how oft cloth turn their fate;
He's now a captive that was king of late.
What is't in wealth great treasures to obtain?
No, that's but labor, anxious care, and pain.
He heaps up riches, and he heaps up sorrow,
It's his today, but who's his heir tomorrow?
What then? Content in pleasures canst thou find?
More vain than all, that's but to grasp the wind.
The sensual senses for a time they please,
Meanwhile the conscience rage, who shall appease?
What is't in beauty? No that's but a snare,
They're foul enough today, that once were fair.
What is't in flowering youth, or manly age?
The first is prone to vice, the last to rage.
Where is it then, in wisdom, learning, arts?
Sure if on earth, it must be in those parts;
Yet these the wisest man of men did find
But vanity, vexation of mind.
And he that knows the most doth still bemoan
He knows not all that here is to be known.
What is it then? to do as stoics tell,
Nor laugh, nor weep, let things go ill or well?
Such stoics are but stocks, such teaching vain,
While man is man, he shall have ease or pain.
If not in honor, beauty, age, nor treasure,
Nor yet in learning, wisdom, youth, nor pleasure,
Where shall I climb, sound, seek, search, or find
That *summum bonum* which may stay my mind?
There is a path no vulture's eye hath seen
Where lion fierce, nor lion's whelps have been,
Which leads unto that living crystal fount,
Who drinks thereof, the world doth nought account.
The depth and sea have said " 'tis not in me,"
With pearl and gold it shall not valued be.
For sapphire, onyx, topaz who would change;
It's hid from eyes of men, they count it strange.
Death and destruction the fame hath heard,
But where and what it is from heaven's declared;
It brings to honor which shall ne'er decay,
It stores with wealth which time can't wear away.
It yieldeth pleasures far beyond conceit,

And truly beautifies without deceit.
Nor strength, nor wisdom, nor fresh youth shall fade,
Nor death shall see, but are immortal made.
This pearl of price, this tree of life, this spring,
Who is possessed of shall reign a king.
Nor change of state nor cares shall ever see,
But wear his crown unto eternity.
This satiates the soul, this stays the mind,
And all the rest, but vanity we find.

1:12–14 I the Preacher was king over Israel in Jerusalem. And I gave my heart to seek and search out by wisdom concerning all things that are done under heaven: this sore travail hath God given to the sons of man to be exercised therewith. I have seen all the works that are done under the sun; and, behold, all is vanity and vexation of spirit.

Ecclesiastes

Derek Mahon

God, you could grow to love it, God-fearing, God-
 chosen purist little puritan that,
for all your wiles and smiles, you are (the
 dank churches, the empty streets,
the shipyard silence, the tied-up swings) and
 shelter your cold heart from the heat
of the world, from woman-inquisition, from the
 bright eyes of children. Yes, you could
wear black, drink water, nourish a fierce zeal
 with locusts and wild honey, and not
feel called upon to understand and forgive
 but only to speak with a bleak
afflatus, and love the January rains when they
 darken the dark doors and sink hard
into the Antrim hills, the bog meadows, the heaped
 graves of your fathers. Bury that red
bandana and stick, that banjo. This is your
 country, close one eye and be king.
Your people await you, their heavy washing
 flaps for you in the housing estates—
a credulous people. God, you could do it, God
 help you, stand on a corner stiff
with rhetoric, promising nothing under the sun.

2:15–16 Then said I in my heart, As it happeneth to the fool, so it happeneth even to me; and why was I then more wise? Then I said in my heart, that this also is vanity. For there is no remembrance of the wise more than of the fool for ever; seeing that which now is in the days to come shall all be forgotten. And how dieth the wise man? as the fool.

A Spirit Appeared to Me

Herman Melville

A spirit appeared to me, and said
'Where now would you choose to dwell?
In the Paradise of the Fool,
Or in wise Solomon's hell?'

Never he asked me twice:
'Give me the Fool's Paradise.'

3:1–8 To every thing there is a season, and a time to every purpose under the heaven: A time to be born, and a time to die; a time to plant, and a time to pluck up that which is planted; A time to kill, and a time to heal; a time to break down, and a time to build up; A time to weep, and a time to laugh; a time to mourn, and a time to dance; A time to cast away stones, and a time to gather stones together; a time to embrace, and a time to refrain from embracing; A time to get, and a time to lose; a time to keep, and a time to cast away; A time to rend, and a time to sew; a time to keep silence, and a time to speak; A time to love, and a time to hate; a time of war, and a time of peace.

Times go by Turns

Robert Southwell

The loppèd tree in time may grow again;
Most naked plants renew both fruit and flower;
The sorriest wight may find release of pain,
The driest soil suck in some moistening shower;
Times go by turns and chances change by course,
From foul to fair, from better hap to worse.

The sea of fortune doth not ever flow,
She draws her favors to the lowest ebb;

Her tide hath equal times to come and go,
Her loom doth weave the fine and coarsest web;
No joy so great but runneth to an end,
No hap so hard but may in time amend.

Not always fall of leaf nor ever spring,
No endless night yet not eternal day;
The saddest birds a season find to sing,
The roughest storm a calm may soon allay;
Thus with succeeding turns God tempereth all,
That man may hope to rise yet fear to fall.

A chance may win that by mischance was lost;
The net that holds no great, takes little fish;
In some things all, in all things none are crossed,
Few all they need, but none have all they wish;
Unmeddled joys here to no man befall,
Who least hath some, who most hath never all.

5:6–7 Suffer not thy mouth to cause thy flesh to sin; neither say thou before the angel, that it was an error: wherefore should God be angry at thy voice, and destroy the work of thine hands? For in the multitude of dreams and many words there are also divers vanities: but fear thou God.

ECCLESIASTES

G. K. CHESTERTON

There is one sin: to call a green leaf gray,
  Whereat the sun in heaven shuddereth.
There is one blasphemy: for death to pray,
  For God alone knoweth the praise of death.

There is one creed: 'neath no world-terror's wing
  Apples forget to grow on apple-trees.
There is one thing is needful—everything—
  The rest is vanity of vanities.

5:8–20 If thou seest the oppression of the poor, and violent perverting of judgment and justice in a province, marvel not at the matter: for he that is higher than the highest regardeth; and there be higher than they.

Moreover the profit of the earth is for all: the king himself is served by the field. He that loveth silver shall not be satisfied with silver; nor he that loveth abundance with increase: this is also vanity. When goods increase, they are increased that eat them: and what good is there to the owners thereof, saving the beholding of them with their eyes? The sleep of a labouring man is sweet, whether he eat little or much: but the abundance of the rich will not suffer him to sleep.

There is a sore evil which I have seen under the sun, namely, riches kept for the owners thereof to their hurt. But those riches perish by evil travail: and he begetteth a son, and there is nothing in his hand. As he came forth of his mother's womb, naked shall he return to go as he came, and shall take nothing of his labour, which he may carry away in his hand. And this also is a sore evil, that in all points as he came, so shall he go: and what profit hath he that hath laboured for the wind? All his days also he eateth in darkness, and he hath much sorrow and wrath with his sickness.

Behold that which I have seen: it is good and comely for one to eat and to drink, and to enjoy the good of all his labour that he taketh under the sun all the days of his life, which God giveth him: for it is his portion. Every man also to whom God hath given riches and wealth, and hath given him power to eat thereof, and to take his portion, and to rejoice in his labour; this is the gift of God. For he shall not much remember the days of his life; because God answereth him in the joy of his heart.

from A PARAPHRASE OF PART OF THE BOOK OF ECCLESIASTES

HENRY HOWARD, EARL OF SURREY

Chapter 1

I, Solomon, David's son,   King of Jerusalem,
Chosen by God to teach the Jews,   and in his laws lead them,
Confess, under the sun   that everything is vain;
The world is false; man he is frail,   and all his pleasures pain.
Alas! what stable fruit   may Adam's children find
In that, they seek by sweat of brows   and travail of their mind.
We that live on the earth,   draw toward our decay;
Our children fill our place awhile,   and then they vade away.
Such changes make the earth,   and doth remove for none;
But serves us for a place to play   our tragedies upon.

* * *

I, that in David's seat   sit crowned and rejoice;
That with my sceptre rule the Jews,   and teach them with my voice,
Have searched long to know   all things under the sun;

To see how in this mortal life, a surety might be won.
This kindled will to know; strange things for to desire.
God hath graft in our greedy breasts a torment for our hire.
The end of each travail forthwith I sought to know;
I found them vain, mixed with gall, and burdened with much woe.

* * *

Chapter 4

When I bethought me well, under the restless sun
By folk of power what cruel works unchastised were done;
I saw where stood a herd by power of such oppressed,
Out of whose eyes ran floods of tears, that bathéd all their breast;
Devoid of comfort clean, in terrors and distress;
In whose defence none would arise such rigor to repress.
Then thought I thus; "Oh Lord! the dead whose fatal hour
"Is clean run out more happy are; whom that the worms devour:
"And happiest is the seed that never did conceive;
"That never felt the wailful wrongs that mortal folk receive."
And then I saw that wealth, and every honest gain
By travail won, and sweat of brows gan grow into disdain;
Through sloth of careless folk, whom ease so fat doth feed:
Whose idle hands do nought but waste the fruit of other seed.
Which to themselves persuade that little got with ease
More thankful is, than kingdoms won by travail and misease.
Another sort I saw without both friend or kin,
Whose greedy ways yet never sought a faithful friend to win;
Whose wretched corpse no toil yet ever weary could;
Now glutted ever were their eyes, with heaps of shining gold.
But, if it might appear to their abused eyen,
To whose avail they travail so, and for whose sake they pine;
Then should they see what cause they have for to repent,
The fruitless pains and eke the time that they in vain have spent.
Then gan I thus resolve — "More pleasant is the life
"Of faithful friends that spend their goods in common, without strife;"
For as the tender friend appeaseth every grief,
So, if he fall that lives alone, who shall be his relief?
The friendly feres lie warm in arms embraced fast;
Who sleeps alone, at every turn doth feel the winter blast.
What can he do but yield, that must resist alone:
If there be twain, one may defend the t'other overthrown.
The single twined cords may no such stress endure
As cables braided threefold may, together wreathed sure.
In better far estate stand children, poor and wise,

Than aged kings, wedded to will, that work without advice.
In prison have I seen, or this, a woful wight
That never knew what freedom meant, nor tasted of delight;
With such unhoped hap in most despair hath met,
Within the hands that erst wore gyves to have a scepter set.
And by conjures the seed of kings is thrust from state,
Whereon a grieved people work oft-times their hidden hate.
Other, without respect, I saw of friend or foe
With feet worn bare in tracing such, whereas the honors grow.
And at death of a prince great routs revived strange,
Which fain their old yoke to discharge, rejoiced in the change.
But when I thought, to these as heavy even or more
Shall be the burden of his reign, as his that went before;
And that a train like great upon the dead attend,
I gan conclude, each greedy gain hath its uncertain end.

* * *

Chapter 5

When that repentant tears hath cleansed clear from ill
The charged breast; and grace hath wrought therein, amending will;
With bold demands then may his mercy well assail
The speech man saith, without the which request may none prevail.

* * *

With feigned words and oaths contract with God no guile;
Such craft returns to thine own harm, and doth thyself defile.
And though the mist of sin persuade such error light,
Thereby yet are thy outward works all dampened in his sight.
As sundry broken dreams us diversely abuse,
So are his errors manifold that many words doth use.
With humble secret plaint few words of hot effect,
Honor thy Lord; allowance vain of void desert, neglect.

* * *

Naked as from the womb we came, if we depart,
With toil to seek that we must leave, what boot to vex the heart?
What life lead testy men then, that consume their days
In inward frets, untempered hates, at strife with some always.
Then gan I praise all those, in such a world of strife,
As take the profit of their goods, that may be had in life.
For sure the liberal hand that hath no heart to spare
This fading wealth, but pours it forth, it is a virtue rare.
That makes wealth slave to need, and gold become his thrall,

Clings not his guts with niggish fare, to heap his chest withal;
But feeds the lusts of kind with costly meats and wine;
And slacks the hunger and the thirst of needy folk that pine.
No glutton's feast I mean in waste of spence to strive;
But temperate meals the dulled spirits with joy thus to revive.
No care may pierce where mirth hath tempered such a breast:
The bitter gall, seasoned with sweet, such wisdom may digest.

7:15–16 All things have I seen in the days of my vanity: there is a just man that perisheth in his righteousness, and there is a wicked man that prolongeth his life in his wickedness. Be not righteous over much; neither make thyself over wise: why shouldest thou destroy thyself?

Address to the Unco Guid, or the Rigidly Righteous

Robert Burns

My son, these maxims make a rule,
And lump them ay tegither;
The Rigid Righteous *is a fool,*
The Rigid Wise *anither:*
The cleanest corn that e'er was dight
May hae some pyles o' caff in;
So ne'er a fellow-creature slight
For random fits o' daffin.
Solomon.—Eccles. ch. vii. vers. 16.

O ye wha are sae guid yoursel,
Sae pious and sae holy,
Ye've noght to do but mark and tell
Your Neebours' fauts and folly!
Whase life is like a weel-gaun mill,
Supply'd wi' store o' water,
The heaped happer 's ebbing still,
And still the clap plays clatter.

Hear me, ye venerable Core,
As counsel for poor mortals,
That frequent pass douce Wisdom's door
For glaikit Folly's portals;
I, for their thoughtless, careless sakes
Would here propone defences,
Their donsie tricks, their black mistakes,
Their failings and mischances.

Ye see your state wi' theirs compar'd,
And shudder at the niffer,
But cast a moment's fair regard
What maks the mighty differ;
Discount what scant occasion gave,
That purity ye pride in,
And (what's aft mair than a' the lave)
Your better art o' hiding.

Think, when your castigated pulse
Gies now and then a wallop,
What ragings must his veins convulse,
That still eternal gallop:
Wi' wind and tide fair i' your tail,
Right on ye scud your sea-way;
But, in the teeth o' baith to sail,
It maks an unco leeway.

See Social-life and Glee sit down,
All joyous and unthinking,
Till, quite transmugrify'd, they're grown
Debauchery and Drinking:
O would they stay to calculate
Th' eternal consequences;
Or your more dreaded h-ll to state,
D-mnation of expences!

Ye high, exalted, virtuous Dames,
Ty'd up in godly laces,
Before ye gie poor Frailty names,
Suppose a change o' cases;

A dear-lov'd lad, convenience snug,
A treacherous inclination—
But, let me whisper i' your lug,
Ye're aiblins nae temptation.

Then gently scan your brother Man,
Still gentler sister Woman;
Tho' they may gang a kennin wrang,
To step aside is human:
One point must still be greatly dark,
The moving *Why* they do it;
And just as lamely can ye mark,
How far perhaps they rue it.

Who made the heart, 'tis He alone
Decidedly can try us,
He knows each chord its various tone,
Each spring its various bias:
Then at the balance let's be mute,
We never can adjust it;
What's done we partly may compute,
But know not what's resisted.

7:24 That which is far off, and exceeding deep, who can find it out?

In Ecclesiastes I Read

J. P. White

In Ecclesiastes I read,
"That which is far off and exceeding deep,
Who can find it out?"
Who can tell the earth's tale of wearing down,
building up, erosion, creation,
a swirl of embers breathing amethyst and tourmaline,
a suffering bounded by the four baleful rivers of Hell
and a sun that will one day collapse,
engulfing it in one long dragon breath of dying out?
The ancients said earth was immovable—
that every daffodil and sequoia
was fixed in its own sky-blue mirror.

Now we know this planet is like others,
restless, driven, continually torn apart
and reassembled by a shifting of plates
grinding beneath the surface like nervous molars.
The globe itself a work in progress
with its iced poles wandering
and its fires bubbling below the seas.
Even its path through space
is an egg-shaped, elliptical orbit, hardly circular.
It is here on what used to be called solid ground
that we live—fragile, torn by our need
for love, food and mercy.
Most of us worried there will be too little time
to light the lamps of our fingers
and walk the narrow path in the rain.
But what of the earth? Who can find it out—
embrace its drifting continents,
who can love it as it is—unfinished,
smudged with the dust of rare constellations,
flickering on and off like a rain-drenched fire in the woods?

9:4–7 For to him that is joined to all the living there is hope: for a living dog is better than a dead lion. For the living know that they shall die: but the dead know not any thing, neither have they any more a reward; for the memory of them is forgotten. Also their love, and their hatred, and their envy, is now perished; neither have they any more a portion for ever in any thing that is done under the sun. Go thy way, eat thy bread with joy, and drink thy wine with a merry heart; for God now accepteth thy works.

KOHELETH

LOUIS UNTERMEYER

I waited and worked
To win myself leisure,
Till loneliness irked
And I turned to raw pleasure.

I drank and gamed,
I feasted and wasted,
Till, sick and ashamed,
The food stood untasted.

I searched in the Book
For rooted convictions
Till the badgered brain shook
With its own contradictions.

Then, done with the speech,
Of the foolishly lettered,
I started to teach
Life cannot be bettered:

That the warrior fails
Whatever his weapon,
And nothing avails
While time and chance happen.

That fools who assure men
With lies are respected,
While the vision of pure men
Is scorned and rejected.

That a wise man goes grieving
Even in Zion,
While any dog living
Outroars a dead lion.

9:11–12 I returned, and saw under the sun, that the race is not to the swift, nor the battle to the strong, neither yet bread to the wise, nor yet riches to men of understanding, nor yet favour to men of skill; but time and chance happeneth to them all. For man also knoweth not his time: as the fishes that are taken in an evil net, and as the birds that are caught in the snare; so are the sons of men snared in an evil time, when it falleth suddenly upon them.

Race and Battle

D. H. Lawrence

The race is not to the swift
but to those that can sit still
and let the waves go over them.

The battle is not to the strong
but to the frail, who know best
how to efface themselves
to save the streaked pansy of the heart from being trampled to mud.

10:1 Dead flies cause the ointment of the apothecary to send forth a stinking savour: so doth a little folly him that is in reputation for wisdom and honour.

from Pleasure: The second Book of Solomon on the Vanity of the World

Matthew Prior

Oft have I said, the praise of doing well
Is to the ear, as ointment to the smell.
Now if some flies perchance, however small,
Into the alabaster urn should fall;
The odors of the sweets enclosed would die;
And stench corrupt (sad change!) their place supply.
So the least faults, if mixed with fairest deed,
Of future ill become the fatal seed:
Into the balm of purest virtue cast,
Annoy all life with one contagious blast.

Lost Solomon! pursue this thought no more:
Of thy past errors recollect the store:
And silent weep, that while the deathless Muse
Shall sing the Just; shall o'er their head diffuse
Perfumes with lavish hand; She shall proclaim
Thy crimes alone; and to thy evil fame
Impartial, scatter damps, and poisons on thy name.

Awaking therefore, as who long had dreamed,
Much of my women, and their Gods ashamed,
From this abyss of exemplary vice
Resolved, as time might aid my thought, to rise;
Again I bid the mournful goddess write
The fond pursuit of fugitive delight:
Bid her exalt her melancholy wing,
And raised from Earth, and saved from passion, sing
Of human hope by cross event destroyed
Of useless wealth, and greatness unenjoyed
Of lust and love, with their fantastic train,
Their wishes, smiles, and looks deceitful all, and vain.

12:1–2 Remember now thy Creator in the days of thy youth, while the evil days come not, nor the years draw nigh, when thou shalt say, I have no pleasure in them; While the sun, or the light, or the moon, or the stars, be not darkened, nor the clouds return after the rain:

Past Thinking of Solomon

Francis Thompson

Wise-Unto-Hell Ecclesiast,
Who sievedst life to the gritted last!

This thy sting, thy darkness, Mage—
Cloud upon sun, upon youth age?

Now is come a darker thing,
And is come a colder sting,

Unto us, who find the womb
Opes on the courtyard of the tomb.

Now in this fuliginous
City of flesh our sires for us

Darkly built, the sun at prime
Is hidden, and betwixt the time

Of day and night is variance none,
Who know not altern moon and sun;

Whose deposed heaven through dungeon-bars
Looks down blinded of its stars.

Yea, in the days of youth, God wot,
Now we say: They please me not.

12:8 **Vanity of vanities, saith the preacher; all is vanity.**

'All is Vanity, Saith the Preacher'

George Noel Gordon, Lord Byron

Fame, wisdom, love, and power were mine,
    And health and youth possessed me;
My goblets blushed from every vine,
    And lovely forms caressed me;
I sunned my heart in beauty's eyes,
    And felt my soul grow tender;
All earth can give, or mortal prize,
    Was mine of regal splendour.

I strive to number o'er what days
    Remembrance can discover,
Which all that life or earth displays
    Would lure me to live over.
There rose no day, there rolled no hour
    Of pleasure unembittered;
And not a trapping decked my power
    That galled not while it glittered.

The serpent of the field, by art
    And spells, is won from harming;
But that which coils around the heart,
    Oh! who hath power of charming?
It will not list to wisdom's lore,
    Nor music's voice can lure it;
But there it stings for evermore
    The soul that must endure it.

12:13–14 Let us hear the conclusion of the whole matter: Fear God, and keep his commandments: for this is the whole duty of man. For God shall bring every work into judgment, with every secret thing, whether it be good, or whether it be evil.

The Conclusion of the Matter

Christopher Smart

Fear God—obey his just decrees,
And do it hand, and heart, and knees;
For after all our utmost care
There's nought like penitence and prayer.

Then weigh the balance in your mind,
Look forward, not one glance behind;
Let no foul fiend retard your pace,
Hosanna! Thou hast won the race.

The Song of SOLOMON

1:1–3 The song of songs, which is Solomon's. Let him kiss me with the kisses of his mouth: for thy love is better than wine. Because of the savour of thy good ointments thy name is as ointment poured forth, therefore do the virgins love thee.

Let Him with Kisses of His Mouth

Anonymous

Let him with kisses of his mouth
Be pleasèd me to kiss.
Because much better than the wine

Thy loving kindness is.
Thy name as poured forth ointment is,
Because of the sweet smell
Of thy good ointments, therefore do
The virgins love thee well.

2:1 I am the rose of Sharon, and the lily of the valleys.

The Reflexion

Edward Taylor

Lord, art thou at the table head above
Meat, medicine, sweetness, sparkling beauties, to
Enamor souls with flaming flakes of love,
And not my trencher, nor my cup o'erflow?
Be n't I a bidden guest? Oh! sweat mine eye:
O'erflow with tears: Oh! draw thy fountains dry.

Shall I not smell thy sweet, oh! Sharons rose?
Shall not mine eye salute thy beauty? Why?
Shall thy sweet leaves their beauteous sweets upclose?
As half ashamed my sight should on them lie?
Woe's me! For this my sighs shall be in grain,
Offered on sorrows altar for the same.

Had not my soul's, thy conduit, pipes stopped been
With mud, what ravishment wouldst thou convey?
Let graces golden spade dig till the spring
Of tears arise, and clear this filth away.
Lord, let thy spirit raise my sighings till
These pipes my soul do with thy sweetness fill.

Earth once was Paradise of Heaven below,
Till inkfaced sin had it with poison stocked;
And chased this Paradise away into
Heavens upmost loft, and it in glory locked.
But thou, sweet Lord, hast with thy golden key
Unlocked the door, and made a golden day.

Once at thy feast, I saw the pearl-like stand
'Tween Heaven and Earth, where heavens bright glory all

In streams fell on thee, as a floodgate and,
Like sun beams through thee on the world to fall.
Oh! Sugar sweet then! My dear sweet Lord, I see
Saints heaven-lost happiness restored by thee.

3:1–2 By night on my bed I sought him whom my soul loveth: I sought him, but I found him not. I will rise now, and go about the city in the streets, and in the broad ways I will seek him whom my soul loveth: I sought him, but I found him not.

The City in which I Love You

Li-Young Lee

And when, in the city in which I love you,
even my most excellent song goes unanswered,
and I mount the scabbed streets,
the long shouts of avenues,
and tunnel sunken night in search of you . . .

That I negotiate fog, bituminous
rain ringing like teeth into the beggar's tin,
or two men jackaling a third in some alley
weirdly lit by a couch on fire, that I
drag my extinction in search of you . . .

Past the guarded schoolyards, the boarded-up churches, swastikaed
synagogues, defended houses of worship, past
newspapered windows of tenements, among the violated,
the prosecuted citizenry, throughout this
storied, buttressed, scavenged, policed
city I call home, in which I am a guest . . .

A bruise, blue
in the muscle, you
impinge upon me.
As bone hugs the ache home, so
I'm vexed to love you, your body

the shape of returns, your hair a torso
of light, your heat

I must have, your opening
I'd eat, each moment
of that soft-finned fruit,
inverted fountain in which I don't see me.

My tongue remembers your wounded flavor.
The vein in my neck
adores you. A sword
stands up between my hips;
my hidden fleece sends forth its scent of human oil.

The shadows under my arms,
I promise, are tender, the shadows
under my face. Do not calculate,
but come, smooth other, rough sister.
Yet how will you know me

among the captives, my hair grown long,
my blood motley, my ways trespassed upon?
In the uproar, the confusion
of accents and inflections,
how will you hear me when I open my mouth?

Look for me, one of the drab population
under fissured edifices, fractured
artifices. Make my various
names flock overhead,
I will follow you.
Hew me to your beauty.

Stack in me the unaccountable fire,
bring on me the iron leaf, but tenderly.
Folded one hundred times and
creased, I'll not crack.
Threshed to excellence, I'll achieve you.

But in the city
in which I love you,
no one comes, no one
meets me in the brick clefts;
in the wedged dark,

no finger touches me secretly, no mouth
tastes my flawless salt,

no one wakens the honey in the cells, finds the humming
in the ribs, the rich business in the recesses;
hulls clogged, I continue laden, translated

by exhaustion and time's appetite, my sleep abandoned
in bus stations and storefront stoops,
my insomnia erected under a sky
cross-hatched by wires, branches,
and black flights of rain. Lewd body of wind

jams me in the passageways, doors slam
like guns going off, a gun goes off, a pie plate
spins past, whizzing its thin tremolo,
a plastic bag, fat with wind, barrels by and slaps
a chain-link fence, wraps it like clung skin.

In the excavated places,
I waited for you, and I did not cry out.
In the derelict rooms, my body needed you,
and there was such flight in my breast.
During the daily assaults, I called to you,

my voice pursued you,
even backward
to that other city
in which I saw a woman
squat in the street

beside a body,
and fan with a handkerchief flies from its face.
That woman
was not me. And
the corpse

lying there, lying there
so still it seemed with great effort, as though
his whole being was concentrating on the hole
in his forehead, so still
I expected he'd sit up any minute and laugh out loud—

that man was not me;
his wound was his, his death not mine.
And the soldier,
who fired the shot, then lit a cigarette—
he was not me.

And the ones I do not see
in cities all over the world,
the ones sitting, standing, lying down,
those in prisons playing checkers with their knocked-out teeth:
they are not me. Some of them are

my age, even my height and weight:
none of them is me.
The woman who is slapped, the man who is kicked,
the ones who don't survive,
whose names I do not know—

they are not me forever,
the ones who no longer live
in the cities in which
you are not,
the cities in which I looked for you.

The only sound now is a far flapping.
Over the National Bank, the flag of some republic or other
gallops like water or fire to tear itself.
Your otherness exhausts me,
everything is punished by your absence.

Where are you
in the cities in which
I love you, the cities
daily risen to work and to money,
to the magnificent miles and the gold coasts?

Morning comes to this city vacant of you.
Pages and windows flare, and you are not there.
Someone sweeps his portion of sidewalk,
wakens the drunk, slumped like laundry,
and you are gone.

You are not in the wind
which someone notes in the margins of a book.
You are gone out of the small fires in abandoned lots
where human figures huddle,
each aspiring its own ghost.

Between brick walls, in a space no wider than my face,
a leafless sapling stands in mud.

In its branches, a nest of raw mouths
gaping and cheeping, scrawny fires that must eat.
My hunger for you is no less than theirs.

At the gates of the city in which I love you,
the sea hauls the sun on its back,
strikes the land, which rebukes it.
What ardor in its sliding heft,
a flameless friction on the rocks.

Like the sea, I am recommended by my orphaning.
Noisy with telegrams not received,
quarrelsome with aliases,
intricate with misguided journeys,
by my expulsions have I come to love you.

Straight from my father's wrath,
and long from my mother's womb,
late in this century and on a Wednesday morning,
bearing the mark of one who's experienced
neither heaven nor hell,

my birthplace vanished, my citizenship earned,
in league with the stones of the earth, I
enter, without retreat or help from history,
the days of no day, my earth
of no earth, I re-enter

the city in which I love you.
And I never believed that the multitude
of dreams and many words was vain.

3:3–11 The watchmen that go about the city found me: to whom I said, Saw ye him whom my soul loveth?. . .Go forth, O ye daughters of Zion, and behold king Solomon with the crown wherewith his mother crowned him in the day of his espousals, and in the day of the gladness of his heart.

from The Most Excellent Song which was Solomon's

Michael Drayton

The Third Chapter

By night within my bed, I roamed here and there,
But all in vain, I could not find my love and friendly fere.
Then straightways up I rose, and searching every street
Throughout the city far and near, but him I could not meet.
The watchmen found me though, to whom I then can say,
Have ye not seen mine own true love, of late come this a way:
Then passing them, I found my love I long had sought,
And to my mother's chamber then, my darling have I brought.
I charge you by the roes and hinds, this vow to me you make,
Ye Jewish daughters, not to call my love till she do wake.
Who's that which doth from wilderness, in mighty smoke appear,
Like the perfumes of odors sweet, which merchants hold so dear.
About the bed of Solomon, behold, there is a band
Of threescore valiant Israelites, which all in armor stand,
All expert men of war, with sword still ready pressed,
Lest foes in night time should approach, when men suspect them least:
King Solomon hath made of Leban' tree so sure,
A palace brave, whose pillars strong are all of silver pure:
The pavement beaten gold, the hangings purple grain,
The daughters of Jerusalem with joy to entertain.
Ye Sion daughters, see, where Solomon is set
In royal throne, and on his head, the princely coronet,
Wherewith his mother first, adorned him (as they say)
When he in marriage linked was, even on his wedding day.

4:10–15 How fair is thy love, my sister, my spouse! how much better is thy love than wine! and the smell of thine ointments than all spices! Thy lips, O my spouse, drop as the honeycomb: honey and milk are under thy tongue; and the smell of thy garments is like the smell of Lebanon. A garden inclosed is my sister, my spouse; a spring shut up, a fountain sealed. Thy plants are an orchard of pomegranates, with pleasant fruits; camphire, with spikenard, Spikenard and saffron; calamus and cinnamon, with all trees of frankincense; myrrh and aloes, with all the chief spices: A fountain of gardens, a well of living waters, and streams from Lebanon.

from EXERCISES IN SCRIPTURAL WRITING

CARL RAKOSI

Sandalwood comes to my mind
when I think of you
and the triumph of your shoulders.
Greek chorus girls came to me
in the course of the day
and from a distance
Celtic vestals too,
but you bring me the Holy Land
and the sound of deep themes
in the inner chamber.

I give you praise
in the language
of wells and vineyards.

Your hand recalls
the salty heat of barbarism.
Your mouth is a pouch
for the accents of queens.
Your eyes flow over
with a gentle psalm
like the fawn eyes
of the woodland.

Your black hair
plucks my strings.

In the foggy wilderness
is not your heart
a hermit thrush?

You are timeless
as the mirrors,
Jewess of the palm country,
isolate as the frost
on the queen of swans.

Now that I have seen
the royal stones and fountains

and the tetrarch's lovely swans,
I am satisfied that you are
a mindful of white birds
in the folly of an old Jew.

Because of the coral
of your two breasts
are the prophets angry
but i have my lips upon them
and the song shall go on.

4:16 Awake, O north wind; and come, thou south; blow upon my garden, that the spices thereof may flow out. Let my beloved come into his garden, and eat his pleasant fruits.

Regeneration

Henry Vaughan

A ward, and still in bonds, one day
          I stole abroad,
It was high-spring, and all the way
     Primrosed, and hung with shade;
     Yet, was it frost within,
          And surly winds
Blasted my infant buds, and sin
     Like clouds eclipsed my mind.

Stormed thus; I straight perceived my spring
          Mere stage, and show,
My walk a monstrous, mountained thing
     Rough-cast with rocks, and snow;
     And as a pilgrim's eye
          Far from relief,
Measures the melancholy sky
     Then drops, and rains for grief,

So sighed I upwards still, at last
          'Twixt steps, and falls

I reached the pinnacle, where placed
I found a pair of scales
I took them up and laid
In th'one late pains,
The other smoke, and pleasures weighed
But proved the heavier grains;

With that, some cried, Away; straight I
Obeyed, and led
Full East, a fair, fresh field could spy
Some called it, *Jacob's Bed;*
A virgin-soil, which no
Rude feet e'er trod,
Where (since he stepped there,) only go
Prophets, and friends of God.

Here, I reposed; but scarce well set,
A grove descried
Of stately height, whose branches met
And mixed on every side;
I entered, and once in
(Amazed to see't,)
Found all was changed, and a new spring
Did all my senses greet;

The unthrift sun shot vital gold
A thousand pieces,
And heaven its azure did unfold
Checkered with snowy fleeces,
The air was all in spice
And every bush
A garland wore; thus fed my eyes
But all the ear lay hush.

Only a little fountain lent
Some use for ears,
And on the dumb shades language spent
The music of her tears;

I drew her near, and found
The cistern full
Of diverse stones, some bright, and round
Others ill-shaped, and dull.

The first (pray mark,) as quick as light
Danced through the flood,
But, th'last more heavy than the night
Nailed to the center stood;
I wondered much, but tired
At last with thought,
My restless eye that still desired
As strange an object brought;

It was a bank of flowers, where I descried
(Though 'twas mid-day,)
Some fast asleep, others broad-eyed
And taking in the ray,
Here musing long, I heard
A rushing wind
Which still increased, but whence it stirred
No where I could not find;

I turned me round, and to each shade
Dispatched an eye,
To see, if any leaf had made
Least motion, or reply,
But while I listening sought
My mind to ease
By knowing, where 'twas, or where not,
It whispered; Where I please.

Lord, then said I, *On me one breath*
And let me die before my death!

5:2 I sleep, but my heart waketh: it is the voice of my beloved that knocketh, saying, Open to me, my sister, my love, my dove, my undefiled: for my head is filled with dew, and my locks with the drops of the night.

My dove, my beautiful one

James Joyce

My dove, my beautiful one,
  Arise, arise!
  The night-dew lies
Upon my lips and eyes.

The odorous winds are weaving
  A music of sighs:
  Arise, arise,
My dove, my beautiful one!

I wait by the cedar tree,
  My sister, my love.
  White breast of the dove,
My breast shall be your bed.

The pale dew lies
  Like a veil on my head.
  My fair one, my fair dove,
Arise, arise!

5:3–6 I have put off my coat; how shall I put it on? I have washed my feet; how shall I defile them? My beloved put in his hand by the hole of the door, and my bowels were moved for him. I rose up to open to my beloved; and my hands dropped with myrrh, and my fingers with sweet smelling myrrh, upon the handles of the lock. I opened to my beloved; but my beloved had withdrawn himself, and was gone: my soul failed when he spake: I sought him, but I could not find him; I called him, but he gave me no answer.

Cant. 5.6 & c.

Elizabeth Singer

Oh! How his pointed language, like a dart,
Sticks to the softest fibers of my heart,
Quite through my soul the charming accents slide,
That from his life inspiring portals glide;
And whilst I the enchanting sound admire,
My melting vitals in a trance expire.
Oh Son of Venus, mourn thy baffled arts,
For I defy the proudest of thy darts:
Undazzled now, I thy weak taper view,
And find no fatal influence accrue;
Nor would fond child thy feebler lamp appear,
Should my bright sun deign to approach more near;
Canst thou his rival then pretend to prove?
Thou a false idol, he the God of Love;
Lovely beyond conception, he is all
Reason, or fancy amiable call,
All that the most exerted thoughts can reach,
When sublimated to its utmost stretch.
Oh! altogether charming, why in thee
Do the vain world no form or beauty see?
Why do they idolize a dusty clod,
And yet refuse their homage to a God?
Why from a beauteous flowing fountain turn,
For the dead puddle of a narrow urn?
Oh carnal madness! sure we falsely call
So dull a thing as man is, rational;
Alas, my shining love, what can there be
On Earth so splendid to out-glitter thee?
In whom the brightness of a Godhead shines,
With all its lovely and endearing lines;
Thee with whose sight mortality once blessed,
Would throw off its dark veil to be possessed;
Then altogether lovely, why in thee
Do the vain world no form or beauty see.

6:1–13 Whither is thy beloved gone, O thou fairest among women? whither is thy beloved turned aside? that we may seek him with thee. My

beloved is gone down into his garden, to the beds of spices, to feed in the gardens, and to gather lilies. . . . Return, return, O Shulamite; return, return, that we may look upon thee. What will ye see in the Shulamite? As it were the company of two armies.

The Hebrew of your poets, Zion

Charles Reznikoff

The Hebrew of your poets, Zion,
is like oil upon a burn,
cool as oil;
after work
the smell in the street at night
of the hedge in flower.
Like Solomon,
I have married and married the speech of strangers;
none are like you, Shulamite.

7:1–8:4 How beautiful are thy feet with shoes, O prince's daughter! the joints of thy thighs are like jewels, the work of the hands of a cunning workman. . . . I charge you, O daughters of Jerusalem, that ye stir not up, nor awake my love, until he please.

The ninth Canticle

George Wither

Thou daughter of the royal line,
How comely are those feet of thine,
    When their beseeming shoes they wear?
The curious knitting of thy thighs,
Is like the costly gems of prize,
    Which wrought by skillful workmen are.

Thy navel, is a goblet round,
Where liquor evermore is found:
    Thy fair and fruitful belly shows
As doth a goodly heap of wheat,
With lilies round about beset;
    And thy two breasts like twinned roes.

Thy neck like some white tower doth rise:
Like Heshbon fishpools are thine eyes,
    Which near the gate Bath-rabbim lie:
Thy nose (which thee doth well become)
Is like the Tower of Libanum,
    Which on Damascus hath an eye.

Thy head like scarlet doth appear,
The hairs thereof like purple are:
    And in those threads the king is bound.
Oh Love! how wondrous fair art thou!
How perfect do thy pleasures show!
    And how thy joys in them abound!

Thou statured art in palm-tree wise:
Thy breasts like clusters do arise.
    I said, Into this palm I'll go;
My hold shall on her branches be,
And those thy breasts shall be to me
    Like clusters that on vines do grow.

Thy nostrils savor shall as well,
As newly gathered fruits do smell:
    Thy speech shall also relish so,
As purest wine, that for my dear
Is fitting drink, and able were
    To cause an old man's lips to go.

I my Beloved's am; and he
Hath his affection set on me.
    Come, well-beloved, come away:
Into the fields let's walk along;
And there the villages among.
    Even in the country, we will stay.

We to the vines betimes will go,
And see, if they do spring or no–
    Or, if the tender grapes appear.
We will moreover go and see
If the pomegranates blossomed be:
    And I my love will give thee there.

Sweet smells, the mandrakes do afford:
And we within our gates are stored

Of all things that delightful be;
Yea, whether new or old they are,
Preparéd they be for my dear;
And I have laid them up for thee.

Would as my brother thou mightst be
That sucked my mothers breast with me:
Oh! would it were no otherwise!
In public then I thee would meet,
And give thee kisses in the street;
And none there is should thee despise.

Then I my self would for thee come,
And bring thee to my mother's home:
Thou likewise thou'ld'st instruct me there.
And wine, that is commixed with spice,
(Sweet wine of the pomegranate juice)
I would for thee, to drink prepare.

My head with his left hand he stayed:
His right hand over me he laid;
And (being so embraced by him)
Said he, I charge you not disease,
Nor wake my Love until she please,
You daughters of Jerusalem.

8:7–10 Many waters cannot quench love, neither can the floods drown it: if a man would give all the substance of his house for love, it would utterly be contemned. We have a little sister, and she hath no breasts: what shall we do for our sister in the day when she shall be spoken for? If she be a wall, we will build upon her a palace of silver: and if she be a door, we will inclose her with boards of cedar. I am a wall, and my breasts like towers: then was I in his eyes as one that found favour.

The Book of Wisdom

Robert Lowell

Can I go on loving anyone at fifty,
still cool to the brief and five-times wounded lives
of those we loathed with wild idealism young?

Though the gods only toss me twenty cards,
twenty, thirty, or fifty years of work,
I shiver up vertical like a baby pigeon,
palate-sprung for the worm, senility—
to strap the gross artillery to my back,
lash on destroying what I lurch against,
not with anger, but unwieldy feet,
ballooning like the spotted, warty, blow-rib toad,
King Solomon croaking, "This too is vanity;
her lips are a scarlet thread, her breasts are towers,"
hymns of the terrible organ in decay.

The Book of the Prophet ISAIAH

1:16–18 Wash you, make you clean; put away the evil of your doings from before mine eyes; cease to do evil; Learn to do well; seek judgment, relieve the oppressed, judge the fatherless, plead for the widow. Come now, and let us reason together, saith the LORD: though your sins be as scarlet, they shall be as white as snow; though they be red like crimson, they shall be as wool.

Beyond Knowledge

Alice Meynell

Into the rescued world newcomer,
    The newly-dead stepped up, and cried,
"O what is that, sweeter than summer
    Was to my heart before I died?
Sir (to an angel), what is yonder
    More bright than the remembered skies,
A lovelier sight, a softer splendour
    Than when the moon was wont to rise?
Surely no sinner wears such seeming
    Even the Rescued World within?"

"O the success of His redeeming!
O child, it is a rescued sin!"

6:8–10 Also I heard the voice of the Lord, saying, Whom shall I send, and who will go for us? Then said I, Here am I; send me. And he said, Go, and tell this people, Hear ye indeed, but understand not; and see ye indeed, but perceive not. Make the heart of this people fat, and make their ears heavy, and shut their eyes; lest they see with their eyes, and hear with their ears, and understand with their heart, and convert, and be healed.

Where the Sun Ends

(Isaiah 6:8)

Peter Davison

"Eastward I go by force; but westward I go free."—Thoreau: "Walking"

Mount. Leave your living to the wise.
Peel out, the highway's for the sun.
Your eyes have pierced the state's disguise,
Your journey has begun.

Shun shelter, offices, the maze
of striving. Genitals tell you true:
Children sing sweeter praise
than senators do.

What held you to the empty day,
the churlish functionary grind
Where unclean lips beseech and bray
their sermons for the blind?

"A hissing tongue, a shuddering door,"
the prophets tell, the thrones attest.
Our hoarsened hymns ignite and roar,
our engines growl toward the West:

Here am I; send me.

11:1–10 And there shall come forth a rod out of the stem of Jesse, and a Branch shall grow out of his roots: And the spirit of the LORD shall rest upon him, the spirit of wisdom and understanding, the spirit of counsel and might, the spirit of knowledge and of the fear of the LORD; And shall make him of quick understanding in the fear of the LORD: and he shall not judge after the sight of his eyes, neither reprove after the hearing of his ears: But with righteousness shall he judge the poor, and reprove with equity for the meek of the earth: and he shall smite the earth: with the rod of his mouth, and with the breath of his lips shall he slay the wicked. And righteousness shall be the girdle of his loins, and faithfulness the girdle of his reins. The wolf also shall dwell with the lamb, and the leopard shall lie down with the kid; and the calf and the young lion and the fatling together; and a little child shall lead them. And the cow and the bear shall feed; their young ones shall lie down together: and the lion shall eat straw like the ox. And the sucking child shall play on the hole of the asp, and the weaned child shall put his hand on the cockatrice' den. They shall not hurt nor destroy in all my holy mountain: for the earth shall be full of the knowledge of the LORD, as the waters cover the sea. And in that day there shall be a root of Jesse, which shall stand for an ensign of the people; to it shall the Gentiles seek: and his rest shall be glorious.

MESSIAH: A SACRED ECLOGUE IN IMITATION OF VIRGIL'S POLLIO

ALEXANDER POPE

Ye nymphs of Solyma! begin the song:
To heavenly themes sublimer strains belong.
The mossy fountains, and the sylvan shades,
The dreams of Pindus and Aonian maids,
Delight no more—O thou my voice inspire
Who touched Isaiah's hallowed lips with fire!
Rapt into future times, the bard begun:
A Virgin shall conceive, a Virgin bear a Son!
From Jesse's root behold a Branch arise,
Whose sacred flower with fragrance fills the skies:
The ethereal spirit o'er its leaves shall move,
And on its top descends the mystic Dove.
Ye heavens! from high the dewy nectar pour,
And in oft silence shed the kindly shower!
The sick and weak the healing plant shall aid,
From storms a shelter, and from heat a shade.
All crimes shall cease, and ancient fraud shall fail;
Returning Justice lift aloft her scale;
Peace o'er the world her olive wand extend,

And white-robed Innocence from heaven descend.
Swift fly the years, and rise the expected morn!
Oh spring to light, auspicious Babe, be born!
See Nature hastes her earliest wreaths to bring,
With all the incense of the breathing spring:
See lofty Lebanon his head advance,
See nodding forests on the mountain dance:
See spicy clouds from lowly Sharon rise,
And Carmel's flowery top perfumes the skies!
Hark! a glad voice the lonely desert cheers:—
"Prepare the way! a God, a God appears";
"A God, a God!" the vocal hills reply,
The rocks proclaim the approaching Deity.
Lo, earth receives him from the bending skies!
Sink down, ye mountains, and ye valleys, rise;
With heads declined, ye cedars, homage pay;
Be smooth, ye rocks; ye rapid floods, give way;
The Savior comes! by ancient bards foretold!
Hear him, ye deaf, and all ye blind, behold!
He from thick films shall purge the visual ray,
And on the sightless eyeball pour the day:
'Tis he th' obstructed paths of sound shall clear,
And bid new music charm th' unfolding ear:
The dumb shall sing, the lame his crutch forego,
And leap exulting like the bounding roe.
No sigh, no murmur the wide world shall hear,
From every face he wipes off every tear.
In adamantine chains shall Death be bound,
And Hell's grim tyrant feel the eternal wound.
As the good shepherd tends his fleecy care,
Seeks freshest pasture and the purest air,
Explores the lost, the wandering sheep directs,
By day o'ersees them, and by night protects;
The tender lambs he raises in his arms,
Feeds from his hands, and in his bosom warms;
Thus shall mankind his guardian care engage,
The promised Father of the future age.
No more shall nation against nation rise,
Nor ardent warriors meet with hateful eyes,
Nor fields with gleaming steel be covered o'er,
The brazen trumpets kindle rage no more;
But useless lances into scythes shall bend,

And the broad falchion in a ploughshare end.
Then palaces shall rise; the joyful son
Shall finish what his short-lived sire begun;
Their vines a shadow to their race shall yield,
And the same hand that sowed, shall reap the field.
The swain in barren deserts with surprise
See lilies spring, and sudden verdure rise;
And start, amidst the thirsty wilds to hear
New falls of water murmuring in his ear.
On rifted rocks, the dragon's late abodes,
The green reed trembles, and the bulrush nods.
Waste sandy valleys, once perplexed with thorn,
The spiry fir and shapely box adorn;
To leafless shrubs the flowering palms succeed,
And odorous myrtle to the noisome weed.
The lambs with wolves shall graze the verdant mead,
And boys in flowery bands the tiger lead;
The steer and lion at one crib shall meet,
And harmless serpents lick the pilgrim's feet;
The smiling infant in his hand shall take
The crested basilisk and speckled snake,
Pleased the green lustre of the scales survey,
And with their forky tongue shall innocently play.
Rise, crowned with light, imperial Salem, rise!
Exalt thy towery head, and lift thy eyes!
See, a long race thy spacious courts adorn;
See future sons, and daughters yet unborn,
In crowding ranks on every side arise,
Demanding life, impatient for the skies!
See barbarous nations at thy gates attend,
Walk in thy light, and in thy temple bend;
See thy bright altars thronged with prostrate kings,
And heaped with products of Sabean springs!
For thee Idume's spicy forests blow,
And seeds of gold in Ophir's mountains glow.
See heaven its sparkling portals wide display,
And break upon thee in a flood of day.
No more the rising sun shall gild the morn,
Nor evening Cynthia fill her silver horn;
But lost, dissolved in thy superior rays,
One tide of glory, one unclouded blaze
O'erflow thy courts: the Light himself shall shine

Revealed, and God's eternal day be thine!
The seas shall waste, the skies in smoke decay,
Rocks fall to dust, and mountains melt away;
But fixed his word, his saving power remains:
Thy realms for ever lasts, thy own MESSIAH reigns!

12:1–6 And in that day thou shalt say, O LORD, I will praise thee: though thou wast angry with me, thine anger is turned away, and thou comfortedst me. . . . Cry out and shout, thou inhabitant of Zion: for great is the Holy One of Israel in the midst of thee.

AN OTHER SONG OF THE FAITHFUL, FOR THE MERCIES OF GOD

MICHAEL DRAYTON

Oh Living Lord, I still will laud thy name,
   for though thou wert offended once with me:
Thy heavy wrath is turned from me again,
   and graciously thou now dost comfort me.

Behold, the Lord is my salvation,
   I trust in him, and fear not any power:
He is my song, the strength I lean upon,
   the Lord God is my loving Savior.

Therefore with joy out of the well of life,
   draw forth sweet water, which it doth afford:
And in the day of trouble and of strife,
   call on the name of God the living Lord.

Extol his works and wonders to the sun,
   unto all people let his praise be shown:
Record in song the marvels he hath done,
   and let his glory through the world be blown.

Cry out aloud and shout on Sion hill,
   I give thee charge that this proclaimed be:
The great and mighty king of Israel,
   now only dwelleth in the midst of thee.

14:12–18 How art thou fallen from heaven, O Lucifer, son of the morning! how art thou cut down to the ground, which didst weaken the nations! For thou hast said in thine heart, I will ascend into heaven, I will exalt my throne above the stars of God: I will sit also upon the mount of the congregation, in the sides of the north: I will ascend above the heights of the clouds; I will be like the most High. Yet thou shalt be brought down to hell, to the sides of the pit. They that see thee shall narrowly look upon thee, and consider thee, saying, Is this the man that made the earth to tremble, that did shake kingdoms; That made the world as a wilderness, and destroyed the cities thereof; that opened not the house of his prisoners? All the kings of the nations, even all of them, lie in glory, every one in his own house.

Lucifer in Starlight

George Meredith

On a starred night Prince Lucifer uprose.
Tired of his dark dominion swung the fiend
Above the rolling ball in cloud part screened,
Where sinners hugged their spectre of repose
Poor prey to his hot fit of pride were those.
And now upon his western wing he leaned,
Now his huge bulk o'er Afric's sands careened,
Now the black planet shadowed arctic snows.
Soaring through wider zones that pricked his scars
With memory of the old revolt from awe,
He reached a middle height, and at the stars,
Which are the brain of heaven, he looked, and sank.
Around the ancient track marched, rank on rank,
The army of unalterable law.

21:9 And, behold, here cometh a chariot of men, with a couple of horsemen. And he answered and said, Babylon is fallen, is fallen; and all the graven images of her gods he hath broken unto the ground.

Babylon

Siegfried Sassoon

Babylon that was beautiful is Nothing now.
Once to the world it tolled a golden bell:

Belshazzar wore its blaze upon his brow;
Ruled; and to ruin fell.
Babylon—a blurred and blinded face of stone—
At dumb Oblivion bragged with trumpets blown;
Teemed, and while merchants strove and prophets dreamed,
Bowed before idols, and was overthrown.

Babylon the merciless, now a name of doom,
Built towers in Time, as we today, for whom
Auguries of self-annihilation loom.

29:11–14 And the vision of all is become unto you as the words of a book that is sealed, which men deliver to one that is learned, saying, Read this, I pray thee: and he saith, I cannot; for it is sealed: And the book is delivered to him that is not learned, saying, Read this, I pray thee: and he saith, I am not learned. Wherefore the Lord said, Forasmuch as this people draw near me with their mouth, and with their lips do honour me, but have removed their heart far from me, and their fear toward me is taught by the precept of men: Therefore, behold, I will proceed to do a marvellous work among this people, even a marvellous work and a wonder: for the wisdom of their wise men shall perish, and the understanding of their prudent men shall be hid.

Isaiah by Kerosene Lantern Light

Robert Harris

This voice an older friend has kept
to patronise the single name he swears by
saying aha, aha to me.

The heresy hunter, sifting these lines
another shrieks through serepax and heroin
that we have a 'culture'.

These are the very same who shall wait
for plainer faces after they've glutted on beauty,
a mild people back from the dead

shall speak the doors down
to the last hullo reaching the last crooked hutch
in forest or forest-like deeps of the town.

These who teach with the fingers and answer
with laughter, with anger, shall be in derision
and the waiting long, and the blue and white days

like a grave in a senseless universe.
I believe this wick and this open book
in the light's oval, and I disbelieve

everything this generation has told me.

34:1–17 Come near, ye nations, to hear; and hearken, ye people: let the earth hear, and all that is therein; the world, and all things that come forth of it. . . .

And he hath cast the lot for them, and his hand hath divided it unto them by line: they shall possess it for ever, from generation to generation shall they dwell therein.

The 34. Chapter of the Prophet Isaiah

Abraham Cowley

Awake, and with attention hear,
    Thou drowsy World, for it concerns thee near;
        Awake, I say, and listen well,
To what from God, I, his loud prophet, tell.
Bid both the poles suppress their stormy noise,
And bid the roaring sea contain its voice.
Be still thou Sea, be still thou Air and Earth,
Still, as old Chaos, before motion's birth,
A dreadful host of judgments is gone out;
        In strength and number more
        Then e'er was raised by God before,
To scourge the Rebel World, and march it round about.

    I see the Sword of God brandished above;
        And from it streams a dismal ray;
            I see the scabbard cast away.
How red anon with slaughter will it prove!
        How will it sweat and reek in blood!

How will the scarlet-glutton be o'er-gorged with his food!
And devour all the mighty feast!
Nothing soon but bones will rest.
God does a solemn sacrifice prepare;
But not of oxen, nor of rams,
Not of kids, nor of their dams,
Not of heifers, nor of lambs.
The altar all the land, and all men in't the victims are,
Since wicked men's more guilty blood to spare,
The beasts so long have sacrificed been,
Since men their birthright forfeit still by sin,
'Tis fit at last beasts their revenge should have,
And sacrificed men their better brethren save.

So will they fall, so will they flee;
Such will the creatures wild distraction be,
When at the final Doom,
Nature and Time shall both be slain,
Shall struggle with Deaths pangs in vain,
And the whole world their funeral pile become.
The wide-stretched scroll of heaven, which we
Immortal as the Deity think,
With all the beauteous characters that in it
With such deep sense by God's own hand were writ,
Whose eloquence though we understand not, we admire,
Shall crackle, and the parts together shrink
Like parchment in a fire.
Th'exhausted sun to th'moon no more shall lend;
But truly then headlong into the sea descend.
The glittering Host, now in such fair array,
So proud, so well appointed, and so gay,
Like fearful troops in some strong ambush ta'en,
Shall some fly routed, and some fall slain,
Thick as ripe fruit, or yellow leaves in autumn fall,
With such a violent storm as blows down tree and all.

And Thou, O cursed Land,
Which wilt not see the precipice where thou dost stand,
Though thou standst just upon the brink;
Thou of this poisoned bowl the bitter dregs shalt drink.
Thy rivers and thy lakes shall so
With human blood o'erflow;

That they shall fetch the slaughtered corpse away,
Which in the fields around unburied lay,
And rob the beasts and birds to give the fish their prey.
The rotting corpse shall so infect the air;
Beget such plagues, and putrid venoms there,
That by thine own dead shall be slain,
All thy few living that remain.
As one who buys, surveys a ground,
So the Destroying Angel measures it around.
So careful and so strict he is,
Lest any nook or corner he should miss.
He walks about the perishing nation,
Ruin behind him stalks and empty desolation.

Then shall the market and the pleading-place
Be choked with brambles and o'ergrown with grass.
The serpents through thy streets shall roll,
And in thy lower rooms the wolves shall howl,
And thy gilt chambers lodge the raven and the owl,
And all the winged ill-omens of the air,
Though no new ills can be foreboded there.
The lion then shall to the leopard say
Brother Leopard come away;
Behold a land which God has given us in prey!
Behold a land from whence we see
Mankind expulsed, His and our common enemy!
The brother leopard shakes himself, and does not stay.

The glutted vultures shall expect in vain
New armies to be slain.
Shall find at last the business done,
Leave their consumed quarters, and be gone.
Th'unburied ghosts shall sadly moan,
The satyrs laugh to hear them groan.
The evil spirits that delight
To dance and revel in the mask of night,
The moon and stars, their sole spectators shall affright.
And if of lost Mankind
Ought happen to be left behind,
If any relics but remain
They in the Dens shall lurk, beasts in the palaces shall reign.

37:15–16 And Hezekiah prayed unto the LORD, saying, O LORD of hosts, God of Israel, that dwellest between the cherubims, thou art the God, even thou alone, of all the kingdoms of the earth: thou hast made heaven and earth. . . .

THE PRAYER OF HEZEKIAH

GEORGE WITHER

Lord of Hosts, and God of Israel!
Thou who between the cherubims dost dwell;
Of all the world thou only art the king,
And Heaven and Earth unto their form didst bring.
Lord bow thine ear; to hear attentive be,
Lift up thine eyes, and deign, Oh Lord, to see
What words Sennacherib hath cast abroad;
And his proud message to the living God.

Lord, true it is, that lands and kingdoms all
Are to the king of Ashur brought in thrall:
Yea, he their gods into the fire hath thrown:
For gods they were not but of wood and stone.
Man's work they were, and men destroyed them have,
Us therefore from his power vouchsafe to save;
That all the kingdoms of the world may see,
That thou art God, that only thou art he.

38:9–15 The writing of Hezekiah king of Judah, when he had been sick, and was recovered of his sickness: I said in the cutting off of my days, I shall go to the gates of the grave: I am deprived of the residue of my years. I said, I shall not see the LORD, even the LORD, in the land of the living: I shall behold man no more with the inhabitants of the world. Mine age is departed, and is removed from me as a shepherd's tent: I have cut off like a weaver my life: he will cut me off with pining sickness: from day even to night wilt thou make an end of me. I reckoned till morning, that, as a lion, so will he break all my bones: from day even to night wilt thou make an end of me. Like a crane or a swallow, so did I chatter: I did mourn as a dove: mine eyes fail with looking upward: O LORD, I am oppressed; undertake for me. What shall I say? he hath both spoken unto me, and himself hath done it: I shall go softly all my years in the bitterness of my soul.

Recogitabo tibi omnes annos meos

William Habington

Time! where didst thou those years inter
Which I have seen decease?
My soul's at war and truth bids her
Find out their hidden sepulcher,
To give her troubles peace.

Pregnant with flowers doth not the Spring
Like a late bride appear?
Whose feathered music only bring
Caresses, and no requiem sing
On the departed year?

The Earth, like some rich wanton heir,
Whose parents coffined lie,
Forgets it once looked pale and bare
And doth for vanities prepare,
As the Spring ne'er should dye.

The present hour, flattered by all
Reflects not on the last;
But I, like a sad factor shall
T' account my life each moment call,
And only weep the past.

My memory tracks each several way
Since reason did begin
Over my actions her first sway:
And teacheth me that each new day
Did only vary sin.

Poor bankrupt conscience! where are those
Rich hours but farmed to thee?
How carelessly I some did lose,
And other to my lust dispose
As no rent day should be?

I have infected with impure
Disorders my past years.
But I'll to penitence inure
Those that succeed. There is no cure
Nor antidote but tears.

38:16–20 O Lord, by these things men live, and in all these things is the life of my spirit: so wilt thou recover me, and make me to live. Behold, for peace I had great bitterness: but thou hast in love to my soul delivered it from the pit of corruption: for thou hast cast all my sins behind thy back. For the grave cannot praise thee, death can not celebrate thee: they that go down into the pit cannot hope for thy truth. The living, the living, he shall praise thee, as I do this day: the father to the children shall make known thy truth. The LORD was ready to save me: therefore we will sing my songs to the stringed instruments all the days of our life in the house of the LORD.

THE SONG OF ESECHIA

JOHN HALL

Unto the gates of hell
I went I should have wend,
Amid my days when as I thought
My years were at an end.

With in my self I said,
I never shall again
Visit the Lord (the Lord I say)
In this life while I reign.

I never look again
Before men to appear,
Nor to behold no worldly wights
That have their dwelling here.

Mine age is folded up
Together at this day:
As one should from the shepherd poor
His cottage take away.

And through my sins my life
Is cut off and undo,
As when the weaver's work is done
His web he cuts atwo.

This pining sickness will
My life in sunder rend,
For in one day I well perceive
My life shall have an end.

Until tomorow yet
I thought to live so long:
But he my bones hath bruised sore
Most like a giant strong.

For in one day thou wilt
Mine end bring on me low:
As swallows chatter in their lay,
Then gan I to do so.

I cried like the crane,
And mourned as the dove:
Directing ever more mine eyes
On high to him above.

O Lord, then said I, though
This sickness doth me press:
O ease thou me for in thy power
It is, the same to cease.

What shall I say, the Lord
His promise made to me,
And he himself performed hath
The same as we may see.

All while I live therefore,
It shall not from my mind,
My bitter life, and how therein
I found him good and kind.

Beyond their years I see
O Lord that men may live,
Which I to all men will declare,
And knowledge will them give.

In those prolonged years
How I in joy do reign:
And that thou causedst me to sleep
And gave me life again.

My pensiveness behold,
As bitter was as gall:
And for my health I longed sore
Out of that woefull thrall.

Thy pleasure was to save
Me from the filthy lake:
For thou O Lord hast all my sins
Out thrown behind thy back.

For hell gives thee no praise,
Nor death magnificence:
And in their grave none praise thy truth,
That parted be from hence.

The Lord hath wrought my health,
Our songs we therefore sure
Will always sing within thy house,
While our life days endure.

40:6–8 The voice said, Cry. And he said, What shall I cry? All flesh is grass, and all the goodliness thereof is as the flower of the field: The grass withereth, the flower fadeth: because the spirit of the LORD bloweth upon it: surely the people is grass. The grass withereth, the flower fadeth: but the word of our God shall stand for ever.

The Steed Bit his Master

Anonymous

The steed bit his master:
How came this to pass?
He heard the good pastor
Cry, "All flesh is grass."

47:1 Come down, and sit in the dust, O virgin daughter of Babylon, sit on the ground: there is no throne, O daughter of the Chaldeans: for thou shalt no more be called tender and delicate.

Babylon

Alfred, Lord Tennyson

Bow, daughter of Babylon, bow thee to dust!
Thine heart shall be quelled, and thy pride shall be crushed:

Weep, Babylon, weep! for thy splendour is past;
And they come like the storm in the day of the blast.

Howl, desolate Babylon, lost one and lone!
And bind thee in sackcloth—for where is thy throne?
Like a winepress in wrath will I trample thee down,
And rend from thy temples the pride of thy crown.

Though thy streets be a hundred, thy gates be all brass,
Yet thy proud ones of war shall be withered like grass;
Thy gates shall be broken, thy strength be laid low,
And thy streets shall resound to the shouts of the foe!

Though thy chariots of power on thy battlements bound,
And the grandeur of waters encompass thee round;
Yet thy walls shall be shaken, thy waters shall fail,
Thy matrons shall shriek, and thy king shall be pale.

The terrible day of thy fall is at hand,
When my rage shall descend on the face of thy land;
The lances are pointed, the keen sword is bared,
The shields are anointed, the helmets prepared.

I call upon Cyrus! He comes from afar,
And the armies of nations are gathered to war;
With the blood of thy children his path shall be red,
And the bright sun of conquest shall blaze o'er his head.

Thou glory of kingdoms! thy princes are drunk,
But their loins shall be loosed, and their hearts shall be sunk;
They shall crouch to the dust, and be counted as slaves,
At the roll of his wheels, like the rushing of waves!

For I am the Lord, who have mightily spanned
The breadth of the heavens, and the sea and the land;
And the mountains shall flow at my presence, and earth
Shall reel to and fro in the glance of my wrath!

Your proud domes of cedar on earth shall be thrown
And the rank grass shall wave o'er the lonely hearthstone;
And your sons and your sires and your daughters shall bleed
By the barbarous hands of the murdering Mede!

I will sweep ye away in destruction and death,
As the whirlwind that scatters the chaff with its breath;
And the fanes of your gods shall be sprinkled with gore,
And the course of your streams shall be heard of no more!

There the wandering Arab shall ne'er pitch his tent,
But the beasts of the desert shall wail and lament;
In their desolate houses the dragons shall lie,
And the satyrs shall dance, and the bitterns shall cry!

55:1–2 Ho, every one that thirsteth, come ye to the waters, and he that hath no money; come ye, buy, and eat; yea, come, buy wine and milk without money and without price. Wherefore do ye spend money for that which is not bread? and your labour for that which satisfieth not? hearken diligently unto me, and eat ye that which is good, and let your soul delight itself in fatness.

The Invitation

George Herbert

Come ye hither all, whose taste
Is our waste;
Save your cost, and mend your fare.
God is here prepared and dressed,
And the feast,
God, in whom all dainties are.

Come ye hither all, whom wine
Doth define,
Naming you not to your good:
Weep what ye have drunk amiss,
And drink this,
Which before ye drink is blood.

Come ye hither all, whom pain
Doth arraign,
Bringing all your sins to sight:

Taste and fear not: God is here
In this cheer,
And on sin doth cast the fright.

Come ye hither all, whom joy
Doth destroy,
While ye graze without your bounds:
Here is joy that drowneth quite
Your delight,
As a flood the lower grounds.

Come ye hither all, whose love
Is your dove,
And exalts you to the sky:
Here is love, which having breath
Ev'n in death,
After death can never die.

Lord I have invited all,
And I shall
Still invite, still call to thee:
For it seems but just and right
In my sight,
Where is all, there all should be.

Ho, everyone that thirsteth

A. E. Housman

Ho, everyone that thirsteth
And hath the price to give,
Come to the stolen waters,
Drink and your soul shall live.

Come to the stolen waters,
And leap the guarded pale,
And pull the flower in season
Before desire shall fail.

It shall not last for ever,
No more than earth and skies;
But he that drinks in season
Shall live before he dies.

June suns, you cannot store them
To warm the winter's cold,
The lad that hopes for heaven
Shall fill his mouth with mould.

60:15–20 Whereas thou hast been forsaken and hated, so that no man went through thee, I will make thee an eternal excellency, a joy of many generations. Thou shalt also suck the milk of the Gentiles, and shalt suck the breast of kings: and thou shalt know that I the LORD am thy Saviour and thy Redeemer, the mighty One of Jacob. For brass I will bring gold, and for iron I will bring silver, and for wood brass, and for stones iron: I will also make thy officers peace, and thine exactors righteousness. Violence shall no more be heard in thy land, wasting nor destruction within thy borders; but thou shalt call thy walls Salvation, and thy gates Praise. The sun shall be no more thy light by day; neither for brightness shall the moon give light unto thee: but the LORD shall be unto thee an everlasting light, and thy God thy glory. Thy sun shall no more go down; neither shall thy moon withdraw itself: for the LORD shall be thine everlasting light, and the days of thy mourning shall be ended.

Hymn 10

William Cowper

Hear what God the Lord hath spoken,
O my people, weak and few;
Comfortless, afflicted, broken,
Fair abodes I build for you:
Thorns of heart-felt tribulation
Shall no more perplex your ways;
You shall name your walls, Salvation,
And your gates shall all be praise.

Then, like streams that feed the garden,
Pleasures, without end, shall flow;
For the Lord, your faith rewarding,
All his bounty shall bestow:

Still in undisturbed possession,
Peace and righteousness shall reign;
Never shall you feel oppression,
Hear the voice of war again.

You no more your suns descending,
Waning moons no more shall see;
But your griefs, for ever ending,
Find eternal noon in me;
God shall rise, and shining o'er you,
Change to day the gloom of night;
He, the Lord, shall be your glory,
God your everlasting light.

63:1–6 Who is this that cometh from Edom, with dyed garments from Bozrah? this that is glorious in his apparel, travelling in the greatness of his strength? I that speak in righteousness, mighty to save. Wherefore art thou red in thine apparel, and thy garments like him that treadeth in the winefat? I have trodden the winepress alone; and of the people there was none with me: for I will tread them in mine anger, and trample them in my fury; and their blood shall be sprinkled upon my garments, and I will stain all my raiment. For the day of vengeance is in mine heart, and the year of my redeemed is come. And I looked, and there was none to help; and I wondered that there was none to uphold: therefore mine own arm brought salvation unto me; and my fury, it upheld me. And I will tread down the people in mine anger, and make them drunk in my fury, and I will bring down their strength to the earth.

What is he, this lordling

Friar William Herebert

What is he, this lordling, that cometh from the fight
With blood-red weed so grisliche y-dight,
So fair y-cointìsëd, so seemly in sight,
So stiflichë gangeth, so doughty a knight?

'I it am, I it am, that ne speak butë right,
Champion to healen mankind in fight.'

'Why then is thy shroud red, with blood all y-ment,
As treaderës in wring with must all besprent?'

The wring I have y-trodden all myself one,
And of all mankind ne was none other wone.
I them have y-trodden in wrath and in grame
And all my weed is besprent with their blood y-same,
And all my robe y-foulëd to their greatë shame.
The day of th'ilkë wrechë liveth in my thought;
The year of meedës yielding ne forget I nought.

I looked all aboutë some helping man;
I sought all the routë, but help n'as there none.
It was mine ownë strengthë that this botë wrought,
Myn ownë doughtinessë that help there me brought.'

'On Godës milsfulness I will bethinkë me,
And herien him in allë thing that he yieldeth me.'

'I have y-trodden the folk in wrath and in grame,
Adreint all with shenness, y-drawn down with shame.'

65:25 The wolf and the lamb shall feed together, and the lion shall eat straw like the bullock: and dust shall be the serpent's meat. They shall not hurt nor destroy in all my holy mountain, saith the LORD.

On Falling Asleep by Firelight

William Meredith

Around the fireplace, pointing at the fire,
As in the prophet's dream of the last truce,
The animals lie down; they doze or stare,
Their hoofs and paws in comical disuse;
A few still run in dreams. None seems aware
Of the laws of prey that lie asleep here, too,
The dreamer unafraid who keeps the zoo.

Some winter nights impel us to take in
Whatever lopes outside, beastly or kind;
Nothing that gibbers in or out of mind
But the hearth bestows a sleepy sense of kin.
Promiscuous hosts, we bid the causeless slime

Come in; its casualness remains a crime,
But metaphysics bites less sharp than wind.

Now, too, a ghostly, gradually erect
Company lies down, weary of the walk—
Parents with whom we would, but cannot, talk,
Beside them on the floor their artifacts:
Weapons we gave them, which they now bring back.
If they see our privilege, they do not object,
And we are not ashamed to be their stock.

All we had thought unkind were all the while
Alike, the firelight says, and strikes us dumb;
We dream there is no ravening or guile
And take it kindly of the beasts to come
And suffer hospitality, the heat
Turns softly on the hearth into that dust
Isaiah said would be the serpent's meat.

66:1–2 Thus saith the LORD, The heaven is my throne, and the earth is my footstool: where is the house that ye build unto me? and where is the place of my rest? For all those things hath mine hand made, and all those things have been, saith the LORD: but to this man will I look, even to him that is poor and of a contrite spirit, and trembleth at my word.

ISAIAH: CHAPTER 66

DAVID ROSENBERG

The Lord speaks
this way
the sky

and all ways behind it
is a royal seat for me
space

is where I rest
and the earth my footrest
in time

where could you build a house
for me
where a place

especially for me to rest
as if I would sleep or abide
there   or there

when I made all this
all of it comes from my hand
all that is came into being

from me
my Lord
is speaking

but I look at man especially
for the man or woman oppressed
poor and powerless

when he knows he is
broken hearted and
filled with humility

his body trembling with care
open to the others
to my words.

66:6–13 A voice of noise from the city, a voice from the temple, a voice of the LORD that rendereth recompence to his enemies. Before she travailed, she brought forth; before her pain came, she was delivered of a man child.

Who hath heard such a thing? who hath seen such things? Shall the earth be made to bring forth in one day? or shall a nation be born at once? for as soon as Zion travailed, she brought forth her children. Shall I bring to the birth, and not cause to bring forth? saith the LORD: shall I cause to bring forth, and shut the womb? saith thy God.

Rejoice ye with Jerusalem, and be glad with her, all ye that love her: rejoice for joy with her, all ye that mourn for her: That ye may suck, and be satisfied with the breasts of her consolations; that ye may milk out, and be delighted with the abundance of her glory. For thus saith the LORD, Behold, I will extend peace to her like a river, and the glory of the Gentiles like a flowing stream: then shall ye suck, ye shall be borne upon

her sides, and be dandled upon her knees. As one whom his mother comforteth, so will I comfort you; and ye shall be comforted in Jerusalem.

Isaiah 66. 11

Francis Quarles

What, never filled? Be thy lips screwed so fast
To th' earth's full breast? For shame, for shame unseize thee:
Thou tak'st a surfeit where thou shouldst but taste,
And mak'st too much not half enough to please thee.
Ah fool, forbear; Thou swallowst at one breath
Both food and poison down; thou drawst both milk and death.

The uberous breasts, when fairly drawn, repast
The thriving infant with their milky flood,
But being overstrained, return at last
Unwholesome gulps composed of wind and blood.
A moderate use does both repast and please;
Who strains beyond a mean draws in and gulps disease.

But, O that mean whose good the least abuse
Makes bad, is too too hard to be directed:
Can thorns bring grapes, or crabs a pleasing juice?
There's nothing wholesome, where the whole's infected.
Unseize thy lips: Earth's milk's a ripened core
That drops from her disease, that matters from her sore.

Thinkst thou that paunch that burlies out thy coat,
Is thriving fat; or flesh, that seems so brawny?
Thy paunch is dropsied and thy cheeks are bloat;
Thy lips are white and thy complexion tawny;
Thy skin's a bladder blown with watery tumors;
Thy flesh a trembling bog, a quagmire full of humors.

And thou whose thriveless hands are ever straining
Earth's fluent breasts into an empty sieve,
That always hast, yet always art complaining,
And whin'st for more than earth has power to give;
Whose treasure flows and flees away as fast;
That ever hast, and hast, yet hast not what thou hast:

Go choose a substance, fool, that will remain
    Within the limits of thy leaking measure;
Or else go seek an urn that will retain
    The liquid body of thy slippery treasure:
        Alas, how poorly are thy labors crowned?
Thy liquours's neither sweet, nor yet thy vessel sound.

What less than fool is Man, to prog and plot,
    And lavish out the cream of all his care,
To gain poor seeming goods, which, being got,
    Make firm possession but a thoroughfare:
        Or if they stay, they furrow thoughts the deeper,
And being kept with care, they lose their careful keeper.

The Book of the Prophet JEREMIAH

3:6 The LORD said also unto me in the days of Josiah the king, Hast thou seen that which backsliding Israel hath done? she is gone up upon every high mountain and under every green tree, and there hath played the harlot.

ISRAEL

CARL RAKOSI

I hear the voice
            of David and Bathsheba
and the judgment
            on the continual
backslidings
            of the Kings of Israel

I have stumbled
on the ancient voice
of honesty
and tremble
at the voice
of my people.

8:19–22 Behold the voice of the cry of the daughter of my people because of them that dwell in a far country: Is not the LORD in Zion? is not her king in her? Why have they provoked me to anger with their graven images, and with strange vanities? The harvest is past, the summer is ended, and we are not saved. For the hurt of the daughter of my people am I hurt; I am black; astonishment hath taken hold on me. Is there no balm in Gilead; is there no physician there? why then is not the health of the daughter of my people recovered?

To God: an Anthem, sung in the Chapel at White-Hall, before the King

Robert Herrick

Verse. My God, I'm wounded by my sin
And sore without, and sick within:
Ver. Chor. I come to Thee, in hope to find
Salve for my body, and my mind.
Verse. In Gilead though no balm be found,
To ease this smart, or cure this wound;
Ver. Chor. Yet, Lord, I know there is with Thee
All saving health, and help for me.
Verse. Then reach Thou forth that hand of Thine,
That pours in oil, as well as wine.
Ver. Chor. And let it work, for I'll endure
The utmost smart, so Thou wilt cure.

12:1 Righteous art thou, O Lord, when I plead with thee: yet let me talk with thee of thy judgments: Wherefore doth the way of the wicked prosper? wherefore are all they happy that deal very treacherously?

THOU ART INDEED JUST, LORD

GERARD MANLEY HOPKINS

Thou art indeed just, Lord, if I contend
With thee; but, sir, so what I plead is just.
Why do sinners' ways prosper? and why must
Disappointment all I endeavour end?
Wert thou mine enemy, O thou my friend,
How wouldst thou worse, I wonder, than thou dost
Defeat, thwart me? Oh, the sots and thralls of lust
Do in spare hours more thrive than I that spend,
Sir, life upon thy cause. See, banks and brakes
Now, leavèd how thick! lacèd they are again
With fretty chervil, look, and fresh wind shakes
Them; birds build—but not I build; no, but strain,
Time's eunuch, and not breed one work that wakes.
Mine, O thou lord of life, send my roots rain.

17:14–18 Heal me, O LORD, and I shall be healed; save me, and I shall be saved: for thou art my praise. . . . Let them be confounded that persecute me, but let not me be confounded: let them be dismayed, but let not me be dismayed: bring upon them the day of evil, and destroy them with double destruction.

JEREMIE .17

JOHN HALL

O Lord I shall be whole in deed,
If I be healed of thee:
If thou vouchsafe now me to save,
Then shall I saved be.

Thou art my prayer and my praise,
I have none other fort:
To give thee thanks for all my help,
To thee I must resort.

Behold those men that say to me
In mockage and in scorn,

Where is the word of God say they?
Let it come us beforne.

Though not withstanding when I led,
Thy flock in godly train,
Into thy ways by violence
I did them not constrain.

Ne yet the death of any man,
I never did desire,
Thou knowst right well that before thee
My tongue was not a liar.

Be not to me too terrible
O Lord, but me refrain:
For thou art he in whom I hope
In peril and in pain.

Confound me not, but confound them
That do my life pursue:
Nor fear me not, but make thou them
To fear and eke to rue.

And pour on them their painful plague
When thou shalt see the time,
And them destroy that have thee done
So detestable crime.

19:14–15 Then came Jeremiah from Tophet, whither the LORD had sent him to prophesy; and he stood in the court of the LORD'S house; and said to all the people, Thus saith the LORD of hosts, the God of Israel; Behold, I will bring upon this city and upon all her towns all the evil that I have pronounced against it, because they have hardened their necks, that they might not hear my words.

Tophet

THOMAS GRAY

Such Tophet was; so looked the grinning fiend
Whom many a frighted prelate called his friend;

I saw them bow and, while they wished him dead,
With servile simper nod with mitred head.
Our Mother-Church with half-averted sight
Blushed as she blessed her grisly proselyte:
Hosannahs rung through Hell's tremendous borders,
And Satan's self had thoughts of taking orders.*

31:18–21 I have surely heard Ephraim bemoaning himself thus; Thou hast chastised me, and I was chastised, as a bullock unaccustomed to the yoke: turn thou me, and I shall be turned; for thou art the LORD my God. Surely after that I was turned, I repented; and after that I was instructed, I smote upon my thigh: I was ashamed, yea, even confounded, because I did bear the reproach of my youth. Is Ephraim my dear son? is he a pleasant child? for since I spake against him, I do earnestly remember him still: therefore my bowels are troubled for him; I will surely have mercy upon him, saith the LORD. Set thee up waymarks, make thee high heaps: set thine heart toward the highway, even the way which thou wentest: turn again, O virgin of Israel, turn again to these thy cities.

Ephraim Repenting

William Cowper

My God, till I received thy stroke
 How like a beast was I!
So unaccustomed to the yoke,
 So backward to comply.

With grief my just reproach I bear,
 Shame fills me at the thought;
How frequent my rebellions were!
 What wickedness I wrought!

Thy merciful restraint I scorned,
 And left the pleasant road;
Yet turn me, and I shall be turned,
 Thou art the Lord my God.

*Gray wrote these lines as a satirical attack on one Reverend Henry Etough, Rector of Therfield, who had incurred the poet's wrath by meddling in the affairs of Pembroke College, Cambridge. "Etough," pronounced "Etoph," became an anagram of Tophet.

"Is Ephraim banished from my thoughts,
    Or vile in my esteem?
"No," saith the Lord, "with all his faults
    I still remember him.

"Is he a dear and pleasant child?
    Yes dear and pleasant still;
Though sin his foolish heart beguiled,
    And he withstood my will.

"My sharp rebuke has laid him low,
    He seeks my face again;
My pity kindles at his woe,
    He shall not seek in vain."

51:10–11 The LORD hath brought forth our righteousness: come, and let us declare in Zion the work of the LORD our God.

Make bright the arrows; gather the shields: the LORD hath raised up the spirit of the kings of the Medes: for his device is against Babylon, to destroy it; because it is the vengeance of the LORD, the vengeance of his temple.

MAKE BRIGHT THE ARROWS

EDNA ST. VINCENT MILLAY

Make bright the arrows,
    Gather the shields:
Conquest narrows
    The peaceful fields.

Stock well the quiver
    With arrows bright:
The bowman feared
    Need never fight.

Make bright the arrows,
    O peaceful and wise!
Gather the shields
    Against surprise.

51:20–23 Thou art my battle ax and weapons of war: for with thee will I break in pieces the nations, and with thee will I destroy kingdoms; And with thee will I break in pieces the horse and his rider; and with thee will I break in pieces the chariot and his rider; With thee also will I break in pieces man and woman; and with thee will I break in pieces old and young; and with thee will I break in pieces the young man and the maid; I will also break in pieces with thee the shepherd and his flock; and with thee will I break in pieces the husbandman and his yoke of oxen; and with thee will I break in pieces captains and rulers.

In Time of 'The Breaking of Nations'

THOMAS HARDY

I

Only a man harrowing clods
In a slow silent walk
With an old horse that stumbles and nods
Half asleep as they stalk.

II

Only thin smoke without flame
From the heaps of couch-grass;
Yet this will go onward the same
Though Dynasties pass.

III

Yonder a maid and her wight
Come whispering by:
War's annals will cloud into night
Ere their story die.

The Lamentations of JEREMIAH

1:1 How doth the city sit solitary, that was full of people! how is she become as a widow! she that was great among the nations, and princess among the provinces, how is she become tributary!

WEDNESDAY OF HOLY WEEK, 1940

KENNETH REXROTH

Out of the east window a storm
Blooms spasmodically across the moonrise;
In the west, in the haze, the planets
Pulsate like standing meteors.
We listen in the darkness to the service of Tenebrae,
Music older than the Resurrection,
The voice of the ruinous, disorderly Levant:
"Why doth the city sit solitary
That was full of people?"
The voices of the Benedictines are massive, impersonal;
They neither fear this agony nor are ashamed of it.
Think . . . six hours ago in Europe,
Thousands were singing these words,
Putting out the candles psalm by psalm . . .
Albi like a fort in the cold dark,
Aachen, the voices fluttering in the ancient vaulting,
The light of the last candle
In Munich on the gnarled carving.
"Jerusalem, Jerusalem,
Return ye unto the Lord thy God."
Thousands kneeling in the dark,
Saying, "Have mercy upon me O God."
We listen appreciatively, smoking, talking quietly,
The voices are coming from three thousand miles.
On the white garden wall the shadows
Of the date palm thresh wildly;
The full moon of the spring is up,
And a gale with it.

1:2–4 She weepeth sore in the night, and her tears are on her cheeks: among all her lovers she hath none to comfort her: all her friends have dealt treacherously with her, they are become her enemies. Judah is gone into captivity because of affliction, and because of great servitude: she dwelleth among the heathen, she findeth no rest: all her persecutors overtook her between the straits. The ways of Zion do mourn, because none come to the solemn feasts: all her gates are desolate: her priests sigh, her virgins are afflicted, and she is in bitterness.

Judah in Exile Wanders

George Sandys

Judah in exile wanders,
Ah, subdued
By vast afflictions and base servitude,
Among the heathen finds no rest.

Ah! see how Sion mourns!
Her gates and ways
Lie unfrequented on her solemn days,
Her virgins weep, her priests lament her fall,
And all
Her sweets convert to gall.

1:5–22 Her adversaries are the chief, her enemies prosper; for the LORD hath afflicted her for the multitude of her transgressions: her children are gone into captivity before the enemy. . . . Let all their wickedness come before thee; and do unto them, as thou hast done unto me for all my transgressions: for my sighs are many, and my heart is faint.

The Lamentations of Jeremy, for the most part according to Tremelius

Chap. I

John Donne

How sits this city, late most populous,
Thus solitary, and like a widow thus!
Amplest of Nations, Queen of Provinces
She was, who now thus tributary is!
Still in the night she weeps, and her tears fall
Down by her cheeks along, and none of all
Her lovers comfort her; Perfidiously
Her friends have dealt, and now are enemy.
Unto great bondage, and afflictions
Judah is captive led; Those nations
With whom she dwells, no place of rest afford,
In straits she meets her persecutors' sword.

Empty are the gates of Sion, and her ways
Mourn, because none come to her solemn days.
Her priests do groan, her maids are comfortless,
And she's unto her self a bitterness.
Her foes are grown her head, and live at peace,
Because when her transgressions did increase,
The Lord struck her with sadness: Th'enemy
Doth drive her children to captivity.
From Sion's daughter is all beauty gone,
Like harts, which seek for pasture, and find none,
Her princes are, and now before the foe
Which still pursues them, without strength they go.
Now in her days of tears, Jerusalem
(Her men slain by the foe, none succouring them)
Remembers what of old, she esteemed most,
Whilst her foes laugh at her, for what she hath lost.
Jerusalem hath sinned, therefore is she
Removed, as women in uncleanness be;
Who honored, scorn her, for her foulness they
Have seen; her self doth groan, and turn away.
Her foulness in her skirts was seen, yet she
Remembered not her end; Miraculously
Therefore she fell, none comforting: Behold
O Lord my affliction, for the Foe grows bold.
Upon all things where her delight hath been,
The foe hath stretched his hand, for she hath seen,
Heathen, whom thou commandst, should not do so,
Into her holy Sanctuary go.
And all her people groan, and seek for bread;
And they have given, only to be fed,
All precious things, wherein their pleasure lay:
How cheap I'm grown, O Lord, behold, and weigh.
All this concerns not you, who pass by me,
O see, and mark if any sorrow be
Like to my sorrow, which Jehovah hath
Done to me in the day of his fierce wrath?
That fire, which by himself is governed
He hath cast from heaven on my bones, and spread
A net before my feet, and me o'erthrown,
And made me languish all the day alone.
His hand hath of my sins framed a yoke
Which wreathed, and cast upon my neck, hath broke
My strength. The Lord unto those enemies
Hath given me, from whom I cannot rise.

He under foot hath trodden in my sight
My strong men; He did company invite
To break my young men; he the winepress hath
Trod upon Judah's daughter in his wrath.
For these things do I weep, mine eye, mine eye
Casts water out; For he which should be nigh
To comfort me, is now departed far;
The foe prevails, forlorn my children are.
There's none, though Sion do stretch out her hand,
To comfort her, it is the Lord's command
That Jacob's foes girt him. Jerusalem
Is as an unclean woman amongst them.
But yet the Lord is just, and righteous still,
I have rebelled against his holy will;
O hear all people, and my sorrow see,
My maids, my young men in captivity.
I called for my lovers then, but they
Deceived me, and my priests, and elders lay
Dead in the city; for they sought for meat
Which should refresh their souls, they could not get.
Because I am in straits, Jehovah see
My heart o'erturned, my bowels muddy be,
Because I have rebelled so much, as fast
The sword without, as death within, doth waste.
Of all which here I mourn, none comforts me,
My foes have heard my grief, and glad they be,
That thou hast done it; But thy promised day
Will come, when, as I suffer, so shall they.
Let all their wickedness appear to thee,
Do unto them, as thou hast done to me,
For all my sins: The sighs which I have had
Are very many, and my heart is sad.

The Book of the Prophet
EZEKIEL

1:15–21 Now as I beheld the living creatures, behold one wheel upon the earth by the living creatures, with his four faces. The appearance of the wheels and their work was like unto the colour of a beryl: and they four

had one likeness: and their appearance and their work was as it were a wheel in the middle of a wheel. When they went, they went upon their four sides: and they turned not when they went. As for their rings, they were so high that they were dreadful; and their rings were full of eyes round about them four. And when the living creatures went, the wheels went by them: and when the living creatures were lifted up from the earth, the wheels were lifted up. Whithersoever the spirit was to go, they went, thither was their spirit to go; and the wheels were lifted up over against them: for the spirit of the living creature was in the wheels. When those went, these went; and when those stood, these stood; and when those were lifted up from the earth, the wheels were lifted up over against them: for the spirit of the living creature was in the wheels.

Live, Evil Veil

John Wheelwright

for Dorothy Day

The Church of Heaven's triumphal Car
by Justice and by Mercy veiled
(Car of wing'd, wheel'd Eyes
Wisdom's pulvery cornbin
winevat, bespattering, of Love)
steeled with mirroring moon and moon
whose spherical rims fall
desiring to climb, and rise
returning to their prime
(each eye-rimmed wheel, a wing'd eyeball)
clangs over empounded flame
with here a saw, and there a hoe
and shadows of smoke like flame.

Thin Wings wire the Crucified's umbra;
other Wings gyre,—His own;
the Pallium sails amid intactile fire;
the Shibboleth hovers over shadows
with here a sickle, and there a scythe
and here and there a hammer.

Shadows, returned to cover
three-fold, double-folded veils,

separately converge
into trine Countenance's radiances;
but starry Messengers behold:
their fires, to these fires, are
as yellow haze to gold,
their joyous innocence
to this lean anger, cold:—
with here a scythe, and there a hammer
and here a saw, and there a saw
and here and there a hoe.

The Eyes swoon while the Wings moan:
"Wake us from our repeating dream
within this clanging bell.
Search the unpaved cage
we pace confined. Cruel Eyes gleam
in sable moon and silver moon;
wake us from our repeating dream
of Hell."
With here a hoe, and there a hoe
and there and there a scythe.
Talons rage to claw the image
of the mirrored, iron Face's
clinging, clanging tongues.
Lion Jaws, to devour the other
(which is a mirrored brother)
call on crispate light to melt
prismatic wires, about them, of Mercy:
(with Justice, below, blackly reflected)
"Wake us from dreams repeated."
(They remain undefeated
recurring days; they will not die.)
"Wake us to fact; dreams lie;
wake us to Grace."
(These snakes, frozen on the waters,
were Wings.
These embers among dark cinders
are blind.)
With here a hammer, and there a sickle
and here a scythe, and there a saw
and here and there a hoe.

Loud, abundant strength of clang
—colorless, colorful, colorless—

(yet similar in righteousness)
shakes horny hearing
which once caused its song;
until, at length
the Wings revive. The Eyes awake.
The haze divides; the frozen Lake
of fire melts to spiral Space
where Justice (that doubles Satan's Face)
clung and clangs
as the hammer strikes, and the sickle swings;
and (as Watchers dreamt) it clings
to the Car's veiled Cross
in whose dead embrace
dead
Man hangs.

10:1–19 Then I looked, and, behold, in the firmament that was above the head of the cherubims there appeared over them as it were a sapphire stone, as the appearance of the likeness of a throne. And he spake unto the man clothed with linen, and said, Go in between the wheels, even under the cherub, and fill thine hand with coals of fire from between the cherubims, and scatter them over the city. And he went in in my sight. . . . And it came to pass, that when he had commanded the man clothed with linen, saying, Take fire from between the wheels, from between the cherubims; then he went in, and stood beside the wheels. And one cherub stretched forth his hand from between the cherubims unto the fire that was between the cherubims, and took thereof, and put it into the hands of him that was clothed with linen: who took it, and went out. . . .

The Burning Wheel

Aldous Huxley

Wearied of its own turning,
Distressed with its own busy restlessness,
Yearning to draw the circumferent pain —
The rim that is dizzy with speed —
To the motionless centre, there to rest,
The wheel must strain through agony
On agony contracting, returning
Into the core of steel.
    And at last the wheel has rest, is still,

Shrunk to an adamant core:
Fulfilling its will in fixity.
But the yearning atoms, as they grind
Closer and closer, more and more
Fiercely together, beget
A flaming fire upward leaping,
Billowing out in a burning,
Passionate, fierce desire to find
The infinite calm of the mother's breast.
And there the flame is a Christ-child sleeping,
Bright, tenderly radiant;
All bitterness lost in the infinite
Peace of the mother's bosom.
But death comes creeping in a tide
Of slow oblivion, till the flame in fear
Wakes from the sleep of its quiet brightness
And burns with a darkening passion and pain,
Lest, all forgetting in quiet, it perish.
And as it burns and anguishes it quickens,
Begetting once again the wheel that yearns —
Sick with its speed — for the terrible stillness
Of the adamant core and the steel-hard chain.
And so once more
Shall the wheel revolve till its anguish cease
In the iron anguish of fixity;
Till once again
Flame billows out to infinity,
Sinking to a sleep of brightness
In that vast oblivious peace.

23:1–49 . . . Therefore, O Aholibah, thus saith the Lord GOD; Behold, I will raise up thy lovers against thee, from whom thy mind is alienated, and I will bring them against thee on every side; The Babylonians, and all the Chaldeans, Pekod, and Shoa, and Koa, and all the Assyrians with them: all of them desirable young men, captains and rulers, great lords and renowned, all of them riding upon horses. And they shall come against thee with chariots, wagons, and wheels, and with an assembly of people, which shall set against thee buckler and shield and helmet round about: and I will set judgment before them, and they shall judge thee according to their judgments. And I will set my jealousy against thee, and they shall deal furiously with thee: they shall take away thy nose and thine ears; and thy remnant shall fall by the sword: they shall take thy sons and thy daughters; and thy residue shall be devoured by the fire.

They shall also strip thee out of thy clothes, and take away thy fair jewels. Thus will I make thy lewdness to cease from thee, and thy whoredom brought from the land of Egypt: so that thou shalt not lift up thine eyes unto them, nor remember Egypt any more. . . .

Aholibah

ALGERNON CHARLES SWINBURNE

In the beginning God made thee
    A woman well to look upon,
Thy tender body as a tree
    Whereon cool wind hath always blown
    Till the clean branches be well grown.

There was none like thee in the land;
    The girls that were thy bondwomen
Did bind thee with a purple band
    Upon thy forehead, that all men
    Should know thee for God's handmaiden.

Strange raiment clad thee like a bride,
    With silk to wear on hands and feet
And plates of gold on either side:
    Wine made thee glad, and thou didst eat
    Honey, and choice of pleasant meat.

And fishers in the middle sea
    Did get thee sea-fish and sea-weeds
In colour like the robes on thee;
    And curious work of plaited reeds,
    And wools wherein live purple bleeds.

And round the edges of thy cup
    Men wrought thee marvels out of gold,
Strong snakes with lean throats lifted up,
    Large eyes whereon the brows had hold,
    And scaly things their slime kept cold.

For thee they blew soft wind in flutes
    And ground sweet roots for cunning scent;
Made slow because of many lutes,
    The wind among thy chambers went
    Wherein no light was violent.

God called thy name Aholibah,
    His tabernacle being in thee,
A witness through waste Asia;
    Thou wert a tent sewn cunningly
    With gold and colours of the sea.

God gave thee gracious ministers
    And all their work who plait and weave:
The cunning of embroiderers
    That sew the pillow to the sleeve,
    And likeness of all things that live.

Thy garments upon thee were fair
    With scarlet and with yellow thread;
Also the weaving of thine hair
    Was as fine gold upon thy head,
    And thy silk shoes were sewn with red.

All sweet things he bade sift, and ground
    As a man grindeth wheat in mills
With strong wheels alway going round;
    He gave thee corn, and grass that fills
    The cattle on a thousand hills.

The wine of many seasons fed
    Thy mouth, and made it fair and clean;
Sweet oil was poured out on thy head
    And ran down like cool rain between
    The strait close locks it melted in.

The strong men and the captains knew
    Thy chambers wrought and fashioned
With gold and covering of blue,
    And the blue raiment of thine head
    Who satest on a stately bed.

All these had on their garments wrought
    The shape of beasts and creeping things
The body that availeth not,
    Flat backs of worms and veinèd wings,
    And the lewd bulk that sleeps and stings.

Also the chosen of the years,
    The multitude being at ease,

With sackbuts and with dulcimers
    And noise of shawms and psalteries
    Made mirth within the ears of these.

But as a common woman doth,
    Thou didst think evil and devise;
The sweet smell of thy breast and mouth
    Thou madest as the harlot's wise,
    And there was painting on thine eyes.

Yea, in the woven guest-chamber
    And by the painted passages
Where the strange gracious paintings were,
    State upon state of companies,
    There came on thee the lust of these.

Because of shapes on either wall
    Sea-coloured from some rare blue shell
At many a Tyrian interval,
    Horsemen on horses, girdled well,
    Delicate and desirable,

Thou saidest: I am sick of love:
    Stay me with flagons, comfort me
With apples for my pain thereof
    Till my hands gather in his tree
    That fruit wherein my lips would be.

Yea, saidest thou, I will go up
    When there is no more shade than one
May cover with a hollow cup,
    And make my bed against the sun
    Till my blood's violence be done.

Thy mouth was leant upon the wall
    Against the painted mouth, thy chin
Touched the hair's painted curve and fall;
    Thy deep throat, fallen lax and thin,
    Worked as the blood's beat worked therein.

Therefore, O thou Aholibah,
    God is not glad because of thee;
And thy fine gold shall pass away
    Like those fair coins of ore that be
    Washed over by the middle sea.

Then will one make thy body bare
        To strip it of all gracious things,
And pluck the cover from thine hair,
        And break the gift of many kings,
        Thy wrist-rings and thine ankle-rings.

Likewise the man whose body joins
        To thy smooth body, as was said,
Who hath a girdle on his loins
        And dyed attire upon his head—
        The same who, seeing, worshipped,

Because thy face was like the face
        Of a clean maiden that smells sweet,
Because thy gait was as the pace
        Of one that opens not her feet
        And is not heard within the street—

Even he, O thou Aholibah,
        Made separate from thy desire,
        Shall cut thy nose and ears away
And bruise thee for thy body's hire
        And burn the residue with fire.

Then shall the heathen people say,
        The multitude being at ease;
Lo, this is that Aholibah
        Whose name was blown among strange seas,
        Grown old with soft adulteries.

Also her bed was made of green,
        Her windows beautiful for glass
That she had made her bed between:
        Yea, for pure lust her body was
        Made like white summer-coloured grass.

Her raiment was a strongman's spoil;
        Upon a table by a bed
She set mine incense and mine oil
        To be the beauty of her head
        In chambers walled about with red.

Also between the walls she had
        Fair faces of strong men portrayed;

All girded round the loins, and clad
With several cloths of woven braid
And garments marvellously made.

Therefore the wrath of God shall be
Set as a watch upon her way;
And whoso findeth by the sea
Blown dust of bones will hardly say
If this were that Aholibah.

33:30–33 Also, thou son of man, the children of thy people still are talking against thee by the walls and in the doors of the houses, and speak one to another, every one to his brother, saying, Come, I pray you, and hear what is the word that cometh forth from the LORD. And they come unto thee as the people cometh, and they sit before thee as my people, and they hear thy words, but they will not do them: for with their mouth they shew much love, but their heart goeth after their covetousness. And, lo, thou art unto them as a very lovely song of one that hath a pleasant voice, and can play well on an instrument: for they hear thy words, but they do them not. And when this cometh to pass, (lo, it will come,) then shall they know that a prophet hath been among them.

EZEKIEL

JOHN GREENLEAF WHITTIER

They hear Thee not, O God! nor see
Beneath Thy rod they mock at Thee;
The princes of our ancient line
Lie drunken with Assyrian wine;
The priests around Thy altar speak
The false words which their hearers seek;
And hymns which Chaldea's wanton maids
Have sung in Dura's idol-shades
Are with the Levites' chant ascending.
With Zion's holiest anthems blending!

On Israel's bleeding bosom set,
The heathen heel is crushing yet;
The towers upon our holy hill
Echo Chaldean footsteps still.
Our wasted shrines,—who weeps for them?

Who mourneth for Jerusalem?
Who turneth from his gains away?
Whose knee with mine is bowed to pray ?
Who, leaving feast and purpling cup,
Takes Zion's lamentation up?

A sad and thoughtful youth, I went
With Israel's early banishment;
And where the sullen Chebar crept,
The ritual of my fathers kept.
The water for the trench I drew,
The firstling of the flock I slew,
And, standing at the altar's side,
I shared the Levites' lingering pride,
That still, amidst her mocking foes,
The smoke of Zion's offering rose.

In sudden whirlwind, cloud and flame,
The Spirit of the Highest came!
Before mine eyes a vision passed,
A glory terrible and vast;
With dreadful eyes of living things,
And sounding sweep of angel wings,
With circling light and sapphire throne,
And flame-like form of One thereon,
And voice of that dread Likeness sent
Down from the crystal firmament!

The burden of a prophet's power
Fell on me in that fearful hour;
From off unutterable woes
The curtain of the future rose;
I saw far down the coming time
The fiery chastisement of crime;
With noise of mingling hosts, and jar
Of falling towers and shouts of war,
I saw the nations rise and fall,
Like fire-gleams on my tent's white wall.

In dream and trance, I saw the slain
Of Egypt heaped like harvest grain.
I saw the walls of sea-born Tyre
Swept over by the spoiler's fire;
And heard the low, expiring moan

Of Edom on his rocky throne;
And, woe is me! the wild lament
From Zion's desolation sent;
And felt within my heart each blow
Which laid her holy places low.

In bonds and sorrow, day by day,
Before the pictured tile I lay;
And there, as in a mirror, saw
The coming of Assyria's war;
Her swarthy lines of spearmen pass
Like locusts through Bethhoron's grass;
I saw them draw their stormy hem
Of battle round Jerusalem;
And, listening, heard the Hebrew wail
Blend with the victor-trump of Baal!

Who trembled at my warning word?
Who owned the prophet of the Lord?
How mocked the rude, how scoffed the vile,
How stung the Levites' scornful smile,
As o'er my spirit, dark and slow,
The shadow crept of Israel's woe
As if the angel's mournful roll
Had left its record on my soul,
And traced in lines of darkness there
The picture of its great despair!

Yet ever at the hour I feel
My lips in prophecy unseal.
Prince, priest, and Levite gather near,
And Salem's daughters haste to hear,
On Chebar's waste and alien shore,
The harp of Judah swept once more.
They listen, as in Babel's throng
The Chaldeans to the dancer's song,
Or wild sabbeka's nightly play,
As careless and as vain as they.

* * *

And thus, O Prophet-bard of old,
Hast thou thy tale of sorrow told!
The same which earth's unwelcome seers
Have felt in all succeeding years.

Sport of the changeful multitude,
Nor calmly heard nor understood,
Their song has seemed a trick of art,
Their warnings but the actor's part.
With bonds, and scorn, and evil will,
The world requites its prophets still.

So was it when the Holy One
The garments of the flesh put on!
Men followed where the Highest led
For common gifts of daily bread,
And gross of ear, of vision dim,
Owned not the Godlike power of Him.
Vain as a dreamer's words to them
His wail above Jerusalem,
And meaningless the watch He kept
Through which His weak disciples slept.

Yet shrink not thou, whoe'er thou art,
For God's great purpose set apart,
Before whose far-discerning eyes,
The Future as the Present lies!
Beyond a narrow-bounded age
Stretches thy prophet-heritage,
Through Heaven's vast spaces angel-trod.
And through the eternal years of God!
Thy audience, worlds!—all things to be
The witness of the Truth in thee!

37:1–6 The hand of the LORD was upon me, and carried me out in the spirit of the LORD, and set me down in the midst of the valley which was full of bones, And caused me to pass by them round about: and, behold, there were very many in the open valley; and, lo, they were very dry. And he said unto me, Son of man, can these bones live? And I answered, O Lord GOD, thou knowest. Again he said unto me, Prophesy upon these bones, and say unto them, O ye dry bones, hear the word of the LORD. Thus saith the Lord GOD unto these bones; Behold, I will cause breath to enter into you, and ye shall live: And I will lay sinews upon you, and will bring up flesh upon you, and cover you with skin, and put breath in you, and ye shall live; and ye shall know that I am the LORD.

The End

Wilfred Owen

After the blast of lightning from the east,
The flourish of loud clouds, the Chariot Throne;
After the drums of time have rolled and ceased,
And by the bronze west long retreat is blown,

Shall Life renew these bodies? Of a truth
All death will he annul, all tears assuage?—
Or fill these void veins full again with youth,
And wash, with an immortal water, Age?

When I do ask white Age he saith not so:
"My head hangs heavy weighed with snow."
And when I hearken to the Earth, she saith:
"My fiery heart shrinks, aching. It is death.
Mine ancient scars shall not be glorified,
Nor my titanic tears, the seas, be dried."

37:23–25 Neither shall they defile themselves any more with their idols, nor with their detestable things, nor with any of their transgressions: but I will save them out of all their dwellingplaces, wherein they have sinned, and will cleanse them: so shall they be my people, and I will be their God. And David my servant shall be king over them; and they all shall have one shepherd: they shall also walk in my judgments, and observe my statutes, and do them. And they shall dwell in the land that I have given unto Jacob my servant, wherein your fathers have dwelt; and they shall dwell therein, even they, and their children, and their children's children for ever: and my servant David shall be their prince for ever.

Meditation Twelve

Second Series

Edward Taylor

Dull. Dull indeed! What shall it e'er be thus?
    And why? Are not thy promises, my Lord,
Rich, quickening things? How should my full cheeks
    To find me thus? And those a lifeless word?
    My heart is heedless: unconcerned hereat:
    I find my spirits spiritless, and flat.

Thou courtst mine eyes in sparkling colors bright.
Most bright indeed, and soul enamoring,
With the most shining sun, whose beams did smite
Me with delightful smiles to make me spring.
Embellished knots of love assault my mind
Which still is dull, as if this sun ne'er shined.

David in all his gallantry now comes,
Bringing to tend thy shrine, his royal glory,
Rich prowess, prudence, victories, sweet songs,
And piety to pencil out thy story;
To draw my heart to thee in this brave shine
Of typic beams, most warm. But still I pine.

Shall not this lovely beauty, Lord, set out
In dazzling shining flashes 'fore mine eye,
Enchant my heart, love's golden mine, 'til't spout
Out streams of love refined that on thee lie?
Thy glory's great: Thou David's kingdom shalt
Enjoy for aye. I want and that's my fault.

Spare me, my Lord, spare me, I greatly pray,
Let me thy gold pass through thy fire until
Thy fire refine, and take my filth away.
That I may shine like gold, and have my fill
Of love for thee; until my virginal
Chime out in changes sweet thy praises shall.

Wipe off my rust, Lord, with thy wisp me scour,
And make thy beams perch on my strings their blaze.
My tunes clothe with thy shine, and quavers pour
My cursing strings on, loaded with thy praise.
My fervent love with music in her hand
Shall then attend thyself, and thy command.

The Book of DANIEL

**2:1–3 And in the second year of the reign of Nebuchadnezzar, Neb-
uchadnezzar dreamed dreams, wherewith his spirit was troubled, and his
sleep brake from him. Then the king commanded to call the magicians,**

and the astrologers, and the sorcerers, and the Chaldeans, for to shew the king his dreams. So they came and stood before the king. And the king said unto them, I have dreamed a dream, and my spirit was troubled to know the dream. . . .

Nebuchadnezzar

Elinor Wylie

My body is weary to death of my mischievous brain;
I am weary forever and ever of being brave;
Therefore I crouch on my knees while the cool white rain
Curves the clover over my head like a wave.

The stem and the frosty seed of the grass are ripe;
I have devoured their strength; I have drunk them deep;
And the dandelion is gall in a thin green pipe;
But the clover is honey and sun and the smell of sleep.

2:31–33 Thou, O king, sawest, and behold a great image. This great image, whose brightness was excellent, stood before thee; and the form thereof was terrible. This image's head was of fine gold, his breast and his arms of silver, his belly and his thighs of brass, His legs of iron, his feet part of iron and part of clay.

Nebuchadnezzar's Dream

John Keats

Before he went to feed with owls and bats
Nebuchadnezzar had an ugly dream,
Worse than an Hus'if's when she thinks her cream
Made a Naumachia for mice and rats.
So scared, he sent for that 'Good King of Cats'
Young Daniel, who soon did pluck the beam
From out his eye, and said 'I do not deem
Your sceptre worth a straw—your Cushions old door-mats'.
A horrid nightmare similar somewhat
Of late has haunted a most valiant crew
Of loggerheads and Chapmen—we are told

That any Daniel though he be a sot
Can make their lying lips turn pale of hue
By drawling out 'ye are that head of Gold.'

3:13–15 Then Nebuchadnezzar in his rage and fury commanded to bring Shadrach, Meshach, and Abednego. Then they brought these men before the king. Nebuchadnezzar spake and said unto them, Is it true, O Shadrach, Meshach, and Abednego, do not ye serve my gods, nor worship the golden image which I have set up? Now if ye be ready that at what time ye hear the sound of the cornet, flute, harp, sackbut, psaltery, and dulcimer, and all kinds of musick, ye fall down and worship the image which I have made; well: but if ye worship not, ye shall be cast the same hour into the midst of a burning fiery furnace; and who is that God that shall deliver you out of my hands?

On the Three Children in the Fiery Furnace

Henry Colman

Ye glorious Jove-born imps how you rejoice
Your heavenly Sire to hear your swanlike voice
Chant forth (in spite of death) his sacred praise,
Behold the flames dance at your powerful lays
And fear to hurt you, fire for love of you
Shall become cold as ice, yet shall renew
Its natural fierceness to destroy your foes,
Angels shall guard you so, you shall not lose
The smallest hair, and though but three are bound
In spite o'th'tyrant-king there shall be found
A fourth, (all walking loose) whose glorious face
Shall fright th'insulting monarch, and his base
Shallow-brained Sophi; thus both can, and will
Th'eternal work for his own servants still.
The water shall be parted, and shall stand
On each side like a wall, while on dry land
Through it the saints shall pass, the earth shall yield
Suddenly choice delights, and every field
Through which they go shall groan under the weight
Of natures choicest fruit, the fire shall straight
Lay off its native burning, and shall be
Ready to serve such without injury,
At mid-day shall the sun stop his career

And ten degrees shall back again retire,
The heavens, and stars by course, shall war and fight
Against all such as keep them from their right,
And all the elements with one consent
Shall strive to shield, and guard the innocent,
This is th'Almighty's work, and none but he
Did in the burning flames preserve these three.
And didst thou thus for them because in thee
Alone, they trusted? Lord instruct thou me
Also I humbly beg, that I may love,
And trust in thee alone, then though thou prove
Me by the flame, the sword, or plague I dare
Build on thy mercy, and despise all fear
Even in the midst of death; thy only name
Shall arm me 'gainst the rack, plague, sword, and flame.

5:24–30 Then was the part of the hand sent from him; and this writing was written. And this is the writing that was written, MENE, MENE, TEKEL, UPHARSIN.

This is the interpretation of the thing: MENE; God hath numbered thy kingdom, and finished it. TEKEL; Thou art weighed in the balances, and art found wanting. PERES; Thy kingdom is divided, and given to the Medes and Persians.

Then commanded Belshazzar, and they clothed Daniel with scarlet, and put a chain of gold about his neck, and made a proclamation concerning him, that he should be the third ruler in the kingdom.

In that night was Belshazzar the king of the Chaldeans slain.

To Belshazzar

George Noel Gordon, Lord Byron

Belshazzar! from the banquet turn,
    Nor in thy sensuous fulness fall;
Behold! while yet before thee burn
    The graven words, the glowing wall,
Many a despot men miscall
    Crowned and anointed from on high;

But thou, the weakest, worst of all—
Is it not written, thou must die?

Go! dash the roses from thy brow—
Grey hairs but poorly wreathe with them;
Youth's garlands misbecome thee now,
More than thy very diadem,
Where thou hast tarnished every gem:—
Then throw the worthless bauble by,
Which, worn by thee, even slaves contemn;
And learn like better men to die!

Oh! early in the balance weighed,
And ever light of word and worth,
Whose soul expired ere youth decayed,
And left thee but a mass of earth.
To see thee moves the scorner's mirth:
But tears in Hope's averted eye
Lament that even thou hadst birth—
Unfit to govern, live, or die.

BELSHAZZAR HAD A LETTER –

EMILY DICKINSON

Belshazzar had a Letter –
He never had but one –
Belshazzar's Correspondent
Concluded and begun
In that immortal Copy
The Conscience of us all
Can read without its Glasses
On Revelation's Wall –

6:19–24 Then the king arose very early in the morning, and went in haste unto the den of lions. And when he came to the den, he cried with a lamentable voice unto Daniel: and the king spake and said to Daniel, O Daniel, servant of the living God, is thy God, whom thou servest continually, able to deliver thee from the lions? Then said Daniel unto the king,

O king, live for ever. My God hath sent his angel, and hath shut the lions' mouths, that they have not hurt me: forasmuch as before him innocency was found in me; and also before thee, O king, have I done no hurt. Then was the king exceeding glad for him, and commanded that they should take Daniel up out of the den. So Daniel was taken up out of the den, and no manner of hurt was found upon him, because he believed in his God. And the king commanded, and they brought those men which had accused Daniel, and they cast them into the den of lions, them, their children, and their wives; and the lions had the mastery of them, and brake all their bones in pieces or ever they came at the bottom of the den.

NEBUCHADNEZZAR'S KINGDOM-COME

DAVID ROWBOTHAM

Daniel in the lion's den
Confounded those who cast him in,
The priests and kings of Babylon
So like the beasts he prayed among.

The god of the land they stole him from
In Nebuchadnezzar's kingdom-come
Gave him mercy and release,
And undefiled he found his peace.

Now in the dens of Babylons
That lure or steal believing ones,
With tawny thoroughness the beasts
Spring as the prides of kings and priests.

For in the present kingdoms-come
The ancient gods are rendered dumb;
To be devoured is Daniel's doom,
And mauled angels stumble home.

Now prayer provokes the savagery
Which priests and kings in beasts set free
On captured innocence in the den,
Confounding deities, not men.

7:1–8 In the first year of Belshazzar king of Babylon Daniel had a dream and visions of his head upon his bed: then he wrote the dream, and told the sum of the matters. Daniel spake and said, I saw in my vision by night, and, behold, the four winds of the heaven strove upon the great sea. And four great beasts came up from the sea, diverse one from another. The first was like a lion, and had eagle's wings: I beheld till the wings thereof were plucked, and it was lifted up from the earth, and made stand upon the feet as a man, and a man's heart was given to it. And behold another beast, a second, like to a bear, and it raised up itself on one side, and it had three ribs in the mouth of it between the teeth of it: and they said thus unto it, Arise, devour much flesh. After this I beheld, and lo another, like a leopard, which had upon the back of it four wings of a fowl; the beast had also four heads; and dominion was given to it. After this I saw in the night visions, and behold a fourth beast, dreadful and terrible, and strong exceedingly; and it had great iron teeth: it devoured and brake in pieces, and stamped the residue with the feet of it: and it was diverse from all the beasts that were before it; and it had ten horns. I considered the horns, and, behold, there came up among them another little horn, before whom there were three of the first horns plucked up by the roots: and, behold, in this horn were eyes like the eyes of man, and a mouth speaking great things.

from The Locusts, or Apollyonists

Phineas Fletcher

Canto 3, stanzas 17–20

Say Muses, say; who now in those rich fields
Where silver Tibris swims in golden sands,
Who now, ye Muses, that great scepter wields,
Which once swayed all the earth with servile bands?
Who now those Babel towers, once fallen, builds?
    Say, say, how first it fell, how now it stands?
    How, and by what degrees that city sunk?
Caesars to change for friars, a monarch for a monk?

Th' Assyrian Lion decked in golden hide,
Once grasped the nations in his lordly paw:
But him the Persian silver Bear defied,
Tore, killed, and swallowed up with ravenous jaw;
Whom that Greek Leopard no sooner spied,

But slew, devoured, and filled his empty maw:
    But with his ravened prey his bowels broke;
    So into four divides his brazen yoke.
Stol'n bits, thrust down in haste, do seldom feed, but choke.

Meantime in Tybris fen a dreadful beast
With monstrous breadth, and length seven hills o'er-spreads:
And nursed with daily spoils and bloody feast
Grew up to wondrous strength: with seven heads,
Armed all with iron teeth, he rends the rest,
And with proud feet to clay and mortar treads.
    And now all earth subdued, high heaven he braves,
    The head he kills, then 'gainst the body raves:
With saintly flesh he swells, with bones his den he paves.

At length five heads were fallen; the sixth retired
By absence yields an easy way of rising
To th' next, and last: who with ambition fired,
In humble weeds his haughty pride disguising,
By slow, sly growth unto the top aspired:
Unlike the rest he veils his tyrannizing
    With that Lamb's head, and horns: both which he claims;
    Thence double reign, within, without he frames:
His head the Lamb, his tongue the Dragon loud proclaims.

8:13 Then I heard one saint speaking, and another saint said unto that certain saint which spake, How long shall be the vision concerning the daily sacrifice, and the transgression of desolation, to give both the sanctuary and the host to be trodden under foot?

A Vision of Beasts

JOHN HEATH-STUBBS

Four winds contend on the sea's face,
Lashing the spray to warhorses and chariots;
Out of the maelstrom the beasts of history
Surface in beauty and cruelty –
Ancient empires, panther-spotted, lion-tawny;
They scud on the waves with airy pinions;
And the brutal and barbarous bear
Sucking the marrow from cracked bones.

And then that last, graceless amorphous anomaly
Horned, tusked, bristled, woolly,
Splay-footed, hoofed, clawed. Where he treads
Suppressed groans, where he rolls
The stink of pollution, where he roots,
Our bread is tasteless with sorrow, and in his tracks
A straggling tail of discarded rubbish.

How long, till the Human Being
Comes, riding the clouds,
In naked perfection of geometry,
To the throne of God, from whence
A cataract of hydrogen
Streams incandescent through the galaxies?

THE MINOR PROPHETS

HOSEA 4:1–7 Hear the word of the LORD, ye children of Israel: for the LORD hath a controversy with the inhabitants of the land, because there is no truth, nor mercy, nor knowledge of God in the land. By swearing, and lying, and killing, and stealing, and committing adultery, they break out, and blood toucheth blood. Therefore shall the land mourn, and every one that dwelleth therein shall languish, with the beasts of the field, and with the fowls of heaven; yea, the fishes of the sea also shall be taken away. Yet let no man strive, nor reprove another: for thy people are as they that strive with the priest. Therefore shalt thou fall in the day, and the prophet also shall fall with thee in the night, and I will destroy thy mother. My people are destroyed for lack of knowledge: because thou hast rejected knowledge, I will also reject thee, that thou shalt be no priest to me: seeing thou hast forgotten the law of thy God, I will also forget thy children. As they were increased, so they sinned against me: therefore will I change their glory into shame.

MY PEOPLE ARE DESTROYED FOR LACK OF KNOWLEDGE

JONES VERY

For lack of knowledge do my people die!
No fell diseases in our land abound,
No pestilential vapors fill the sky,
No drought or barrenness has cursed the ground;
The harvest-fields are white on every side,
For God has given to all with liberal hand;
To none His sun and rain has He denied,
But with abundance blessed our fruitful land.
But Him who gives to all, they have not known!
His truth, His mercy, and unfailing love;
Who sends not on one favored race alone
His gifts and mercies from the heavens above;—
Therefore the land doth mourn; and, day by day,
War wastes our fields and doth the people slay!

HOSEA 6:1–4 Come, and let us return unto the LORD: for he hath torn, and he will heal us; he hath smitten, and he will bind us up. After two days will he revive us: in the third day he will raise us up, and we shall live in his sight. Then shall we know, if we follow on to know the LORD: his going forth is prepared as the morning; and he shall come unto us as the rain, as the latter and former rain unto the earth.

O Ephraim, what shall I do unto thee? O Judah, what shall I do unto thee? for your goodness is as a morning cloud, and as the early dew it goeth away.

DISORDER AND FRAILTY

HENRY VAUGHAN

When first thou didst even from the grave
And womb of darkness beckon out
My brutish soul, and to thy slave
Becam'st thy self, both guide, and scout;
          Even from that hour
Thou gotst my heart; And though here tossed
     By winds, and bit with frost
          I pine, and shrink
          Breaking the link

'Twixt thee, and me; And ofttimes creep
Into th' old silence, and dead sleep,
Quitting thy way
All the long day,
Yet, sure, my God! I love thee most.
Alas, thy love.

I threaten heaven, and from my cell
Of clay, and frailty break, and bud
Touched by thy fire, and breath; Thy blood
Too, is my dew, and springing well.
But while I grow
And stretch to thee, aiming at all
Thy stars, and spangled hall,
Each fly doth taste,
Poison, and blast
My yielding leaves; sometimes a shower
Beats them quite off, and in an hour
Not one poor shoot
But the bare root
Hid under ground survives the fall.
Alas, frail weed!

Thus like some sleeping exhalation
(Which waked by heat, and beams, makes up
Unto that comforter, the sun,
And soars, and shines; but ere we sup
And walk two steps
Cooled by the damps of night, descends,
And, whence it sprung, there ends,)
Doth my weak fire
Pine and retire,
And (after all my height of flames,)
In sickly expirations tames
Leaving me dead
On my first bed
Until thy sun again ascends.
Poor, falling star!

O, is! but give wings to my fire,
And hatch my soul, until it fly
Up where thou art, amongst thy 'tire
Of Stars, above infirmity;
Let not perverse,

And foolish thoughts add to my bill
  Of forward sins, and kill
    That seed, which thou
    In me didst sow,
But dress, and water with thy grace
Together with the seed, the place;
    And for his sake
    Who died to stake
His life for mine, tune to thy will
    My heart, my verse.

JONAH 1:17–2:10 Now the LORD had prepared a great fish to swallow up Jonah. And Jonah was in the belly of the fish three days and three nights.

Then Jonah prayed unto the LORD his God out of the fish's belly, And said, I cried by reason of mine affliction unto the LORD, and he heard me; out of the belly of hell cried I, and thou heardest my voice. . . . But I will sacrifice unto thee with the voice of thanksgiving; I will pay that that I have vowed. Salvation is of the LORD.

And the LORD spake unto the fish, and it vomited out Jonah upon the dry land.

THE SONG OF JONAH IN THE WHALE'S BELLY

MICHAEL DRAYTON

In grief and anguish of my heart, my voice I did extend,
Unto the Lord, and he thereto, a willing ear did lend:
Even from the deep and darkest pit, and the infernal lake,
To me he hath bowed down his ear, for his great mercies' sake.
For thou into the middest, of surging seas so deep
Hath cast me forth: whose bottom is so low and wondrous steep.
Whose mighty wallowing waves, which from the floods do flow,
Have with their power up swallowed me, and overwhelmed me though.
Then said I, lo, I am exiled, from presence of thy face,
Yet will I once again behold, thy house and dwelling place.
Waters have encompassed me, the floods enclosed me round,
The weeds have sore encumbered me, which in the seas abound.
Unto the valleys down I went, beneath the hills which stand,
The earth hath there environed me, with force of all the land.

Yet hast thou still preserved me, from all these dangers here,
And brought my life out of the pit, oh Lord my God so dear.
My soul consuming thus with care, I prayed unto the Lord,
And he from out his holy place, heard me with one accord.
Who to vain lying vanities doth wholly him betake,
Doth err also, God's mercy he doth utterly forsake.
But I will offer unto him the sacrifice of praise,
And pay my vows, ascribing thanks unto the Lord always.

THE RIBS AND TERRORS . . .

HERMAN MELVILLE

The ribs and terrors in the whale,
    Arched over me a dismal gloom,
While all God's sun-lit waves rolled by,
    And lift me to a deeper doom.

I saw the opening maw of hell,
    With endless pains and sorrows there;
Which none but they that feel can tell—
    Oh, I was plunging to despair.

In black distress, I called my God,
    When I could scarce believe Him mine,
He bowed His ear to my complaints—
    No more the whale did me confine.

With speed He flew to my relief,
    As on a radiant dolphin borne;
Awful, yet bright, as lightning shone
    The face of my Deliverer God.

My song for ever shall record
    That terrible, that joyful hour;
I give the glory to my God,
    His all the mercy and the power.

JONAH 3:1–4:4 And the word of the LORD came unto Jonah the second time, saying, Arise, go unto Nineveh, that great city, and preach unto it the preaching that I bid thee. So Jonah arose, and went unto Nineveh, according to the word of the LORD. Now Nineveh was an exceeding great

city of three days' journey. And Jonah began to enter into the city a day's journey, and he cried, and said, Yet forty days, and Nineveh shall be overthrown.

So the people of Nineveh believed God, and proclaimed a fast, and put on sackcloth, from the greatest of them even to the least of them. For word came unto the king of Nineveh, and he arose from his throne, and he laid his robe from him, and covered him with sackcloth, and sat in ashes. And he caused it to be proclaimed and published through Nineveh by the decree of the king and his nobles, saying, Let neither man nor beast, herd nor flock, taste any thing: let them not feed, nor drink water: But let man and beast be covered with sackcloth, and cry mightily unto God: yea, let them turn every one from his evil way, and from the violence that is in their hands. Who can tell if God will turn and repent, and turn away from his fierce anger, that we perish not? And God saw their works, that they turned from their evil way; and God repented of the evil, that he had said that he would do unto them; and he did it not.

But it displeased Jonah exceedingly, and he was very angry. And he prayed unto the LORD, and said, I pray thee, O LORD, was not this my saying, when I was yet in my country? Therefore I fled before unto Tarshish: for I knew that thou art a gracious God, and merciful, slow to anger, and of great kindness, and repentest thee of the evil. Therefore now, O LORD, take, I beseech thee, my life from me; for it is better for me to die than to live.

Then said the LORD, Doest thou well to be angry?

JONAH

RANDALL JARRELL

As I lie here in the sun
And gaze out, a day's journey, over Nineveh,
The sailors in the dark hold cry to me:
"What meanest thou, O sleeper? Arise and call upon
Thy God; pray with us, that we perish not."

All thy billows and thy waves passed over me.
The waters compassed me, the weeds were wrapped about my head;
The earth with her bars was about me forever.
A naked worm, a man no longer,
I writhed beneath the dead:

But thou art merciful.
When my soul was dead within me I remembered thee,

From the depths I cried to thee. For thou art merciful:
Thou hast brought my life up from corruption,
O Lord my God. . . . When the king said, "Who can tell

But God may yet repent, and turn away
From his fierce anger, that we perish not?"
My heart fell; for I knew thy grace of old—
In my own country, Lord, did I not say
That thou art merciful?

Now take, Lord, I beseech thee,
My life from me; it is better that I die . . .
But I hear, "Doest thou well, then, to be angry?"
And I say nothing, and look bitterly
Across the city; a young gourd grows over me

And shades me—and I slumber, clean of grief.
I was glad of the gourd. But God prepared
A worm that gnawed the gourd; but God prepared
The east wind, the sun beat upon my head
Till I cried, "Let me die!" And God said, "Doest thou well

To be angry for the gourd?"
And I said in my anger, "I do well
To be angry, even unto death." But the Lord God
Said to me, "Thou hast had pity on the gourd"—
And I wept, to hear its dead leaves rattle—

"Which came up in a night, and perished in a night.
And should I not spare Nineveh, that city
Wherein are more than six-score thousand persons
Who cannot tell their left hand from their right;
And also much cattle?"

In a Blind Garden

David Shapiro

The whale
is a room
A light blue room

a blind garden
The skulls make room too
And what is the whale
behind you
It's a complex note
When the whale strains
The little fish die
must die like a school
of lances trained on
our friend of two openings
a blowhole a slippery
prey pointed like a joint
in a design of teeth
Can you guess
which whale
Imagine you are a
whale: what a waste
of captured energy
Jonah sulking
like light in a pyramid

and the summer eats
through you like an
island or like
an island whale
with a huge watery tongue
pushing Jonah to that
elusive depth
where the jaw's
sounds pierce him
ear to ear: it is
fear, fear of the bottom
fear of the crashing filter
of these open mouths
skinning us, squeezing
us and gulping our happy eyes
Jonah stands naked in the
room with no solutions
throwing lots like a blanket

and the whale also drowns
like he/she slightly singing
The first part to break
is the hole tightly closed

Next the subject
Next the streamlined shape
As we are young
we have reached the zero surface
Mother's nipple our first meal
nurses for two years
the richest of all animals
Jonah, grow on this
rich milk
in the unique ribs
collapsing under pressure
like Nineveh of grime
The airplane learns
the song is almost continuous
and the prophet's perfume
is then engraved with a picture
The scratches are filled with soot

In a blind garden
think of the whale
as helping Jonah
a joke in poor taste
in relation to a lack
of consciousness of nonsense
Now think of Nineveh
of madness and associated cities
Dear whale of my youth
you are alive and I am swallowed
Now think of a rotting palm
of a rotting royal palm
under which you dream
of a curse like sperm or teeth
of a continuing city's fine song
that can never be heard
by idiotic ears

the prophet's a skeleton now
what about a coral skull
or a coral penis
or coral without the body
We must blind one another
like pollen in the bright
sun's dust Mercifully
mercy concludes the story

Your dreams are those
of a young architect
You don't want to be seen, but to inspect
the curious architecture
of the island bird's throat
as you grow aware of the
increasing dark green ground
of the truncated future

MICAH 3:1–7 And I said, Hear, I pray you, O heads of Jacob, and ye princes of the house of Israel; Is it not for you to know judgment? Who hate the good, and love the evil; who pluck off their skin from off them, and their flesh from off their bones; Who also eat the flesh of my people, and flay their skin from off them; and they break their bones, and chop them in pieces, as for the pot, and as flesh within the caldron. Then shall they cry unto the LORD, but he will not hear them: he will even hide his face from them at that time, as they have behaved themselves ill in their doings. Thus saith the LORD concerning the prophets that make my people err, that bite with their teeth, and cry, Peace; and he that putteth not into their mouths, they even prepare war against him. Therefore night shall be unto you, that ye shall not have a vision; and it shall be dark unto you, that ye shall not divine; and the sun shall go down over the prophets, and the day shall be dark over them. Then shall the seers be ashamed, and the diviners confounded: yea, they shall all cover their lips; for there is no answer of God.

A Dream Question

THOMAS HARDY

I asked the Lord: 'Sire, is this true
Which hosts of theologians hold,
That when we creatures censure you
For shaping griefs and ails untold
(Deeming them punishments undue)
You rage, as Moses wrote of old?

When we exclaim: "Beneficent
He is not, for he orders pain,
Or, if so, not omnipotent:
To a mere child the thing is plain!"
Those who profess to represent
You, cry out: "Impious and profane!" '

He: 'Save me from my friends, who deem
That I care what my creatures say!
Mouth as you list: sneer, rail, blaspheme,
O manikin, the livelong day,
Not one grief-groan or pleasure-gleam
Will you increase or take away.

'Why things are thus, whoso derides,
May well remain my secret still. . . .
A fourth dimension, say the guides,
To matter is conceivable.
Think some such mystery resides
Within the ethic of my will.'

NAHUM 2:1–10 He that dasheth in pieces is come up before thy face: keep the munition, watch the way, make thy loins strong, fortify thy power mightily. For the LORD hath turned away the excellency of Jacob, as the excellency of Israel: for the emptiers have emptied them out, and marred their vine branches. The shield of his mighty men is made red, the valiant men are in scarlet: the chariots shall be with flaming torches in the day of his preparation, and the fir trees shall be terribly shaken. The chariots shall rage in the streets, they shall justle one against another in the broad ways: they shall seem like torches, they shall run like the lightnings. He shall recount his worthies: they shall stumble in their walk; they shall make haste to the wall thereof, and the defence shall be prepared. The gates of the rivers shall be opened, and the palace shall be dissolved. And Huzzab shall be led away captive, she shall be brought up, and her maids shall lead her as with the voice of doves, tabering upon their breasts.

But Nineveh is of old like a pool of water: yet they shall flee away. Stand, stand, shall they cry; but none shall look back. Take ye the spoil of silver, take the spoil of gold: for there is none end of the store and glory out of all the pleasant furniture. She is empty, and void, and waste: and the heart melteth, and the knees smite together, and much pain is in all loins, and the faces of them all gather blackness.

NAHUM 2. 10

FRANCIS QUARLES

She's empty: hark, she sounds: there's nothing there
But noise to fill thy ear;

Thy vain enquiry can at length but find
A blast of murmuring wind:
It is a cask, that seems as full as fair
But merely tunned with air:
Fond youth, go build thy hopes on better grounds:
The soul that vainly founds
Her joys upon this world but feeds on empty sounds.

She's empty: hark, she sounds: there's nothing in't,
The spark-engendering flint
Shall sooner melt, and hardest raunce shall first
Dissolve and quench thy thirst;
Ere this false world shall still thy stormy breast
With smooth-faced calms of rest:
Thou mayst as well expect Meridian light
From shades of black-mouthed night,
As in this empty world to find a full delight.

She's empty: hark, she sounds; 'tis void and vast;
What if some flattering blast
Of flatuous honor should perchance be there,
And whisper in thine ear:
It is but wind, and blows but where it list,
And vanishes like a mist:
Poor honor earth can give! What generous mind
Would be so base to bind
Her Heaven-bred soul a slave to serve a blast of wind?

She's empty: hark, she sounds; 'tis but a ball
For fools to play withal:
The painted film but of a stronger bubble,
That's lined with silken trouble:
It is a world, whose work and recreation
Is vanity and vexation?
A hag, repaired with vice-complexion, paint,
A quest-house of complaint:
It is a saint, a fiend; worse fiend, when most a saint.

She's empty: hark, she sounds: 'tis vain and void.
What's here to be enjoyed,
But grief and sickness, and large bills of sorrow,
Drawn now, and crossed tomorrow?
Or what are men, but puffs of dying breath,
Revived with living death?
Fond lad, O build thy hopes on surer grounds
Then what dull flesh propounds:
Trust not this hollow world, she's empty: hark, she sounds.

HABAKKUK 3:1–19 A prayer of Habakkuk the prophet upon Shigionoth. O LORD, I have heard thy speech, and was afraid: O LORD, revive thy work in the midst of the years, in the midst of the years make known; in wrath remember mercy. . . . The LORD God is my strength, and he will make my feet like hinds' feet, and he will make me to walk upon mine high places.To the chief singer on my stringed instruments.

A Song of the Faithful

MICHAEL DRAYTON

Lord, at thy voice, my heart for fear hath trembled,
Unto the world (Lord) let thy works be shown:
In these our days now let thy power be known,
And yet in wrath let mercy be remembered.

From Teman lo, our God you may behold,
The holy one from Paran mount so high:
His glory hath clean covered the sky,
And in the earth his praises be enrolled.

His shining was more clearer than the light,
And from his hands a fullness did proceed,
Which did contain his wrath and power indeed.
Consuming plagues and fire were in his sight.

He stood aloft and compassed the land,
And of the nations doth diffusion make,
The mountains rent, the hills for fear did quake,
His unknown paths no man may understand.

The Morians tents even for their wickedness,
I might behold the land of Midian:
Amazed and trembling like unto a man,
Forsaken quite, and left in great distress:

What, did the rivers move the Lord to ire?
Or did the floods his majesty displease:
Or was the Lord offended with the seas,
That thou camest forth in chariot hot as fire.

Thy force and power thou freely didst relate,
Unto the tribes thy oath doth surely stand,
And by thy strength thou didst divide the land,
And from the earth the rivers separate.

The mountains saw, and trembled for fear,
The sturdy stream, with speed forth passed by,
The mighty depths shout out a hideous cry,
And then aloft their waves they did uprear.

The sun and moon amid their course stood still,
Thy spears and arrows forth with shining went,
Thou spoilest the land, being to anger bent,
And in displeasure thou didst slay and kill.

Thou wentest forth for thine own chosen's sake,
For the safeguard of thine annointed one;
The house of wicked men is overthrown,
And their foundations now go all to wrack.

Their towns thou strikest by thy mighty power,
With their own weapons, made for their defence:
Who like a whirlwind came with the pretence,
The poor and simple man quite to devour.

Thou madest thy horse on seas to gallop fast.
Upon the waves thou ridest here and there:
My entrails trembled then for very fear,
And at thy voice, my lips shook at the last.

Grief pierced my bones, and fear did me annoy,
In time of trouble, where I might find rest:
For to revenge, when once the Lord is pressed,
With plagues he will the people quite destroy.

The fig-tree now no more shall sprout nor flourish,
The pleasant vine no more with grapes abound:
No pleasure in the city shall be found:
The field no more her fruit shall feed nor nourish.

The sheep shall now be taken from the fold,
In stall of bullocks there shall be no choice.
Yet in the Lord my Savior I rejoice,
My hope in God yet will I surely hold.

God is my strength, the Lord my only stay,
My feet for swiftness, it is he will make
Like to the hinds, who none in course can take:
Upon high places he will make my way.

ZEPHANIAH 1:14–18 The great day of the LORD is near, it is near, and hasteth greatly, even the voice of the day of the LORD: the mighty man shall cry there bitterly. That day is a day of wrath, a day of trouble and distress, a day of wasteness and desolation, a day of darkness and gloominess, a day of clouds and thick darkness, A day of the trumpet and alarm against the fenced cities, and against the high towers. And I will bring distress upon men, that they shall walk like blind men, because they have sinned against the LORD: and their blood shall be poured out as dust, and their flesh as the dung. Neither their silver nor their gold shall be able to deliver them in the day of the LORD'S wrath; but the whole land shall be devoured by the fire of his jealousy: for he shall make even a speedy riddance of all them that dwell in the land.

THE DAY OF JUDGEMENT

JONATHAN SWIFT

With a whirl of thought oppressed
I sink from revery to rest.
An horrid vision seized my head,
I saw the graves give up their dead.
Jove, armed with terrors, burst the skies,
And thunder roars, and lightning flies!
Amazed, confused, its fate unknown,
The World stands trembling at his throne.
While each pale sinner hangs his head,
Jove, nodding, shook the heavens, and said,

"Offending race of human kind,
By nature, reason, learning, blind;
You who through frailty stepped aside,
And you who never fell—through pride;
You who in different sects have shammed,
And come to see each other damned;
(So some folks told you, but they knew
No more of Jove's designs than you)
The World's mad business now is o'er,
And I resent these pranks no more.
I to such blockheads set my wit!
I damn such fools! Go, go, you're bit."

HAGGAI 1:4–6 Then came the word of the LORD by Haggai the prophet, saying, Is it time for you, O ye, to dwell in your ceiled houses, and this house lie waste? Now therefore thus saith the LORD of hosts; Consider your ways. Ye have sown much, and bring in little; ye eat, but ye have not enough; ye drink, but ye are not filled with drink; ye clothe you, but there is none warm; and he that earneth wages earneth wages to put it into a bag with holes.

HAGGAI

JOHN CHAGY

Shealtiel, governor of Judah,
And Jehozadak, his friend, the high priest,
Had no time for prophecies. But their sons,
Zerubbabel and Joshua, listened,
And there was fear in their hearts as Haggai
Admonished them. "Your fathers say the time
Has not yet come to build the second Temple,
Therefore the Lord has kept the heaven back.
The drought upon the land has starved the cattle,
Withered the fig-tree, dried the pomegranate.
Your hands are calloused and weary with labor
Yet your wives and little ones go hungry.
The Jews run every man for his own house
And so are scattered, weak and separate
Even in Jerusalem, without a Temple.
Last night I heard the Lord of hosts again,

He bade me stir your hearts to build His House.
Then in a dream I saw the Temple site;
The Temple stood there on that highest hill
More glorious than any of our buildings.
From within I heard the sound of pipes and oboes,
Trumpets, harps, shofars, cymbals and singers—
The leader had the sweetest voice in Israel.
The Lord appointed me His messenger
To urge you and the remnants of the people
To consider your ways and hearken unto the Lord.
And from the day the Temple's completed
The acorn and vines and olive-trees shall blossom
And in this land there shall be peace again.
Israel's one home is in the House of the Lord."

ZECHARIAH 1:7–11 Upon the four and twentieth day of the eleventh month, which is the month Sebat, in the second year of Darius, came the word of the LORD unto Zechariah, the son of Berechiah, the son of Iddo the prophet, saying, I saw by night, and behold a man riding upon a red horse, and he stood among the myrtle trees that were in the bottom; and behind him were there red horses, speckled, and white. Then said I, O my lord, what are these? And the angel that talked with me said unto me, I will shew thee what these be. And the man that stood among the myrtle trees answered and said, These are they whom the LORD hath sent to walk to and fro through the earth. And they answered the angel of the LORD that stood among the myrtle trees, and said, We have walked to and fro through the earth, and, behold, all the earth sitteth still, and is at rest.

IN A MYRTLE SHADE

WILLIAM BLAKE

O, how sick and weary I
Underneath my myrtle lie,
Like to dung upon the ground
Underneath my myrtle bound.

Why should I be bound to thee,
O my lovely myrtle tree?
Love, free love, cannot be bound
To any tree that grows on ground.

Oft my myrtle sighed in vain
To behold my heavy chain.
Oft my father saw us sigh,
And laughed at our simplicity.

So I smote him and his gore
Stained the roots my myrtle bore.
But the time of youth is fled,
And grey hairs are on my head.

ZECHARIAH 1:18–21 Then lifted I up mine eyes, and saw, and behold four horns. And I said unto the angel that talked with me, What be these? And he answered me, These are the horns which have scattered Judah, Israel, and Jerusalem. And the LORD shewed me four carpenters. Then said I, What come these to do? And he spake, saying, These are the horns which have scattered Judah, so that no man did lift up his head: but these are come to fray them, to cast out the horns of the Gentiles, which lifted up their horn over the land of Judah to scatter it.

from *JUBILATE AGNO*

CHRISTOPHER SMART

For I prophesy that we shall have our horns again.
For in the day of David Man as yet had a glorious horn upon his forehead.
For this horn was a bright substance in colour and consistence as the nail of the hand.
For it was broad, thick and strong so as to serve for defence as well as ornament.
For it brightened to the Glory of God, which came upon the human face at morning prayer.
For it was largest and brightest in the best men.
For it was taken away all at once from all of them.
For this was done in the divine contempt of a general pusillanimity.
For this happened in a season after their return from the Babylonish captivity.
For their spirits were broke and their manhood impaired by foreign vices for exaction.
For I prophesy that the English will recover their horns the first.
For I prophesy that all the nations in the world will do the like in turn.

For I prophesy that all Englishmen will wear their beards again.
For a beard is a good step to a horn.
For when men get their horns again, they will delight to go uncovered.
For it is not good to wear any thing upon the head.
For a man should put no obstacle between his head and the blessing of Almighty God.
For a hat was an abomination of the heathen. Lord have mercy upon the Quakers.
For the ceiling of the house is an obstacle and therefore we pray on the house-top.
For the head will be liable to less disorders on the recovery of its horn.
For the horn on the forehead is a tower upon an arch.
For it is a strong munition against the adversary, who is sickness and death.
For it is instrumental in subjecting the woman.
For the insolence of the woman has increased ever since man has been crest-fallen.
For they have turned the horn into scoff and derision without ceasing.
For we are amerced of God, who has his horn.
For we are amerced of the blessed angels, who have their horns.
For when they get their horns again they will put them upon the altar.
For they give great occasion for mirth and music.
For our Blessed Saviour had not his horn upon the face of the earth.
For this was in meekness and condescension to the infirmities of human nature at that time.
For at his second coming his horn will be exalted in glory.
For his horn is the horn of Salvation.
For Christ Jesus has exalted my voice to his own glory.
For he has answered me in the air as with a horn from Heaven to the ears of many people.
For the horn is of plenty.
For this has been the sense of all ages.
For Man and Earth suffer together.
For when Man was amerced of his horn, earth lost part of her fertility.
For the art of Agriculture is improving.
For this is evident in flowers.
For it is more especially manifest in double flowers.
For earth will get it up again by the blessing of God on the industry of man.
For the horn is of plenty because of milk and honey.
For I pray God be gracious to the Bees and the Beeves this day.

ZECHARIAH 9:9–11 Rejoice greatly, O daughter of Zion; shout, O daughter of Jerusalem: behold, thy King cometh unto thee: he is just, and having salvation; lowly, and riding upon an ass, and upon a colt the foal of an ass. And I will cut off the chariot from Ephraim, and the horse from Jerusalem, and the battle bow shall be cut off: and he shall speak peace unto the heathen: and his dominion shall be from sea even to sea, and from the river even to the ends of the earth. As for thee also, by the blood of thy covenant I have sent forth thy prisoners out of the pit wherein is no water.

MEDITATION SEVENTY-SEVEN

Second Series

EDWARD TAYLOR

A state, a state, oh! dungeon state indeed.
In which me headlong, long ago sin pitched:
As dark as pitch; where nastiness doth breed:
And filth defiles: and I am with it ditched.
A sinfull state: This pit no water's in't.
A bugbear state: as black as any ink.

I once sat singing on the summit high
'Mong the celestial choir in music sweet:
On highest bough of paradisal joy;
Glory and innocence did in me meet.
I as a gold-finched nighting-gale, tuned o'er
Melodious songs 'fore glory's palace door.

But on this bough I tuning perched not long:
Th'infernal foe shot out a shaft from Hell;
A fiery dart piled with sins poison strong:
That struck my heart, and down I headlong fell:
And from the highest pinnacle of light
Into this lowest pit more dark than night.

A pit indeed of sin: No water's here:
Whose bottom's furthest off from Heaven bright.
And is next door to Hell gate: to it near:
And here I dwell in sad and solemn night.
My gold-finched angel feathers dappled in
Hells scarlet dye fat, blood red grown with sin.

I in this pit all destitute of light
Crammed full of horrid darkness, here do crawl
Up over head, and ears, in nauseous plight:
And swinelike wallow in this mire and gall:
No heavenly dews nor holy waters drill:
Nor sweet air breeze, nor comfort here distil.

Here for companions, are fears, heart-aches, grief,
    Frogs, toads, newts, bats, horrid hob-goblins, ghosts,
Ill spirits haunt this pit: and no relief:
    Nor cord can fetch me hence in creatures coasts.
    I who once lodged at Heaven's palace gate
    With full fledged angels, now possess this fate.

But yet, my Lord, thy golden chain of grace
    Thou canst let down, and draw me up into
Thy holy air, and glory's happy place,
    Out from these hellish damps and pit so low.
    And if thy grace shall do't, My harp I'll raise,
    Whose strings touched by this grace, will twang thy praise.

ZECHARIAH 13:1 In that day there shall be a fountain opened to the house of David and to the inhabitants of Jerusalem for sin and for uncleanness.

THE FOUNTAIN

WILLIAM COWPER

There is a fountain filled with blood,
    Drawn from Immanuel's veins;
And sinners, plunged beneath that flood,
    Lose all their guilty stains.

The dying thief rejoiced to see
    That fountain in his day;
And there may I, as vile as he,
    Wash all my sins away.

Dear dying Lamb, thy precious blood
    Shall never lose its power,
Till all the ransomed church of God
    Be saved,—to sin no more.

E'er since, by faith I saw the stream,
    Thy flowing wounds supply,
Redeeming love has been my theme,
    And shall be,—till I die.

Then in a nobler, sweeter song,
I'll sing thy power to save;
When this poor, lisping, faltering tongue
Lies silent in the grave.

Lord, I believe thou hast prepared
(Unworthy though I be)
For me a blood-bought free reward,
A golden harp for me!

'Tis strung, and tuned, for endless years,
And formed by power divine,
To sound in God the Father's ears
No other name but thine.

MALACHI 4:2 But unto you that fear my name shall the Sun of righteousness arise with healing in his wings; and ye shall go forth, and grow up as calves of the stall.

EASTER WINGS

GEORGE HERBERT

Lord, who createdst man in wealth and store,
Though foolishly he lost the same,
Decaying more and more,
Till he became
Most poor:
With thee
O let me rise
As larks, harmoniously
And sing this day thy victories:
Then shall the fall further the flight in me.

My tender age in sorrow did begin:
And still with sicknesses and shame
Thou didst so punish sin,
That I became
Most thin.
With thee
Let me combine,
And feel this day thy victory:
For, if I imp my wing on thine,
Affliction shall advance the flight in me.

Index of Titles

INDEX OF FIRST LINES

Index of Poets